Freedom and Socialism   Uhuru na Ujamaa

An informal picture of
PRESIDENT JULIUS K. NYERERE

JULIUS K. NYERERE

Freedom	Uhuru
and	na
Socialism	Ujamaa

A SELECTION FROM
WRITINGS AND SPEECHES
1965-1967

DAR ES SALAAM

OXFORD UNIVERSITY PRESS
NAIROBI LONDON NEW YORK

OXFORD UNIVERSITY PRESS

ELY HOUSE, DOVER STREET, LONDON W I

Glasgow New York Toronto Wellington Melbourne
Ibadan Nairobi Dar es Salaam Lusaka Addis Ababa
Delhi Bombay Calcutta Madras Karachi Lahore Dacca
Kuala Lumpur Singapore Hong Kong Tokyo

P. O. BOX 72532, NAIROBI, KENYA

Printed and made in Tanzania, East Africa
by Tanzania Litho Ltd., Arusha

TO

THE PEOPLE

Contents

Illustrations

ix

Contents List by Subject

Preface

In the Preface to *Freedom and Unity* I said that producing a book of this kind is a collective effort, and that I was therefore indebted to very many people. Circumstances of book preparation and production have not changed in the intervening three years, so I can only repeat my acknowledgement and my thanks.

During the period covered by the speeches and writings of this book, the people of Tanzania have accepted a new commitment which demands even greater efforts than the struggle for independence. This commitment to socialism was vocalized by the Tanganyika African National Union National Executive, and by myself and other leaders of TANU and the Afro-Shirazi Party. But the words really represent a translation into general principles, and into policy formulations, of questions and ideas expressed in our villages and our towns. It is therefore no cliche for me to say that this book has sprung out of the people of this United Republic. The ideas expressed here are an attempt to formulate and to express in policy-making terms the basic ideals and desires of the masses of the people of Tanzania. It is they who have inspired the thought; it is they who have accepted the proposals and ideas; and it is they who will express their approval by the work they do in implementation.

To my colleagues in Government, and in the TANU and Afro-Shirazi Parties, I am, of course, particularly indebted. It is with them that detailed discussions have been held, and it is they who have spread these definitions and ideas throughout the country. Without their energy and enthusiasm the questions and ideas of the peasants and workers would remain unanswered.

Although the members of the Public Services of Tanzania have not been involved directly in the policy-making discussions which precede the kind of new commitment Tanzania has undertaken, I would like to take this opportunity to express our nation's deep indebtedness to them. Had we continued along the road to capitalism, the members of our Civil Service, Local Government Service, our Army and Police, our doctors, auditors, administrators, and so on, might well have been among the privileged class of Tanzanians. By our commitment to socialism we have given them all more work, at the same time as we have closed their road to individual wealth. It is a tribute to their great patriotism, and to their loyalty, that they have accepted the people's will and worked without ceasing for our national objectives. Our present measure of success, and that of the future, is and will be to a large extent due to their efforts.

As always particular individuals have made special contributions to the task of preparing this book for publication. To Miss Joan Wicken, my Personal Assistant, who has done the research and much else to help in this work I would like to express my appreciation. I am also indebted in turn to Miss Betty Hughes, Miss Joan Saxelby, and Miss Esther Mwinyimvua, who have typed the drafts and final versions of the speeches and documents to prepare the book for the printers. Thanks are also due to Mrs. Barbara Broome who prepared the Index.

Finally, I wish to acknowledge the kindness of editors and publishers who have allowed me to include works originally written for their publications; and to congratulate the photographers of the Tanzania Information Service whose fine photographs illustrate this book.

August 1968.   J. K. N.

Introduction

The Introduction to a collection of speeches and writings could usefully be a description of the events and changing circumstances of the period during which they were produced. But it is not my intention to provide such a background. To a large extent the items in this book explain their own context, and the events or developments which provoked them; for the rest I think the preliminary paragraphs give sufficient information to make their inclusion intelligible. Instead I propose to enlarge upon the socialist goal which Tanzania has accepted as its objective, and upon the manner in which Tanzania can progress towards this goal.

The Tanganyika African National Union has been formally committed to socialism since it revised its constitution almost immediately after Tanganyika's independence in December 1961. Much of the legislation and many of the policies adopted by the different Governments—both before and after the Union with Zanzibar—reflected that commitment. Yet it gradually became clear that the absence of a generally accepted and easily understood statement of philosophy and policy was causing problems, and some Government and Party actions were having the effect of encouraging the growth of non-socialist institutions, values, and attitudes. This was happening because the implications of our broad commitment to socialism were not understood. The adoption of the Arusha Declaration early in 1967 therefore marks an important step forward for Tanzania. For this Declaration, together with subsequent policy statements, provides some definition of what socialism demands of our country, and especially of its leaders.

But the Arusha Declaration is only a beginning. Tanzania is not now a socialist country; it is only a country whose people have firmly committed themselves to building socialism. The actual work has barely begun. For socialism is not built by Government decisions, nor by Acts of Parliament; a country does not become socialist by nationalizations or grand designs on paper. It is more difficult than that to build socialism, and it takes much longer.

UJAMAA IS TANZANIAN SOCIALISM

What does socialism mean for us? How can we move towards it? The answer to these questions is in some ways implicit in the word we have chosen to describe our goal. For there was nothing accidental in our selection of the word 'ujamaa' to define our socialist policies; nor did this word result solely from the desire to find a Swahili equivalent for the word 'socialism'. Swahili is a growing language and continues to incorporate foreign words into its vocabulary when necessary; indeed we talk of the policies of some other countries as being 'kisoshalisti'. The word 'ujamaa' was chosen for special reasons. First, it is an African word and thus emphasizes the African-ness of the policies we intend to follow. Second, its literal meaning is 'family-hood', so that it brings to the mind of our people the idea of mutual involvement in the family as we know it.

By the use of the word 'ujamaa', therefore, we state that for us socialism involves building on the foundation of our past, and building also to our own design. We are not importing a foreign ideology into Tanzania and trying to smother our distinct social patterns with it. We have deliberately decided to grow, as a society, out of our own roots, but in a particular direction and towards a particular kind of objective. We are doing this by emphasizing certain characteristics of our traditional organization, and extending them so that they can embrace the possibilities of modern technology and enable us to meet the challenge of life in the twentieth century world.

This emphasis on growth from traditional patterns of social living means that we shall be trying to create something which is uniquely ours, and by methods which may be unique to Tanzania. This does not invalidate our claim to be building socialism.

Socialism is international; its ideas and beliefs relate to man in society, not just to Tanzanian man in Tanzania, or African man in Africa. But just because it is a universal concept so it must also relate to Tanzanian man in Tanzania. And if it is to do this, it must be able to encompass us as we are—as our geography and our history have made us. It must not demand the remoulding of man to a single pattern, regardless of whether man has been born in Uzanaki or Hunan, Colchester or Uppsala. The universality of socialism only exists if it can take account of men's differences, and be equally valid for all of them. And it can. For the universality of socialism does not imply a single, world-wide uniformity of social institutions, social habits, or social language. There is no reason why a dozen fully socialist societies should not have a dozen different methods of organizing themselves, a dozen different sets of customs relating to social intercourse, and a dozen different styles of political address and description. It is by no means necessary to call people 'comrade' in order to be socialist; it is not necessary to insist upon a civil marriage ceremony in a socialist society; it is by no means certain that a centralized economy is an inherent part of socialist organization. It is my contention that socialist societies in different parts of the world will differ in many respects even when they are fully developed instead of being, as now, at different stages on the road to socialism. The differences between these societies will reflect both the manner of their development, and their historical traditions.

It would be absurd to suggest that because differences will exist between different socialist societies in different parts of the world, that therefore 'socialism' has no meaning, or that it is too vague a concept to be sensibly adopted as the social goal of a young country. For there are certain universal values and essential characteristics which would be found in every socialist society, and which would not be found in non-socialist societies. It is the existence of these values and characteristics which define a socialist society. They will not necessarily be found in a society which is still creating socialism; a society in transition is, by definition, short of the goal. But the more of these values and characteristics which can be observed in the workings of any community the nearer it is to becoming socialist. The gap between the reality and the goal will show the distance which has still to be travelled and the work which still has to be done. A brief examination of these essential elements of socialism will demonstrate to those who know Tanzania the amount of hard work which our country still has to perform.

WHAT IS A SOCIALIST SOCIETY?

What should we look for when trying to determine whether a particular society is socialist? What are the universal characteristics and values which would underlie differences of institution and organization in a socialist society?

First, and most central of all, is that under socialism Man is the purpose of all social activity. The service of man, the furtherance of his human development, is in fact the purpose of society itself. There is no other purpose above this; no glorification of 'nation', no increase in production—nothing is more central to a socialist society than an acceptance that Man is its justification for existence.

In one sense, all the other characteristics of socialism follow from this. But in view of the historical development of mankind, one more thing has to be stated categorically. The word 'man' to a socialist, means all men—all human beings. Male and female; black, white, brown, yellow; long-nosed and short-nosed; educated and uneducated; wise and stupid; strong and weak; all these, and all other distinctions between human beings, are irrelevant to the fact that all members of the society—all the human beings who are its purpose—are equal.

The equality of man may or may not be susceptible to scientific proof. But its acceptance as a basic assumption of life in society is the core and essence of socialism. No one who qualifies his belief in the equality of man is really a socialist. A society is not socialist if, in its organization, or its practices, it discriminates, or allows discrimination, between its members because of their parentage, their place of birth, their appearance, their religious beliefs, or anything other than their behaviour in relation to their fellows. The existence of racialism, of tribalism, or of religious intolerance, means that a society is not socialist—regardless of whatever other attributes it may have. A society in which all men are of equal account will probably be socialist, because socialist organization is really the means by which the diversity of mankind is harnessed to the common benefit of all men. Socialism, as a system, is in fact the organization of men's inequalities to serve their equality. Their equality is socialist belief.

The upholding of human dignity could be expected to follow automatically from these two basic characteristics of a socialist society. For a society cannot acquiesce in the abasement or humiliation of its own purpose; on the contrary, a man-centred society would promote the dignity and the growth to excellence of all the human beings who are members of it. Indeed, it could not draw boundaries around itself in this matter. A socialist society would seek to uphold human dignity everywhere; and however limited its capacity in this respect, it could never act in such a manner as to be itself responsible for the denial of any man's humanity.

Democracy is another essential characteristic of a socialist society. For the people's equality must be reflected in the political organization; everyone must be an equal participant in the government of his society. Whatever devices are used to implement this principle, the people (meaning all the members of the society equally) must be sovereign, and they must be able to exert their sovereignty without causing a break-down of the law and order, or of the administration in their society. There must, in other words, be some mechanisms by which the people exert their will peacefully, and achieve changes in the laws which govern them; they must be able to change the personnel in positions of leadership within the framework of the normal workings of the social system. It is difficult to see how this could be achieved without the existence of some system of free elections if the society is so large that direct democracy (the direct government by all the people) is impossible. But elections are not the beginning and end of democracy. The freedom of the people to choose their own representatives is important, but it is equally important that the people's representatives should possess the freedom and the power to exert effective control over those sectors of the social organization for which they have been given responsibility. And none of these things is possible unless every other aspect of society—its economic, social and legal organization—is such as to emphasize and serve man's equality. A political democracy which exists in a society of gross economic inequalities, or of social inequality, is at best imperfect, and at worst a hollow sham.

A socialist society, therefore, will consist of workers —and only of workers. Every member will contribute, by his work, to the total of wealth and welfare produced by the society, and he will receive a return in proportion to his efforts and his contribution to the well-being of the community. Only small children, the men and women who are too old to work, and the sick, are exempt from the responsibility to work. To everyone else this duty, and this right, belongs.

For work is not only a duty to society; it is also a right of every human being, and anyone who is deprived of the opportunity to do something useful for himself, his fellow citizens, and his society, needs and merits some compensation. The child needs food, love, and care; that is obvious and unquestioned. The sick and crippled need an opportunity to do whatever is within their power, and also the willing gift of such food, clothing and shelter as they are unable to provide for themselves. And the society has a responsibility also towards any person whom it deprives of an opportunity to earn his own living. Under socialism there could not be a group of 'permanently unemployed'; but technological changes, and the economic flexibility which must exist in a developing community, may mean that some individuals need support while they are receiving new training, or—especially in a country like Tanzania— until the first harvest when they return to the land.

Apart from these groups, however, everyone in a socialist society will be a worker. Unless this is so socialism cannot exist; it would collapse through its own poverty. But the word 'worker' in this context means anyone who works; he may be a peasant working on his own shamba, a member of a co-operative farming group, or a woman looking after her small children and the family home. None of these people receive wages for their activity, but they do contribute to the total output of goods and welfare. Nor is it necessary to make a distinction between a wage-earner whose work involves much physical labour, and one who works in an office or carries managerial or professional responsibilities. All who contribute to the society by their work are workers.

It follows from this that in a socialist society there will be no exploitation of one man by another. There will be no 'masters' who sit in idleness while others labour on 'their' farms or in 'their' factories. Nor will there be too great a degree of inequality between the incomes of different members of the society. It is arguable that an especially clever man, or an especially hard-working man, contributes more to the society than one who does not have these qualities, and that he is therefore entitled to receive greater remuneration. But can any one man do work which is 100 times more valuable than that of another? It is true that for some jobs to be done effectively certain extra facilities are needed by the worker; a teacher or an administrator, for example, will need a place where he can study quietly, will need to be able to obtain books of a certain type, and so on. But does anyone need a palace while another receives only a 'bedspace'?

There is, however, another form of exploitation which a socialist society would avoid, and to which it may be especially prone. A man who cheats his fellows by dishonesty, who fails to do a full day's work, or who fails to co-operate with his fellows because he wants to bolster his own personal interests, is exploiting other men. Society has as much a right, and a duty, to prevent these kinds of exploitation as it has to prevent the exploitation which arises from individual ownership of the means of production and exchange.

For this is another characteristic of a socialist community. It would be so organized that the tools of production and the mechanisms of exchange are firmly under the control of the people. Control in this context does not only mean regulation in the negative sense of stopping people from doing certain things. It also means the power to do positive things—to expand a factory, to build a new one in a particular place, to invest in a risky enterprise, etc. It seems almost certain that this will normally involve public ownership at least of the key points of the economy, and one would therefore expect a socialist society to be distinguished from a non-socialist society in this matter of ownership of the economy. It may be, however, that particular societies can devise some other means of securing effective and positive control over their economy in such a manner as to preclude exploitation. This would be unusual, but if they can, that society could still be recognized as socialist, provided that the other essential characteristics of socialism exist.

It may be necessary to add that public ownership can be of many types, and it has a purpose. The purpose is to ensure that there is no exploitation in the economy, and no built-in tendency towards inequalities. It could therefore be ownership by the people through the instrument of their elected central government, or their local government; or it could be expressed through co-operatives, or other group organizations. The appropriate form would vary both according to the technology concerned, and according to the other practices and desires of the society. The essential point is that no individual or group of individuals would be able to hold to ransom either the society as a whole, or other individuals, by means of their exclusive control of an instrument which is necessary to the increasing well-being of the community.

Obviously this does not preclude private ownership of the things which pertain to the individual worker, or to the family. Such a suggestion is simply put forward to frighten the timid men and to mislead those trying to find an alternative to the social evils of capitalism. A farmer can own his hoe, a carpenter can own his hand-saw; any worker can own the tools which he uses by himself as a supplement to his own hands. Similarly, a family can own the house in which it lives, the furniture and equipment which increase the comfort of its members, and so on. The question of public ownership arises when men have to co-operate together in the pursuit of a particular objective. When the tool has to be used by two men it must be owned equally; when the product is necessary for the decent life of others they must be involved in the control over it. Any suggestion that socialism involves the nationalization or community ownership of every artifact of life is the suggestion of a fool or a mischief-maker.

There is another bogeyman which is used to frighten people, and that is the suggestion that individual freedom does not exist under socialism. The purpose of socialism is to enlarge the real freedom of man, to expand his opportunity of living in dignity and well-being. An obviously essential part of this is that the laws of the society shall be known, be applied equally, and that people shall not be subject to arbitrary arrest, or persecution by the servants of the society. The Rule of Law is a part of socialism; until it prevails socialism does not prevail. By itself the Rule of Law does not bring socialism; but you cannot have socialism without it, because it is the expression of man's equality in one facet of social living.

The final characteristic of a socialist society which must be listed here is the social values it emphasizes. In a feudal or aristocratic system, birth is a matter of the highest importance; if you are born of certain parents you have social respect as well as economic advantages accorded to you as of right. In a capitalist system, individual wealth is the most important single criterion for respect, and the competitive spirit is acclaimed as a paramount social virtue—in practice if not in theory. The social values of a socialist society will be very different from either of these. First, both the organization and the teaching will emphasize man's co-operative spirit—his desire to work in harmony with his friends and neighbours—not his personal aggressiveness. Second, it will reserve its highest respect and its highest prizes for those whose life and work demonstrate the greatest service, not the greatest personal acquisitiveness. Comparative wealth will not be the criteria on which a man is judged by his fellows. Success in a socialist society will imply that a man has earned the respect, admiration, and love of his fellow citizens, by his desire to serve, and by the contribution he has made to the well-being of the community.

All these things together are the hallmark of a socialist society. When you find them you have found a society which is socialist. When you find some but not others, you have found a society which is partly socialist—or which has the elements of socialism in it. And when you find a deliberate attempt being made to build these values and organizational systems, then you have found a society which is working towards socialism.

SOCIALISM AND THE PRODUCTION OF WEALTH

Both before and since the Arusha Declaration, the Government and Party in Tanzania have been emphasizing the need to increase output —to increase the production of wealth. We shall continue to do this, because *in our circumstances* an increase in the amount of goods produced and available for social services, for distribution, and for investment, is a socialist purpose. Our country is bedevilled by its present poverty; people are sick, ignorant, and live in very poor conditions, because we do not produce enough wealth to be able to eradicate these evils. We have to increase our production of goods if we are to enable everyone to live in conditions of human dignity. At present not even complete equality in the distribution of the available wealth would do this; our national income per head is something between Shs. 400/- and Shs. 460/- per year. An increase in production must have a very high priority in our social plans; it is the cornerstone for all our other ambitions.

It is necessary to stress this because the production of wealth for its own sake is not a socialist purpose. The purpose of production must always be the greater well-being of man; goods must be produced because they are useful and make life better. To Tanzanians that looks very obvious; indeed, most Tanzanian citizens may wonder what I am talking about, because it is so obvious that extra food, bricks, roofing, ovens, chairs, tables, beds, clothing, and so on and so on, will make life better. Yet we are still in danger of being attracted by the idea of 'wealth' as represented by all the consumer goods we see advertised in foreign magazines (and even Tanzanian ones), or in the films, etc. We are still in danger of accepting the idea that the greatest production of consumer goods is the criterion by which a nation, or an economic system, should be judged.

A socialist does not look at things that way. He asks, what sort of production? What is it that is being produced? Under what conditions? And what effect does it have, on balance, on the society as a whole? To a socialist, therefore, there is no virtue in 'creating a market' for something which people have never thought of wanting and really have no need for, but which someone hopes to make a profit by producing. This happens all the time in capitalist societies; it is an inherent part of them. There are very many examples which could be given; I will mention only two. In some societies it is a matter of pride, I am told, to buy an electric tooth-brush—presumably the energy required to clean one's mouth properly is beyond the strength of well-fed men and women! An even more useless object which manufacturers were trying to persuade the people of another capitalist country to buy was something called a 'non-spill' tray, which was said to enable you to swing a tray holding glasses of liquid without spilling a drop! Advertisements to promote the sale of such things are a normal part of capitalist society; their newspapers, television, etc. make every attempt to suggest to people that they will be 'old-fashioned' if they do not acquire the object in question. In other words, an attempt is made to make people discontented without the thing which is being 'promoted', so that they will buy it—if they have enough money. This is called 'creating a market', and 'creating a market' is said to be an inherent part of 'progress', of increasing the national income, and of 'free consumer choice'.

A socialist will not be impressed by such values, nor even by the talk of people 'exercising their freedom as consumers', if, at the same time as these things are being produced and sold, other human values are being ignored or sacrificed. For the incredible thing is that in the same countries which encourage this kind of 'market creation', other people are living in conditions of great poverty, educational facilities are starved of funds, and completely free hospital care for everyone is said to be too expensive for the community to bear! The production of wealth for the benefit of man—that is production for socialist purposes—would have rather different results. Electric tooth-brushes and non-spill trays—if they were produced at all—would not be produced until after these more basic needs had been met.

To a socialist, the first priority of production must be the manufacture and distribution of such goods as will allow every member of the society to have sufficient food, clothing and shelter, to sustain a decent life. Other goods would be produced only if they in some way hastened the day when this goal was reached. Apart from these basic needs of man, a socialist society would put much emphasis on the production of socially advantageous goods. It would concentrate on better educational facilities, medical care, places of community activity like libraries, community centres, parks, etc. It would devote resources also to social values which have nothing to do with production—things like improving the hours and conditions of work, or maintaining and improving the natural beauties of the world in which we live. Of course, some care, money, and energy has to be spent on these non-consumer products even before the basic job is complete, because they affect the way people will be able to live. Thus, for example, when building new houses in a town it is necessary to plan for public spaces and leave room for community buildings even if you cannot build them immediately; it is necessary to provide minimum educational and health services as far as you can; and it is essential to spend that minimum amount of money which is necessary to prevent the destruction of that natural beauty or wild life which could never be replaced if it was once allowed to disappear.

In a socialist society, therefore, man as a consumer is not 'king'. Instead man is recognized as a human being who desires human dignity, who is a consumer both privately and socially, and who is also a producer. For socialism involves an acceptance of the fact that man's life in society cannot be divided up into bits. A man is concerned with his life as a whole; if he is starving it is no use expecting him to be happy because he has the freedom to vote every few years, or if he is well-fed it is no use expecting him to be happy as a slave. Under a socialist society men come together to try and organize the community in which they live so that all their different needs and all their co-operative social values are considered, with priority being given to those which are most urgent—but without any being destroyed.

In Tanzania the increased output of wealth so that all our people may live decently is the most urgent thing. But we cannot allow this need to destroy our belief in human equality and human dignity. On the contrary, we have to organize our expansion of wealth in such a way as to give the maximum possible emphasis to these other values.

SOCIALISM IS SECULAR

The fact that socialism is concerned with all aspects of man's life in society does not mean that man as an individual ceases to exist. Every person is unique; there are some things which are, and which must be, private to himself. Society has the right where necessary to regulate, encourage, or discourage, those actions of individuals which affect other members of the society. It has no business in relation to things which are by nature or by method entirely personal. Once a man has fulfilled his responsibilities to the society, it is nothing to do with socialism whether he spends his spare time painting, dancing, writing poetry, playing football, or just sitting. Nor is it any business of socialism if an individual is, or is not, inspired in his daily life by a belief in God, nor if he does, or does not, attend a place of religious worship—or pray elsewhere.

Socialism is concerned with man's life in *this* society. A man's relationship with his God is a personal matter for him and him alone; his beliefs about the hereafter are his own affair. These things have nothing to do with anyone else as long as he does not indulge in practices which adversely affect the similar private rights of other members of the society. Thus, for example, a man's belief that he should pray at specified hours of the day and night wherever he happens to be is a matter for him, and no one else has the right to interfere. But a religion which involved human sacrifice, or demanded the exploitation of human beings, could not be allowed to carry out these practices.

Socialism's concern about the organization of life on earth does not involve any supposition about life elsewhere, or about man's soul, or the procedures for fulfilling the will of God or Gods.

Socialism is secular. It has nothing to say about whether there is
a God. Certainly it rests on the assumption of the equality of
man, but people can reach this conclusion by many routes. People
can accept the equality of man because they believe that all men were
created by God, they can believe it because they feel that the scientific evidence supports such a conclusion, or they can accept it simply
because they believe it is the only basis on which life in society can
be organized without injustice. It does not matter why people
accept the equality of man as the basis of social organization; all
that matters is that they do accept it.

This means that socialism cannot require that its adherents be
atheists. There is not the slightest necessity for people to study
metaphysics and decide whether there is one God, many Gods, or
no God, before they can be socialist. It is not necessary to try and
decide whether there is an after-life, or what kind, before you can
be a socialist. These questions are important to man, but irrelevant
to socialism; trying to bring them into the discussion about socialism
simply causes quarrels between socialists, and thus weakens the
struggle for the things they all support. What matters in socialism
and to socialists is that you should care about a particular kind of
social relationship on this earth. Why you care is your own affair.
There is nothing incompatible between socialism and Christianity,
Islam, or any other religion which accepts the equality of man on
earth.

The fact that socialism and religion are two different things does
not mean that socialism is anti-religious. In a socialist society the
members of the community would be free to be religious, and to
follow whatever religion they wish; the society would try very hard
not to make a decision which outrages the religious feelings of any
of its members, however small in numbers the group may be.
There are times, however, when this cannot be done—for example
if questions of public health arose in an urban society out of certain
religious burial practices. But even then, every effort would be made
to reach agreement with the people concerned; the religious feelings
would always be taken into account.

This necessity for religious toleration arises out of the nature of
socialism. For a man's religious beliefs are important to him, and the
purpose of socialism is Man. Socialism does not just seek to serve
some abstract thing called 'the people'; it seeks to maximize the

benefit of society to all the individuals who are members of it. It is thus the essentially personal nature of religious beliefs which makes it necessary for socialism to leave religious questions alone as far as possible—which makes it necessary that socialism should be secular. And being secular involves trying to avoid upsetting deeply held religious beliefs however stupid they may appear to non-believers. The wearing of long hair, the erection of statues to the religious heroes or saints, the pouring of libations, the ban on music and dancing—all these things appear at best irrelevant to those who do not follow the religion concerned, but they are important to those who do. And because they are important to these believers, a socialist society will not interfere. It will not force people to cut their hair, nor allow others to be forced to wear their hair long. It will not prohibit libations, although it may ask that they be poured where they will not damage public property. It will not force people to dance, even if the society has agreed that its people should do a period of National Service which normally includes dance activity. It will protect the statues from wilful damage. It will allow genuine conscientious objection to the bearing of arms, and so on. Always socialism will try to enlarge freedom, and religious freedom is an essential part of man's liberty.

THERE IS NO THEOLOGY OF SOCIALISM

There is, however, an apparent tendency among certain socialists to try and establish a new religion—a religion of socialism itself. This is usually called 'scientific socialism' and the works of Marx and Lenin are regarded as the holy writ in the light of which all other thoughts and actions of socialists have to be judged.

Of course, this doctrine is not presented as a religion; its proponents are often most anxious to decry religion as the 'opium of the people', and they present their beliefs as 'science'. Yet they talk and act in the same manner as the most rigid of theologians. We find them condemning one another's actions because they do not accord with what the priests of 'scientific socialism' have decided is the true meaning, in modern terms, of books written more than 100 years ago. Indeed we are fast getting to the stage where quarrels between different Christian sects about the precise meaning of the Bible fade into insignificance when compared with the quarrels of those who claim to be the true interpreters of Marxism-Leninism!

This attempt to create a new religion out of socialism is absurd. It is not scientific, and it is almost certainly not Marxist—for however combatant and quarrelsome a socialist Marx was, he never claimed to be an infallible divinity! Marx was a great thinker. He gave a brilliant analysis of the industrial capitalist society in which he lived; he diagnosed its ills and advocated certain remedies which he believed would lead to the development of a healthy society. But he was not God. The years have proved him wrong in certain respects just as they have proved him right in others. Marx did not write revealed truth; his books are the result of hard thinking and hard work, not a revelation from God. It is therefore unscientific to appeal to his writings as Christians appeal to the Bible, or Muslims to the Koran.

The works of Marx and Lenin are useful to a socialist because these men thought about the objective conditions of their time and tried to work out the actions necessary to achieve certain ends. We can learn from their methods of analysis, and from their ideas. But the same is true of many other thinkers of the past. It is no part of the job of a socialist in 1968 to worry about whether or not his actions or proposals are in accordance with what Marx or Lenin wrote, and it is a waste of time and energy to spend hours— if not months and years—trying to prove that what you have decided is objectively necessary is really in accordance with their teachings. The task of a socialist is to think out for himself the best way of achieving desired ends under the conditions which exist now. It is his job to think how to organize society, how to solve a particular problem, or how to effect certain changes, in a manner which will emphasize the importance of man and the equality of man.

It is especially important that we in Africa should understand this. We are groping our way forward towards socialism, and we are in danger of being bemused by this new theology, and therefore of trying to solve our problems according to what the priests of Marxism say is what Marx said or meant. If we do this we shall fail. Africa's conditions are very different from those of the Europe in which Marx and Lenin wrote and worked. To talk as if these thinkers provided all the answers to our problems, or as if Marx invented socialism, is to reject both the humanity of Africa and the universality of socialism. Marx did contribute a great deal to socialist thought. But socialism did not begin with him, nor can it end in constant reinterpretations of his writings.

Speaking generally, and despite the existence of a few feudalistic communities, traditional Tanzanian society had many socialist characteristics. The people did not call themselves socialists, and they were not socialists by deliberate design. But all people were workers, there was no living off the sweat of others. There was no very great difference in the amount of goods available to the different members of the society. All these are socialist characteristics. Despite the low level of material progress, traditional African society was in practice organized on a basis which was in accordance with socialist principles.

These conditions still prevail over large areas of Tanzania—and indeed in many other parts of Africa. Even in our urban areas, the social expectation of sharing what you have with your kinsfolk is still very strong—and causes great problems for individuals! These things have nothing to do with Marx; the people have never heard of him. Yet they provide a basis on which modern socialism can be built. To reject this base is to accept the idea that Africa has nothing to contribute to the march of mankind; it is to argue that the only way progress can be achieved in Africa is if we reject our own past and impose on ourselves the doctrines of some other society.

Nor would it be very scientific to reject Africa's past when trying to build socialism in Africa. For scientific thinking means finding out all the facts in a particular situation, regardless of whether you like them or not, or whether they fit in with preconceived ideas. It means analysing these facts, and then working out solutions to the problems you are concerned with in the light of these facts, and of the objectives you are trying to achieve. This is what Marx did in Europe in the middle of the nineteenth century; if he had lived in Sukumaland, Masailand, or Ruvuma, he would have written a different book than *Das Kapital*, but he could have been just as scientific and just as socialist. For if 'scientific socialism' means anything, it can only mean that the objectives are socialist and you apply scientific methods of study in working out the appropriate policies. If the phrase does not mean that, then it is simply a trap to ensnare the unwary into a denunciation of their own nature and therefore into a new form of oppression. For a scientist works to discover truth. He does not claim to know it, nor is he seeking to discover truth as revealed—which is the job of the theologian. A scientist works on the basis of the knowledge which has been accumulated empirically, and which is held to be true until new experience demonstrates otherwise, or demonstrates a superior truth which takes precedence in particular situations.

A really scientific socialist would therefore start his analysis of the problems of a particular society from the standpoint of that society. In Tanzania he would take the existence of some socialist values as part of his material for analysis; he would study the effect of the colonial era on these attitudes and on the systems of social organization; he would take account of the world situation as it affects Tanzania. After doing all that he would try to work out policies appropriate for the growth of a modern socialist state. And he could well finish up with the Arusha Declaration and the policies of ujamaa!

A scientific socialist could do all this with or without a knowledge and understanding of Marx and Lenin—or for that matter Saint-Simon, Owen or Laski. Knowledge of the work and thinking of these and other people may help a socialist to know what to look for and how to evaluate the things he sees; but it could also mislead him if he is not careful. Equally, a knowledge of history may help him to learn from the experience of others; a knowledge of economics will help him to understand some of the forces at work in the society. But if he tries to use any of these disciplines or philosophies as a gospel according to which he must work out solutions he will go wrong. There is no substitute for his own hard work and hard thinking.

For example, a study of the work of past socialist thinkers and of history and economics appears to have led some people to argue that Tanzania can only become socialist if it first goes through the stage of capitalism. Yet it is difficult to believe that they thought about the objective conditions of this country when coming to this conclusion. (It is also difficult to believe that they understand the principles of socialism—the attitude of mind it requires!) Certainly Tanzania was part of the Western capitalist world while it was under colonial domination, but it was very much on the fringe. Certainly our independent nation inherited a few capitalist institutions, and some of our people adopted capitalist and individualistic ideas as a result of their education or their envy of the colonial representatives whom they encountered. But the masses of the people did not become capitalist, and are not filled with capitalist ideas. By far the largest part of our economy is not organized on capitalist lines. Indeed, whenever we try to help Africans to become capitalist shopkeepers, capitalist farmers, industrialists, etc., we find that most of them fail because they cannot adopt the capitalist practices which are essential to commercial success! Yet rather than give up their theories, these dogmatists often attribute these African failures to the machinations of a racial minority—thus revealing their racialism and non-socialist beliefs—instead of recognizing that capitalism demands certain attributes among its practitioners which the majority of our people have never been forced to acquire.

Under these circumstances what would be the sense in working to create capitalism, with all the individualism, social aggressiveness, and human indignities which it involves? These attributes would have to be fought against, and the organizations of capitalism destroyed or reformed, when you finally decided that the task of building socialism could be begun. And when should opposition to capitalism be started? If capitalism must precede socialism, how far does it have to go before it can be replaced?

Capitalism would only have to precede socialism if there was some reason to believe that the people will fail to solve the problems of production except by capitalist methods. It is certainly true that capitalism can lead to the high output of goods and services—no socialist would dispute that. But there is very little evidence to support the contention that only through capitalism can a satisfactory level of production be attained; indeed there is an increasing amount of evidence with which to refute such a statement. Countries like the USSR, East Germany, China, and North Korea may differ in their approach to socialism, but they are certainly not capitalist, and they do produce the goods their people need. North Korea, for example, may not be able to compare with the state of New York in the provision of television sets, cars, and fashion clothes; but it has electrified something like 98 per cent of its villages, and 86 per cent of its farm houses, and it has built new and improved houses for about two thirds of its rural families in the space of eight years. In other words, the priorities of production may be different, and the emphasis given to economic output as against other values may vary, but North Korea has shown that production can be organized in a non-capitalist manner. If it can be done once, what reason is there to believe that it cannot be done again?

The real truth is that the principles of socialism are relevant to all human society at all stages of technology and social organization. But their application has constantly to be worked out afresh according to the objective conditions prevailing in the time or place. There is no book which provides all the answers to these problems of application; there is no 'socialist road map' which depicts all obstacles and provides a path through or around them. In fact we have no alternative but to hold fast to the principles of socialism—to understand its characteristics—and then apply the accumulated knowledge of man to the continuing and changing problems of man. And we have to do this as best we can, without the infinite knowledge which belongs to God and which would provide the answers to all our problems. There is no magic formula, and no short cut to socialism. We can only grope our way forward, doing our best to think clearly—and scientifically—about our own conditions in relation to our objectives.

THERE IS NO MODEL FOR US TO COPY

In 1965 Tanzania adopted its own form of democracy—we rejected the Western model and said it was not appropriate for our circumstances despite the fact that all our constitutional development had until then been based on it. We looked at different democratic systems round the world, and studied the work of different thinkers, and we asked ourselves two questions. First, what is the purpose of democratic systems? And second, what are the conditions of Tanzania, and what special problems face the country? Then we worked out a system of one-party Government which seemed to us to include the essential elements of democracy at the same time as it provided for unity and strength in Government, and took account of our poverty, our size, our traditions, and our aspirations. The resultant constitution is not perfect; but it suits us better than any system operating elsewhere, and we believe that it safeguards the people's sovereignty at the same time as it enables the effective and strong Government so essential at this stage of our development.

When we introduced this new system, we were criticized for 'abandoning democracy', and even now these charges are still heard. The criticisms came mostly from the traditional democracies of the West; even some of our sympathizers felt that we had taken a step backwards in our development. In response to this criticism we tried to explain what we were trying to do and why we thought our new system was both democratic and suitable for our conditions. But having done that we did not worry about what the Western countries said or what democratic theorists said. For in rejecting the idea that we had to follow the 'Westminster model' if we wanted to be democratic, we had also overcome the psychological need to have a certificate of approval from the West in relation to our political system. We did not reject this idea of an accolade from the West because we were critical of the political systems operating in Western countries. On the contrary, there was much that we admired in them, and we learned a great deal from them. But we acted as intelligent and thoughtful citizens of Tanzania who wanted democracy to be a continuing reality in our own country.

What we have done in relation to democracy we have also to do in relation to socialism. It is not intelligent to reject an accolade from the West on democracy in order to seek one from the East on socialism. Socialism is about people, and people are the products of their history, education, and environment. It is absurd to assume that while democracy has to be adapted to the circumstances of the country in order that the people's will shall be effective, socialism can just be copied from somewhere else. Admiration of some facets of democracy in Britain, Sweden, and elsewhere did not lead us to imitation. Equally we should be able to admire certain things which have been done in China, Russia, Korea, Yugoslavia, and so on, without assuming that any of these countries provide a model for us to copy.

Unfortunately some of our people—often the ones who were most insistent that we should not copy the democracy of the West—are now judging our socialist policies and progress by what Moscow or Peking have done, and are demanding that we do something because it has proved useful in one of these places. They get upset if the communist parties of these countries express disapproval (either explicitly or implicitly), because they believe that the model for socialism already exists there, and that we can only be really socialist if we have earned a 'certificate of approval' from the guardians of this model. Such people are refusing to think for themselves. They are saying that the perfect answer to the problems of man in society is already known, and all we have to do is to copy others. Once again, they are saying that Africa has nothing to contribute to the world and all good things come from elsewhere. And then, in their insecurity, they look for a 'certificate of socialist approval' from the country or party which they believe has these answers.

We must avoid this attitude. It is neither patriotic nor sensible to deny the need for Western approval and in the next breath to seek an accolade from the East. Tanzania does not need a certificate of approval about its internal policies from any outside group. The only approval our policies need is the approval of the Tanzanian people. We shall get that if we succeed in dealing with our own problems in a way which is suitable to our present circumstances and acceptable to the people's beliefs and understanding at any one time. True Tanzanians will worry about what the Tanzanian people think, not what anyone else thinks. True Tanzanian socialists will worry about how the Tanzanian people can move in the quickest possible time towards a society where socialist principles find their fullest expression. They will not worry about the approval or disapproval of other socialists in matters which are of exclusive concern to us.

Of course it would be stupid to allow an insistence on working out our own policies to develop into a rejection of the lessons we can learn from the experiences of other countries and the ideas of other people. To say that Tanzania does not need certificates of approval from this country or that does not mean that we cannot learn from non-Tanzanians. This kind of automatic rejection of something because it is said by an American or Chinese, or done in Britain or Poland, is as much a reflection of an inferiority complex as the automatic acceptance of what they say or do.

Why should Tanzania not learn from the agricultural communes of China? Their experience could promote thought and ideas about our own rural organization, provided that we go to learn, and proceed to think—not to copy. Why can we not learn from the Korean success in rural transformation in comparison with continuing difficulties in other Communist countries? Do the Cuban experiments in adult education have nothing to teach us? Agricultural organization, rural transformation, adult education, are all problems we have to deal with in Tanzania; why should we not study the techniques used by other men to see if they could usefully be adapted to meet our needs, or if they provide a clue to the solution of a difficulty we are experiencing?

Nor do we have to confine our attention to development in communist countries. The co-operative settlements of Israel, the co-operative organizations of Denmark and Sweden, have all accumulated great experience which we could learn from. Even the most avowedly capitalist countries have something to teach us—for example, the techniques by which they encourage workers to increase their output. We do not have to adopt these blindly, but we could usefully consider whether, or to what extent, these techniques are acceptable to a socialist society. And what of the freedom for individuals to express their beliefs and ideas about government, about policies, about organization? Is there nothing valuable for us in this freedom? Even if individual freedom to vote and organize does not have the exclusive importance which advocates of capitalism appear to give it, surely it is a reflection of one facet of man's equality and therefore important to a socialist? How far can we achieve this kind of freedom and equality in our circumstances without sacrificing other freedoms and equalities?

We in Tanzania are a part of mankind. We have to take our place in the world. We would be stupid to reject everything or everyone coming out of the West because that is the home of capitalism; we would be stupid to reject everything the communists do. We are trying to build ujamaa—socialism—which is neither of these things. We can learn from both—and from other political systems—without trying to copy or seeking for their approval. Our task is to look first at our own position and our own needs, and then to consider other experience and other suggestions in the light of our requirements. We should not put ourselves into blinkers as though we were a horse which could not be trusted to see what is going on elsewhere. We should be willing to learn from our fellow men, and we should contribute to the common pool of knowledge and experience. We can do this if we use our brains—that is, if we THINK.

THE UNIVERSALITY AND DIVERSITY OF SOCIALISM

What does all this amount to? It is an expression of belief that man can only live in harmony with man, and can only develop to his full potential as a unique individual, in a society the purpose of which is Man, which is based on the principles of human equality, and which is so organized as to emphasize both man's equality and his control over all the instruments of his life and development.

It is a statement that because men are different, and because different communities and societies have had different histories, live in different geographical conditions, and have developed different customs and systems of belief, therefore the road to socialism and the institutions through which socialism is ultimately expressed will be different. It is a statement insisting that the progress of one man or group of men does not make it unnecessary for other men and other groups to think for themselves. It is an assertion that there are no natural laws of human development which we have only to discover and apply in order to reach the Nirvana of a perfect socialist society; on the contrary, that it is by deliberate design that men will build socialist societies, and by deliberate design that they will maintain socialist principles in a form which seems to them to be good. It is an assertion of man's unity and also his diversity; the validity of certain basic principles for social living, and the variety of their expression. It is a statement that one will not recognize or define a socialist society by its institutions or its statements, but by its fundamental characteristics of equality, cooperation, and freedom.

THE TRANSITION TO SOCIALISM

By definition, however, the characteristics which identify a socialist state will not exist in their entirety in a state which is trying to build socialism. If the institutions, and the attitudes, of socialism existed it would be socialist; until then it is inevitable that at least some of the essential elements of socialist society will be missing. This is true whether the commitment to socialism is linked with revolution, or whether it follows peaceful political development.

Socialism does not spring ready-made out of the womb of violence. Even the most successful and popular revolution inevitably leaves behind it a legacy of bitterness, suspicion and hostility between members of the society. These are not conducive to the institutions of equality, and make it difficult to build a spirit of co-operation between the whole people. In particular there is always a fear that those who suffered during the revolution may be looking for an opportunity of revenge; there is the memory of injury and bereavement deliberately inflicted, which poisons the relations between men within the society. A violent revolution may make the introduction of socialist *institutions* easier; it makes more difficult the development of the socialist *attitudes* which give life to these institutions.

This is not to say that violent revolutions are always wrong or irrelevant to socialism. Sometimes they are a regrettable necessity because they are the only way to break the power of those who prevent progress towards socialism. But violence is a short cut only to the destruction of the institutions and power groups of the old society; they are not a short cut to the building of the new. For even if change is secured through the violent overthrow of a feudal or a fascist society, the new life has still to be built by and with people who lived in the old society and who were shaped by it even if they reacted against it. The necessity for a violent revolution brings its own problems to the building of socialism; they may be different problems from those experienced by the states which are fortunate enough to be able to move peacefully from one kind of social system to another, but they are nonetheless real.

In fact those who talk as if violence must always and everywhere precede socialism, and who judge a country to be developing towards socialism only if violence has occurred, are almost certainly not socialist in their own attitudes. For violence cannot be welcomed by those who care about people. It is a very serious matter because of the misery and suffering it involves for human beings; it should only be accepted as a necessity when every other road forward is completely blocked and cannot be cleared by persistence, by public determination, or by other expressions of the majority will. Violence itself is the opposite of a socialist characteristic. Brigands can govern by violence and fear; dictatorships can establish themselves and flourish. Socialism cannot be imposed in this way, for it is based on equality. It denies the right of any individual or any small minority, to say, 'I know and the others are fools who must be led like sheep'. Leadership can be given—and indeed must be given—in a socialist state. But it must be the people's leadership, which they accept because ultimately they control it. Socialist leadership is of the people; it cannot be imposed by force or tyranny.

This means that where a violent revolution was a necessary precondition for the establishment of an opportunity to begin the work of building socialism, the early period of transition towards this goal will have certain kinds of non-socialist characteristics. There may well be suspicions, fear, illegalities, and an absence of political freedom; there may be something of a vacuum in effective administration even as brave attempts are made to create the groundwork of socialist economic organizations.

If, on the other hand, the transition out of the old society can be effected by non-violent means, different non-socialist characteristics will be evident as the work of building is in process. There will be many remnants of the preceding social organization; many old habits may continue simply because social upheaval has not forced people to think about them; and old attitudes and behaviour may still be dominant in people holding responsible positions. These things create difficulties for socialist progress just as the aftermath of a revolution creates difficulties. By whichever method the conditions for building socialism are established, a visitor could look at the society in transition and deny its socialism, or its progress, by pointing to characteristics which are non-socialist, or even antisocialist.

This is as true in Tanzania as elsewhere, and indeed our Union provides examples of the difficulties of both kinds of transition. In Zanzibar the revolution cleared many obstacles from the path of socialism, but it created other difficulties and fears. On the mainland, where political circumstances obviated the necessity for violence, we are able to try to build socialism by evolution—by dealing with the problems one by one in accordance with the consensus of opinion and our capacity at any one time. But this, too, has its difficulties, and the danger that self-seeking men will be able to mislead the people into opposing the struggle forward. And in both parts of the Union we have still to ensure that new privileged groups do not grow out of the post-independence and post-revolutionary forces.

The solution to all these problems depends upon the growth of socialist understanding and socialist attitudes among the people. In particular it depends upon the speed and success with which the concepts of human equality and the people's sovereignty are accepted by the society and the leadership in the society. Institutions can help to spread these ideas and encourage their expression, but they do not in themselves provide an answer. Thus, for example, the Permanent Commission of Enquiry provides machinery through which members of the public can complain against petty tyranny of leaders and officials, but its effectiveness depends upon the willingness of the people to make and to substantiate their complaints, as well as the willingness of Government and Party personnel to correct wrongs which reduce the people's sovereignty. Or, again, the leadership qualifications are aimed at emphasizing the identity of the leadership and the people, but they can only restrict behaviour negatively—and their intentions can be evaded. There is, in fact, no substitute for the individual moral courage of men; everything ultimately depends upon the determination of the people to be judges over those to whom they have entrusted positions of responsibility and leadership. The only way in which leadership can be maintained as a people's leadership is if the leaders have reason to fear the judgement of the people.

The people's purposes in society, however, will only go forward smoothly when they exercise their power over leadership in a calm and deliberate manner—and when the institutions of the society enable them to do so. And the people have to understand their own power, and its importance to their future; they have to understand the basic principles of socialism. Only then will they be able to avoid being used by the jealousies and envies of individuals who seek to exploit, for their own ambition's sake, the honest mistakes of individual leaders. Only then will the people be able to avoid the blandishments of those who, for their own benefit, pretend that there is a short cut to socialism and to prosperity which the existing leaders stand in the way of. The people's will must be sovereign; but it will only lead them to the equalities and dignities of socialism if they exert that sovereignty with an understanding of socialism.

THE PROBLEMS OF BUILDING SOCIALISM IN AN EX-COLONIAL COUNTRY

There are particular problems about this in an ex-colonial country like Tanzania. For to build socialism you must have socialists—particularly in leading positions. It is not enough that our people's traditional life should have been based upon socialist principles; that is good, but it is necessary that the leaders in modernization should also accept those principles and be able to apply them in the very different technological and international conditions of the twentieth century. Further, it is essential that the people should be aware of the new socialist objective and what it means to them.

Yet in Tanzania the great mass campaigns of the 1950s and early 1960s were for independence. We campaigned against colonialism, against foreign domination. We did not campaign against capitalism or for socialism. Creating still more difficulties was the fact that the colonialism we fought against was that of a people who happened to be of a different racial group than ourselves. It was fatally easy to identify the thing you were fighting against as people of this other race—the Europeans. It is true that we in Tanzania campaigned on the grounds of human equality; that has helped us. But the problem Africa knew was that of discrimination against the African majority. We therefore asked, 'Why are there no African District Commissioners, administrators, supervisors, secretaries, etc.?', and often this was transposed into, 'Why are there European or Asian—this and that?'. Humanity took second place in this struggle very often; even when political leaders said on public platforms and elsewhere that they would never countenance reverse discrimination after independence, this was sometimes interpreted as a manoeuvre designed to avoid the heavy hand of the colonial authority! Almost throughout Africa, therefore, the first and most vocal demand of the people after independence was for Africanization. They did not demand localization—indeed, the most popular thing would have been for leaders to deny citizenship to non-black residents. Still less did the people demand socialization; they simply demanded the replacement of white and brown faces by black ones. The leaders could therefore receive applause if they replaced white, or brown, capitalists by black ones. Capitalism was the system which the masses knew in the modern sector, and what they had been fighting against was that this modern sector should be in alien hands.

It was not only the masses who looked upon things in this way; many leaders of the independence struggle themselves saw things in these terms. They were not against capitalism; they simply wanted its fruits, and saw independence as the means to that end. Indeed, many of the most active fighters in the independence movement were motivated—consciously or unconsciously—by the belief that only with independence could they attain that ideal of individual wealth which their education or their experience in the modern sector had established as a worthwhile goal. It is in this fact that lies the paradox of the changing classifications given to different African leaders by the capitalists of the colonial territories. For the 'extremist' of the independence period was sometimes the man who was saying, 'Kill the whites' because he wanted what they had for himself. In such a case (if he survives) the 'extremist' may well become a great defender of capitalism after independence, and he will then probably be reclassified as a 'moderate'! Similarly, the independence campaigner who opposed the murder of non-Africans could either have been deeply religious, or he could have been a socialist. If he was the latter, his classification by the capitalists after independence is liable to change from 'moderate' to 'extremist' or 'communist'!

This lack of ideological content during the independence struggle often served to maintain unity among the anti-colonialist forces, or to prevent a diversion of energies into the difficult questions of socialist education. (It was not always selfishness which made leaders think only in terms of Africanizing the capitalist economy of the colonialists; often they had no knowledge of any alternative). But it can present a serious problem in the post-independence period. Once they have power, some of the leaders whom the people have learned to know and trust will think their nationalism demands expropriation of non-Africans in favour of African citizens; the more sophisticated may deny this but think of economic development in terms of expanding capitalism with the participation of Africans.

Such leaders as these may well identify the progress they have promised the people with the increasing wealth of the few; they will point to African-owned large cars and luxurious houses, and so on, as evidence of growing prosperity and of their own devotion to the cause of national independence. It was on this basis, for example, that some Tanzanian leaders criticized the Arusha Declaration. They said that the leadership qualifications prevented Africans from becoming landowners and businessmen, while Asians and Europeans could continue in these fields as they had done before independence. These critics thus demonstrated their conviction, firstly, that Asian citizens could not or should not desire to hold responsible positions in the society; and secondly, that exploitation was only wrong when carried out upon the masses by people of a different race. Incidentally, they were also showing that they wished to use positions of power for private gain, because almost the only way in which Africans could get the capital to become landlords or capitalists was by virtue of their office or their seniority in the public service. (There were exceptions to this general rule, because there had been isolated instances before independence of Africans establishing themselves in business or modern farming. But in general it was the post-independence accession to power which enabled Africans to enter the capitalist system as owners or employers instead of as workers).

The perpetuation of capitalism, and its expansion to include Africans, will be accepted by the masses who took part in the independence struggle. They may take the new wealth of their leaders as natural and even good—for a time they may even take a reflected pride in it. This may go on for a long period if economic circumstances of the country allow a simultaneous lightening of the general poverty—or even if the conditions of the masses remain static. This public acceptance of African capitalism will be obtained because the people have learned to trust their nationalist leaders, and will wish to honour them. Also there will inevitably be new jobs and opportunities for a good number of the most active, vocal and intelligent of those who might otherwise have led criticism. And on top of that, there will be an end to stupidities like interference with traditional African customs by a foreign Government. But, sooner or later, the people will lose their enthusiasm and will look upon the independence Government as simply another new ruler which they should avoid as much as possible. Provided it has been possible to avoid any fundamental upset in their traditional economic and social conditions, they will then sink back into apathy —until the next time someone is able to convince them that their own efforts can lead to an improvement in their lives!

It is comparatively easy to get independence from a colonial power—especially one which claims to base its national morality on the principles of freedom and democracy. Everyone wants to be free, and the task of a nationalist is simply to rouse the people to a confidence in their own power of protest. But to build the real freedom which socialism represents is a very different thing. It demands a positive understanding and positive actions, not simply a rejection of colonialism and a willingness to co-operate in non-co-operation. And the anti-colonial struggle will almost certainly have intensified the difficulties.

During the campaign for independence a number of developments were probably inevitable, or were unavoidable except at great cost. First, is the fact that racialism has been allowed to grow—and may even have been indirectly encouraged during the process of simplifying the issues at stake. In Tanzania the masses remained remarkably free from this disease— and are still free. But many of the leaders suffered from discrimination themselves, and some have been unable to achieve that degree of objectivity which would enable them to direct their hatred towards discrimination itself instead of at the racial group which the discriminators represented. Yet racialism is absolutely and fundamentally contrary to first principle of socialism—the equality of man.

Second, the most active, and therefore the most popular, of the nationalist leaders may have been people without a socialist conviction. They may either have never had an opportunity to study the problems and possibilities of social and economic organization, or they may even have been people who were motivated by a personal desire for the fruits of capitalism.

Third, all the national Party organization and education were geared to defeating colonialism and to opposing people of another race who happened to be in positions of power. This means that once idependence is achieved, and the key positions of power have been Africanized, there is a grave danger that the Party will loose support and will atrophy. The people—and even many of the leaders—may feel that the Party has achieved its purpose; once independence has been attained there is no point in the effort required to sustain it.

All these things mean that after independence the work of building socialism has to be started from the beginning. The people have to be shown another goal— the goal of socialism—and they have to learn that only by extending their efforts for this second purpose will they really benefit from the effort they have already made.

To do this new task a strong Party organization is as essential as it was before independence, but it involves a serious and conscious effort on the part of the leaders. In particular they have to act deliberately so as to emphasize their identification with the people, and so as to remain one of them. During the independence struggle this was no problem: the leaders lived with the people, and were as poor as the masses whom they led. They had no choice in the matter and no particular temptation. In the struggle for socialism the position is different: often the leaders have to live in more comfortable surroundings if they are to do their new Government tasks efficiently, and they are also faced with all the temptations of power. Yet to be effective leaders in this second phase of the freedom struggle, it is essential that they should turn their backs on these temptations; they have to act like socialists and be prepared to account to the people for all the personal wealth which they deploy.

However, it is not only leaders who must be involved in the building of socialism. There must be an active adult education system which is directed at helping the people to understand the principles of socialism and their relevance to real development and freedom. There must be local institutions of socialism—co-operative societies which are under the effective control of the members, ujamaa villages, and so on. These are as essential to the building of ujamaa as the Government action which secures control of the key points of the economy for the people at the same time as it mobilizes all the resources of skill and experience which are available. In addition, new economic, social and political institutions must be created which will stress the equality of all men regardless of race or tribe, and which will enable the people to make their voices heard throughout the society. Yet all this must be done under conditions which safeguard these infant institutions, and the young state, from subversion. These things must be achieved while the people are protected against the manipulation of those who are so arrogant that they wish to enforce their own judgement of what is 'the good life'.

This is a formidable—though not exhaustive—list of work to be done even when stated in such broad and general terms. It becomes much more difficult when translated into practice—when you begin to work out the details which appear insignificant but which can make all the difference to success or failure. The difficulties are exacerbated in Africa where the responsibilities and temptations of new nationhood coincide with a great shortage of educated people, of finance, and of committed, modern, and thinking socialists. But these same difficulties also provide unique opportunities. Because a new nation has been created, the people are ready and anxious for change—they only need leadership based on human respect. And the absence of large financial resources—once it is understood and accepted—forces a concentration on the abilities and the importance of men rather than money, and thus orientates the society towards the development of man instead of material wealth. The very magnitude of the problem creates a challenge, and the major difficulty is to relate the hard, detailed work, and the long-drawn-out struggle forward, to the ultimate goal.

In Tanzania we have begun the work of building socialism. So far all that we have really achieved is some success in showing people that there is another goal to work for now that our independence exists. For the rest we have tried to prevent the growth of new and stronger groups with a vested interest in capitalism; we have established some of the institutions through which the people can speak; and we have just begun to search out and help the local experiments in modern socialism. We have defined our policies in education, in rural development, and have listed our expectations of leadership. But we are NOT a socialist society. Our work has only just begun. Of particular priority are the outstanding tasks of socialist adult education, and of strengthening the people's self-confidence and pride. These are the essential preliminaries to real freedom from the abuse of power, and from the dangers of manipulation by ambitious, dishonest, and selfish men. They are also fundamental to the people's active participation in, and control of, the development of a new society.

The ultimate success in the work of building socialism in Tanzania —as elsewhere—depends upon the people of this nation. For any society is only what the people make it. The benefit to the people of a socialist society will depend upon their contribution to it—their work, their co-operation for the common good, and their acceptance of each other as equals and brothers.

To the extent that we in Tanzania succeed in the struggle to which we have committed ourselves, so we shall be taking our place in the march of humanity towards peace and human dignity. For too long we in Africa—and Tanzania as part of Africa—have slept, and allowed the rest of the world to walk round and over us. Now we are beginning to wake up and to join with our fellow human beings in deciding the destiny of the human race. By thinking out our own problems on the basis of those principles which have universal validity, Tanzania will make its contribution to the development of mankind. That is our opportunity and our responsibility.

August 1968   J.K.N.

1

Tanzania's Long March is Economic

At the state banquet in honour of Premier Chou En Lai on 4 June 1965, President Nyerere began by paying tribute to the guest and his colleagues for their life of sacrifice, and referred particularly to the Long March undertaken by the beleaguered Red Army in 1934/5. He went on:

...We in Tanzania were more fortunate, but although not put to this kind of test ourselves we are able to appreciate the meaning of such determination and such sacrifice. It is with deep sincerity that we salute the achievements of the Chinese people and their leaders. And if our own independence should ever be threatened from any quarter I believe that your example will assist us to find similar courage.

There is, however, another lesson which we can learn from the Chinese revolution. It is that courage, enthusiasm, and endurance are not enough. There must also be discipline, and the intelligent application of policies to the needs and circumstances of the country and the time. There is no single answer which is applicable in all times and at all places. Each country and each generation has to deal with its own problems in its own way, exploiting to the greatest possible advantage such opportunities as are available to it. This means that the different countries of the world will use different methods, and different systems, of economic, social and political organization. It is only by doing so that each of them will achieve the common aim of human progress and betterment.

Yet while our national paths may be different, the unity of mankind and our common aspiration for peace, freedom, and economic well-being, mean that we can and should maintain friendship and mutual co-operation. Both China and Tanzania are now engaged in a new kind of revolutionary battle—the fight against poverty and economic backwardness. For Tanzania, in fact, the 'Long March' is an economic one, and the enemy we have to fight does not kill us with bullets, but weakens us with disease, tempts us to slothfulness, and encourages us to indulge in the boastfulness of conspicuous consumption when all our energies are needed for the work ahead. And it is a fact, Mr. Premier, that in this respect too, we can learn from China. The singlemindedness with which the Chinese people are concentrating on development was the thing which most impressed me during my visit to your great country. The conscious and deliberate frugality with which your people and your Government efficiently and joyfully conduct their affairs was a big lesson for me, and through me for my people. I believe we shall begin to apply that lesson.

Before I sit down there is one other thing I wish to mention. I have said that Tanzania's Long March is an economic one; but this is not the whole truth. While we use every possible weapon against our poverty, we have at the same time to guard the sovereignty and the integrity of our United Republic against any who wish to take advantage of our current need in order to get control over us.

Happily we shall enter into agreements and contracts for trade and economic assistance with friendly peoples and nations from all parts of the globe. But from no quarter shall we accept direction, or neo-colonialism, and at no time shall we lower our guard against the subversion of our Government or our people. Neither our principles, our country, nor our freedom to determine our own future are for sale.

And there is more to it than that. Tanzania is not yet wholly free; because Africa is not wholly free. We cannot concentrate all our energies on the economic battle until that situation is remedied. We are still hoping, and still working, to see that freedom gained by peaceful means. But we know that whatever happens, freedom for the whole of Africa must be won. And Africa is determined to win it.

Mr. Premier, the People's Republic of China and the United Republic of Tanzania are different in many important respects—and in particular in our size and potential importance in the world. But our peoples also have many things in common. Among these are a desire for peace, freedom, economic development, and mutual friendship. I am therefore proud, on behalf of Tanzania, to salute the people of your great country, the Chairman of your Party—Mao Tse Tung—and you yourselves, our guests here this evening.

2

Dissolving the Independence Parliament

This address to the National Assembly was delivered, in Swahili, on 8 June 1965. In it, the President recommended the One–Party Constitutional Proposals, and then went on to speak at length about the progress and requirements of economic development.

Under our constitution it is my privilege sometimes to address this House directly instead of through my Ministerial colleagues. I do so today for two reasons.

In the first place I wish to inform you that it is my intention to dissolve Parliament at the end of this present sitting. As citizens of an independent country our people in mainland Tanzania will then have their first opportunity to select their representatives in Parliament for the coming five years. Fundamental changes have taken place since 1960 when the last election was held. This Parliament has been responsible, in co-operation with the Government and the people, for effecting a constitutional revolution in our national status, and for beginning the much longer process of effecting an economic revolution. But there is much more work ahead of us, and it is now time that the people of this Republic should have an opportunity once again to select the persons who will speak for them.

My second task today is to ask this House to consider the proposals for implementing a one-party state, which will later be submitted to you in the form of Constitutional Amendments and related Bills. And it is in this context of learning from the past that I ask this House to study the Budget and other matters which will be submitted to you by the Minister for Finance.

THE ONE-PARTY STATE PROPOSALS

TANU was formed, and received the overwhelming support of the people of Tanganyika, because of certain basic political principles. Its purpose was to bring democracy to Tanganyika, and by so doing to establish the independence of this nation and the opportunity for the people to determine and control their own development. That remains the purpose of TANU, and it is on the basis of this principle that you are being asked to establish a one-party system by law.

Since 1958, in election after election, the overwhelming national support of TANU has been increasingly demonstrated. The United Tanganyika Party was destroyed by the votes of the people; the African National Congress failed to safeguard even its candidates' deposits; only one independent candidate has ever been elected to this House in opposition to TANU—and he was one of those rare exceptions which truly prove the rule: he was a member of TANU who continued to recruit members for TANU even during the very campaign in which he was opposing TANU's official candidate. The people are united behind their national movement.

In consequence of this a candidate supported by TANU is automatically elected; the people want a TANU representative. Yet, because we have been operating in the context of a multi-party system the people have no choice as to which TANU candidate. This means that our procedures are, in practice, endangering both democracy and unity; if the people always acquiesce in the TANU candidate who is submitted to them by the Party machinery they are losing their effective power over the representative and his actions. If they oppose him they are in danger of giving sustenance to the enemies of our national unity and bringing into jeopardy the future of the principles which they wish to defend. We have thus come to a position where the maintenance of institutions and procedures which were supposed to safeguard the practice of democracy, and which are appropriate to a multi-party system, in fact eliminates the people's choice of their representative.

It was to remedy this situation that the TANU Annual Conference decided, in 1963, to establish a democratic one-party system by law. A Presidential Commission was set up to consider what constitutional and other changes were necessary to implement this objective. Its report is now before you, together with a Government White Paper which incorporates the amendments decided upon by the

Party and the Government. Before the end of this Parliament the legislation necessary to implement the proposals will be submitted for your consideration.

If, as I hope, you support the measures which will be put before you, this Parliament will then be responsible for four major constitutional developments in its five years of existence, three of which are directly related to the institutions and system of Government. The independence constitution of Tanganyika was worked out by TANU in co-operation with the colonial power; it was obviously and directly influenced by the practices of democracy in Britain. There was nothing very wrong in that; in the light of our history it was an appropriate starting point. But the institutions of a democratic government must reflect the national culture, and the national ambitions, of the country in which they are working. Therefore, in 1962, we ourselves worked out the republican constitution under which we have since governed ourselves. The proposals now before this House are a further effort to develop for ourselves institutions which suit our own conditions, and our own ambitions.

I do not believe there is anything wrong in making these changes in our fundamental law—in our constitution. In July 1961 I said that in relation to the form of our future society, and in relation to our political institutions, we must 'grope our way forward.' This means that we must learn by thinking about our own experience, and about that of other people. We refuse to adopt the institutions of other countries even where they have served those countries well—because it is our conditions that have to be served by our institutions. We refuse to put ourselves in a strait-jacket of constitutional devices—even of our own making. The constitution of Tanzania must serve the people of Tanzania. We do not intend that the people of Tanzania should serve the constitution.

Certainly the constitution must not be treated lightly. Any change in it must be carefully considered and fully debated to see whether we really believe it will achieve the purpose we desire. I believe that the proposals now before you are the product of this kind of careful thought; the Commission's report is, in fact, a document which deserves to have a place in international political history. It was prepared after nation-wide consultations with the people, and it has since been discussed—and amended—by TANU.

In asking for your approval of the White Paper and the consequent legislation, let me make it clear that I am not claiming that this is the final answer for us. We believe that these proposals will help to ensure the people's control over a strong central Government. But faults may be revealed in practice, or the circumstances in which our political institutions work may change. We should be making a big mistake if we treated the amended constitution as a sacred text, which must not be criticized or amended under any circumstances.

The constitution of Tanzania, both in the past and in the future, is sacred in one sense only. That is the sense in which it provides a framework within which—and only within which—both the Government and the laws can be changed at the will of the people. To attempt to change either the laws or the Government outside that framework—that pattern of procedure—is treason to our country. But it would be stupidity if mistaken notions of the immutability of the constitution made the people themselves feel unable to change their constitution even if experience shows that it is not able to facilitate the principles it is supposed to serve.

The amendments and changes in law which are in the White Paper and are submitted for consideration do not at all change the nation's basic principles. We remain committed to democracy; Government believes that these changes will permit it to operate more effectively. We recognize and rejoice in the fact that democracy can only operate on the basis of the equality of every citizen of the Republic; Government believes that these proposals will strengthen the political equality of all Tanzanian citizens. We believe that there are certain ethical principles which must lie at the basis of any society, and any nation, and which its institutions should serve. In the National Ethic an attempt has been made to spell these out for Tanzania, and the Government believes that the application of these principles will receive support from the political changes it is recommending

It is not my intention now to list the changes which are proposed. I wish to draw your attention to only a few points which I believe to be fundamental to the proposals. The first is the nature of the Party which will be the single political organization of this state. It will be a mass Party through which any citizen who accepts TANU's basic principles can participate in the process of Government. This provision is in line with the history of TANU, and is a basic factor in the Government's proposals for a one-party democracy.

The second point I wish to mention is the changes which are proposed in the method of selecting candidates for this House and for local government, and for electing the Members. The provision that the people shall have a choice between two TANU candidates is designed to eliminate the present apparent conflict between, on the one hand, freedom to choose the representative, and, on the other hand, the preservation of national unity. The unique procedures through which it is proposed that these candidates shall be selected and submitted to the judgement of the people are designed to avoid sowing the seeds of permanent division—even between individuals—while at the same time giving the people a good opportunity to know and assess the character and ability of those who are asking for their votes.

Thirdly, I wish you to consider carefully the different method which is proposed for the election of the President of this United Republic. The powers of the President under our constitution are very great indeed; in addition he represents in his person the unity and dignity of our nation. It is necessary that this National Assembly should make quite clear its views on this matter.

Finally, on these political developments, I wish to commend to you the proposal to establish a Permanent Commission on the Abuse of Power. The nature of our economic problems in Tanzania demands that many officers of the Government, the Party, and the law itself, should be entrusted with great powers over other individuals. At the same time our recent history, and the educational backwardness of the majority of our people mean that automatic checks on abuse of power are almost non-existent. To the people in the villages and scattered homesteads of our wide country, it is the policeman, the magistrate, the TANU official or the Government officer, who represents Government in their everyday life. And in the District and Regional Headquarters it is the Commissioner who wields direct and effective power in a manner which affects the life of our fellow citizens. This is inevitable and necessary. Only by entrusting real responsibility to such people can our nation be transformed. But we have to recognize that these powers can be—and have been —abused. And the sufferers are the people on whose behalf Government is, and should be, conducted.

It is intended that the Commission on the Abuse of Power should receive and investigate complaints by the people of this country, and that it should submit reports and make recommendations to the President. The people will have direct access to it. The Government believes that the operation of such a Commission should help to make a reality of the political equality of all our people, and of their individual freedom within the context of our socialist society.

ECONOMIC PLAN SURVEY

I have talked for a long time about these political matters. But as we have said on very many previous occasions, our political organization is only one aspect of the heavy task ahead of us. It must assist us to retain and expand personal freedom and human dignity and, at the same time, it must enable us to develop the economy of the country. For only if we do this shall we really build the kind of life our people wish to live. It is on this subject which I now wish to speak.

Almost one year ago we began to implement the Five-Year Development Plan for Tanganyika. It is now time for us to make a first assessment of the Plan in practice, and to examine our failures and the reason for them, so that we can take any steps which are necessary for improvement.

This means that we must ask ourselves the question, 'Have we been succeeeding in our aim to develop the country at the maximum possible speed?' For this was the purpose of the Plan: to increase the national wealth of Tanganyika as quickly as is consistent with the maintenance of our national independence and our people's control over their own economy.

What progress have we made?

An overall survey of the economy will be made by the Minister for Finance when he speaks in two days' time. But on the basis of the first nine months of the Plan one thing is certain—our people have the right to claim that they have been playing their part. This is illustrated by the fact that voluntary nation-building work which was done between 1 July 1964 and 1 April 1965 has resulted in new assets for this country worth more than £900,000. We have 316 miles of new feeder roads and 97 small bridges; 664 additional classrooms; 134 clinics; and 49 co-operative stores. All of these service facilities have been built as part of the Plan, so that teachers are available for the classrooms, and medical personnel for the clinics and so on. Further, 18,542 acres of communal farms have been cleared and planted; 517 miles of irrigation funnels dug, and more than 5,000 fishponds established—all things which are directly related to increased production and better food for the people concerned.

That is not a complete list of the work done, but it is an inspiring one. For it represents the determination of our people, and their willingness to keep working for their own betterment. Self-help schemes on a nation-wide basis were first launched in 1962; that this work is still being done in 1965 shows that our enthusiasm for development is no flash in the pan, but a basic factor in the growth we shall achieve.

The great increase in cash crops is another indication of this. Despite our complete inability to control the rains so that not all efforts bring the results we would like to see, cotton, coffee, and cashew nuts have all been grown in greatly increased quantities by our peasant farmers this year. Some other crops have suffered more from the weather conditions, but everywhere in the country the farmers have demonstrated their willingness to play their part in the work which has to be done.

The Five-Year Plan, however, recognized that this kind of effort is not in itself sufficient if our nation is to make the maximum progress we desire. Programmes of intention, and of desire, supported by encouragement, were laid down for both the public sector of our economy, and for the private sector.

The amount of private investment which has taken place over the past year is, quite frankly, a disappointment to us. We have special tax concessions to encourage new investment; we have investment guarantees for bringing capital into the country; and we have many other arrangements designed to encourage private enterprise of a character which will serve our nation. Yet the level of private investment does not appear to be as great as that provided for in the Plan. We have to do some more thinking about this, and see if there are legitimate complaints and problems which could yet be dealt with or whether it is largely a matter of misunderstanding.

To say that we are disappointed in this field is, however, simply another way of saying how important a part the private sector has to play in our Plan. It does not imply a failure; on the contrary private investment during 1964 was 19 per cent higher than in 1963—a figure which included almost £10 million worth of machinery and equipment, as well as a considerable revival in residential building. This is good; all I am saying is that we must have even more. The most obvious lesson of this first year's experience is the need for greater self-reliance.

At this point it is appropriate that I should mention the work of the National Development Corporation, for this is a bridge between private and public investment, and is already showing signs of making vast contributions to our economy. The NDC was formed only in January of this year, and absorbed the old Tanganyika Development Corporation, and the Agricultural Corporation. It has also taken over from the Treasury the Government investment folios in Williamson's Diamond Mines, Tanganyika Packers, and Nyanza Salt Mines; and in a very short while the NDC will probably be the largest single business organization in Tanzania, and certainly the one with the largest spread of interest.

The NDC is a body established by Government, owned by Government, controlled by a board of directors on which there are six Ministers and four other persons nominated by Government, and with the sole purpose of securing for the people of this country the maximum economic development. The NDC is not only the Government investor, it is also a socialist organization, for it is the people's institution of economic ownership and expansion. All its profits are reinvested; it pays tax to the Treasury like any other company, but there are no shareholders.

This does not mean that the NDC is, or should be, sole owner of what it participates in. Its job is to promote maximum development, and to use its own resources to achieve the greatest possible growth in our economy.

This it is doing. Despite its few months of existence the Corporation already has under close investigation with different private enterprise partners, projects involving £1,800,000 of NDC money, and more than £6 million of outside money. When these plans come to fruition this will mean that by investing less than £2 million the NDC will have promoted investment in Tanzania worth £8 million— and we anticipate that this will be achieved within the next 18 months.

The National Development Corporation does, in fact, represent a radical new approach to investment by Government and the people. It has further promotion plans which will be announced in due course.

It is not possible for me to speak at similar length on other aspects of investment in the public sector. The Ministers will each have an opportunity to detail their efforts and the results they have achieved. Broadly speaking, however, it is true that in financial terms we moved very slowly at the beginning of the Plan period, but that the pace increased rapidly during the third quarter. All the indications are that this higher rate of development is being maintained in the present and final quarter of the first Plan year.

Certain physical developments the House is aware of. The Hale hydro-electric station is now operating; it was not part of the Five-Year Plan, but the power from it is an important factor in our ability to establish new industries in the area served by it. Work on the oil refinery and the Nyumba ya Mungu Dam is proceeding, and a number of other smaller industrial units have come into production. More are in the advanced planning stage.

One of the most notable new constructions during the past year has been the expansion of the University College. Something like £1 million has been spent on College buildings in the past twelve months—and it has been well and economically spent so that we have every right to be proud of that institution and to make heavy demands on those who have the privilege of attending it.

It is in fact true to say that over the whole field of education great advance has been made. The Teacher Training College in Dar es Salaam has begun to operate in large and magnificent new buildings —although it has not yet been formally opened—and work or advanced planning is proceeding on four other Teachers' Colleges in Morogoro, Marangu, Mpwapwa and Butimba. But even before these new colleges are ready the number of secondary school leavers who are entering teacher training has risen by 200 in the past year—which means an increase of more than 50 per cent over last year. In addition, the first 51 students have now begun their three-year diploma course at the Morogoro Agricultural College, where the commercial demonstration farm is already well developed, and the college buildings are under construction.

These developments (like all higher education advances) are the product of earlier expansion lower down the scale. In fact they are the result of our consistent concentration on secondary school expansion ever since TANU assumed control of the Government in 1960. This policy must be maintained for some time yet, but we can now see the possibility of early improvement in both the quality and the quantity of our primary schools. In the meantime the secondary school at Kibaha, which is part of the Nordic Tanganyika Project, opened in February with Class 1 and Class 5 students; the new buildings for Tanga Secondary School are just starting, and school buildings at Korogwe and Shinyanga are due to start shortly.

Housing construction in the capital is also well under way, through the efforts of the National Housing Corporation. Some 900 houses have been completed, and hundreds more are in process of construction. The Government is now anxious to spread this work to other towns. A small start has been made at Morogoro, Tabora, Tanga, Mtwara, Songea, and Shinyanga, but we have not yet solved the problems of real development in those areas.

At this stage, however, it is productive investments upon which we should be concentrating our efforts. Important among these for the future are the Village Settlement Schemes, and of these there are now 23 under the control of the Rural Settlement Commission as against 10 a year ago. At present 3,311 farmers are involved, but in the coming year this number is expected to increase to 7,500. More important, about 10,000 acres have been planted with cash crops in the existing schemes, and about 138,000 acres of land have been, or are being, cleared ready for the next planting season.

Most of these new settlements are making good progress, but we have learned a number of lessons from this early experience. In particular we intend to reduce the capitalization of these villages. To burden the farm with very heavy debts at the outset, and at the same time to make it appear that Government can provide all services, is not the best way of promoting activity. In future we shall increasingly help by providing the economic services, leaving the development of the social services in the form of housing, etc., to the initiative and energies of the farmers as their work brings its return. The individual no less than the nation must learn the lesson of greater self-reliance.

All these are notable advances, but they are not enough. We have not been able to carry out, or even start, all the projects which were included in the first year of the Plan. In the public sector, despite a great increase in public investment over 1963, it is unlikely that we shall have achieved much more than 55 per cent of the Plan target for 1964/65. Why is this?

Firstly, our slow start is in part attributable to the fact that when the Plan period began we were rather like the athlete who arrives breathless at the starting post. The Plan was published only in May and the take-off date was 1 July. In that period it was impossible to negotiate finance and get projects ready to start.

But this will not recur; what is more serious is that some of the assumptions upon which the feasibility of the Plan was based have not been validated during this first period. This is true as regards both men and money.

First of all, I stated last year that in Government service alone we should have to recruit about 500 people with high level skills from outside the country. Despite a continuing rigid examination of these requirements we do not appear likely to be able to make any large reduction in them. It is true that our manpower programme is resulting in students receiving their higher education in fields of need, so that by 1968 we shall have increasing numbers of professional and technically qualified Tanzanians. But although this, combined with manpower utilization studies, reduces the original estimate, new developments in other areas of the Plan have almost balanced the reduction. Yet over the last twelve months we have in fact barely recruited enough people to balance loss through contracts ending and retirements. Clearly further efforts have to be made in this field. At the moment we are in danger of having delays at two different points because of this one difficulty. The first is in the execution of new projects, and the second is in drawing up the projects in a form which will enable them to be submitted for financing. Some countries' loan applications are so complicated that often we are probably slow in getting financial assistance because we don't have the people able to make the proper applications!

There are two things which are at present reducing the damage done by the gaps. Firstly, many of our existing officers are working hours of unpaid overtime and straining themselves to the limit. Secondly, an increase in the number of volunteers of high qualifications has enabled us to use some of them in operation posts. But these remedies are not sufficient, and as our expansion proceeds we shall find ourselves in increasing difficulty. In this field, therefore, we have to make further efforts. And—as I have said before—all of us in the nation can help. The best advertisement when you are trying to attract people to come and work, is the contentment of the existing expert personnel. Each one of them should not only feel satisfied that he is doing a worthwhile job—that will be true. But if he is to be happy working here, and encourage others to do likewise, he must also feel that he is among friends, who give respect to him and his responsibilities just as they demand respect for themselves.

Let me add, before I leave this subject, that one thing we have managed to do in our recruitment is to spread the area of recruitment. We now have working here in Tanganyika people from ten countries as different as Russia, Yugoslavia, Canada, USA, China, etc. In addition we currently have applications for technical help lodged with a total of 17 countries. I hope this will not frighten any of the more nervous Members of this House who fear the effect of our overseas recruitment!

The other factor which has delayed certain projects is money! On the question of overseas aid there is nothing new for me to say. We have made clear our need for it, our appreciation of it when it is given, and our determination that it shall not affect our national independence. The aid which we are now using in our different development projects is in full conformity with that requirement of our independence in all fields. I think that must be recognized by all of us.

At the same time there are other things which must be accepted and understood by us. The first is that there are more countries looking for economic assistance than there are countries willing or able to give it. This means that the donor countries can be, and will be, selective in the projects they agree to help, and even in the countries they agree to help.

This often imposes delays. We have to prepare detailed applications for project assistance and submit these for consideration. At the end of some months it may be that the donor country decides against helping that project—which they have every right to do. Then application has to be made to another country. In the meantime no progress is possible; we cannot order materials nor recruit staff, nor even prepare the ground. This has been the position with a large number of the projects in the Plan which Honourable Members will doubtless ask about.

The second point is that when foreign countries do agree to give assistance to particular projects they usually prefer to help those which have a large 'import content'—that is, those where the total cost includes a large element of payment for goods which have to be imported, rather than payment of local wages or payment for goods which can be produced internally.

This means that the easiest projects to finance are those which do not employ large numbers of local people and do not promote great internal demand for the products of our new factories. It also means that quite often finance becomes available from overseas according to factors other than our own order of priorities. In consequence there is a danger that our Plan progress will get out of balance if we depend too heavily on overseas assistance. The lesson again is an obvious one. *Kujitegemea zaidi.*

The third factor is that when assistance is given for a project it is frequently partial and conditional. Very often a foreign country agrees to meet only the import costs of a project, and on condition that we ourselves can find the money for the local costs. We always endeavour to get some contribution to the local costs, and many of our friends have been responsive to this problem. But the effect of this can be that we could obtain, for example, the machines which a factory needs, but that we are unable to use them because we do not have the money to build the factory or meet the initial outlay on raw materials.

The solution to all these problems is to increase the local contribution to development financing. We are a poor country but we shall remain poor unless we strain ourselves to the utmost in this matter. In the long run the use of our resources is what matters most in development. It is unreasonable to ask others to help us if we are not doing everything possible to help ourselves.

There are two sides to this. Firstly there is the problem of making available for development all the money which is not essential for current consumption. And secondly, there is the question of how we spend the money which we raise.

We can raise local money for development by two means; through taxation, and through savings. A man is saving in this sense if he is investing in factories or farms which will contribute to our development. But not many of us have that amount of money, or the skills which are necessary to save in this form. It is for this reason that the Government launched the National Savings Bonds earlier this year. Amounts as small as Shs. 10/- can now be lent to the Government for a seven-year period, during which this money can be used for development; at the end of that time the individual will receive Shs. 14/- for every Shs. 10/- he invested. These are generous terms, but I think the Minister for Finance will confirm that the sale of bonds has started quite slowly. Again, in November last year the Government issued $6\frac{3}{4}$ per cent Government stock which matures in 1970/71; we have so far received less than half a million pounds by this means.

Even if these savings schemes do win greater support in the coming months, we have to recognize that they are not going to solve our problem of local development finance. And we must find this money. That means local taxation. From our salaries, if we are wage-earners, or from our produce if we are farmers, we must raise the money which will help us to develop our resources.

When we as a nation decided to adopt the Plan we bound ourselves to make the sacrifices which were necessary to achieve it. I said last year that this Plan is a challenge to the nation—as big a challenge as that which we faced to achieve Uhuru. We have therefore to accept the necessity to tax ourselves beyond the point which is normally accepted in more developed societies in times of peace. Because we are not in times of peace; we are at war—at war with our poverty.

There are two more things which are relevant to this problem of finding the local resources necessary for development. The first is that the return anyone receives for his work must be related to the contribution which he makes to our society. NUTA and the Government together have achieved great improvements in the wages and conditions of the workers of this country, although the conditions of the lowest paid workers are still a long way below those which we wish to see. But wage and income increases affect the real cost of the goods and services produced unless they are directly related to increases in productivity. This has not always happened in the past. It must happen in the future. An urgent need now is for a wages and incomes policy to be worked out for this country. In the coming months this will be a preoccupation of the Government in the light of our twin objectives of socialism and development.

The second factor is the need for much more financial discipline within the Government itself, and in the Civil Service, than there has been up to now. On every single issue we have to consider whether the same objective could not be achieved more cheaply, or if the advantage of the more expensive method is really worth the extra cost involved. As I said in my Union Day broadcast, it is extremely stupid for Tanzania to act as if she were a wealthy country, and hope to impress people by display. All that we achieve when we spend large sums of money on trying to impress people is that we make them doubt the sincerity of our claim to be fighting poverty, or we make them think we are a bunch of idiots.

In addition, it is necessary for the Government to insist that all users of public funds should comply with General Orders and Financial Orders and Instructions regarding expenditure control. I expect the Public Accounts Committee of this House to take appropriate action in any cases of financial irregularity arising out of failure to observe these rules. We cannot afford to be as lax in this matter as we have been in the recent past. Only if we really tighten our financial discipline in all respects will the people's money be properly looked after and used to the greatest advantage to our nation.

Our watchword must be 'frugality'. This must run through the whole expenditure of Government. It is in this light that I have decided to institute immediately two minor economies. Firstly, from today no spirits will be served at any Government reception; only tea, coffee, beer, or soft drinks. Secondly, from today no car, except for 4-wheel drive vehicles, will be bought for any Government official or politician at a price higher than £900 c.i.f. Dar es Salaam and most will be expected to cost less than that.

These economies are small ones, but the total saving to Government in a single year will run into many thousands of pounds. Further, they are not unreasonable, and will not make our work less efficient. I expect them to be followed by other similar economies in every Government office throughout the country, and we shall welcome any suggestions which can be made by Members of this House, or other citizens of our United Republic.

Mr. Speaker, I ask the Members of this House, in this, their last meeting, to live up to the standard of responsibility to our nation which they have observed throughout the life of this Parliament.

On behalf of the people of Tanzania, I express gratitude to every Member, and to you yourself, for the work which has been done over the past five years. And I wish for every Member a continuing opportunity to serve this nation, either in this House or in some other field of endeavour. *Uhuru na Kazi*.

3

Relations with the West

During his visit to London for the 1965 *Commonwealth Conference, President Nyerere was invited to address the International Press Club, which he did at a luncheon on* 23 *June* 1965.

... I am grateful for the opportunity to re-state one or two things which, although obvious to us, do not appear to be equally obvious to other people!

The first of these is that the nationalist movement in Tanzania is still a nationalist movement; it has not changed its character nor its objectives. The difference between the position now and that which existed in 1954 when TANU was formed, is that we now have the opportunity and the responsibility to try and bring those objectives into being.

We stand for democracy now as we did eleven years ago; with our new one-party constitution we are trying to make this a practical reality for every one of our citizens without destroying the unity which is our nation's greatest development asset. We stand for equality now as we did at the beginning of TANU, and the discrimination which for so long disfigured my country is now considerably less than it was—in some respects it has disappeared altogether.

We stand for unity in Africa. In particular we still urgently desire an East African Federation. If Mzee Kenyatta today says he is ready, then we will federate tomorrow. We stand fast on the principle of national freedom; we do not believe that we ourselves can be secure in our freedom while our neighbours continue to be under colonial rule.

We stand for the economic and social betterment of the people; the Five-Year Development Plan and the efforts the people are making to implement this Plan are eloquent evidence of the determination and our progress in this respect.

I am provoked into saying these things because of the overseas reaction there has been to certain decisions made by the independent Government of my country. Towards the end of last year independent Tanzania invited seven Chinese technicians to train our reorganized army in the use of the weapons we were getting from that country. There has been an exchange of state visits between my country and the People's Republic of China; I addressed a mass rally in Peking, and Premier Chou En Lai addressed a public meeting in Dar es Salaam. Also—I am pleased to say—China has given us a grant of £1 million, and made credits available to us totalling more than £10 million.

Ever since these events began to take place large sections of the Western press, and some Western politicians, have been examining us through microscopes to see whether we have been—as they would put it—'contaminated' by these contacts. I gather that even the suits I wear have been adduced as evidence of pernicious Chinese influence!

Frankly I find this anxiety about the health of Tanzania sometimes funny, sometimes irritating, and always odd.

When I spoke to the United Nations General Assembly immediately after Tanganyika's independence in December 1961, I made it clear that our foreign policy would be based on the principles of non-alignment. I said that we wanted to be friends with all nations on the basis of national equality and sovereignty, and of mutual respect. Until that date Tanganyika had not been non-aligned. It had been administered by Britain, and was therefore obviously and clearly part of the Western Bloc. We are still part of the Western Bloc. There cannot be many international organizations which are more Western, or under greater Western influence, than the Commonwealth.

If we are to be non-aligned we have to make friends with Eastern Bloc countries, because we had no contact with them before independence. We knew, and after independence were friendly with, the British, the Americans, the Germans, and many other Western peoples who had visited our country, sent missionaries, businessmen, and so on. But people from the Eastern Bloc were strangers to us; they did not visit us nor we them; they did not trade with us; all our news of them came through the words of those who opposed their whole philosophy.

What is so strange, therefore, about our new contacts with communist countries? Are we capitalist because we trade with Britain and America? Are we capitalist because the bulk of our overseas experts come from this country or other Western powers? If not, why do we become communist when we begin to trade with China and Russia, and begin to use the services of their experts? Sometimes I wonder whether the Western countries are not rapidly developing an inferiority complex towards the Eastern countries, and China in particular.

But in any case, even if we in Tanzania had people from communist countries in the same proportion as we have people from the West, why would that make the West so concerned about our 'independence'? For years we have been reminding the world that one third of Africa does not have any independence or democracy. I cannot honestly claim that this fact seems to worry the Western press or the Western politicians very much. I can assure you that it worries us.

The continuation of colonialism and racialism in the Portuguese colonies, in Southern Rhodesia, and in South Africa is a daily affront to all the principles of democracy, equality, national freedom, and African unity on which we stand. And it is the thing which really ought to be worrying the West very much indeed, because it is these matters which will really affect the relations of the West with Africa —not a handful of army technicians and a few factories and farms run by communist experts. Because we in Tanzania, and the people of Africa as a whole, are determined that colonialism shall go. We are as determined about this as Britain was that Hitler's forces should be pushed out of Holland, Belgium, France and all the other war-time occupied countries. The continued occupation of Africa angers us just as much as the German occupation of these countries worried you. Do not let our present weakness deceive you on this, because you would be making a very big mistake.

As far as we are concerned there is only one question which remains to be settled. Is freedom for the rest of Africa to be obtained peacefully or by violence? Are the peoples of Mozambique, Southern Rhodesia and the rest, to be helped through a short transitional period in which power is transferred with co-operation, or do they first have to spill their blood—and that of the imperialists? It is the West which has to answer that question, and it is upon that answer that Africa's future relations with the West will really depend.

Mr. Chairman, I have stated this on several occasions and I can assure you that the reason is not that I like hearing my own voice. And it is absurd to think that a poor country like Tanzania can threaten the West. When I say this I am simply stating another obvious fact. Let me spell out the situation.

The southern part of Africa is governed by powers which claim to be part of the Western Bloc, and which are accepted by their allies as part of the 'free world'. This is not denied. Africa is determined that Africa shall be governed by Africa. That also is undeniable. Therefore if the Western powers accept the democracy they claim to uphold, then all of them must logically accept Africa's position, not only as a fact to be taken into account, but also as a ust cause. In that case they have no alternative but to help Africa to achieve its objective peacefully and with the minimum of disorganization.

If the West is not willing to do this then the Western countries will be fighting against Africa; for it is difficult to see how they can be neutral. You are not being neutral if you continue to sell arms and other economic weapons to Portugal on the grounds that she is a member of NATO, while Portugal is using her arms and such economic strength as she has in an effort to retain control of her colonies. Such a policy would be recognized by Africa, and by any objective observer, as being hostile to Africa. Our reaction would have to be to get arms ourselves. And as we do not make them we would have to get them from those who were willing to supply them—which would be the communist countries.

There are enough examples in the world to show what would happen then. The West would 'discover' that Portugal was fighting an 'anti-communist war', and in the spirit of a crusader it would come to her assistance. The result would be that the nationalist forces of Africa would be fighting the West. Not because Africa wanted to, but because it wants freedom, and because the West is opposing that freedom, or failing to take the steps necessary to help Africa achieve it without the risk of war.

Finally let me say this. I do not believe that the fears I have outlined would come to pass because the other Western countries are *unable* to influence Portugal, and the other powers concerned. They may have to shake themselves a little, but that's all. Does anyone really believe that little, decadent Portugal, and minority governments in Southern Rhodesia and South Africa, could stand out against determined pressure from the other powers of the Western Bloc? My fear is that these things will come to pass because the West is not *willing* to do something. Because, perhaps, they spend so much time wondering about how willing Africa's leaders are to sell their new independence to the East, that they have not time left to realize that Africa's leaders are still willing to pay a price to obtain Africa's independence from the West.

4

Tanzania Unjustly Accused

In laying the foundation stone for the East African Common Ser-
vices Organization Building in Dar es Salaam on 15 July 1965,
the President began by outlining the process of decision-making which
led up to it. He concluded by acknowledging the work done by differ-
ent individuals and groups, but also said, inter alia:

. . . This project, therefore, is nearly five years old and is intended
to enable the Common Services to be more efficiently administered
in Tanzania.

I have given this brief history in order to dispel some of the rub
bish which is being allowed to circulate in East Africa these days
It seems that there is nothing we can do in Tanzania, however
reasonable and however logical, without being accused of breaking
up East African unity. Rumours are now going round that the
erection of this building in Dar es Salaam heralds the breaking up of
EACSO.

Uganda can ask for the dissolution of the East African University
and we will hear the most muted mention of this fact in East Africa;
Kenya can unilaterally reverse a decision of the Common Services
Authority and there will be no mention of this anywhere. Tanzania
argues patiently and for years that as long as we fail to federate it is
inevitable for the East African states to have separate currencies
and to work out some adjustment in the working of the Common
Market. This provokes some silly people in East Africa, who have
no shame, into accusing Tanzania of taking orders from China and
endangering East African unity.

I have often examined the list of our accusers. I am left with the
strong impression that it does not consist of people who are or have
been particularly enthusiastic about East African unity. It consists

mainly of foreigners and opportunists who will today be for Federation and tomorrow against it, depending upon their personal interests rather than the interests of East Africa as a whole.

I want to take this opportunity to re-state Tanzania's position. We stand for Federation now as we have always stood for Federation. Nothing has happened in East Africa to shake our firm faith in a united East Africa. I still believe that there is nothing on which the masses and the intellectuals of East Africa are more united than in their desire for a united East Africa. The failure of East Africa to federate is therefore a great shame. So, I repeat, *we* prefer Federation. But if our neighbours prefer a looser form of co-operation in the form of the Common Market and the Common Services, I pledge Tanzania's full co-operation in maintaining the Common Market and the Common Services. In the course of this co-operation we shall grow up and learn to accept both the advantages and the headaches of this kind of neighbourly co-operation.

In particular we must learn to examine each of our present and future fields of co-operation on its own merits. We must outgrow the habit of blackmail, of saying, 'If you do so-and-so, we shall do so-and-so'—irrespective of the merits of the case. Blackmail is never a healthy basis for co-operation. This tender seed of co-operation in East Africa must be nursed by all of us.

I have found it necessary to say these things because of the great importance that I attach to continued co-operation in East Africa. This co-operation has a significance beyond East Africa itself . . . .

5

Treatment of Leprosy

On 26 July 1965, the President opened the Mwena Leprosarium in Mtwara Region. He used the opportunity to explain the treatment possibilities of this disease, as well as to express appreciation of humanitarian actions by people abroad.

. . . There was a time, not very long ago, when to be afflicted with leprosy was to face certain death, preceded by social ostracism. Each of the tribes of our country had its own way of dealing with the victims of this disease, but all of us were very much afraid of it, and excluded the sufferers from the community.

Now, thanks to medical advance, and thanks also to the devoted work of many people in the field, this is no longer true. Leprosy can be cured; in addition, if it is diagnosed and treated early enough, the terrible disfigurements from which people used to suffer can be avoided. And in very many cases patients can be treated while they live at their homes, along with their families.

Nonetheless, despite all these advances the treatment of this disease is a long one, and residential treatment is frequently necessary at least for a period. Further, in a large underdeveloped country like Tanzania, many sufferers are still not treated early enough. This means that it is difficult for them always to remain happily in their own community—particularly as not all of our people realize the new discoveries in treatment.

For these reasons the opening of this new leprosarium is very much to be welcomed. For a long time there has been a centre for leprosy patients in this area, but it is Sister Lia Schwartzmueller who is really responsible for the present fine development. Sister Lia came to this area in 1952, and for twelve years was working with the patients, helping them with what facilities she could find, and at the same time raising interest in Europe for the extension. During that whole time Sister Lia took no leave, and worked without thought for herself until last year she suffered from a stroke and a heart attack. Her devotion to our service is an example to every citizen of this country, and I am very happy that she is with us today.

... This new centre will provide accommodation for almost 700 in-patients; there is a hospital for 105 patients where sufferers can have the treatment they need; and in addition there is a primary school, recreation hall, and space for evening classes. Finally there is an agricultural plot of about 350 acres where patients can take part in the growing of their own food and thus maintain their self-respect.

These buildings have to be financed. More than $3\frac{1}{4}$ million shillings have been spent on them up to now. And none of that money has been found by Tanzania. For all the buildings we see here today we are indebted to the German Leprosy Association, which has its headquarters in Wuerzburg in the Federal Republic.

On behalf of the patients here; and on behalf of all the people of this United Republic, I would like to express our very deep gratitude to this Association and to all the German people who have contributed to it. We in Tanzania can recognize this kind of need, but it is quite impossible for us to meet it. We accept gladly this evidence of man's humanity to man, and only wish that all those responsible for today's ceremony could be here to receive personally our thanks.

But there is more cause for our gratitude than the buildings. It now costs about Shs. 220,000/- every year to keep this leprosarium running. The Government contributes a very small part of this. Almost all the costs are met by the Catholic Mission of the Benedictine Fathers here, and by other charitable organizations in the Western world.

Ladies and gentlemen, I hope that those of you who represent organizations and individuals who help to maintain this centre will convey our thanks to all those responsible. Thanks are indeed a small exchange for this kind of gift, but I believe in fact that the donors will find their greatest satisfaction in the consiousness of a good job being done.

... This is a Christian mission, but the leprosarium is not for Christians only—the majority of the patients are in fact adherents to the Muslim faith. I do not believe there is anything wrong in this, on either side. On the contrary, I believe it is a recognition that whatever our particular beliefs about God and His prophets we can best worship Him by living together, and working together, in harmony, and in His service . . . .

6

Problems of East African Co-operation

The Central Legislative Assembly, consisting of representatives of the three East African Parliaments, meets alternately in the three capitals, and normally begins by receiving a message from the appropriate Head of State, outlining Agreements or Recommendations from the East African Authority (which is the three Presidents sitting together). In 1964 a number of difficulties between the three countries had led to widespread rumours that the system of economic co-operation was about to break up, and President Nyerere therefore brought the problem into the open when addressing the Central Legislative Assembly meeting in Dar es Salaam on 10 August 1965. Shortly after this meeting the three leaders met in Mombasa and decided to set up the Philip Commission, charging it with the task of working out new machinery of co-operation.

It is with pleasure that I welcome the Central Legislative Assembly to its meeting in Dar es Salaam. I hope that your stay in our Tanzanian capital will be an enjoyable one, and that in your work here you will be able to contribute to the further strengthening of East African brotherliness and unity.

Unfortunately, since the last Assembly meeting it has not been possible for an East African Authority meeting to be held. This means that I have no Authority message to communicate to this meeting, and no proposals to make to you on behalf of the three East African leaders.

I am aware that this regrettable report may well be used to support allegations that East African co-operation is in disarray, and in grave danger of collapsing. I hope that the Members of this

Assembly will refuse to give countenance to such reports, for I assure you that they are untrue. Kenya, Tanzania, and Uganda are as united in their objectives as they have ever been, and as determined to work together for the benefit of all the peoples in East Africa.

There have, of course, been differences of opinion between our three sovereign nations in recent months. It would be surprising if there had not. But there is no reason at all to believe that East African co-operation is about to collapse. It is sustained by our overwhelming will for unity; we shall not let the present problems overwhelm us. As Mark Twain once said: 'The report of my death was an exaggeration'. The same is true of East African unity.

Nonetheless, I propose today to speak frankly about some of our difficulties, because it is not sufficient for us to rely on our desire for continued and expanded unity, and therefore to ignore practical difficulties which are now being experienced. Such complacency could be very dangerous. For although the spirit of unity can be a very effective lubricant for organizational machinery, it is not itself a substitute for machinery. And just as no machine can run without oil, so a bad machine uses up and wastes large quantities of it, and still breaks down so frequently that it is finally abandoned. The important thing for us in East Africa, as for a mechanic, is to learn the correct lessons from the first sign of trouble, and take the appropriate action.

This is what we have to do now. We have no lack of aspiration for unity, nor any absence of understanding about the advantages of unity in Africa. Throughout our three countries the intellectuals and masses are united on this subject, and no politician would now dare to stand up and oppose East African unity. But we are in danger of treating the will as if it were the deed.

The truth is that we do not in fact have unity in East Africa, and it is now clear that it cannot be achieved as easily as we once hoped and expected. What we do have is such economic integration between our sovereign states that frictions are inevitable in the absence of efficient decision-making machinery. On top of that, we have such close historical connections between our respective nationalist movements that we tend to take each other's understanding for granted. Consequently we East African countries have less institutional political contact than each of us has with countries which are much further away, and with whom we have far fewer common interests. If we were all content merely to maintain the economic status quo of pre-1961 these things would not matter very much. But in fact each of our nations is committed to rapid economic, social and political development—every aspect of which reverberates throughout our whole region.

In fact, of course, economic co-operation between Kenya, Tanzania, and Uganda has never been without its difficulties or its allegations of unfair advantage for one or other country. The present difficulties are by no means the first that East Africa has experienced. They do, however, take place in a different political context than earlier difficulties.

In the past there was always one ultimate authority which had the power to settle disputes between the three territorial Governments, and which had the ability to enforce whatever decision was made. In colonial times our countries were as separate as now, but they had a common master. A decision on any matter could always be obtained, and always had to be accepted even by the country which disagreed with the decision. This ceased to be the case in December 1961, when Tanganyika became independent.

As our three countries obtained their separate independence, the single ultimate authority ceased to exist. Whereas the colonial territorial authority was replaced by a national Government in each case, no single East African arbiter replaced the final rule of Whitehall in the case of East African affairs. Instead, the ultimate authority became the three-headed East African Authority, and absolute unanimity of decision between sovereign states had to be obtained on all matters connected with our Common Services and our Common Market.

It is important to be clear what this means; if the three leaders cannot agree unanimously on a proposal, then no action is possible at all—unless one or other of us unilaterally breaks the agreements and conventions which are the foundation of our co-operation. In other words, if and while discussion fails to result in agreement or acceptable compromise, then each of our three nations has a veto power in relation to certain developments in the other two. This veto—which can be exercised by failure to answer as well as by an adverse decision—can be ignored; the Authority has no enforcement machinery. But this can only be done at the risk of destroying our whole complex of economic co-operation.

The requirement of unanimity, however, is not easy to achieve despite our great will to co-operate. Each of our three Governments is answerable to the people of its own country. Each of them is beset with the urgent needs of one part of the total East African area. In Authority meetings, therefore, and in all our joint meetings, each Member can look at the interests of East Africa as a whole only to the extent that these do not conflict fundamentally with the requirements of his own nation's immediate needs. We Members are leaders of democratic Governments, and must balance the long-term need for unity with our immediate need for action, in just the same way as we have internally to balance the long-term need for large capital investment against urgent social needs. Ultimately we are not in fact 'East African' leaders, but leaders of states in East Africa; and regional loyalty has sometimes to come second to our national responsibilities.

It is true that the common poverty, and the historical links of East Africa, mean that there is broad agreement about the road ahead, and a large area of agreement on practical co-operation. When we get unduly worried about the recently publicized difficulties it is a good thing to stop and consider the wide range of things which are going ahead without any conflict whatsoever. These do not receive any publicity. But it is necessary to recognize, too, that there are areas of potential friction.

There are many differences in the structure of the common poverty of our three states; in one, urban unemployment is the most pressing problem; in another, the almost complete absence of an industrial sector of the economy. There are differences in the quantity and quality of the educational facilities we each inherited from our colonial past, and differences in the administrative machines. All these, and the many other detailed differences which have resulted from separate colonial histories, mean that each of our territorial Governments has to have different priorities of action, and to some extent a different approach to the problems before it. It is therefore inevitable that at any one time there may be genuine clashes of interest, with one nation feeling a positive need to take steps which the others cannot approve. Usually, with patience and compromise, agreement can be reached. But sometimes patience will be exhausted before this has been achieved, and sometimes the conflict—taken in isolation—permits no mutually agreeable solution.

Let me illustrate my point by explaining Tanzania's problems (because they are problems which I understand better) in certain matters relating to the Common Market. The pattern of European settlement in East Africa, together with other fortuitous circumstances, meant that Nairobi developed as an industrial and commercial centre for the whole area. Firms were established there and expanded their operations to sell goods throughout East Africa. Tanzania obtained virtually no industries of her own, but built up a sizeable export capacity in certain primary commodities. At the same time some of her crops—like wheat—were prohibited from entering Kenya. The prohibition was laid down by the same colonial authority which established and maintained the common market in industrial goods, but I am told it still continues.

The result has been that in 1961 Kenya exported goods worth £8.9 million to Tanganyika, and imported goods only to the value of £1.8 million. In 1964 Tanzania's imports from Kenya had risen to £13.3 million, and her exports to Kenya were worth £4.1 million. This meant that the deficit on Tanzania's trade with Kenya had increased from £7.1 million to £9.2 million.

In other words, the colonial economic pattern meant that Tanganyika was a free market for Kenya, and the surplus she earned on overseas trade with other countries was not promoting her own development. Further, any money which the independent Government now borrows for infrastructural development leaks away. Instead of the secondary effects of investment being felt in the country which has the obligation to repay any loan, the increase in the effective market is felt mainly by Tanzania's partners in the Common Market. Because of the common tariff arrangements, and the free inter-East African trade, Tanzania cannot buy in the cheapest market abroad, and equally, she cannot protect her own infant industries against competition from long-established and large-scale firms in Kenya, and—to a lesser extent—in Uganda.

This situation did not result from evil machinations by the people or Governments of our neighbouring territories. It was a historically determined fact and still remains as a fact. But as far as Tanzania was concerned, it meant that her own development was hamstrung. Without the establishment of an industrial base Tanzania will never achieve a stable economy or reach the take-off point of economic growth. If the present pattern continues—and it is obviously not self-correcting—Tanzania would never be able to guarantee the financing of the basic social and public services which her people rightly demand.

This is a very basic and urgent question for Tanzania, which her Government must deal with if it is to fulfil its responsibilities to the people. But obviously any move to correct the position may well have short-term adverse effects on Kenya's efforts to overcome her pressing unemployment problem. This is, therefore, a difficult matter for the East African countries. Nonetheless, as soon as it became clear that there was no immediate prospect of Federation Tanzania had to press for some agreed East African action. And in March 1964, the meeting at Kampala did achieve agreement on the principles of corrective action. Unfortunately this Agreement has not yet been ratified by our Governments.

As the months went by without ratification Tanzania felt that she had no option but to take action on her own, though in accordance with the principles agreed at the Kampala meeting. Temporary quotas have therefore been set on the import of certain items from Kenya, with the sole object of promoting their production locally. The total imports affected by these quotas to date account for only £2 million out of the 1964 deficit of £9.2 million. This is an indication that Tanzania is taking only the very minimum action, and only when it becomes absolutely imperative for her own development. It is important to realize, too, that on the basis of the 1964 figures, even if these decisions cut imports from Kenya by as much as £2 million—which is most unlikely—Tanzania would still be the largest national importer of Kenya goods in the whole world.

We will be happy to continue in this first place; but it is also useful to reflect on the fact that Tanzania cannot be a large trading partner for anyone if she remains for ever poor. Our efforts to develop our economy are intended to make this a more profitable market. Our trading partners as well as ourselves will benefit if we succeed. And certainly the twentieth century international experience demonstrates quite clearly that trade increases fastest between countries which are equally wealthy and developed, not between industrial nations on the one hand, and primary producers on the other. It is ironic that it should be necessary to stress with regard to ourselves a basic economic fact which the underdeveloped countries as a whole have been pointing out in world trade conferences for many years.

Let me stress again that Tanzania understands the economic problem of her neighbours, and deeply regrets any temporary complication which her own need creates. We have tried to avoid it. Although our problem was clear to us long before our independence, we took no action until 1964 because we hoped the matter could be dealt with in the framework of an East African Federation. For a time we were willing and able to accept the status quo, and all its disadvantages to us, as a necessary price to pay for East African unity. But in the absence of any progress or any hope of an early Federation, we had no alternative but to seek actively for an equalization of the advantages and disadvantages of the Common Market. Only when our efforts failed to bring practical agreement on an East African basis did we, very reluctantly, take steps on our own.

I have expanded on this Tanzanian problem, but it would be wrong to give the impression that it is only one country which experiences difficulty with the present arrangements, or which has taken its own action. The recent grant to Pan-American Airways of temporary landing rights in Nairobi was contrary to two separate unanimous decisions of the East African Authority. But clearly, Kenya felt in the end that she could not afford to lose the advantages she expected from such a decision, despite our common fears about the effect of such landing rights on the prosperity of our jointly-owned East African Airways.

I could give other examples of the economic problems which the three-headed Authority is unable to deal with satisfactorily at present. But my purpose is not to raise discussion on particular issues—and I hope that this Assembly will not go over this ground all over again. These examples have merely been used to illustrate the difficulty which the present lack of organic unity brings to East African co-operation.

The trouble is, of course, that each difficulty of this kind uses up our stock of emotional unity. Kenya clearly feels extremely bitter about Tanzania's pressure to restrict the freedom of entry into the Tanzanian market. Tanzania, on her side, feels that if East Africa does not federate there must be some effort to accept the inevitable consequences of such failure. Similarly, Tanzania feels let down by what she regards as a weakening of the airline which the three countries own jointly, while Kenya feels that we have failed to appreciate her needs in relation to this Pan-American proposal.

Unfortunately, once this sort of resentment begins to be felt there are plenty of people only too anxious to emphasize the differences and difficulties between us, and exaggerate them until they become suspicions and hostility. Genuine difficulties like those I have quoted are a godsend to such people, and we have evidence that they are being used in the campaign to divide us in East Africa. In just the same way every difference of emphasis and expression in our international policies is used to sow misunderstanding between us. Who has not heard the suggestion that Tanzania is under Chinese influence, or that Kenya is under American? (Uganda so far appears to have escaped these allegations, doubtless on the principle of dealing with one thing at a time! Uganda's time will obviously come one day.) There are suggestions made to Kenya that Tanzania is preparing to replace imports from her by imports from China. There are suggestions being made to Tanzania that Kenya is deliberately worsening Tanzania's non-aligned image overseas so as to gain an economic advantage. In isolation these suggestions would be dismissed out of hand; but when our real problems give rise to friction and misunderstanding, would it not be natural that eventually we should each begin to wonder whether they have some basis?

It is now clear that the pressures of our separate domestic problems can bring us, more easily than we would have thought possible a few years ago, to a position where we are prepared to believe slanders about each other. And this is the greatest danger of all; for if we take that road it is not only East African Federation which is gone for all time. So too has economic co-operation, and so has our ambition for continent-wide unity.

It is vital that we analyse our position properly, without being bemused by propaganda. We have to face the fact that our present difficulties have nothing to do with one or other country being a stooge of East or West. They arise out of our peculiar combination of unity in economic affairs, and disunity in the machinery of responsibility and decision-making. Then we have to deal with one or other side of this equation, and bring it into balance.

Tanzania believes very strongly that every effort must be made to maintain our economic unity, and our Common Services. The real security and the real development of our separate territories, as well as the area as a whole, needs unity in East Africa as a preliminary to the unity of our continent. It is for this reason that we remain so anxious for the establishment of a sovereign federal East African state. Only by such a transfer of sovereignty can one authority be established with overall powers in matters of East African concern. We should then have a single voice in the international world; it would be infinitely more difficult for anyone to play us up against each other. In a Federation short-term clashes of economic interest could be settled by a body which was responsible to the peoples of the whole area. And this same sovereign body could ensure that each of our particular poverty problems was tackled in co-operation, while at the same time our joint resources were used to tackle the basic underlying problems which are common to us all.

It is, however, by now clear that Federation will not be achieved this year or next. We very much regret this. But we must face up to it. And we have to decide what we do instead; for we cannot stay where we are. One thing which all of us agree about is that our poverty can only be overcome by economic planning. We must therefore be in a position where there is either one Federal Development Plan, or where each of the separate states has the power, as well as the responsibility, to make and implement a national Development Plan.

It was this need which caused Tanzania to take the lead in calling for the establishment of separate national currencies. We found that it is impossible to control our economy and achieve the maximum development while our currency and credit was outside our control. This was not a sudden realization that financial control is necessary for economic planning. It was a recognition that our decision in 1961 to remain within the common currency area was based on a false premise—the expectation that control would be able to be exercised on a federal basis when the other two territories became, in their turn, independent.

In fact, the whole existing machinery of East African co-operation was established in the expectation of rapid Federation. It was regarded as an interim arrangement by the then Tanganyika Government, and I think also by the nationalist movements of Kenya and Uganda. It depends entirely on the goodwill and brotherly spirit between our peoples and our leaders, and it makes no provision for the conflicting responsibilities which at times face us. Nonetheless it has served us well and we have made many advances under it.

But if we continue to rely only on the existing arrangement we shall continue to deal with each problem separately, and there is a grave danger that we shall continue to quarrel about things which are urgent for one or other of us. This will mean that our existing co-operation will be jeopardized, and Federation itself will get further and further away as our relations deteriorate. Instead we must recognize the current difficulties for what they are—symptoms of a deficiency in our present arrangements. We must then work out realistic arrangements for co-operation and joint activity, short of Federation, which acknowledge our separation for the time being and the consequent needs of our separate sovereignties and development plans.

It is true, of course, that any treaty of co-operation and joint activity reduces the individual national power of decision and involves a voluntary surrender by the sovereign authority of some of its day-to-day power. This we have to accept. I have pointed out before that if three men co-operate to build a boat, they can each enlarge their freedom to travel in safety on the sea and can each obtain a larger catch of fish. But at the same time their joint ownership of the boat restricts their individual freedom to dispose of the boat unilaterally. This is surely accepted by everyone. If it were not, there would be no point in talking about East African co-operation at all.

I am convinced that this fact is not challenged in East Africa, and that each of our countries is willing to accept its implications. What we need is simply a better system for regulating the use of the boat so that each owner gets the maximum and fair return. I believe this can be done, and am confident that if we can get the institutions right, our area of inter-East African co-operation may be expanded. It may even be that in looking again at the practical questions of co-operation we shall be able to make a fresh approach to the objective of Federation.

But however that may be, we can and we must act now to oil the wheels of our relationship so as to cut out any possibility of friction in the testing years ahead. If, after examination, we feel that national planning demands a little loosening of some of our ties, and if we are not prepared for the alternative surrender of national sovereignty, then it would be better to accept that fact. What we must not do is allow ourselves to drift into a position where our spirit of unity is replaced by mutual suspicions.

Mr. Speaker, I do appeal to this Assembly to help East Africa. We have only ourselves upon whom we can depend to promote the unity and development of our continent of Africa, and this part of it to which we belong. At your meeting here, and when the Members return to their homes, this Assembly can play a very important part in furthering the cause of unity. For this is not simply a question of Governments; we are all individually involved. It is not appropriate that we should indulge in mutual recrimination or abuse. It is necessary that we go forward together and tackle the basic problems. If I may use a Tanzanian slogan to this East African gathering, I would say, 'It can be done; play your part.'

7

Unemployment is no Problem

On 16 August 1965, President Nyerere laid the foundation stone of the Kibo Match Factory in Moshi. After welcoming the initiative of the private promoters, especially in their choice of location, the President referred to the question of unemployment in the area.

. . . Let me, at this point, offer a word of warning. The factory will employ only 40 workers on each shift—despite the capital investment of £125,000. By itself it will not, therefore, solve an 'unemployment problem'. But I myself am not convinced that we in Tanzania yet suffer from this problem. We have, and shall have increasingly, people coming out of primary schools who cannot get wage employment. But this does not mean that they have no work they can do.

In the past there was a tendency for young people—and even their parents—to assume that having an education meant leaving the land and taking wage employment. What is more, it was expected that anyone of Standard VIII and above should work in an office. Unfortunately, too many of our people still have this attitude. It is time that we dropped it, and realized that this is an independent country, with no room for colonial attitudes of mind.

Why is it that in highly developed countries like America, Britain, and Germany, you find university graduates working as farmers? It is because they realize that education is intended to make a person better able to do whatever job is important and profitable, both to himself and his country. The national prosperity of countries like Germany is based on the fact that they have educated people in all fields of activity, and that a man knows that his schooling can be used in the fields and on a factory floor, as well as on a desk. But we sometimes seem to take our ideas from the fact that the colonial civil servants had degrees, and worked in offices, as though that was the whole truth instead of reflecting only a small part of the British economic organization. In fact we also had—and still have—expatriate Agricultural Officers who have been through university. In Kenya, many of the European settlers were men with high academic qualifications and I think we should realize that as a result Kenya's agriculture is much more advanced than that of Tanzania.

It is necessary that we should realize that our young people out of school are not disqualified from being farmers. They are qualified to be better farmers, and better citizens. In this area in particular it ought to be obvious that prosperity can come from careful husbandry. And if there is a land shortage here, that is certainly not true of our nation as a whole.

Mr. Chairman, I have digressed from my theme. But I think you will agree that this factory will succeed to the extent that it works in harmony with the rest of our society, so perhaps my last point is not really out of place. . . .

8

Election Broadcast

The Presidential and mainland Parliamentary Elections were held under the new one-party constitution in September 1965. President Nyerere did not on this occasion campaign through the country, but addressed the nation by radio on 10 September.

On the 21, 23 and 26 September—that is before the end of this month—the people of Tanzania will have their first opportunity to elect the President of the United Republic. Until now I have been President of our nation because at the time of the Union between Tanganyika and Zanzibar it was agreed that the person who had been elected President of Tanganyika in 1962 should be the head of the Union. Now the people of the mainland and the people of the islands, acting as one, will decide whether they wish me to continue to be President of our country.

At the same time as this election is held, the people on the mainland will also have an opportunity to choose their Member of Parliament from among the two people who have been presented to them by TANU.

I want to talk about both these elections tonight, but before I do so I want to stress their importance for all of us. Free elections in an independent country give meaning to independence, because it is through them that we govern ourselves, and decide what sort of country ours will become. When we elect the President and the Parliament of the United Republic we are deciding what will be the laws of our country, how much tax we will pay in order to get public and social services, and who will talk on our behalf with foreign countries, as well as very many other things.

This is what we were claiming for ourselves when we campaigned for independence. We said that we had a right to run our own country in accordance with our own desires, and that no man had the right to govern another. We won that right for ourselves; elections are an occasion on which we exercise it. They are the means through which we choose, and later call to account, the people who have the responsibility of making laws, and leading us. There is no other way in which we can freely govern ourselves because—as we know very well—life in any community brings duties as well as rights. We cannot all do just as we like all of the time. Real freedom therefore means that a man has the right to join with his fellows, on terms of equality and absolute freedom, in deciding what are the citizen's duties and rights, and what proportion of our time and our wealth shall be devoted to common activities for the benefit of our future, and so on.

In very small societies, like the village, this self-government can be effected through community discussions, where every adult joins in, and the group talk until they have reached agreement. Then everyone knows that he has participated in his own government, and knows the decision and how it was arrived at.

Clearly this method is not possible when very large communities are involved, and some other method has to be found whereby each individual can have the same freedom to express his views, and after which a decision can be reached. In a democratic country like Tanzania there are many ways through which this is done. One of the most important for us is through membership of TANU or the Afro-Shirazi Party, and participation in the free discussion at Party meetings. But there are many other ways; it can be done through joining in the discussions of the Village Development Committees, through active membership of NUTA, the co-operative societies and the UWT, through writing to the Members of Parliament, and to the newspapers.

By any and all of these methods every citizen of our country can make sure that his ideas are heard and understood. But in addition to all these methods of exerting democratic rights, there is the basic right of a citizen to choose his representative in Parliament, and to choose his President. This is done periodically; our next opportunity will be through the elections which are to be held later this month.

To be eligible for a vote, and not to have registered as a voter is a very bad waste of a citizen's freedom. To have registered as a voter, so that you have a voter's card, and not to go to the polling place on election day and record your vote would be very stupid indeed.

Our elections this month will be of a new kind, different from any of those which have gone before. All the candidates for the Parliamentary seats are TANU candidates, endorsed by the National Executive of the Party. And the Presidential candidate is the joint TANU and Afro-Shirazi candidate, chosen at a joint meeting of the two Parties.

This is a very important change from previous elections. In the past when the people went to vote they were choosing between TANU and another political party, or between TANU and an individual who opposed TANU. Over and over again the people chose TANU, and voted for the candidate that the TANU Executive had selected. But this meant that the people never really had an effective choice of the individual who represented them. The system was such that by choosing the policy they wanted—the TANU policy—they then had no real choice of the individual who was to speak for them within the context of the policy.

Only in one case were the people ever so determined about individuals that they over-rode the TANU Executive and that was where the two candidates were both supporting the same TANU policies. But usually, even if the people did not like an individual, they voted for him because they wanted to support the Party.

Under our new one-party constitution this problem no longer exists. As a nation we have accepted the principles and policies of TANU as the basis for our future national development. It is therefore now possible for the people to choose between *individuals* who are standing for election in their area. The people can decide for themselves which of the two is best qualified by character and ability to represent them in the national councils of our land. But candidates in each constituency where there is a contest—which is 101 out of the 107 in Tanganyika—have been approved by the Party; both are committed to the basic principles of TANU and to the TANU Creed. The purpose of the meetings, of the radio talks, and other campaign processes, is therefore to give you an opportunity to judge the men themselves, their sincerity, their spirit of service, and their ability to do the job properly.

The same thing is true of the Presidential Election, although in this case only one candidate is being put forward by the TANU and Afro-Shirazi Parties for the consideration of the people. This does not mean that the people are not able to reject me as the future President if they think it would be better for the country if there was a new President. Those who do not wish me to be President of Tanzania for the next five years have simply to put a tick in the space on the ballot paper underneath where it says 'Hapana'—that is, underneath the shaded space. If the majority of the people who voted do this, then the two Parties will meet again and select another name to put before you for your consideration; another Presidential Election will be held, and as soon as you have chosen another person he will take over from me.

I am explaining this point not because I want the people to reject the TANU/Afro-Shirazi recommendation that I should be the President again. I hope that a very large majority of people will agree with the Party on its selection, because it is a very important matter—perhaps the most important single choice our two Parties make. Therefore, if the Parties have not chosen according to your wishes then they are out of touch with the people as a whole, and this would be very bad. But it is important that everyone should understand that the President of this country is the people's President, chosen by them, and responsible to them for his actions. Therefore the people have, and must have, absolute freedom to vote for or against the man who is put forward by the two Parties. The voting is secret so that a voter's choice may be quite free and not influenced by fear or anything except his own judgement.

But every citizen should use his vote. Any person holding this responsible position of President in Tanzania is carrying on his work on behalf of the people, and he can only do it well if the people fully and wholeheartedly support him, and if they show that they do. If, therefore, you as a voter feel that I should continue as President, I hope you will go to the polls and vote for me by putting your tick on the Presidential ballot paper under the word 'ndiyo'—that is, underneath the black spot. The more people who do this the more help I receive in doing my work properly, and the more obvious it is to people from other countries that I really do speak for Tanzania, and in accordance with the wishes of the people of Tanzania. But if you do not think I am the right person, then it is your duty to vote 'Hapana', and to ask the Parties to make another recommendation. What you must not do is assume that it does not matter. Your vote does matter very much indeed.

I am saying all these things, which most of you know already, because it is my duty as your President to uphold the constitution of this country. The constitution gives to the people an absolutely free choice in their voting according to law. If your votes go against me I shall accept your decision. If you endorse the Party choice— as I hope you will—I will then accept the heavy responsibilities of President from you again.

If you elect me, I will then once again do my best to serve my country, and to lead the people of Tanzania in the long and hard fight against poverty, ignorance, and disease. I will strive to work with you, the people, in maintaining the complete independence of our country from outside control. And I will uphold the laws and the constitution of this country, and the sovereignty of the people. At the same time I shall continue to work for the unity and liberation of Africa, and for the closer co-operation between Tanzania and her neighbouring states.

More than this I do not think it is necessary for me to say about my own candidature. You have had many opportunities to hear me speak, and on many different subjects. You know my views and my attitudes. I think we know each other. I ask you to consider carefully whether you think I have done well as your President, and whether you think I shall do well in the future. And if you can then do so with a clear conscience I ask you to vote 'ndiyo' on polling day.

Having spoken about the Presidential Election which will be taking place throughout Tanzania, let me now speak briefly about the General Election which is taking place on the mainland. The voters in this election will be choosing the person who will be their Member of Parliament for the next five years. What is the job that a Member has to do?

Firstly, he is the representative of the people in the National Assembly. He must speak on their behalf when new laws are being considered; he must bring the people's problems to the Government for consideration; he must join with his fellow Members in supporting the Government when he believes it is acting correctly, and in criticizing it when he thinks some other action would be more in the national interest. And in addition to this work of putting the views of the people to the Government, a Member of Parliament has also to explain to the people in his constituency what the Government is doing and why.

A Member of Parliament is elected from each constituency, and therefore has a special responsibility to the people of his area. But he is not only the Member for—let us say—Moshi. He is a Member of the National Assembly, and as such he has to consider the interests of the nation as a whole as well as those of his own particular area. He can, and should, state the particular needs of his own area; but ultimately he must act in Parliament and outside as a representative and spokesman of our nation as a whole.

What qualifications are therefore needed if a person is to become a good Member of Parliament? According to the constitution every candidate must be a citizen of the Republic, a loyal member of TANU, of sound mind, and over 21 years old. Every candidate who is asking for your support fulfils these qualifications. But you will wish to consider other things as well.

It is necessary that an effective Member of Parliament should be able to express clearly the people's views to the Government, and explain the Government's efforts and problems to you. But he must not simply be a competent spokesman; even more important he must also be able to understand the problems of our nation, and be able to consider various suggestions which are made to overcome them. I should add that this understanding is not simply a question of education; that can help, but what matters very much is character, intelligence, honesty, and a willingness to learn.

Let me add one more thing about this election. The only purpose of the election symbols is to make it easy for illiterate voters to record their vote without help from the Presiding Officer—although he will still help them if they ask for assistance. The symbols are simply a means of identification—no more than that. It is by chance only that a particular candidate was given a nyumba or a jembe as his symbol, and voters will be choosing a man, not a thing.

In addition there is one other matter which I hope everyone will remember. All the candidates are TANU candidates and our national unity need not be, and must not be, impaired by these elections. There is no reason why the candidates and their different supporters should not be good friends; you may like a person very much, and think highly of him, but still not agree that he is the best possible Member of Parliament. There must be no quarrelling or recriminations during or after these elections; once the people have made their choice everyone has to work together in their different jobs.

For although it is an honour to be elected Member of Parliament, it is no disgrace to stand for election and then to fail. Nor does failure prove that a man was wrong to stand for election; by standing he enabled the people to choose and express their will.

It is because of the importance of unity that the election regulations forbid the use of tribalism and racialism in the campaign, and forbid any candidate to appeal on grounds of religion or sex. There are, however, many ways in which clever and unscrupulous people can make such appeals without doing so openly. It is my belief that our people so much value our national unity that they will react strongly against those who bring in these matters by any means whatsoever.

Finally, let me pay tribute to the election supervisors who have left their homes, and are travelling with the candidates in different areas so as to ensure that the elections are conducted fairly and according to law. These supervisors are doing a vital job for our democratic country; I hope they are everywhere being treated with proper respect, and that they in their turn will strictly enforce the regulations. I hope the supervisors will also ensure that the people understand their freedom to vote how they please, both in the General and the Presidential Elections, and that they understand the method by which they should record their wishes.

Mabibi na Mabwana; we have a lot of work ahead of us in Tanzania. Through these elections we shall be choosing who is to lead us; who is to be our President, and who are to be the mainland Members of Parliament during the next five years. Use your vote wisely and after careful thought. But do not fail to use it.

Thank you. *Uhuru na Kazi.*

9

Congress on African History

In his opening speech at the International Congress on African History on 26 September 1965, President Nyerere stressed the relevance of, and the interest in, historical research in Africa.

On behalf of the Government of Tanzania, and with a great deal of personal pleasure, I welcome you all to this Conference on African History. I hope that you will be happy in our University College, and that its facilities will assist you to have a successful conference.

Although you will spend most of your time on this Hill, however, I hope that the attractions of the campus, and of discussions with your colleagues, will not prevent you from seeing something of Dar es Salaam—and even of Tanzania—while you are in our country. If you require one, you even have an excuse for such excursions!

It so happens that today has been the final polling day in the first one-party elections of our United Republic. And, in a few days' time, we shall embark on a further stage of the political evolution of our nation with the swearing in of the President—that is, assuming that the TANU candidate receives a majority of affirmative votes—and the inauguration of a new Cabinet. These events are at present probably classified in academic parlance as 'political science'; but in a few years' time you will find them included in the history you have to write about and teach!

In fact, it is not only in jest that I suggest these landmarks in the development of Tanzania are of interest to the conference delegates. Neither am I trying to seduce you away from your work, or implying a lack of interest in the subjects you will be discussing here. I am simply suggesting that the past and present are one; and that an understanding of both is necessary for the specialists of each time period. For any student of life and society, past and present are merely two aspects of a single thing. The continuity of life is maintained throughout—and despite—change, both in societies and in individuals; although reformers sometimes wish it were not so, and revolutionaries pretend otherwise! Different as are the lives of modern Africans from those of our grandparents, still we and our ancestors are linked together indissolubly. Our present day attitudes and reactions cannot be properly understood without reference to the economy, social organization, and religious basis of the society of fifty years ago; and so on back through time. But equally, I believe that great light can be thrown on the recent past, and then backwards, by an understanding of the aspirations and attitudes of present day Africa.

To say this is not to imply that there is no need for specialists in history and the different ages and branches of history. It is simply a reminder that life is a single whole, and that knowledge is not gained if we hug it to ourselves like a prized personal possession. It must be thrown like a pebble into the pool of wisdom so that the soft matter and the ragged edges can be worn away, until only the hard grain of truth remains. It is the accretion of all these grains, from thousands of different sources as regards time and discipline, which builds a platform for longer vision, and which can ultimately increase our understanding of the phenomenon which is man, and the future he can make for himself. In this connection, therefore, no aspect of knowledge is unrelated to the others; past and present are fused, and the different academic disciplines are but segments of one whole.

Thus it is that this conference will gain greatly by the presence of people from so many different parts of the world, who have different specialities and methods of approach to the subject of African history. For you are not starting right from the beginning. Because of the work which has already been done, there is one thing which this conference will not have to discuss. That is the contention that Africa has no history! The days when this was seriously suggested by intelligent men and women have now passed. Your problem at this conference is more likely to arise from the uncoordinated and sometimes undisciplined nature of the evidence; and from the number and variety of books and articles published in recent years.

The new consciousness that we have a history, and the amount of study which it needs and deserves, is not confined to Africa. The emergence of independent African states over the last two decades has meant that the rest of the world feels a need to understand this continent in a way which was unnecessary when we were simply colonial subjects. This new interest should not be dismissed as an aspect of neo-colonialism; on the contrary, it is a recognition that we in Africa are now equals whom the world cannot disregard. Conversely, as we Africans are involved in the world, and desire to take our full place in its councils, we must welcome this interest, and co-operate with it.

It is also true that we can benefit from this interest in our past. The fact that people from all over the world, and many different institutions, are involved in the work of re-discovering our history, means that there is a wide variety of experience and techniques which can be used in the investigations. We do not become confined by the traditional study methods of any one university or country; neither do we have to start from the beginning ourselves, or do the whole labour on our own.

At the same time it is natural and right that Africa's new universities and institutions should from now on take a leading part in this work. The primary sources are here, in Africa, and the primary interest is not really other people's desire to understand us, but our own desire to understand ourselves and our societies, so that we can build the future on firm foundations.

I have said that the primary sources of our history are here in Africa, and I do so deliberately. This does not mean I am ignorant of the great amount of written material which is only available in the archives of other countries. Neither does it imply that I believe there are inexhaustible supplies of written documents in this continent only waiting to be found and studied. What I am really referring to is the mass of localized unwritten historical knowledge, which has to be searched for, collected, checked, and written into a comprehensive story.

This is a difficult and time-demanding task, and requires the cross-checking of many different kinds of evidence. It may be—you will know whether this is so—that new tools of historical research, and many different approaches, have to be used. But I hope that one of the things this conference will do is find ways in which the contributions of different academic specialists can be co-ordinated, and effectively used for historical purposes.

But whatever the method, the vital thing is that we should be able to develop a really African history. Up to now the world's knowledge of this continent—and even modern Africa's knowledge —has been drawn almost exclusively from the outside. Most people who study our history at educational institutions throughout the world, still learn of the 'discovery of Africa', and the journeys of the great explorers. They learn of the slave trade, and the European invasions; they analyse the economic motivations and effects—on Europe—of these events. But it is only in very recent years that the continuously changing pattern of African life, and the effect on that pattern of these external events, has really begun to be appreciated. And it is only when these things are looked at from Africa outwards that an 'African history' will develop. It is this task which has recently been begun, and which I believe this conference can promote and assist.

Further, your review of the historical writing and research of recent years can provide a basis for valuable expressions of opinion on what now needs to be done, and with what priorities. I believe that in this forward-looking discussion the Africans among you have a very special responsibility. Because they are of this continent, and concerned so intimately with its future as well as its past, the citizens of Africa should be able to indicate where our needs for historical knowledge press most heavily upon us.

But if Africans have special—though not exclusive—understanding in that field, the questions which have then to be formulated, and the means through which they can be asked, are matters which call for the combined experience and knowledge of everyone.

All this means that there are many fundamental questions which will have to be considered at this congress. What are the African concepts of the past? Of what objective value is the history which was passed from generation to generation in traditional societies, and how can it most accurately be collated? What is the historical value of the artifacts of the more recent past in the light of this oral evidence, and vice versa? What of the historical writings of African Islam, which have been so neglected by European studies of this continent?

These are basic questions of interest to all Africa. I admit, however, that we in Tanzania are particularly interested in the possibilities of a combined literate and oral approach, because this appears to have great relevance to the re-discovery of our own history. It is possible that the Islamic Swahili Chronicles, together with the traditions of our non-literate tribes, could combine to give concrete evidence of a past about which we can now only conjecture from half-knowledge.

Accumulation of facts, however, is only part of the problem. There is also the necessity for interpretation of those facts—that is, for an attempt to explain their meaning. It is at this point that I think the conference could most easily dissolve into disputation unless the emphasis on *Africa's* need, and interest in *Africa's* history is most strongly maintained. I am not saying that the 'non-alignment' of Africa's policies is strictly applicable to your subject of discussion. But I am asking that those who adhere to the Marxist philosophy of history, and those who adhere to various Western philosophies, should both examine honestly the strict applicability of their approach to our problems. An exchange of pre-formulated views would be a waste of a great opportunity; what is required here is a discussion and a thinking aloud, by scholars of different persuasions, about the extent to which their own approach has proved valid and useful in the context of African evidence of history. If this can be done frankly, the future direction of African historical research and interpretation will derive great benefit from your meetings here.

The many questions about future work which will be raised at this conference should not, however, be allowed to mask the amount of lost historical knowledge which has been regained during the last few years. Your sessions which take stock of the results so far achieved will undoubtedly be fascinating, and will constitute a valuable professional exchange. But I hope that they will also be useful to teachers and members of the public who will attend your evening lectures, and to the educationalists of Africa who are among your conference members.

This is my final point. Important as are your discussions about techniques, and valuable as you will each find the exchange of information about results so far achieved, your work will have limited importance unless its results can be disseminated. It is the present and future citizens of Africa, and of the world, who must achieve the understanding which a knowledge of African history can bring. The new knowledge, as it is acquired, must reach our schools and colleges in a form which is useful and understandable. The fact that this knowledge has gaps in it, which are filled with conjectures based on limited evidence, is no great problem. It can be a stimulus to interest and future work by an increasing number of African students. And it is when this happens that African attitudes, insights, and questionings, will really begin to shape the growth of African historical research and writing.

Ladies and Gentlemen, this conference grew out of an initiative promoted by the Society of African Culture. It was organized by the University College of Dar es Salaam, with the full co-operation of my Government. It was paid for by the Tanzanian Government with the help of a generous contribution from UNESCO. A large number of people have thus been involved, and we in Tanzania are very grateful to all those who have helped to bring the conference into being.

Perhaps, however, I should explain one thing. We in Tanzania have devoted what is for us a lot of time and money in organizing this gathering. We have done so for one reason only: because we believe that a knowledge and understanding of African history is important for the growth of our continent. We have not, Mr. Principal, invited distinguished guests from all over the world in the expectation—or hope—that they will finish with a declaration of support for conclusions and resolutions which we have already formulated. We have asked them to come and help in the search for knowledge; to help in the formulation of the right questions, and in the collation of existing experience.

On behalf of the Government, and—if I may change my hat for a moment—as Visitor of the University College, I thank you all for responding to our invitation. I give you our good wishes for a useful and successful conference.

Thank you.

10

Opening of the New National Assembly

On 12 *October* 1965, *President Nyerere addressed the first meeting of the newly elected National Assembly, which consisted of the* 107 *elected Members, plus* 10 *Members nominated by the President, plus Members nominated from Zanzibar and the Regional Commissioners as* ex officio *representatives.*

Mr. Speaker, Honourable Members.

First allow me, Mr. Speaker, to congratulate you on your election to your high and responsible office. Your selection by Members of this House is a tribute to you, and to your friendly but firm and impartial chairmanship of the last National Assembly.

Secondly, I wish to congratulate all the Members of this House who have been sent here by people who freely expressed their choice in the recent elections. An honour and a responsibility have been accorded to you. In the coming years you have to justify this trust, and I am confident that you will exert your minds and your energies for that purpose.

At the same time I think it important to express, on behalf of the Government and the people, thanks to all those who contested the recent elections on the mainland and who were defeated. On this occasion they have not been chosen as Members of Parliament; but this does not mean that the defeated persons have no contribution to make to the development of Tanzania. There is work to be done on our land, and in our new industries; every kind of work which is honourably undertaken and fulfilled is a service to our nation.

It is important that everyone should understand that there is no shame in being defeated in a free election; when two people stand for one seat it is inevitable that one should be rejected. By standing every candidate assisted the workings of our democracy; shame enters into the matter only if those who are defeated in lawfully conducted elections do not work loyally for our nation in the whole-hearted acceptance of the wishes of the people. I do not believe anyone will betray the principles of our democracy in such a manner.

Before I proceed to the body of my address today, there are two other groups of people whom I wish to congratulate, and thank. The election supervisors did a magnificent job in almost every area; scrupulously fair, they ensured that all candidates had an equal opportunity to present themselves to the people, and that the elections were conducted with dignity. As a result of this experience we can say definitely that the system of supervisors is a very good one in our circumstances. We are all indebted to the people who carried out this arduous but responsible task. Their efforts were well supplemented by the Party leadership at the local level. Thousands of Party officials and activists worked very hard and very well to make this election a democratic success. I am confident everyone will agree with me that those efforts were worth while.

The real burden of the election, however, fell upon you, Mr. Speaker, upon your office, and in particular, upon the two Clerks to this National Assembly. It is, perhaps, a good thing for Members of Parliament to reflect for a moment on the work which a simple decision of this House can involve. The total registered electorate for the two elections was 3,359,714. There were 208 mainland Parliamentary candidates, endorsed by the TANU National Executive, and 101 contested seats. In addition, there was the Presidential Election throughout the United Republic.

Work in your office, Mr. Speaker, started with the appointment of the election supervisors, their movement to the constituencies they were covering, the arrangement of transport, accommodation, and subsistence allowance for the 321 people in all different parts of the country. But that was only the beginning. A total of 7 million ballot papers had to be printed and distributed to the correct places; 3 million Parliamentary Election manifestos—of 101 different kinds—had to be edited, checked, and distributed to the relevant constituencies. Seven thousand four hundred polling stations had to be organized and manned; 10,000 ballot boxes prepared and distributed even after it had been found impossible to get sufficient ballot boxes manufactured to enable all the voting to take place on one day.

All this work was done magnificently, and the inevitable break-downs were minor ones. It was done so well because thousands of people threw their whole energies into making a success of it: printers, transporters, administrators, police and clerks. There was no clock-watching, just devotion to duty whatever it demanded. On behalf of the people I very sincerely and wholeheartedly thank all those who were involved.

The purpose of all this activity was to make Tanzania a really democratic country in which Theodore Parker's definition of democracy as 'Government of all the People by all the people, for all the people' is really applicable. We have claimed, and I think we were justified, that the Governments of this nation since before independence have been representative of the people's wishes. But we have to recognize that none of them, until now, has been based on the free and equal choice of all our citizens.

The election we have just conducted is the fifth which has taken place on the mainland. It was fundamentally different from all those which preceded it, and the results can only be understood in the light of that fact.

In 1958 and 1959 we had the first elections in Tanganyika, half of the country being involved each year. The franchise was—to put it mildly—a restricted one; less than 60,000 people were registered as voters. Yet in fact quite a small proportion of those registered voters had an opportunity to record their choice. The overwhelming support given for TANU and TANU supported candidates in 1958 meant that the following year most of those individuals who opposed TANU decided that it was not worth contesting the seat. As a result, and taking the two years together, only 24,000 people actually voted in our first 'national' elections.

The same pattern repeated itself in 1960 when the franchise was a little wider. Almost 900,000 people registered as voters; but in only 11 constituencies was there more than one candidate for a seat, so that less than 100,000 people actually went to the polls to express their choice.

In 1962 we had, for the first time, an election on the basis of adult suffrage, when the first President of Tanganyika was chosen. Yet even then the number of people who voted was comparatively small. One million eight hundred thousand people registered as voters, but only 64 per cent of these went to the polls, so that less than 1,200,000 people actually took an active part in choosing their President.

In the election we have just finished, 2,266,000 people recorded their choice for their Member of Parliament; 2,612,000 recorded their approval or disapproval of the Presidential candidate. Now we can truly say that we have a Parliament and a President chosen by all the people.

But it is not in relation to numbers alone that we have become more democratic. Firstly, in the past elections certain seats were reserved for minority racial groups, and certain individuals had to stand as 'Europeans' or as 'Asians'. We must acknowledge that through that system we had some very good Members of Parliament; I am pleased to see that some of them are again with us. But this time they contested the elections as individual Tanzanian citizens, on equal terms with all other candidates. This is a fundamental change to conform with our principles of equality. It was welcomed most of all, I think, by those whom the former constitution singled out as a separate group.

There is, however, another factor which was even more important in the circumstances of Tanzania in making this election meaningful to the people. For in one sense it can be said that no real choice was offered to the people in the 1958 and 1960 elections. They were offered a choice between the struggle for independence with TANU, or opposition to the forces of nationalism and human equality. It was like asking a man to choose between freedom and slavery— the answer is so obvious that no choice is really involved at all. In the event our people made their attitude clear at the beginning, and after that had comparatively little interest in constantly repeating such an obvious choice.

The fact that this basic question was repeated, however, meant that the Party had no alternative but to stand as one solid group. If the people voted they were then forced to vote for or against TANU. They had virtually no choice of which individual within TANU should represent them. They could normally only reject an individual by appearing to reject TANU. This position was changed at the recent elections; the people were able to record their judgement on individuals without their basic loyalty to TANU being called into question. The choice before them became a real one.

The importance of this ability to choose must not be underestimated. It means that every Member of Parliament is now forced to remember in all his actions that the people are his masters. This is no longer a matter of theory; individuals can no longer take refuge from the people's anger behind the shield of the Party. They stand to be judged by what they themselves do, and by what the people assess to be their character, and their attitude.

The casualty rate among the previous Members of Parliament has been a heavy one, and it includes many people who did very good work for the movement in the past. I want to pay tribute to those individuals now, and to thank them on behalf of all the people for the contribution they made to our successful struggle for freedom. I think everyone will join me in that tribute. Nothing can take away the honour which was earned by the founder members of TANU and those other Members who suffered in the independence struggle. I do not believe our people wish to take away that honour.

But elections are not a vote of thanks. It would be quite wrong to elect a person to Parliament because in the past they have done good work. The elections choose people for the future. Those who have just been elected will not be able to call for an expression of gratitude in five years' time, however well they do the work which is now before them. They will have to account for their actions, and show that the people's trust was not misplaced. But they will then have—once again—to ask for a vote of confidence.

All this means that there is no personal security for Members of Parliament, for members of the Government, or even for the President. Politics is, and must be looked upon as, a field of service, not as a means of earning a living. While a person is serving the nation in this way he must receive enough pay to live on and to do his work properly. Whether or not the person continues to be a Member of Parliament depends entirely on the wishes of those whom he serves, i.e. the voters.

It is of vital importance that all of us—people and politicians alike —should understand this. There can be no complaint against the people's choice. It may be that in addition to those who voted for certain nationally known but defeated candidates, others also feel that the people made a mistake in certain places. Let me make it quite clear. If the people did make a mistake it is their right to do so. They themselves choose their representatives in this Parliament. It is arrogance for anyone to think they can choose on behalf of the people better than the people can choose for themselves. Freedom to choose without fear or pressure is the very essence of democracy. It includes the freedom to choose wrongly in the eyes of any particular group, or even in the eyes of history, or of God.

In our system, however, it is not enough that the Parliamentary Elections should be completely free. If we are to have democracy in our nation the Party must also be democratic. TANU and the Afro-Shirazi Party are absolutely central to our system of government. It is the National Conference and the National Executive which finally select which of the many persons nominated shall actually be submitted to the people's choice. It is these organs of the Party which lay down the basic principles of our national policy.

It is therefore of fundamental importance that all citizens of Tanzania who are willing to accept the aims and objects of the Party, as set out in Article II of the Party Constitution, should be able to join the Party, and should be encouraged to do so. If our Party drifts into becoming an elitist organization, with special privileges for founder members or others, then democracy in Tanzania will die. Within the Party, as in national institutions, the members must have absolute freedom to choose their representatives in the highest offices. Further, they must be able, both directly and through those representatives, to express their views on basic policy questions.

In the coming months particular attention will be paid to these matters. TANU has always had a vital role to play in the Government of this country, but I think it is true that there has been some uncertainty about what this role required of the members and the Party leaders. Under the new constitution the integration of TANU and Government machinery makes it possible for closer co-operation to develop without the danger of overlapping. By our new system we have demonstrated finally that the old conflicts between TANU and the Civil Service, and between TANU and the institutions of central Government, are out of date. The colonialism which engendered these conflicts is dead as far as Tanzania is concerned. We can now put its attitudes behind us and concentrate on building our country in accordance with our own desires.

If we learn their lessons correctly, the national elections which we have just had can teach us many things about the wishes of the people, and the attitudes they desire to see among their leaders. We must objectively examine the results and see if we can find the reasons for them; then we can see what corrections of emphasis—if any—are required in our policies and in our behaviour.

But already I think there are two things which can be seen from the results. Firstly, the people of Tanzania have rejected racialism. Members of the Party and non-members, all have accepted in practice the TANU pledge—'I believe in the universal brotherhood of man'. They have justified our stand on principle in relation to the racial discrimination which was practised in this country in the past, and which is enshrined in the policies of the minority governments of South Africa and Southern Rhodesia. Further, and this we must learn; they have demanded that the servants of the people must be good servants, efficient and capable, and of any colour or ancestry. In the present world situation this is something of which Tanzania can be very proud. It is also something which we must live up to and maintain. A citizen of this country is a citizen: that is enough. Let us never forget that fact, and let no one of us ever again betray the people by acting as if there were different classes of citizens.

The second lesson of the elections, which is already obvious, is that there had not been enough practical recognition of the need to keep in constant touch with the people. Too many of us assumed that because we are of the people we therefore knew what the people wanted. We did not exert ourselves to go to the people from our homes and find out what are their problems in the changing situation. We did too little to help them understand what was being done and why. In fact we have been saying that the people are sovereign, but we have not been acting as their servants should act and constantly going back to account for our actions and hear their views.

The Members of this new Parliament must learn that lesson. They must listen to the people, and talk with them. This is not just a question of holding public meetings, and giving magnificent speeches. It means working with the people on the self-help projects, taking part in educational activities, constantly travelling, and discussing the affairs of the nation, the Region, and the village.

I fully realize that it is not possible for a Member of Parliament to go to every part of his constituency every few weeks. Even more difficult is it for Ministers and other Government personnel to keep in close touch. But the people are not stupid; they know that in a large constituency they cannot individually expect to be able to see their Member all the time; and they know that a Minister has to act on behalf of the nation as a whole. But they do rightly demand that their representative shall work, and not relax in his home in between sessions of this House.

Keeping in contact with the people is, in fact, one of the most important functions of a Member of Parliament. If a Member really works hard in the constituency he will be able to act as a bridge between people and Government for the transmission of ideas; both from the people and to the people. He will be able to explain to the people what Government is trying to achieve, and how they can use the machinery which has been set up to help in the development of the country and the betterment of the people's lives. He will also be able to explain to Government how new measures are working, and how best the people can be helped to help themselves, or what is worrying them.

The job of the Members of Parliament is, in fact, three-fold. They have to act as a bridge; they have jointly to deliberate on new legislation; and they have to keep the Government actively devoted to the people's interests by their intelligent criticism.

This last thing is vital. Members of Parliament have the right to question Ministers on any subject which comes within their jurisdiction; they have the right to demand answers. It is part of the Minister's job to be able to answer and explain the policies of the Government as a whole and the Ministry for which he is responsible. He must also be able to account for all the actions which are done by the civil servants in his Ministry. Until the Minister has fulfilled his responsibilities in these matters it is impossible for the Members to explain things to their constituents. Through their questions, as much as in debate, Members can help the Government to ensure that the people are being served properly, that their freedom is safeguarded, and that their attempts to work for national development are promoted.

Questions, however, do not always have to be asked and answered on the floor of the House. Members have the right to write to Ministers asking them to look into certain things, asking for co-operation in certain endeavours, or simply asking for information. But it is important that Members should realize that their questions must be based on accurate information, that their requests for co-operation should only be forwarded to the Minister when the normal machinery is unable to assist, and where their information needs cannot be supplied by any other means. Before Members come to the Ministers they have a duty to investigate a subject for themselves, to study published documents, and to understand the possibilities. Most important of all, Members must not under any circumstances attack a member of the Civil Service in this House. If they believe a civil servant is acting wrongly and that injustice is in consequence being done it is the Minister whom Members must call to account. Then it is his task to investigate and, if necessary, to invoke the disciplinary procedures against the Government servant.

These same considerations apply also to the consideration of legislation which is submitted to the National Assembly. The Members must study the proposals, and the reasons for them. They must seek to understand whether the proposals being made will serve their expressed purposes, and whether the purposes are in themselves good ones. Only if careful study is undertaken will Members be able to do this work properly.

But it is very important that proper thought, and thorough debate should be given to legislation. There will be no Whips operating in this House; Government will submit Bills for you to consider and pass or reject. Occasionally, on major issues—the Budget is an obvious example—the Government will inform the Members that the Government is committed to a Bill and will appeal to the people if the Assembly rejects it. The people, the National Assembly, the National Executive Committee, and the Government are all partners in the political field, with their own special fields of responsibility and special fields of interest. It is therefore possible that occasionally there will be a division of opinion about the desirability of a particular piece of legislation. In such cases, provided that both sides are honest, and are able to advance arguments to support their views, the people will be better served by reconsideration of the proposal than by an automatic affirmative vote.

This possibility, however, only makes it more important that Members of Parliament should study the responsibilities they have, and should carefully examine the experiences of the past, and of other countries. The members of the six Standing Committees of the

Assembly will have particular responsibilities in the fields which they cover. But all Members might well consider the desirability of specializing in particular fields of interest rather than trying to know a little of everything and therefore mastering nothing. If this is done Parliament and Government together can make a great contribution to the development of our nation.

There are two more points I wish to make before I go on to discuss the composition of my Government, and the policy we shall pursue in the coming years.

The duties of Members of our new Parliament, which I have outlined, mean that they will be subjected to great temptations. Families, friends, and even acquaintances, will ask Members to use their influence so that this man can get a job he wants, another a loan, and so on. Sometimes people will give presents, or allow credit, hoping to put the Member under a moral obligation to them. But whether or not money is passed, this is corruption. It perverts justice, and if allowed to spread would destroy our nation.

Therefore, in accordance with my duties under the constitution, I shall insist that corruption in any form is exposed to the gaze of the people. Where appropriate, prosecution will follow. Members of this House, and of the Government, will be well advised not only to resist corruption, but also to conduct themselves in such a manner that it is obvious that they are not corrupted.

The other point I wish to make is this. Fulfilling the wishes of the people does not always mean taking the most popular course. Some things always have to be done which are unpopular, and sometimes they are the right things to do. Members of Parliament must have the courage to follow their own consciences on basic issues even if they know the cost of doing so will be the people's displeasure, and defeat at the next election. Always, of course, politicians must try to convert others when they feel strongly; always a man who takes an unpopular stand must be prepared to explain and argue. But if he cannot convince others that he is right, or himself that his view is wrong, then his duty to our people demands that he sacrifice his personal comfort and his personal position to what he believes to be right. Members of Parliament are not delegates; they are representatives. Their whole being must be given to the service of the people; but the one thing they must not sacrifice is their self-respect. That must be bound up with the pursuit of what they believe to be right.

This is the policy I have tried to pursue in forming my new Government, and in making my nominations to this House. Let me explain.

We have just had a popular election of the Members of this House. The people have exerted their right to choose their representatives, and no one has the right to ignore their decision, to circumvent it, or to over-ride it. The President on his part has the constitutional right to nominate to this House ten Members, in addition to those from Zanzibar. In one case I have nominated a person who was defeated in the election, and I have made him a Minister.

In making this appointment I wish it to be quite clear that I am not criticizing the voters of Mwanza East; I am not saying they were wrong, nor challenging them. They were electing their representative, and I welcome him here along with all other new Members. As I have already said, we have no right to question this decision; indeed it is my duty to safeguard the people's right to choose. But it is also my duty to form a Government of Tanzania. In general I have, and I will, appoint Ministers from among the elected Members of Parliament. But the President has the constitutional power to appoint ten people to be Members of this House; and if he thinks it necessary he may then legally appoint Ministers from among the nominated Members. In fact in the past there were three Junior Ministers who were nominated Members of Parliament. It is one thing to say the electors have the right to reject as their representative a person who is a Minister; it is another to say the person they elect can become a Minister. Where a person has in my view fulfilled his national responsibilities in an exemplary fashion, and where his particular services are badly needed in the immediate future, it is then my duty to put him in a position to continue to serve the nation as a whole where and while he is needed. Although, therefore, I understand the criticisms on principle, I have appointed the Hon. Paul Bomani as Minister for Economic and Development Planning and he is on an equal footing with all other members of my Government.

The other nominations which I shall make will be consistent with this policy. As a general rule I will not appoint a person who has been defeated in the election, sorry as I am to see some familiar faces missing from this Assembly.

There are only two other points I wish to make with reference to the new Government. Firstly, Economic and Development Planning has again been made a separate Ministry. It was brought into my office in 1964 because its function and its importance were not sufficiently understood. This is no longer true. The change does not imply any reduction in the importance of this work. On the contrary, I expect to preside myself at the Economic Committee of the Cabinet, and I expect that Committee to be more active than it has been in the past. I believe that at the present stage this method of organization into a separate Ministry will be the most efficient way of operation.

Secondly, the separation of the responsibility for Regional Administration, and the appointment as Minister of the Secretary General of the Party, is designed primarily to improve efficiency. It does, however, also facilitate greater co-operation between the Party and the Government administrations. It is another indication of the central importance of the Party in our new structure of Government.

Both of these changes, in other words, are organizational matters, designed to help us as a nation to pursue our basic objectives. These are the achievement of an economic and social revolution in the lives of the people of Tanzania, in accordance with their wishes, and with their full and free co-operation.

The basic policies of the Government have not, in fact, changed at all. The personnel is slightly different, and the responsibilities of the different people have changed. But it is a TANU Government now as it was a TANU Government before the election.

There are two major pieces of legislation which will be submitted to the National Assembly in the current session although not at this meeting. Both of them are, in a sense, unfinished business, but business which must be very carefully examined in all its implications before it is enshrined in a Bill.

Plans are now being worked out for the changes which will be necessary to bring the local government structure into line with the one-party constitution of the Union Government. In the meantime no local government elections will be held. In preparing this Bill the Government is anxious to benefit from our recent experience of democratic elections, so as to ensure that the same principls aree carried over into the local government field. It is Government's desire that the local elections shall be as meaningful to the people as the General Election was, and that at the same time the efficient administration of local authorities shall be ensured.

The other piece of constitutional machinery for which proposals will be submitted to Parliament is in connection with the Permanent Commission of Enquiry which must be established under Chapter VI of the Interim Constitution of Tanzania. I have already stated my intention to appoint Chief Erasto Mang'enya as Chairman of this very important Commission. Parliament has yet, however, to prescribe the duties and powers of this Commission in so far as they are not laid down in the Constitution. I am confident that when the Bill is submitted to this House all Members will consider it carefully and seek to help the Government make the Commission effective. We all know that there have been cases of abuse of power by persons in responsible positions. We must all be conscious, too, that while these continue our people do not live in conditions of complete freedom and justice such as they and we desire. I believe that through the work of this Commission the number of these abuses can be reduced, and that where they do occur the perpetrators can be discovered and disciplined and the sufferers relieved. If we succeed in this intention one further guarantee of freedom for our people will be instituted, without there being any possibility of licence hindering our national unity and development.

Apart from these political matters the most important work of my Government and of this Parliament will be in connecton with our economic development. We must still further increase our rate of progress, and we must check again that all which we have done is working for the benefit of the people. The administration of certain aspects of marketing is clearly in need of examination, and the workings of co-operatives are not always such that they receive the support of the people whom they are intended to serve. In these cases it is not enough to condemn the private traders and the capitalists; we must also examine our own system. For the principle of co-operation is clearly a good one, and consistent with our policy of direct ownership by the producers of their own commercial outlets. Yet it is not enough that the principles be right; first of all the farmers demand that their crops be marketed efficiently and that they get a good price for them. This is not always happening. The same is true of our consumer co-operative organization. In both cases we must see what can be done to improve administration. The co-operation of the Members of Parliament in this connection will be of great value to the Government.

One very important outstanding matter in connection with the implementation of our Development Plan is the adoption of a Wages Policy. The Government's proposals in this respect will be submitted to a meeting of this National Assembly. Plans are now being prepared, but it is not an easy matter. They have to be so designed that both our wage-earners and our farmers receive a fair share of the wealth which is produced in Tanzania, and that both benefit fairly from the progress which our hard work brings.

There is one further general aspect of our development to which we must give increasing attention. We need, and are working hard to obtain, certain large-scale modern factories and modern industries. But we have not up to now been really exploiting the possibilities which exist for small and locally-based industrial undertakings, where the amount of capital required is small and the managerial skill necessary can be more easily acquired by our own people. It is the intention of the Government to give further consideration to the possibility of developing this kind of lower level industrial undertaking. For it is not essential that in every field we produce on a national basis at one central point. Nor is it essential that we should always use the most modern equipment in the world. It is better to use an ox-drawn plough than a digging stick; where mechanics are not available and farms are of medium size it is better to use such a plough than spend money on a tractor. The same thing applies to industry. It is also relevant that in the National Development Corporation we have an instrument which can be used to assist in the establishment of this kind of undertaking.

But although outside capital would not be very much needed for practical propositions of that kind, it is still essential for other parts of the Five-Year Development Plan. In the course of this Parliament, Ministers will be able to give Members some indication of the help we have so far been promised, and the help we have so far actually received. I recommend these figures to your attention; they do not always conform to the public understanding of the position. Ministers will continue to seek outside capital and technical assistance for our Development Plans where this is necessary. In particular we shall be anxiously examining, on behalf of the East African Governments, all possibilities which may arise and which would enable us to make rapid and efficient progress with our ambition to build a railway link between Lusaka and Dar es Salaam.

At no time in our search for overseas assistance, however, will we compromise our national independence or our policies of non-alignment in international quarrels which do not concern us. We are neither capitalist nor communist in philosophy; we are not part of the Eastern Bloc, nor of the Western Bloc. We are Tanzanians, and part of Africa.

It will be a continuing and active policy of this Government to seek to enlarge the areas of co-operation with our neighbouring states. We shall continue to seek greater African unity. We continue to desire to merge our nationhood into an East African Federation, but we are also realists, and in the absence of that Federation will take the necessary steps to ensure the development of our own Union.

In fact, our foreign policy has not changed at all with the change of Government. In particular we remain as we have always been, very firm supporters of the United Nations. This organization represents the greatest hope for peace in the world, and Tanzania will continue to uphold its principles and its rulings in all her international policies. We are well aware of the imperfections of the United Nations; its powers are too limited for the work which it could usefully do. But that is no reason for abandoning it; it is a reason for strengthening it, and Tanzania will assist as she can in that direction.

In particular we believe that the United Nations will be greatly strengthened when the People's Republic of China is admitted to her rightful place as a member of the United Nations. It is folly to pretend that the government of 650 million people of that Republic does not exist, and that all those people are represented in the international councils of the world by the authorities who control the 11 million people of Taiwan. Tanzania will therefore continue to work actively for the admission of the People's Republic of China into the United Nations.

There is another international organization of which Tanzania is a member, and to the principles of which she is committed. During the election campaign I said that if Britain acquiesced in independence for Rhodesia without insisting first on majority rule in that country, then Tanzania would leave the Commonwealth. That remains true. But it was not said lightly or easily. It is not a threat to Britain, for Britain does not own the Commonwealth. It is no more a threat to Britain than to Ghana, India, or Canada. It is rather a test of our own adherence to the principles we say we believe in. And it would be a rather feeble test if we did not value our membership of the Commonwealth.

On the principle of majority rule before independence there can be no compromise at all. We are not yet satisfied that the British Government is insisting on the achievement of majority rule before independence. But I want to make it clear that I regard the principle to be of more importance than the timing. It is infinitely more important to have the right solution than a quick solution. And it is infinitely preferable to have a peaceful solution than to have the peoples of Rhodesia suffer the horrors of war. For historical reasons the situation in that colony is a very difficult one; it would be easy to spend our time in discussing the betrayals of the principles of human equality which have made it so, but that would be fruitless. What matters now is that the situation should be put right.

Because I believe that we must seize any chance which remains to us, I have informed the British Prime Minister that, as long as the principle is maintained, Tanzania would do all in her power to co-operate in securing a transition to majority rule, and then to independence. As I see it, there are three things which could contribute to the peaceful attainment of majority rule.

Firstly, we must recognize the fact I have stated: that the right solution is much more important than a quick solution.

Secondly, the advancement of the people of Rhodesia will be greatly assisted by the unity of the nationalist forces of that colony. It is a disgrace that two African political parties should compete in the face of the danger which exists.

Thirdly, I believe that the possibilities of a peaceful transition to majority rule will be much increased in Rhodesia if the nationalist leaders—provided they are not locked up in prisons or detention camps—should show a willingness to use constitutional methods of struggle if these are available to them. I do not see that this is any great problem. The whole of Africa prefers to use constitutional methods for political development; it is only when these are suppressed that other methods are considered. We know that no constitutional advance could satisfy the nationalist forces unless it gives independence on the basis of majority rule. But this is no reason for not accepting interim steps, and working them, so long as the final goal remains open.

I do not say these things in ignorance of the difficulties which face our brothers in Southern Rhodesia. But I think that if the constitutional path is open to the smallest degree it should be used. For years TANU struggled without having the ultimate goal publicly accepted by the colonial power; but we persisted. When constitutional advances of any kind were proposed, we accepted them and participated in their workings—regardless of how far they fell short of our demands.

If these three points are accepted we in Tanzania believe that progress may be possible in Southern Rhodesia. And it must be clear that we will give sympathetic consideration to any request which is made to us for help in furthering the cause of freedom and equality in that part of Africa.

Let me add one more thing on this subject. In the last few days the talks between the British Prime Minister and the Prime Minister of Southern Rhodesia have ended in failure. The British Government, despite its difficult internal political situation, has refused to give way to the demands of the colonial minority government. We very much welcome this stand and congratulate Mr. Wilson and his colleagues on the political courage they have shown. I hope that this is an indication that the principle of no independence before majority rule has been accepted, despite the British refusal to use these words.

The dangers of a unilateral declaration of independence are, however, still very real. It is my hope that the discussions in London will have caused the Rhodesian authorities to think again on this matter, and that they will realize instead that the entire Rhodesian people—both black and white—will gain from an acceptance of the principles of democratic independence and a planned movement towards their implementation. If the Rhodesian white people would accept these principles, I do not think they would find Africa unsympathetic to their genuine, though baseless, fears. It is no part of African socialism to replace one type of racial discrimination by another. As we are trying to show in Tanzania, we want Africa to be free, and all her citizens—whatever their colour or their race—equal in human dignity.

In this connection I wish to make clear our attitude to the leaders of the Rhodesian people who are now in Dar es Salaam, and I hope these leaders will take note of what I am saying. We expect members of the nationalist forces who are in our country to act and to talk as responsible people and to recognize the desires of humanity.

Sometimes when they speak they sound as if they were anxious that there should be a fight in Rhodesia. The rest of us in Africa are working extremely hard and doing our best to safeguard the principles we stand by while avoiding a violent struggle. We may fail; and a fight may become inevitable. We hope it does not; but if it does I want to make it quite clear that the fighting will take place in Rhodesia and the fighting will be led from Rhodesia and in Rhodesia. It is absurd to expect that a grim fight can be led from the comfort of Dar es Salaam. The right place for these leaders is with Joshua Nkomo and Ndabaningi Sithole and the masses in Rhodesia.

Mr. Speaker, I have not gone into detail about the legislative programme which will be submitted to this National Assembly; nor about the path we as a nation have to follow. The former omission will be rectified as the Ministers bring their proposals to the House. The latter omission is the deliberate avoidance of re-petition of things which have been said many times. My main purpose today was to welcome the new Members of the House, and give some guidance about the relationship between Members of Parliament and the Government of Tanzania under our revised Interim Constitution.

Let me conclude, therefore, by saying again that the people expect the Members of the National Assembly to act on their behalf; to question the Government on its purposes and its administration; to co-operate with the other institutions of our society to ensure the freedom and progress of our people. And most of all, the people of Tanzania demand that the Members of this House shall serve their interests, those of our United Republic, and of Africa; and that they shall ensure that the Government does likewise.

I thank you all. May God be with you in your work.

11

Agriculture is the Basis of Development

When President Nyerere laid the foundation stone of the permanent buildings at the Morogoro Agricultural College on 18 November 1965, studies had already started there. In his speech the President paid tribute to those who had contributed to the overseas capital and technical assistance which had enabled work to start so quickly. He went on:

. . . Agricultural progress is the basis of Tanzanian development.

This truth is said so often that people forget it. They almost don't listen; the words become part of the atmosphere, and have no impact any more. To talk of the importance of agriculture is like playing a record which has been heard too often.

Yet it remains true. Agricultural progress is indeed the basis of Tanzanian development—and thus of a better standard of living for the people of Tanzania.

What we have to do is to vary the manner of telling this truth. We have to make it understood, and meaningful. There is now only one way we can do that. We have to demonstrate by actions that better agricultural methods are possible, and that they mean a better standard of living. We have to show, and not say; we have to act, not talk.

That is the importance of this College.

We need in this country more citizens who know the methods of modern productive agriculture, and who are both prepared and able to undertake the hard work which is involved in increasing our agricultural output. This College is intended to give the technical knowledge to citizens who come here anxious to serve our country by their intelligent hard work. I believe it can fulfil this task.

This is not a job for weaklings. People should not come to this College if they want work which is easy or ostentatious. It is not meant for them. It is meant for MEN. It is meant for citizens who care about our country and the people in it, and who are prepared to face the fact that in this world progress comes through the patient application of hard work.

At the end of the course here the successful students will obtain an agricultural diploma. This is a sign of their intentions. Unless it is backed up by practical work, it is no use at all. The farmers—the mass of the people of our country—will not change their traditional methods because someone with a diploma comes and tells them that change is good. It is not a piece of paper our farmers are interested in; it is their own standard of living, and the progress of our country. If the mass of our farmers are to learn from those who graduate from this College, they will learn because they have confidence in the abilities of the graduates. They will get this confidence by seeing, with their own eyes, the work which is done by the graduates.

The most effective classroom is an efficient farm. The most effective teachers are the efficient farmers. The graduates of this College will be judged by their practical success once they have graduated. This is as it should be. An agriculturalist should not be a man with clean, soft hands. He must be a practical man, who uses his hands at the same time as he uses his head.

Our farmers now produce an ever-increasing amount of crops by sheer hard work and sweat. The hard work and sweat will remain. But by using the knowledge which can be gained at this College, it will be possible for us to increase still further the products of our land, and to gradually bring to the people of Tanzania a decent and secure standard of living. This must be the objective of this College.

Earlier I said this is not a time for words. Neither do I propose to say very much more today. I have very great expectations from this College; it is one of the most important of the institutions which are now growing up in our country. I am myself confident that the students here will justify the responsibility they are being given, and will fulfil the hopes which we have placed in this College. Already I am pleased to hear that students here—although in temporary buildings and suffering many discomforts—are identifying themselves with the people in the surrounding districts. It is right and good that students having an opportunity to come to an institution of higher learning should try to help their countrymen by teaching literacy and other things. I hope this kind of activity will continue and increase. Then our country will progress, and the reputation of our nation will be increased by its educational institutions . . . .

12

The Importance and Pleasure of Reading

On 29 November 1965, President Nyerere opened a printing works and book warehouse in Arusha, which is a pleasant town in Northern Tanzania at the foot of Mount Meru. In his speech the President stressed the value of numbers of small investments. He went on:

... From a social and economic point of view it is better if our industrial development is scattered throughout the United Republic. In so far as there is a choice, we in Tanzania would infinitely prefer to see many small factories started in different towns of our country rather than one big factory started in any one of them. Such a dispersal means that we are saved very many social problems of too rapid growth in any one city, and from the consequent break-up of all our traditional social organization; it promotes agriculture in the different Regions of our country by providing local markets of wage-earners, and a communication centre; and it spreads an understanding and familiarity with the possibilities and requirements of modern living and modern working.

But although I have no ambition to see our capital city—or any other town—become a great soul-less mass, in which people live in isolation while crowded among their fellow citizens, there is only one way in which this can be avoided. That is by having new industrial enterprises scattered throughout our nation.

... Now let me confess to a special pleasure that it is a book store and book printing works which we are today opening in Tanzania. Book production is economically important to us. We spend a lot of money on education and the greater the number of the necessary books which can be printed and published within the country, the less will be the short-term cost of this investment in people. We shall save foreign currency if our schools can be supplied with books which are printed here. When we pay for these books we shall also be paying wages to our own people and thus promoting further development within our territory rather than abroad. These are important factors and it was not without design that the Government, in Mr. Curtis' words, dropped 'certain broad hints' to the printing company to encourage them to expand their operations in this country.

At the same time I have to admit to personal pleasure at the thought of good book production taking place in our country. Stored in books is the accumulated knowledge of man and the earth he lives in, as well as the literature of different civilizations. In time I hope that our own African traditional stories and cultures will also be fully available in this form, and I was pleased to hear Mr. Moshi say that new books are being encouraged on these subjects. But in the meantime the books which are available can teach us, can inspire us, or can refresh our minds with the pleasure of a good story well told. Books can break down the isolation of our lives and provide us with a friend wherever we may be.

I think we have to try very hard in Tanzania to cultivate the habit of reading among our young people and among our newly literate citizens. It is a fact which we must recognize, that in dealing with the modern world children in Europe have two big advantages over our own children. One is the familiarity with mechanical things; the other, and perhaps even more important one, is familiarity with books. Too often in our own society a person who sits down to read is accused of being lazy or of being unsociable. This attitude we must change. When we get to the position where a man and wife can sit together in the evening each reading or reading to each other, and when their children are encouraged to learn out of school by reading books which are easily available, then we shall have made a big break-through in our development . . . .

13

The Judiciary and the People

On 7 December 1965, President Nyerere addressed the opening session of the Judges' and Resident Magistrates' Conference in Dar es Salaam.

Mr. Chief Justice, Gentlemen.

Let me first say that I am sorry our time together has had to be reduced by the need and pleasant duty to welcome the President of Somalia when he arrives later this morning for a state visit to Tanzania.

The time available will, however, suffice for me to say how much I welcome the decision to hold this conference. All aspects of our national life are changing very rapidly, and it is important that all responsible servants of the people should be clear about their duties and opportunities for service in the developing situation. Further—and I am sure you do not need me to point this out—the different facets of our national life and administration must keep in balance. It is impossible for the judiciary to continue to operate in the colonial tradition when everything else in the society is changing. What is necessary, instead, is for the basic purposes of our judicial system to be understood so that the implementation processes of those basic purposes can be adapted to the new society, and the fundamental principles thus preserved.

At the same time there are severely practical and immediate matters for you to consider. I am pleased that you will be discussing problems of judicial administration and of securing some degree of uniformity in sentences for comparable crimes. For whatever judicial system is operating in a country—however perfect it is in theory—injustice will result from a break-down in the day-to-day work of answering letters, preparing files—and of paying salaries!

It is also true that justice cannot be said to prevail in a nation when the cost of committing a crime depends entirely on the place where it was committed, or the luck of which Judge has been hearing the case. Obviously there are disadvantages in always laying down precisely what punishment must be given for particular crimes. That could prevent justice, as it prevents the circumstances of the crime being taken into account. But I hope your discussions will lead to a common approach being worked out, so that differences of degree in punishment do not become so great that in effect they become differences of kind.

It is my hope, therefore, that in all these questions the Judges and Resident Magistrates here will pool their ideas, and—to use an African concept—that you will talk until you agree, at least on the immediate practical questions. We in Tanzania need you to be very frank at this conference. We want you all to put forward for the consideration of your colleagues, and—through the Chief Justice— of the Government, your views on all of the many matters which impinge on the effectiveness of your work.

This is very important. For the work of the judiciary is nothing less than the maintenance of respect for law in this country. Judges are, and must be, nothing less than the buttress wall supporting the individual justice for which our people struggled when they fought for national independence. You do not control legislation; but your actions, together with those of the police, can make that legislation effective or meaningless. Unless your work is done properly none of the objectives of our democratic society can be implemented.

Justice demands many things. It demands that the innocent be assured of personal security; and also that the guilty should be punished. It demands impartiality between individual citizens—that the law should be the same for all. And it demands an understanding by the judiciary of the people, and by the people of the judiciary; for without this mutual understanding the people's basic sense of justice in their relations with each other may be outraged by the very instrument which they have created to implement justice.

I do not know whether there will be time at this conference for all these matters to be discussed thoroughly. It may be that some can only be referred to in passing, and deferred for greater consideration later. It may be that relative failure and success in different aspects of the work will dictate your priorities. In that case let me make it clear that I hope you will discuss the failures and what can be done about them, without wasting time on congratulations!

And when you are discussing difficulties or failures I hope that you will be prepared to go to the root of the matter if necessary. You should be ready to consider how things can be put right; do the problems demand a complete revision of our system of justice, or can they be dealt with by this and succeeding conferences? For example—and it is a layman's example—our criminal courts at present operate on the basis that the accused is innocent until proved guilty, and the 'proving' or otherwise can be entirely a matter for lawyers, without the individual doing or saying anything. Do we reach the truth this way, or is the inquisitorial technique, which I am told operates in countries such as France, more appropriate to our circumstances? Or some other change?

And is it possible that we need some amendment to our system of justice in order to avoid the wealthy taking advantage of technical loopholes which clever and expensive lawyers can find in most legislation? Or would such amendment open such dangerous possibilities for the Rule of Law that we have to accept these things as an inevitable blemish on a fundamentally sound system?

I am not pretending to answer such questions as these; nor have I necessarily asked the most fundamental ones. Least of all do I wish to imply that there is something basically wrong with the system of justice now operating in Tanzania. I am simply asking you, the experts, to think about fundamental questions as well as day-to-day problems. I am saying, do not be afraid of the implications of any problem. I do this because justice for our people is a matter of great concern to the Government, and you are the people who should advise us how best to safeguard it.

We must all of us always remember that the entire purpose of all our activity is service to the people. This applies to Judges and Magistrates as much as to any other public official. And it presents peculiar challenges to you.

I said earlier that Judges do not legislate. That is true. But it is also true that in practice you are often called upon to interpret the law. In doing so you will sometimes—because of the importance of uniformity throughout the nation—be deciding whether the law is to fulfil one purpose or another. Your decision will then stand until and unless Parliament later decides to pass new legislation on the matter.

In pointing this out I am not criticizing Judges, nor implying that they are in any way exceeding their responsibilities. If the law is at any point open to two or more interpretations, and you have to decide a case, then there is no alternative but to make a choice.

Yet this fact makes the identification of the judiciary with the aspirations of the people very important indeed. Someone once said that justice is most effectively administered when the Judges are neutral men from a different society, or different place, than the people who come before them. This is not a stupid statement. But while it highlights one aspect of a Judge's responsibilities, it ignores others which are equally important.

A 'neutral' Judge who is unaffected by the powers and conflicts of local personalities, and who knows none of them, is therefore uninfluenced by contrasting manners and enthusiasms and will perhaps find it easier to be impartial in his administration of justice. He is beholden to no one, and therefore can ignore the importance, or wealth, of anyone brought before him on a criminal charge, or involved in a civil case. That is the truth underlying the suggestion that Judges should come from outside the society, and remain outside it.

But in fact this sort of neutrality—this impartiality—does not have to rest on such a base. For it must rest ultimately on the integrity of the man who is made a Judge; on his own conviction that justice is the right of every human being. And we do in practice assist the Judges by making them 'independent' of power politics. There is a separate hierarchy and system of command for the judiciary, and once a man is appointed it is extremely difficult to displace him. These things are intended to help secure impartiality.

But they must not do more. They must not lead to the belief that a Judge can be, or should be, 'neutral' on the basic issues of our society. The fact that Judges interpret the law makes it vital that they should be part of the society which is governed by the law. Their interpretation must be made in the light of the assumptions and aspirations of the society in which they live. Otherwise their interpretation may appear ridiculous to that society, and may lead to the whole concept of law being held in contempt by the people.

In a one-party state like Tanzania some of the problems of identification with the people are easier than in nations which are more divided, or where the political system stresses diversity more than unity. But because our legal training and traditions emanate from multi-party democracies we do not always take full advantage of the opportunities provided by our national unity. It is understandable that in a country divided between 'Labour', 'Conservative', and 'Liberal', the Judge should be expected to refrain from membership of political parties, and certainly from activity in them. But why should that attitude be adopted here, where we have only one Party?

Quite clearly Judges must avoid becoming involved in any internal Party power conflicts—if there should ever be any! Clearly also they cannot themselves compete for Party or national political office. But why should they not take part, on equal terms with other members, in the discussions about basic policy of our national movement? Why should they not join with other members in nation-building activities when these take place at a time outside their hours of work?

It is only by being an active part of our society that our judiciary can play its full part in shaping the development of our society. What better place to teach, both by example and by precept, the fundamental principles of the Rule of Law than at Party meetings and Party activities? Our national unity allows us to use this opportunity for sowing an understanding of the requirements of justice, and for learning about the people's meaning when they talk of justice.

At present, of course, many members of our judiciary are not citizens of Tanzania. I realize that this makes complete participation impossible. But the Chief Justice himself, and many other non-Tanzanians, have demonstrated that it is possible for servants of the people to join the people in the march forward, simply by demonstrating a desire to participate. You have to make your anxiety to be of use, your desire to understand and be understood, absolutely clear to our people. Then, sooner or later, the opportunity will come.

Mr. Chief Justice, I have spoken for longer than I intended. I have raised many different hares for your Judges and Resident

Magistrates to chase after. I hope that I have not also been the cause of confusion in your discussions! For we want this conference to be a great success. That is to say, we want it to be useful to the participants, and thus to the Government and people of Tanzania.

14

The Honour of Africa

For several years President Nyerere had been actively concerned with the situation in Rhodesia, and had been working through diplomatic channels to try and get from the British Government of the day a commitment to the principle of majority rule before independence. In June 1965, the President had disassociated himself from that part of the Commonwealth Conference Communique which referred to Rhodesia because the British Government had refused to make this commitment even privately.

Following the unilateral declaration of independence by the Smith regime in Rhodesia, a Ministerial Meeting of the Organization of African Unity was held in Addis Ababa and, on 2 December 1965, passed a resolution calling upon all African states to break diplomatic relations with Britain if concrete steps to bring down the Smith regime had not been taken before 15 December. President Nyerere addressed the National Assembly on Tuesday, 14 December 1965, at 5 p.m., on this subject, and the following day diplomatic relations between the two countries were brought to an end.

My purpose today is to explain the policies and attitudes of the Tanzanian Government one month after the illegal declaration of independence by the racist minority government in Southern Rhodesia

AFRICA'S OBJECTIVES

The policies of Tanzania, and of Africa, in relation to Southern Rhodesia, have always had one object, and one object only. That was, and is, to secure a rapid transition to independence on the basis of majority rule. On this subject every action we have taken, every speech we have made, has been intended to further that purpose. We have no other.

The declared policy of the British Government—successive British Governments—in relation to all her colonies has been the same. Our past disagreements with Britain have been on the basis of her performance in particular places at particular times—not really on the basis of ideas. The basic friendship between our two countries, and between Africa and Britain, has been based on our belief that underlying any current disagreement was a present-day, similar purpose, of bringing all colonial territories—including those dominated by white minorities—to democratic independence.

THE CHARGE AGAINST BRITAIN

Why then is Africa now quarrelling with Britain to the extent that Africa has said if certain things are not done by the 15 December—tomorrow—we shall break diplomatic relations with that country? When the enemy is the Smith regime in Southern Rhodesia, why are we breaking relations with Britain when she says that she is an enemy of the Smith regime?

There is a very simple reason. In an ordered society, when a man is wronged by an illegal act he does not, and should not, take the law into his own hands. He applies to the law, and to those responsible for enforcing the law, for redress. And he expects that action will be taken to relieve him of the wrongs which he is suffering because of an illegal action. It is by such procedures that peace and justice are maintained within states. It is by similar procedures that international peace and justice can be maintained between states. Nations which are wronged by the action or inaction of another nation call upon the nation responsible to relieve them of their wrong; or they call upon the United Nations for assistance against the country responsible.

If an individual who is suffering from a continuing illegal act finds that the organs of law and order fail to act in his defence, what is he supposed to do? Even more, if those organs which are meant to protect him appear to be helping the criminal instead, what must his reaction be? He will say—and he will be entitled to say—'This is enough; I will have nothing more to do with you unless and until you demonstrate to my satisfaction that you propose doing something effective against those who continue to wrong me.'

That is the meaning and implication of the resolution passed by the Organization of African Unity Foreign Ministers at Addis Ababa. Africa is saying to Britain, 'This is enough'.

Mr. Speaker, this is a very serious thing for one country to say to another. It is still more serious when 36 countries say it through an organization for unity which they have themselves established. The people of Africa, and indeed the people of Britain themselves, are entitled to ask for an explanation. They need to understand the evidence which causes Africa to say to the British Government—'This is enough'. Before Africans can support their leaders on such a serious matter they must be sure that Britain is the country responsible in law for the wrong to Africa, and the country which must therefore undertake to remove that wrong. They must be sure too, that any failure is a failure of intent and not merely an inefficiency of execution.

I believe these two charges against Britain must be made, and can be sustained, in relation to the events in Southern Rhodesia. I believe further that it is Africa's inescapable duty to make these charges, and to take action in accordance with the evidence.

Let me make the charges clear. Africa maintains that Southern Rhodesia is at present a colony of the United Kingdom, and that ultimate responsibility for events there resides, in consequence, with the Government of the United Kingdom in London. That government may delegate its responsibility if it wishes, but it cannot escape it; if it entrusts its responsibility for the government of Southern Rhodesia to other people, then it is responsible for their actions. If the British Government disagrees with what is being done by those to whom it has entrusted power, then it must replace those people. If those people assume powers which have not been entrusted to them, then the British Government must reassert its authority and get rid of those who have usurped its power.

The first charge is thus that Britain is the right place to go to for redress. The second charge is that Britain has not shown serious determination either to get rid of those in Southern Rhodesia who have usurped British power, or to replace them by representatives of the people. For it is not the independence of Rhodesia that Africa is complaining about; it is independence under a racialist minority government.

What is the evidence to support those charges?

BRITAIN'S RESPONSIBILITY

Southern Rhodesia is a British colony; its constitution is subject to the will of the British Parliament. As an international entity Southern Rhodesia does not exist. Internationally, by both law and custom, there exists only Britain and its colony.

The colony of Southern Rhodesia has been self-governing since 1923; for 43 years increasing *de facto* power has been exerted by a government based in Salisbury. But the constitution under which that government operated reserved certain powers to the British Government and Parliament in London. The fact that successive British Governments did not use their powers to prevent acts which were contrary to the interests of the African people does not alter the existence of these 'Reserved Powers', nor the ultimate responsibility of the British Government for the actions of the Southern Rhodesian government.

In saying this there is no need to argue abstract cases in law. Britain herself accepts responsibility for Southern Rhodesia. More, she claims that responsibility. Britain claims that she, and she alone, can decide what is to be done about Southern Rhodesia. The only time she has ever used the veto in the United Nations was when Ghana proposed a resolution which would have blocked the transfer to the Southern Rhodesian government of the Air Force which had been built up by the defunct Federation of Rhodesia and Nyasaland. In the Commonwealth Conferences of 1964 and 1965, the Government of Britain maintained this stand, and it was conceded by the rest of the Commonwealth—including the African members. And only just over a week ago—on 6 December 1965—Mr. Wilson, the Prime Minister of Britain, is reported to have said once again, 'Rhodesia is Britain's responsibility'.

There is thus no dispute between Britain and Africa about the British responsibility. What then of the manner in which that responsibility has been, and is being, exercised?

BRITISH RECORD

I do not propose to go back further than October 1964 in an examination of the British record. The record before that date is a shameful one; time after time the interests of the African majority were subjected to the selfish power hunger of the settler minority. Even after 1947, when other colonies in Africa began to feel some hope of ultimate freedom, the settlers of Southern Rhodesia were able to extend their sway. In return for some concessions on the periphery of power, some verbal acceptance of the theory of 'partnership', they were able to secure dominance in a federation of Rhodesia with the countries which are now Zambia and Malawi. In 1961, with the tide running hard against them, and when they were concerned to try and save their federation, they still managed to secure a constitution for Southern Rhodesia which entrenched minority power while only appearing to make some concessions to the African population. And in 1963, at the break-up of the federation, they secured into their own hands the real instruments of power—the aeroplanes, the equipment, and the administration of the Army and the Air Force.

For the settler government of Southern Rhodesia even this was not enough. In 1963, and even more in 1964, they began to demand independence for themselves.

That was the position in October 1964. It was an extremely difficult position for anyone to deal with. The effects of mistakes, errors, or sins, do not disappear because one regrets them; they create their own difficulties and reduce the area of possible movement. It is legitimate to sympathize with the problem facing anyone assuming responsibility for Southern Rhodesia in October 1964. Africa did sympathize. Tanzania did sympathize. We sympathized the more because we felt that a new element had entered into the situation, and that there was hope that the long series of betrayals would end and be replaced by some attempt to implement the principles of human justice.

A good start was made. On 27 October 1964, the Prime Minister of Britain said openly to Mr. Smith, the Prime Minister in a British colony, that a unilateral 'declaration of independence would be an open act of defiance and rebellion, and it would be treasonable to take steps to give effect to it'. These strong words meant that Africa was heartened despite the fact that the statement went on to speak only of the economic consequences of such a declaration.

In November, however, the Smith government called for a referendum in support of independence for Southern Rhodesia under the 1961 constitution. He received 58,000 votes in support. I ask that this House should take particular note of that number; it is less than the total registered voters in the Dar es Salaam South constituency of Tanzania. And even that vote was only obtained after Mr. Smith had said that he was not asking for a vote in support of an illegal decleration of independence!

Threats of illegal action nonetheless continued to come from Salisbury, and apart from warnings about what would happen if they were carried out, nothing was done to those who made the threats. Indeed, by the end of the year there were indications from London that independence might be granted without majority rule. Mr. Bottomley, the British Commonwealth Secretary, was reported as saying, 'We must be satisfied that the basis on which independence is to be granted is acceptable to the people as a whole.' This ambiguous statement was clearly deliberate, and it succeeded in one of its designs. Africa thought that this was merely a tactical move, an endeavour to avoid provoking Smith before Britain was ready to deal with him.

There is no need for me to dwell on the long months of negotiation, threat, and counter-threat, between Britain and Smith in the first ten months of this year. It is sufficient to remember that Mr. Smith went to London once, and that Mr. Wilson went once to Salisbury, in addition to two other ministerial visits from the metropolitan capital to the colony. To these negotiations Africa had no objection; on the contrary, it welcomed them as indicating that Mr. Wilson was genuine in his desire to avoid UDI and was not going to complicate the issue by standing on his dignity.

But while Africa accepted Britain's willingness to negotiate it had cause to get increasingly worried about the content of the negotiations. There were two causes for this unease; one of them has already proved to be justified, and the other has increased in intensity.

Although UDI was declared to be an act of rebellion there was a studious avoidance by British Ministers of the statement that the rebellion would be brought down by all necessary means, including the use of force. The Smith group were never faced with that prospect. On several occasions British Ministers said, 'We shall not use force to impose a constitutional solution' to the Rhodesian situation. They never went further. Africa worried, and waited.

Even more serious for Africa was the deliberate vagueness about the ultimate objective of the negotiations and the opposition to UDI.

MAJORITY RULE

Africa does not oppose UDI because it wishes Southern Rhodesia to remain for ever a colony of Britain. And it certainly does not find the maintenance—or the reassertion—of the 1961 constitution an acceptable goal. The goal of Africa is independence on the basis of majority rule for Southern Rhodesia. Its opposition to UDI is because the hope of attaining majority rule, peacefully and reasonably quickly, is compromised by the usurpation of power from a country which is, at least in general principle, committed to that goal for its colonies. Africa would have been equally opposed to a legal granting of independence to Southern Rhodesia if this were done before majority rule had been attained.

Yet Britain's 'five principles' which had to be met before independence would be granted by the British Government did not specify the existence of majority rule. On the contrary, they clearly showed that if certain 'safeguards' were enshrined in a document, then majority rule would not be insisted upon. There was only one ambiguous statement in principle five which many genuine people—including African leaders—believed provided a safeguard. Principle five stated that 'any basis proposed for independence must be acceptable to the people of Rhodesia as a whole'. Many of our friends said that the people of that colony could not possibly agree on an independence without majority rule, and that therefore, so long as this principle was maintained, Rhodesia would not become completely a second South Africa without hope of peaceful progress.

Tanzania was less sanguine; in the Commonwealth Conference I therefore demanded that the words '*independence on the basis of majority rule*' be included in the final communique. They were not included; and in consequence Tanzania disassociated itself from the Southern Rhodesia section of the communique. Our friends thought us needlessly suspicious. But it was quite clear to us that the British Government was willing to grant independence on the basis of minority rule.

Now it is one month after the minority government of Rhodesia has seized power. There is no longer, surely, any problem about 'not complicating the negotiations' or 'allowing Britain to go step by step in her discussions'. But have we yet had the assurance which Tanzania sought in June? The answer is no. The 1961 constitution remains in being, with some few powers having been resumed by the Government in London. This resumption having been forced upon Britain by Smith! Let me quote Mr. Wilson, the Prime Minister of the United Kingdom, speaking in the House of Commons, London, on 23 November 1965—12 days after the rebellion. He said (as reported in the *Times*):

'While we have power to revoke or amend sections of the 1961 constitution we have said we have no present intention of revoking it as a whole, and I cannot at this stage foresee circumstances in which we would do so.'

Mr. Wilson went on to deal with the role of this constitution in what he calls 'the resettlement period'. He said:

'When the Governor is able to report that the people of Rhodesia are willing and able to work on constitutional paths, we are prepared to work together with their leaders to make a new start. For this purpose the 1961 constitution remains in being, though the House will realize the need for those amendments which are required to prevent its perversion and misuse such as we have seen in the last fortnight, and those amendments, too, which are needed to give effect to the five principles to which all parties in this House have subscribed.'

It is perfectly true, Mr. Speaker, that later in the same speech Mr. Wilson said:

'All along we have made it plain—we did all throughout the negotiations—that while guaranteed and unimpeded progress to majority rule is the policy of all of us, we do not believe it can be immediate. . . But all of us are committed to an early attempt by the Rhodesian people to pronounce on their own future. That was the reason for the suggested referendum and for the Royal Commission.'

The thing which I notice in the last statement, Mr. Speaker, is that this was not an assurance about majority rule; it was an assurance against majority rule. There is still no statement that independence will be given only on the basis of majority rule.

At the end of last week the British Broadcasting Corporation news service reported that Mr. Wilson had suggested that after all, when British authority was re-established in Southern Rhodesia, there might be a period of direct rule by the Governor with advisers from all races. As this would mean the end of the 1961 constitution I had a moment of hope; we would begin over again. But the report went on to say that Mr. Wilson stressed that majority rule could not come for a very long time—and still there was no suggestion that independence would be held up until this majority rule had finally been attained.

I have spent a long time on this matter because it is important that one thing should be understood. In this matter of objective it is not the timing which is causing Africa to become so angry; we could argue about time. Our anger and suspicion arise from the fact that Britain is not even now—14 December 1965—committed to the principle 'independence only on the basis of majority rule.'

I must, however, now move to the question of whether Britain has shown serious determination to get rid of those in Southern Rhodesia who have usurped her power. Africa maintains that she has not.

At this point let me make one thing clear. Africa is not hungry for blood. We do not demand that British troops should die in Southern Rhodesia; we do not demand that Smith's forces should die. If this matter can be settled peacefully no one will be more happy than Africa. But IT MUST BE SETTLED. Further, it must be settled QUICKLY. Great principles are at stake. But that is not all. It is also true that the safety of Africa, and particularly of Zambia, is at stake. Africa will therefore co-operate with any EFFECTIVE and determined attempt to deal with Smith without bloodshed; we shall support any proposal which reduces the danger of fighting to the minimum. But we cannot acquiesce in token action, or in inaction. Africa contends that this is what we have had from Britain since 11 November. She has done the very minimum, and left an African state—an African state friendly to Britain—to live under threat to its livelihood from the rebels.

What has Britain done since 11 November?

On that date Mr. Wilson used some strong words: he said, 'It is an illegal act, ineffective in law; an act of rebellion against the Crown and against the constitution as by law established'. But he then went on to instruct the civil servants of Southern Rhodesia to 'stay at their posts but not to assist in any illegal acts.' He was unable to explain how they could do that when they were serving an illegal government.

As regards the use of force Mr. Wilson repeated his stock phrase despite the changed circumstances. Britain would not use force to impose a constitutional settlement he said, but he went on to say that the British Government 'would give full consideration to any appeal from the Governor for help to restore law and order'. Mr. Wilson refrained from explaining how the law could be more broken than it had been by the usurpation of power, that is to say, by treason. He refrained later from explaining how the Governor was to transmit his appeal once the telephone had been taken from him as well as all the furniture of his office, his staff and his transport.

Instead Mr. Wilson obtained the approval of the British Parliament for economic action against the regime. Capital exports to Southern Rhodesia were stopped; exchange restrictions were imposed; Commonwealth preference was suspended, and a ban was imposed on the British import of Rhodesian tobacco and sugar. The British Foreign Secretary was sent to the United Nations to secure international support for these actions.

The United Nations was highly critical: it demanded further action. Finally, on 20 November Britain accepted a Security Council resolution which included this phrase: 'Calls upon all states . . . to do their utmost in order to break all economic relations with Southern Rhodesia, including an embargo on oil and petroleum products. In response to this resolution first the USA, and then the Federal Republic of Germany, have both turned back cargoes of sugar coming from Rhodesia to fulfil the 1965 quota of that country.

The reaction of the country which claims responsibilty for Rhodesia has been rather different. On 23 November Mr. Wilson spoke to the House of Commons, saying, 'We are going to study all aspects of trade and oil . . . we are not going in for a trade embargo or oil embargo alone.' And in explanation of this he said that there are many difficulties and 'there is the position of Zambia to be considered'! That Zambia had supported the resolution appeared irrelevant to the British Prime Minister, who clearly thought he knew the business of that independent African state better than President Kaunda. On 1 December Mr. Wilson again said, 'We are not contemplating an oil embargo immediately.'

What is Africa expected to think of this mockery of a UN resolution which was already—at Britain's insistence—less than a firm, binding declaration of determination to defeat Smith?

On 1 December, however, Mr. Wilson announced new and much sterner economic measures against Rhodesia. Ninety-five per cent of Rhodesia's exports to Britain were then blocked, and financial measures taken which could have had a fairly quick and fairly severe effect on the economy of that colony. But Mr. Smith of Rhodesia was yesterday reported to have said that these have come too late to affect Rhodesia's economy. I do not believe that he is bluffing. He has had weeks in which to prepare for these measures. But the timing is not my only criticism. I have argued that economic sanctions against Rhodesia will not work as long as South Africa is allowed to trade freely with the rebel colony. And it is Britain which has blocked obligatory sanctions under Chapter 7 of the UN Charter.

COMMITMENT TO ZAMBIA

This brings me to my basic criticism of the British approach. It is a half-hearted approach, but one which leaves Zambia to pay a heavy price.

If effective and obligatory economic measures are instituted, and if alone they can bring down the Smith regime reasonably quickly and allow a new start to be made on the road to independence on the basis of majority rule, then on that basis I should be willing to support them: ON ONE CONDITION. That condition is that Zambia is not left alone to take the consequences of this procedure.

No African state is more concerned than Zambia that the Smith regime shall be defeated. No African President is more concerned that this shall be done without bloodshed and without unleashing a racial or ideological war. We in Tanzania join him in both these ambitions. But the power supplies of the Zambian copperbelt are in rebel hands; the power station of the Kariba Dam has been occupied by troops of the rebel regime. Is Dr. Kaunda expected to sit quiet while increasing economic pressure on the rebels makes them more and more desperate, until they finally use their power to interfere with his power supply? What happens to his own economy, and his own peace meantime?

In November, a week after UDI, Dr. Kaunda called for British troops to guard the Kariba Dam. A British representative was sent to Lusaka to discuss this request. Later the British Commonwealth Secretary was sent to Lusaka. The reason? That Britain was only prepared to send troops on conditions—and the conditions amounted to the defence of Rhodesia against attack quite as much as the defence of Zambia against attack from the rebels.

Dr. Kaunda accepted a Royal Air Force contingent because it was essential that his own country have some answer to the Southern Rhodesian and South African planes on his border. But, in the face of tremendous pressure, he has refused to accept ground forces under the conditions which Britain is imposing.

But the fact remains that the British Government has been more willing to use Zambia's difficulties as an excuse for inaction, than it has been to use them as a reason for action. For a long time before 11 November, discussions about 'contingency planning' proceeded between Zambia, Britain and her allies, and Tanzania. When I opened this Assembly in October I said that Tanzania 'will give sympathetic consideration to any request which is made to us for help in furthering the cause of freedom and equality.'

What was this for if not to protect Zambia from the effects of any actions against an illegal Southern Rhodesia regime? And why is it not being used?

Let me make one thing clear at this point. Whatever happens as regards our relations with Britain, our commitment to Zambia remains. We continue to be ready to allow the transit of any goods or personnel, from any place, needed by Zambia to protect her interests and pursue the fight against Smith at the same time.

No one can drive a wedge between Zambia and Tanzania: neither can anyone hide behind Zambia's needs when they are trying to evade their responsibilities.

Mr. Speaker, that is an outline of the charge against the British Government. I could amplify it and speak much longer. I do not think it is necessary. I believe that I have shown that Africa has reason for its action, reasons for saying that the British Government has not shown serious determination either to get rid of those in Southern Rhodesia who have usurped British power, or to replace them by representatives of the people. I believe that I have further shown that in so far as Britain has taken action which will, in the longer term, cause difficulties for the Smith regime, she has failed to safeguard the interests of that independent African state which stands in hourly threat from that regime. She has failed to live up to the responsibilities she has claimed, and she has failed to protect—or allow others to protect—an independent state which is threatened because of her failure to immediately overthrow the rebel regime.

THE ADDIS ABABA RESOLUTION

For these reasons I say that African action directed at Britain is both necessary and appropriate. Africa is entitled to say to this responsible authority, 'Act now, or allow others to act, or take the consequences.'

This is what the Addis Ababa resolution said. If Britain did not act against Smith before the 15 December African states would break diplomatic relations with Britain.

Let me now move to a consideration of that resolution, and the consequent responsibilities for Africa.

The wording of the resolution can be—and has been—criticized. It called for Smith to be brought down by the 15 December. We are told—maybe correctly—that in 13 days this is impossible. But African states are not the fools that some people take them to be. To take an extreme example, it would clearly be absurd for Africa to break diplomatic relations with Britain if by the 15th British troops were moving towards Rhodesia. Africa clearly would not do such a stupid thing. But it is not necessary even for things to have gone as far as that. If Britain has by the 15th demonstrated that at last she means to fulfil her responsibilities, and that she is prepared to pay the price in protecting others if she chooses a slower method, then again it would be absurd for Africa to take action against Britain.

I have myself suggested two things which Britain could do to demonstrate her determination. I understand her preference for economic sanctions; I even share it. But I have said that if she wants this time she must in the meantime protect Zambia. She must apply the full pressure of economic measures, and while these are taking effect she must safeguard Zambia's power supplies by occupying the Kariba Dam and power station. This, Tanzania—and I believe every other African state—would recognize as willingness to act against Smith.

I have further suggested that, as long as the Kariba situation is safeguarded, it does not matter if the action taken is British. Let her call for the help of the United Nations in dealing with Smith. Let her, for example, ask the United Nations to apply Chapter 7 of the Charter which deals with the mandatory use of force by all members—economic or military force. This would give Britain time to allow economic sanctions to work; it would also give Africa the assurance that military force is not ruled out if it becomes necessary.

This is my interpretation of the Addis Ababa resolution. I believe it is Africa's interpretation. I have no reason to believe that any other African state is going to be more illiberal in interpreting that resolution. All we are really asking is that Britain should recognize our interest, and that she should demonstrate to us her determination to defeat the Smith rebellion, and to put Southern Rhodesia once more on the path to democratic independence.

Britain's reaction so far—we have one day to go—has not been encouraging. We have been told that Britain is not going to be pushed around. In a newspaper interview it is reported that Britain's 'not standing idly by' if Zambia's power supplies are cut off by Smith still means 'acting without bloodshed'. And worst of all, because it is an action not words, an oil tanker, hired by a firm in which the British Government hold 51 per cent of the shares, has been told by the same British Government that it may continue on its way taking two weeks' supply of oil to Rhodesia.

Can Africa fail to implement its resolution?

AFRICA'S RESPONSIBILITY TO AFRICA

Do African states meet in solemn conclave to make a noise? Or do they mean what they say? The purpose of that resolution was to show that Africa requires action against Smith; if that action is not taken do we then shrug our shoulders and slink away without showing that Africa at least knows the meaning of the words it uses? Can we—the African states—honourably do nothing to implement our own resolution, or would failure to do so not mean that we are improving on Britain's example of using big words and doing—in our case—absolutely nothing? Britain at least has imposed economic sanctions after her big words. If we fail to implement our resolution we shall have done nothing—less than nothing.

If we ignore our own resolution, neither our suffering brethren in Rhodesia, in Mozambique, in Angola, in South Africa, in South West Africa, nor the broad masses of the people of Africa, or for that matter the non-African members of the United Nations Organization could ever trust Africa to honour a pledge solemnly undertaken by Africa's leaders. Smith will rejoice; Verwoerd will rejoice; Salazar will rejoice. Where can we hide ourselves for shame?

The Addis Ababa resolution did just one thing which the Accra meeting of Heads of State had not done. At Accra we resolved on a series of measures to be taken under certain circumstances. At Addis Ababa the Foreign Ministers of those same Heads of State selected one of those measures and put a date to it. Which of us can say we are not committed to carrying it out?

There are in fact two states in Africa which can absolve themselves if they wish. One is Malawi; the other is a state outside East and Central Africa. Both of these registered reservations, either at Accra, or at Addis Ababa, or both. There is one other state which no sane person could ask to implement it. That is Zambia. Zambia is bearing enough suffering in Africa's cause; far from asking her to accept more, Africa must try to reduce Zambia's present problems by being firm with Britain and Smith.

I make no pretence that the implementation of this resolution will be easy. There are a few states in Africa for whom it is, perhaps, a matter of form. But for many of us the economic cost may be high. We cannot tell exactly how high. But how can we criticize Britain for not being willing to pay the price of freeing Southern Rhodesia and meantime helping Zambia, if we ourselves are not prepared to pay a price to show our own determination? It is easy to call on others for sacrifice. Those who call on Britain without being ready themselves are guilty of a degree of hypocrisy which is unequalled up to now in Africa.

It is said that there is no point in paying this price, because it will have no effect. It will not secure the result we want. Mr. Speaker, I do not think the British Government would agree. No country wishes to be cut off from Africa—free Africa—at this point in our history. They know as well as we do that we are economically and militarily weak. They also know that united we have a strength at the United Nations and elsewhere. If we are prepared to use it, and to be united.

FOR THE HONOUR OF AFRICA

Well, then, it is said, not every African state will in fact implement the resolution, and so there is no point in anyone doing so. Because this is an African commitment, not a commitment for one state or two, or even ten.

Mr. Speaker, I do not understand that line of argument. The Organization of African Unity has twice passed a resolution. Each independent African state is a member of that organization, a sovereign independent member which has voluntarily formed and joined an organization to promote and develop the unity of Africa. They remain sovereign states; Africa is not yet united. Therefore, 36 separate actions have to be taken to implement the resolution instead of only one action. But how can any of us argue that because some other sovereign state may not carry out its obligations, then we will not do so? It is each of us separately which has this obligation; each of us separately which is responsible. It is we ourselves who will have to go to another meeting of the OAU and explain a failure to fulfil a responsibility. For it is our responsibility, and it is not a conditional one. The OAU resolution does not say that this resolution comes into effect once it has been ratified by such and such proportion of states in Africa. One can argue that perhaps it should have done; but it does not. Each separate African state committed itself— with the exceptions I have named—to take action. If we have any respect for international obligations how can we fail to observe our own resolution? If the OAU has any meaning to us, how can we ignore its resolutions?

Earlier I criticized Britain for accepting a United Nations resolution and then failing to implement it. I did not—Africa does not —accept her justification that there is no point in her acting on her own. How then can we use this justification ourselves in relation to another international body of which we have claimed to be loyal members?

Tanzania participated in the resolution at Accra and in the resolution at Addis Ababa. We are committed to this. We are responsible only for the actions of this nation. But for those we, and we alone, are responsible.

The Government feels that Tanzania has no honourable alternative but to abide by that resolution if the conditions are not fulfilled. There is very little time left. I do not intend, on behalf of this country, to take action in accordance with that resolution one minute before we have to do so. We are not proposing to break diplomatic relations with Britain because we wish to do so; we shall do it only if it becomes necessary for our own honour, for the honour of Africa, and as a means of showing our determination never to falter in the campaign against racialism on this continent.

THE RESOLUTION AND THE COMMONWEALTH

I should perhaps add that breaking diplomatic relations with the British Government does not at present mean that Tanzania will be leaving the Commonwealth. The Commonwealth is a multi-national organization, and although it is still true that Britain, for historical reasons, has a very special place in the Commonwealth, it is no longer the British Commonwealth—it is a Commonwealth of free nations. We recognize that because of Britain's special place in this organization, a diplomatic break by any other member with Britain will impose great strains on it. We hope it will be possible for the organization to withstand those strains and still remain true to its principles.

But loyalty to the Commonwealth, and support for its principles, are impossible without loyalty to the Organization of African Unity.

This is a very simple and inescapable fact, and it should be recognized by those African countries which are now asking us to consider the effect on the Commonwealth of a breach with Britain. Disloyalty to one international organization of which a country is a member implies a lack of trustworthiness in relation to all other international organizations. If we are disloyal to the OAU how can we be trusted to be loyal to the Commonwealth—or the United Nations for that matter?

Can a country which has a record of committing itself in an international organization, and then ignoring its own commitment, be respected in other organizations? Will they respect themselves? And will the Commonwealth really be an organization of equals if some members ignore their international commitments while others abide by them?

The time for African states to consider the effect on the Commonwealth of a breach with Britain was before passing the Accra resolution—or at least before the Addis Ababa resolution. Not now. If the African members of the Commonwealth are loyal to the OAU then the Commonwealth has a chance to survive, because its members will respect each other. Otherwise it will be in danger of becoming a shibboleth, and self-respecting heads of Commonwealth countries will go to Commonwealth Conferences only if they enjoy them as a form of relaxation.

I repeat, for the sake of the Commonwealth, as well as for the sake of the OAU, Africa must honour its commitment.

WE OPPOSE RACIALISM

There is one further thing I wish to say, Mr. Speaker, and it is of equal importance with the rest. I ask that every Member of this House accepts full responsibility for ensuring the understanding and the implementation of what I am now about to say.

If it becomes necessary for us to break diplomatic relations with Britain we shall be doing so in support of the principles on which our nation is based. Those principles include anti-colonialism and African unity, and commitment to international obligations. They also include non-racialism. We are not opposing Smith because he is white; we are not proposing action against the British Government because it is a white government. We are opposing Smith because he is a racialist. If there were to be even one person among us who used this time as an excuse to indulge in racialism directed against white people residing here, that would be a betrayal of our country and the cause we are fighting for. This Government of Tanzania deals firmly with treachery.

In the last elections the people of this country demonstrated that they cared about people, not their race or religion. This is a further, and harder, test of that principle. I am confident that the people of Tanzania will again rise to the challenge.

Let me say a further word about British subjects—for by no means all the white people here are British subjects, or of British origin. We do have working in our public services, and in business, a number of people from Britain. Many of them, indeed I suspect most of them, are highly critical of their government on this matter. Most of them, I believe, will be willing to stay and continue to work with us in Tanzania even if diplomatic relations are broken off between the two Governments. I have already stated that we in Tanzania hope that they will stay. Our need for them will be even greater if the carrying out of our Development Plan becomes complicated by a diplomatic break. I realize that some of these expatriate officials may have financial problems if a break comes; we shall do our best to help where this occurs, and at the moment this matter is under very urgent consideration. I realize, however, that even more important to the majority is the atmosphere in which they and their families live and work. I have already given the assurance of the Tanzania Government that their personal safety will not be endangered by their staying on after the British High Commission staff has gone. I am now asking that, in addition, our people should try to make those who stay realize that we understand their personal unhappiness at this quarrel between two Governments with both of which they are involved, and that we appreciate their choosing to continue serving the people of Tanzania. And those, if any, who wish to go must be allowed to go in peace. This is a quarrel between Governments, not between people.

Mr. Speaker, Honourable Members. I do not again expect to address this sitting of the National Assembly. If it becomes necessary I shall ask the Leader of the House to bring a message to you. But I ask you, as always, to conduct any discussions on this very serious matter with a full realization of the importance of your words. You are leaders of our nation; you have a right, indeed a duty, to ask the Ministers for further details of the implications of this decision, this commitment of the Government. You have a right to criticize the Government for making this commitment. I hope you will not—as a body—ask the Government to renounce its commitment. Because it cannot do so and remain the Government. But whatever the House, or the individual members, say, I beg that the words be chosen carefully to serve our objective.

Our objective is the furtherance, on this continent, of justice and peace between men, regardless of race, tribe, or religion.

Mr. Speaker, I ask for the support of this House, and thank you for your attention.

15

New Trading Patterns

In February 1966, *Mr. Gyula Kallai, Chairman of the Council of Ministers of the Hungarian People's Republic, led a trade mission to Tanzania. A state banquet was arranged in the Chairman's honour on* 11 *February* 1966, *at which President Nyerere proposed a toast to 'Our Guests, and the people of Hungary'.*

Mr. Prime Minister, Your Excellencies, Ladies and Gentlemen.

I am never convinced that it is really a sign of goodwill for Tanzania to invite honoured guests to a banquet and then make long speeches at them. I propose therefore to indicate my welcome to our guests this evening in an appropriate manner!

You, Mr. Prime Minister, have come to Tanzania as head of a trade delegation from the Hungarian Republic. We are pleased to welcome you, and particularly for that purpose. For we very much desire to expand the amount of our international trade, and also to widen the trade patterns which our country inherited when it became independent. We shall be happy, therefore, to co-operate in trade expansion plans with any nation which can use the goods we produce, and which can supply us with other things which we need. I believe we shall find that the interests of Hungary and Tanzania coincide at many points, so that it will be to our mutual advantage to increase the trading between our two countries.

We in Tanzania, Mr. Prime Minister, are anxious for only one reason to find new outlets for our goods. That reason is derived from the fact that the entire purpose of this nation is the well-being of the people. We are determined that all Tanzanian people shall be really free, and that involves freedom from the poverty which now afflicts us. By trading on a fair and equal basis with nations all over the world, we believe we can make progress in this fight for a decent standard of living, just as the people of Hungary can benefit from buying our goods and selling us theirs.

This kind of trade expansion does not just happen on its own. It is the responsibility of our Government to lead the work of economic betterment, to make arrangements which will serve the interests of the people, and to guide them in their efforts for progress. We believe that this responsibility will be honoured if other aspects of human freedom are able to be effectively exercised, so that the Government can be forced by the people to be concerned for the people.

We in Tanzania certainly have a very long way to go before we shall begin to be satisfied with our achievement. But we have started well, and we will be happy if co-operation with your country enables both Hungary and Tanzania to make further progress. We value old friendships and old trading partners, but at the same time we are anxious to make new friends, and to establish new avenues of trade.

For this reason, Mr. Prime Minister, it is with pleasure that I greet you as a representative of the Hungarian Government, and it is with pleasure that I propose a toast to you and to the people of your country.

16

Leaders must not be Masters

In February 1966, President Nyerere spent some days on Mafia Island in the course of one of his frequent tours of the country. Before leaving the area, he gave an extempore public speech, in Swahili, which was typical of the kind of teaching which the President always undertakes during his meet-the-people journeys. This translation was made from the tape-recorded text of the speech.

... My aim is to say goodbye to you. But before I do that, I wish to use this opportunity to tell you a few things which may be of benefit to you in days to come. During this visit I have tried to go to almost every part of this island. It is true that I have been here before, but on those past occasions I did not visit as many parts of the island as I have done on this visit. It is also true that when I came here in 1959, I visited Mbweni. But there is a marked difference between the Mbweni I saw in 1959, and the Mbweni I visited on this occasion. Mbweni has changed; there has been some progress, which is the result of the efforts of the inhabitants of Mbweni. In 1959 there was no school there; yesterday I saw some few schools. Their roads are still as bad as they were in 1959. I do not know who is to blame in this matter—whether the Government or the residents at Mbweni. I was shown a big rice farm in the same area and, although it is not yet a good farm, it will be good after some time. This is because nothing has a perfect beginning; time is required for anything to be perfect. The people at Mbweni have already cleared their farm, and have planted it with rice which shows signs of germinating well.

We visited many other farms of this island and saw good progress there. My hope is that this progressive development will continue to improve and become better and better. But I did not give a speech at any of the places I visited. Instead, I encouraged people to ask me questions, or to tell me their problems. This means that this is my first speech since I arrived on this island. I did not make a speech even when I met with your leaders of TANU, UWT, NUTA, and Government departments this morning in that office. I told them to ask me questions about Government and development. From the questions which were asked, I was able to learn a lot of things. Among the questions asked was one on ujamaa. One woman asked me to explain to her the meaning of ujamaa because she did not understand what ujamaa meant, although she had occasionally used the word or had heard other people use it. I tried to answer her question, and I wish to repeat that answer here in public.

I was the first to use the word ujamaa in order to explain the kind of life we wish to live in our country. The word ujamaa denotes the kind of life lived by a man and his family—father, mother, children and near relatives. Our Africa was a poor country before it was invaded and ruled by foreigners. There were no rich people in Africa. There was no person or group of persons who had exclusive claim to the ownership of the land. Land was the property of all the people, and those who used it did not do so because it was their property. They used it because they needed it, and it was their responsibility to use it carefully and hand it over in good condition for use by future generations. Life was easy. It was possible for a man to live with his wife, his children, and other close relatives. Wealth belonged to the family as a whole; and every member of a family had the right to the use of family property. No one used wealth for the purpose of dominating others. This is how we want to live as a nation. We want the whole nation to live as one family.

This is the basis of socialism. Yet we say we want socialism and want to build a socialist state. What do we mean by this? We mean two things. First, that we do not already have what we are looking for. Secondly, we believe that the thing we want is good. If you know that something is bad, you will not waste time trying to get it: it will not benefit you. This means that if we want socialism and aim at developing our country on the basis of socialist principles, it is because we believe that socialism is good.

Let me first explain that many countries are not socialist. Many countries in the world want to be socialist, and different people give different names to this concept of socialism. I have said I chose the word 'ujamaa' to explain socialism. I shall now try to explain why I chose the word ujamaa.

Normally a country is divided into two sections. Some people are called 'masters' and others are called 'servants'. We accept this division of people into classes of 'masters' and 'slaves'. Sometimes we are even content to live with these divisions and to accept them as they are. I will tell you an example which one old man told me. During the German administration a group of people were told to do a certain job. They did not do it. Then they were called to a meeting where their German master told them to divide themselves between 'masters' and 'slaves'. Some of the slaves joined the masters' group, hoping that they would escape punishment if the slaves were going to be punished. After the division, the German master allowed the slaves to go home, but immediately ordered the masters to be caned because they were lazy, and also because they were inducing the slaves to be lazy too. Those slaves who had joined the group of masters regretted their decision.

... Yet it is true that even in countries where such divisions between masters (who cannot be bought like sheep) and servants (who are bought like sheep) are absent, the people are divided into classes. This division exists even though there are no slaves in a country. In such a case the masters have the habit of being served by other people. The wives of masters do not work; they do not cook, or wash clothes, or make their beds. These things are done for them by other people. The masters have cars, but they do not drive them; they are driven. Masters can eat without working despite the fact that a man normally works in order to eat, except if he is ill, crippled, a child, or mad. What these masters are capable of doing is to give instructions to their servants. Sometimes, however, they employ other people to instruct servants on their behalf. The master does not have to do any work; other people will work for him and report to him month after month. They will report to him about the total harvest from one of his farms, and also about the total income obtained through the sale of his crops. These masters live comfortable lives, despite the fact that they do not work.

But this does not mean that all masters are equal; some are more equal than others. There are two groups of masters—the big masters and the little masters. Then there is the group of workers and servants who are often oppressed by the masters. Our aim is to abolish this division of people between masters and servants, and to make every person a master—not a master who oppresses others, but one who serves himself. A person who serves himself is a true master. He has no worries, he has confidence in himself and is confident of his own actions. He dislikes being pushed around and being told what to do. Why should a person who is his own master be pushed into doing work which will not benefit him?

Let me go back to what I said earlier in order to explain what I mean. I said that I did not make speeches at any of the places I had visited on my current tour of this island. Instead, I told the people I met to ask me questions, or to tell me the problems which face them in their everyday lives. It was difficult to get people to ask me questions. They told me they had no problems and that all was well. They were afraid to speak, probably thinking they would be punished. Why should they be punished? In the past years and centuries, we were greatly intimidated and harassed by the colonialists. If you stood before a colonial leader to speak or to ask him a question, you would be harassed by his juniors, who would ask you why you spoke or asked questions. This practice instilled fear in the minds of many citizens. The people did not respect their seniors; they simply feared them. This practice has not ended yet, and it explains why people did not want to tell me their problems when I asked them to. They refused to speak not because they had no problems, but because they were afraid to speak.

This is a bad habit. This is your country. We tell you every day that this is your country and that you have the freedom of speech. If you do not accept your responsibility for this country, I shall claim ownership of it! Any country must be looked after by people. If you do not like to accept the responsibility for looking after this country, I shall get a few clever people, and together we will declare this country to be our property. If we are asked why we are taking it, we shall say you do not want it. But this habit of evading responsibility has been inherited. We have been led to accept the division of men into masters and slaves. Sometimes you hear people talk about themselves as being simply ordinary men. They think their leaders know everything. When you talk to them and explain an issue to them, they will simply say, 'What can we say? You leaders know everything'.

This is a bad habit. You have been brought up badly. We have been treated as slaves and we have accepted that status. This is bad. What is the meaning of leadership? When you are selected to lead your fellow men, it does not mean that you know everything better than they do. It does not even mean that you are more intelligent than they are—especially the elders. Sometimes my own mother calls me and gives me some advice. She tells me not to do this or that. She advises me even in matters of Government. Why must she not advise me? She is a parent and parents are not afraid of their children. She advises me even though she has no formal school education. Why? Does it mean that a person who does not have formal education is a fool? What does education mean? An uneducated man has a brain—given to him by God. Does a man become a goat because he is uneducated? No! Such a person understands the nature of his children; he will know when one of them goes astray. It may be true that I am educated; but how can this mean that I am more intelligent than my mother?

At the moment our aim is to remove fear from the minds of our people. The fear which our people have can be removed from their minds. It was instilled in us by the Portuguese, the Germans, the Arabs, and the British. We have been told that we are not capable of doing this or that, and we have accepted this verdict. We are not even sure where to live. We fear to take decisions. This is why some people tell me to decide things for them on the grounds that we know better. This is not true. You must not fear your leaders. Our aim is to hand over responsibility to the people to make their own decisions. Our leaders are not leaders by birth; they are elected by the people. For why should a person be a leader by birth? Our leaders must be chosen by us. There is no need to have hereditary leaders.

This Area Commissioner is your son. He is not a District Commissioner. If he behaves like a District Commissioner we shall terminate his services. He is not supposed to act like a District Commissioner. He will be making a mistake if he acted as if he were a District Commissioner. We did not want to replace a white DC by a black DC. The Area Commissioner is the servant of the people. He is here to listen to the problems of the people, and to report to us about those problems or the progress being made to remove the problems. I shall keep on urging Tanzanians not to fear their leaders.

If we do not remove fear from our people, and if we do not abolish the two classes of masters and servants from our society, clever people will emerge from among us to take the place of the Europeans, Indians and Arabs. These clever people will continue to exploit our fear for their own benefit. And we leaders can become the clever people. If this happens—that leaders aspire to the positions and privileges enjoyed by colonial leaders—we shall not develop the country on the basis of the equality of all men. Instead, we shall be endangering this country. It will mean that the money we paid to help in the work of removing colonialism will be used to maintain other cleverer Africans capable of oppressing the people more than the colonialists.

This is what is going to happen if you do not remove fear from your minds. You will even lose your property; it will be taken by those who are clever among you. Suddenly you will discover that your Area Commissioner has a farm of 3,000 acres. You will be surprised to hear that even Julius has a 3,000 acre farm. You will be surprised how Julius and the Area Commissioner obtained the farms. And before long you will hear that Regional Commissioner Kitundu has also 3,000 acres of land. This will surprise you more. These farms need not be of the same size because the leaders who own them differ in their status as leaders.

We do not want such a situation to arise. We have stopped TANU leaders from owning farms. We have taken similar steps with other leaders. If we discover that these leaders have farms, we shall ask them. Yesterday we were all poor. If we hear you have a big farm, we shall ask you how you got it. If a person owns a farm of 3,000 acres, he must be aspiring to be a 'master'. What is more, such a person, owning a big farm of 3,000 acres, cannot have time to fulfil effectively the duties of Area Commissioner. If an Area Commissioner has such a large farm, it means he is prepared to employ workers to work on his farm and pay them wages. Where will he get people to work on his farm, and how will he get the money to pay them wages? But even if the money is there, and the workers are there, will there be sufficient land for each of us to have 3,000 acres? I agree that Tanzania is a large country with a small population. But is it true that our country is big enough for each of us to own 3,000 acres of land? The answer is no. And if the answer is no, and we allow a few of us to acquire large farms of 3,000 acres, we are in fact admitting that those who cannot get land will be servants of those who have land. By doing this, are we not dividing people into two classes—masters and slaves? By this action we will not be building socialism. If we give 3,000 acres of land to one man, and fail to give land to another, we shall in effect be making the former person the master and the latter a slave. But why should we do this? If a person says he wants to work for you, why can he not work on his own farm? Does he need to work for you on your farm? That is not socialism. We are going to teach all the people to be their own masters. If we give to one of you a big farm, where will he get the servants to work on it?

Socialism means that no person uses his wealth to exploit others. Just as a father does not use his status to dominate and exploit his wife, children and other relatives, so in a nation the leaders or the fortunate people must not use their positions or their wealth to exploit others. In a small family, the father was respected. He was not feared. Similarly, in a nation it is better to respect leaders than to fear them. Yet respect is a two-way process. Two or more people can respect each other. If one of them ceases to respect the other, they also withdraw their respect for him.

Also, socialism requires all the people to work. The fruits of the labour of the people who lead a socialist life are shared by all on the basis of equality. But everybody must work. It is a shame to be lazy, and those who are lazy are despised by the rest of the community. This means that no man can expect help from his colleagues if he is not willing to help them. It is even true that in order to eat, a man must be willing to work. The rule is that if you work you will eat, but if you do not work you will not eat. Even the old father who appears to eat without doing any work is not exploiting his family. He worked hard during his younger days. He does not work now because he had his turn, and also because the youth respect him for his service when he was young . . . .

17

Rhodesia in the Context of Southern Africa

This article was published in the April 1966 *issue of the American quarterly review* Foreign Affairs *and it is reprinted here by kind permission of the Council on Foreign Relations, Incorporated.*

The deep and intense anger of Africa on the subject of Rhodesia is by now widely realized. It is not, however, so clearly understood. In consequence the mutual suspicion which already exists between free African states and nations of the West, is in danger of getting very much worse.

Before November 11th, 1965, African states, individually and collectively, had frequently expressed their great concern about the position in Southern Rhodesia. But it was with the unilateral declaration of independence by the Smith regime that this concern was transformed into impatient wrath. The catalyst of this changed attitude was the rebellion against British sovereignty. This was not because Africa wished Southern Rhodesia to remain a colony; Africa's earlier demands had been for action to end colonialism. Nor was it evidence of a deep-rooted objection to illegality in the anti-colonial struggle. It is a fact that Africa prefers to use constitutional, legal and peaceful methods in the campaigns for national freedom; but if these fail then other methods are accepted. Thus, for example, an Algerian Government-in-Exile was recognized by many African states long before France conceded independence to that North African state. And at the present time a Government-in-Exile, headed by Holden Roberto, is recognized by the Organization of African Unity as the rightful authority in Angola despite the fact that legally Portugal continues to dominate that area. Africa's objection is to this particular assumption of authority in Southern Rhodesia, not to illegality in general. It would be hypocrisy to pretend otherwise.

The hostility aroused by the Smith declaration of independence is based on a rational interpretation of its purpose and its effects in relation to the total and legitimate goals of Africa. For this rebellion is not an uprising of the people; it represents an attempt to expand the area, and strengthen the hold in Africa, of doctrines which are inimical to the whole future of freedom in this continent. It represents an advance by the forces of racialism, fascism, and indeed, colonialism, in Southern Africa.

To the independent states of Africa this is not a development which can be viewed with Olympian detachment. We are on the frontiers of the conflict with these forces, and our own future demands their defeat. Gradually and somewhat painfully, colonialism and racialism have been pushed out of Northern and Central Africa. But while they remain in this continent none of us can really be free to live in peace and dignity, or be able to concentrate on the economic development which was a large part of the purpose of our political revolution. The Smith declaration of independence represents a counter-attack by these forces, and it is in that context that Africa has reacted, and demands its defeat.

This should not be difficult to comprehend. It may have been possible for the Allied Powers to make peace with Hitler after France, Belgium, and Holland were liberated. They were not prepared to try. Still less were the Jews outside Germany willing to support any compromise which would have left their compatriots under the control of a Nazi regime—even had the ultimate horror of racial extermination been excluded. Both the states concerned, and the peoples who were being treated as racially inferior, realized that the war had to continue until Nazism was politically ended in Europe.

The parallels are almost exact. The separate freedom movements in Africa were but different arms of one liberation process. When Dr. Nkrumah said in 1957 that the independence of Ghana was incomplete until the whole of Africa was free, he spoke a truth which is still valid for all of us. The struggle has to continue until final victory; colonialism must be wiped out in Africa before any post-colonial independent state can feel secure. And no citizen of

Africa—white or black—can live in the comfort of his own self-respect while other African citizens are suffering discrimination and humiliation for being born what they are.

Yet at the present time the Portuguese colonies of Angola and Mozambique, together with South Africa, South West Africa, and Rhodesia, constitute almost one seventh of the land mass of Africa. About 12 per cent of Africa's population lives in these areas. And each of these territories in their different way are governed on the principles of racial inequality and minority domination.

Portugal pretends that her African colonies are really part of Europe, and that she abjures racial discrimination. She claims instead to be in the process of making European Gentlemen out of the African inhabitants of those areas, and talks proudly of the policy of equality for the 'assimilado'. But Africans are not European, could not become European, and do not want to become European. They demand instead the right to be Africans in Africa, and to determine their own cultural, economic, and political future. This right is what Portugal denies. The inhabitants of her colonies can certainly be 'African'; but if they are, then they are subjected to special laws, and special taxation and labour levies; their participation in the functions of their own government is ruled out.

In South Africa there is no longer even the pretence that citizens of different races are equal before the law, or in social and economic rights and duties. The 'separate but equal' concept which was defeated in the United States in 1964, has been defeated in South Africa too; but there, inside Africa, it is the equality aspect which has been abandoned. In providing separate facilities for people of different races, the judges have ruled that the separate schools, housing, waiting rooms and so on, do not have to be of equal standard; it is enough that they are separate. Africans can be—and are—treated as a sub-species of mankind. No legal or political restraint now prevents the white minority government in the Union of South Africa from imposing its harsh, discriminatory will upon the African majority. To be an African is to beg for a permit to live in your own country—or to leave it; it is to need permission to work in a particular place or in a particular job; it is to carry a pass at all times—day and night—and be subjected at any moment to arbitrary arrest. And it is to have no legal means whatsoever to participate in the determination of your own wages and conditions of employment, your own place, or conditions, of living—much less to participate in the governing of your country. To be an African in South Africa is to have permission—unlimited permission—to say 'Yes, Baas'—preferably even then in Afrikaans. It is to have permission to be humiliated by any man, woman, or child, who has a white skin just for the reason that they have a white skin.

It is conditions and attitudes of this kind which free Africa is determined to fight. And there can be no questioning of the fact that (regardless of some reasonable criticisms of particular independent African states), the elimination of colonialism and racial domination in these countries to the South is justified by all the basic principles of mankind. Every principle of national and individual freedom, every principle of human equality, of justice, and of humanity, make it imperative that the rule of the minorities shall be ended. For they are judge, jury, prosecuting counsel, and law-maker in their own dispute. And the question at issue now is whether Rhodesia shall for the foreseeable future be a state governed on that same basis of human inequality, or whether the existing, at present very slightly modified, version of racial domination, shall be replaced by progress towards human justice and equality.

THE POLITICAL SITUATION IN SOUTHERN AFRICA

While Africa is determined that the whole of Southern Africa shall be freed before the struggle ceases, it recognizes that the strategy and tactics of the fight will vary according to the particular circumstances of the three different areas (there are four if South West Africa is counted separately). The monster of 'unfreedom' in Southern Africa has three heads, and although they each draw strength and sustenance from the existence of the others, it remains true that each has its own separate vulnerability to determined assault by the world forces of freedom.

The best armoured, and in many ways the most tragic of the three heads in Southern Africa is the Union of South Africa itself. There, the racialism itself has become a self-justifying religion of survival, which demands ever-increasing ruthlessness to protect its adherents against the hatred it has induced. Its doctrines of superiority are inculcated into the white community from the moment of their birth; its teaching of inferiority dominates the lives of the non-whites from a similar moment. And it is in grave danger—if it has not already done so—of convincing all South Africans that there are not human beings in the world, but whites and non-whites. If it succeeds in this, then there will also one day be learned the dreadful lesson that the whites constitute less than one fifth of the South African population, and that numbers provide strength. Yet because this religion of racialism has already been responsible for so much human humiliation and suffering, only a miracle could provide any real hope of its peaceful reversal and the growth of practical brotherhood. For it has already promoted hatred, and justified fear. It now appears inevitable that sooner or later an overwhelming internal explosion will occur in South Africa and bring the whole present edifice of apartheid to an end; we can only pray that it is not followed by a mere reversal of the racial domination, for that would be the logic of the doctrines which are now being propagated by the South African Government.

But if there is no hope of peaceful change from inside, it remains true that the Union of South Africa is an industrial state, inextricably involved in international commerce. It is also true that the South African Government's policies suffer the expressed disapproval of every major power political organization in the world. This disapproval, however, remains a verbal one; no action is taken to activate it. This is largely because of the international economic links of the capitalist world (and thus international business involvement in apartheid). This economic reluctance to take action is backed up by the fact that South Africa is a legally constituted, internationally recognized, sovereign nation. Fears of the implications of intervention from outside—through the United Nations or by any other means—have thus caused the democratic, and even the anti-colonial, nations of the West, to eschew, on grounds of legality, any deliberate activity designed to reverse the apartheid policies of South Africa. It is claimed that however reprehensible these may be, there must be no outside intervention in the internal affairs of a sovereign state. Legality is given paramountcy over morality. In consequence, the only prospect for the Union of South Africa is long-drawn-out suffering, violence and bitterness. For the struggle will go on until the cause of freedom ultimately triumphs.

The position in relation to Angola, Mozambique, and Portuguese Guinea, is different, This is, or should be, a classic colonial situation.

The problem is that Portugal refuses to live in the twentieth century; she persists in believing that colonialism can be maintained, even by the poorest and most backward of the states of Europe. The problem in this case is, therefore, how to wake up Portugal to the facts of politics in the modern day.

Portugal's European and American allies could, of course, have great influence upon her—particularly if they were prepared to deny her the right to use their military strength in her defence while she uses her own (and their ammunition) in suppressing incipient revolt in her colonies. They could even help her to make the transition to the twentieth century by reviving her internal economy! But if the free countries of the West fail to try, or if they fail to succeed, then Africa will have to pursue this battle on her own, or with what allies she can find. Our own weakness means that we shall have only one way of doing that; by supporting guerilla warfare until, after suffering and destruction, Portugal wakes up to her own realities.

Until November 11th, 1965, there was a hope that Southern Rhodesia would be able to avoid this dreadful path to freedom. Certainly the *de facto* government was a racialistic, racially consti-tuted, minority government. Certainly apartheid under other names restricted the Africans' freedom to choose their place of living and working, and certainly separate educational, health, and other public services, ensured that the Africans maintained their existing lowly position. But the vital difference was that Southern Rhodesia was legally a British colony; British surrender of power to the settler minority had been tragically real, but it stopped short of legal transfer. This meant that although she was faced with difficulties of implementation, Britain was the power responsible for the future in Southern Rhodesia. And Africa took comfort from the fact that Britain's declared policy, in relation to all her colonies, has been to bring them to democratic independence under conditions which safeguard the people from oppression from any quarter.

The legal power and responsibility of Britain therefore meant that Africa expected gradual constitutional advance towards democracy or majority rule. What appeared to be required was to make Britain realize the seriousness of a situation where Southern Rhodesia existed as an outpost of South Africa, but where she operated under the name and responsibility of the British crown. Once this was realized Africa expected that Britain would at last take steps to deal with the white settlers who were misappropriating public power.

AFRICA'S DEMANDS FOR SOUTHERN RHODESIA

In other words, what Africa has been demanding from Britain in relation to Southern Rhodesia is a transition from the white minority domination in government to majority rule and, only after that, independence for the colony. This has been the position of the nationalist forces in the colony; it has been the position of all African leaders. The argument has not been about the timing of this transition—how long it would take, or how many steps are involved—but about the principle of it.

It is in that context that Africa looks at the unilateral declaration of independence by the minority government in Southern Rhodesia; it is because of these reasonable and justified expectations that the Smith move is of such importance. The settler regime has said, in effect, that the very existence of legal restraints upon the minority is unbearable. And as Britain refused to give them independence without asking for some assurances about the future development to majority rule, so they took the independence. And in so doing their leader had the temerity to paraphrase the greatest freedom document of all time—the American Declaration of Independence!

Mr. Ian Smith justified his seizure of power, and his quotations, by claiming that his move was 'anti-colonial', and that his government is the defender of civilized standards—not racialistic at all. He has argued that because countries to the North with a black majority government were granted independence it is unreasonable that Southern Rhodesia should remain a colony after 43 years of 'governing ourselves responsibly'.

The facts do not support Mr. Smith. The facts show that Southern Rhodesia has been governed responsibly only as far as the white community is concerned, and that every aspect of that society is based on racial distinctions to the detriment of the African community. The facts prove, once again, that any elected government is responsive to the electorate, and only to the desires of the electorate; even if its Ministers wish to consider the interests of non-voters they are virtually powerless to do anything really effective.

Writing in *Punch* recently Mr. Smith said, 'Our Parliament is open to all races, our Civil Service offers senior posts on parity terms for all races, our University opens its doors to all races, and our voters' rolls are open to all races. Merit is, and must be, the only criterion. . . .'.

The fact of the matter is that of the 65 seats in Parliament, 50 are elected by the 'A' Roll, and 15 by the 'B' Roll. To get on to the 'A' Roll it is necessary to have an income of £792 per annum, or an income of £330 per annum plus four years' secondary school education (or certain other intermediate combinations). To get on to the 'B' Roll the figures are lower; an income of £264 per annum, or a combination of being over 30 years of age with an income of £132 per annum plus primary education. The registered voters in consequence showed that of the 94,080 people on the 'A' Roll, 89,278 were whites; Africans predominated on the 'B' Roll with more than 10,000 voters as against 1,000 non-Africans on this Roll, but these actual figures are not very revealing as the nationalist organizations called for a boycott of the elections. The comparative population figures show that there are in Southern Rhodesia almost four million Africans, and less than 250,000 people of European descent.

The government of Southern Rhodesia is thus firmly in the hands of the white voters; and is likely to remain so. The 'B' Roll seats are not even sufficient to veto changes in the constitution. Neither are there in fact any Africans in senior positions in the Civil Service; and if there were, the existing legislation would force them to live in the designated 'African Areas' of the towns regardless of their income. And behind all this smokescreen of 'responsibility' and 'merit' is complete segregation, and absolute inequality, in the availability of education.

Schooling for non-African children is compulsory between the ages of 7 and 15 years; and in 1963 there were 19,898 European children in secondary schools out of the 53,000 total European school enrolment. Only 7,045 African pupils were attending secondary schools during that year, and only 81 of these were in Form VI where entrance to the university can be attempted. It is hard to argue that these differences of secondary school attendance are due to differences in innate ability when something like ten times more finance is allocated for each European pupil than each African pupil. The truth is that educational opportunities just do not exist for the African community in the way they do for whites. There are places in the sixth year class for only 50 per cent of the African children who attend school for the first five years; out of those who do pass that hurdle, only 25 per cent will find a place in a secondary school three years later.

It is not my purpose to deny that there are difficulties in providing the educational expansion which is required in Africa now; Tanzania's problems are too real for that. But when this racial distinction is made in educational opportunities it is rank dishonesty to talk of equality of opportunity in other fields which depend on an educational or income qualification. Neither is it realistic to expect the voters (i.e. the people in the upper income brackets, who have reserved educational opportunities for their own children) to break down the racial distinctions which maintain their current privileged position.

Recent history in Southern Rhodesia supports this lack of expectation. Since 1957 there has been a steady electoral move towards political parties and groups which have been most fierce in their declared intention to resist racial integration. The Rhodesian Front, which is the party of the present Smith regime, was elected when it opposed the United Federal Party proposal to amend the Land Apportionment Act (this, among other things, reserves 37 per cent of the land area of the country for European ownership). In its manifesto the Rhodesian Front also declared that it would seek to amend the constitution on the grounds that it would bring about 'premature African dominance', and the manifesto recognized the right of government to 'provide separate amenities for various (racial) groups'.

In fact, since the election successive Rhodesian Front governments have concentrated on political questions, and particularly on the question of independence. In the process they have gained, and used, all the powers of a police state. All African nationalist parties have been banned, and their leaders imprisoned or detained; meetings have been prohibited, demonstrations broken up by police violence. And since independence press censorship has been imposed on all media of public communication, and the harshest penalties imposed for any refusal to bow down to the behests of this minority and illegal administration. The regime has, in fact, moved consistently along the path it laid down for itself; the path which leads directly and in a short time to the imposition in Southern Rhodesia of an unabashed apartheid policy as it is operated in South Africa.

Many of these developments, and certainly the groundwork for them, had taken place before UDI. Independence merely represented a logical further stage; it had to come—legally or otherwise— or there had to be a reversal of direction. What independence under the present minority regime means, therefore, is that the Rubicon has been crossed. If this independence is sustained the hope of a peaceful (even if gradual) development to majority rule has been obliterated. The only hope now remaining is for the rebellion to be defeated by the legal power and a new start made on the road to peaceful progress.

THE INTERNATIONAL IMPLICATIONS OF UDI

The importance of this cannot be overestimated. A successful declaration of independence by the minority government of Southern Rhodesia represents an expansion of racialism and fascism in Africa, and a step backward in the drive for African freedom. It is as though one of the southern states in the United States of America now, in the year 1966, succeeded in enlarging and strengthening the segregation and discrimination within its area of jurisdiction. The reaction of the federal authorities, and of the civil rights organizations, can be easily imagined. They would know that their future was at stake, and that the battle was joined as surely as it was at Fort Sumter in 1861. So it is in Africa.

But the parallel does not stop there. Just as would be the case in America, so in Africa success by the Southern Rhodesian minorities would strengthen the forces of reaction in other parts of the continent. South Africa and Portugal must want the Smith rebellion to succeed. Their interest is one of ideological sympathy; but it is also one of geography. The map of Africa shows their reasons for wanting white domination to be safely entrenched in Southern Rhodesia—just as it indicates the special interest of countries like Zambia and Bechuanaland that it shall not succeed.

Yet although South Africa and Portugal want white domination to be firmly established in Southern Rhodesia, the illegality of the present situation is an embarrassment to them. They cannot afford to intervene actively on the side of Rhodesia unless and until they are certain that the rebellion will succeed. For in supporting the illegal regime they are staking their own future on its success.

South Africa's strongest defence against international criticism of her policies is the legality of her government, the recognized sovereignty of her state, and the doctrine that the internal affairs of any nation are outside the competence of the United Nations or any other international official body. If she openly supports a rebellion against legal authority in another state, then it is infinitely more difficult for her to resist international intervention in her own affairs. Consequently, we have the position where the Verwoerd government claims to stand neutral in the conflict between the sovereign authority (Britain) and the *de facto* authority (the Smith regime) in Southern Rhodesia.

This official neutrality is at the moment possible because the economic sanctions are voluntary acts of each separate nation state. By refusing to participate in these sanctions South Africa is thus breaking no international commitment and infringing neither domestic nor international law. This situation would be changed if the United Nations adopted Chapter 7 of the Charter (even Article 41 alone), which makes sanctions mandatory on all members. South Africa would then either have to co-operate, or she would draw upon herself the international action she is so concerned to avoid. That is to say, she would either have to close her own trade with Southern Rhodesia and be prepared to answer questions about the ultimate destination of goods she is importing, or she would be liable to be included in the area covered by sanctions.

The implications of the present position are well understood by the present South African Government. They account for its failure to give the 'independent' Smith regime all the support it hoped for. Yet it is clear that white public opinion inside South Africa is willing to do at least some of the things the government fears to do—and that the government will not interfere. The 'Oil for Rhodesia' campaign depends for its success on publicity and is thus known outside Southern Africa. There is little doubt, however, that through private business deals with South African firms and citizens, the cutting edge of international sanctions against Southern Rhodesia is being—and will be—blunted. By these means South Africa is able, without risking her own position, to assist the white regime in Southern Rhodesia to survive.

Portugal, too, is hamstrung by the illegality of the present Southern Rhodesian position. She, too, is relying upon legalistic niceties to prevent Western pressure building up against her occupation of Mozambique, Angola and Portuguese Guinea. She can therefore hardly afford to defend and assist a rebellion in the territory of a major European ally. Yet again, it is (to say the least) highly probable that she is giving under-cover assistance to Rhodesia. As Sir Edgar Whitehead, a past Prime Minister of Southern Rhodesia, said in the *Spectator* of January 28th, 'Mozambique could not survive if an African nationalist government took over in Rhodesia, and would be utterly ruined if the Rhodesian economy collapsed'. Sir Edgar went on to refer to the oil refinery at Lourenco Marques, and the assistance which it can give quietly to the Smith regime despite the absence of crude oil for the Umtali refinery. Once again, this position exists because there is no international 'illegality' in trading with Southern Rhodesia. The situation would be changed if Chapter 7 of the United Nations Charter were adopted. For in that case Portugal (even more than South Africa) would be forced by her own needs to cease giving active support to the Smith regime.

South Africa and Portugal are thus unable to give open support to Smith because they depend upon claims of legality to defend their own positions. There is thus a weakness in the racialist Southern African front, which could be exploited by the forces of justice. And it is, in fact, this same question of legality which makes it imperative for Britain and the West generally to use this weakness and to defeat Smith and white domination in Southern Rhodesia.

Successive Western governments have declared their hostility to apartheid, and their adherence to the principles of racial equality. They have frequenty made verbal declarations of their sympathy with the forces in opposition to South African policies. But they have excused their failure to act in support of their words, on the grounds of South Africa's sovereignty. Africa has shown a great deal of scepticism about this argument, believing that it masked a reluctance to intervene on the side of justice when white privilege was involved. Now, in the case of Southern Rhodesia, legality is on the side of intervention. What is the West going to do? Will it justify or confound African suspicions?

So far the West has demonstrated its intentions by the gradual increase of voluntary economic sanctions; there has been a refusal even to challenge South African and Portuguese support for Smith by making sanctions mandatory upon all members of the United

Nations. And there have been repeated statements by the responsible authority that force will not be used except in case of a break-down in law and order—which apparently does not cover the illegal seizure of power! What happens if the economic sanctions fail to bring down the Smith regime is left vague. The suggestion therefore remains that, despite legality, and despite the protestations of belief in human equality, the domination of a white minority over blacks is acceptable to the West.

WHAT DOES AFRICA REQUIRE IN SOUTHERN RHODESIA?

This suspicion about the sincerity of the West can only be eliminated by the defeat of the Smith regime, and a new start being made on the path to majority rule before independence. It would not be enough for Smith to resign and a different 'more liberal', white dominated, independent government to be legally established. If Britain and her allies, with the support of Africa, defeat Smith, then the minimum requirement must be the re-establishment of effective British authority, and an interim government which is charged with the task of leading the colony to majority rule. This will inevitably require the presence of British civil servants and British troops—or, better still, United Nations administrators and forces. Experience in South Africa, and in Southern Rhodesia itself, makes it absurd for anyone to expect Africa to trust Rhodesian whites (even under nominal British sovereignty) with the task of effecting the transition to majority rule.

It is important, too, that there should be a public declaration about the intentions in Southern Rhodesia. It must be made clear that there will be a rapid move (even if in stages) to majority rule, with safeguards for human rights, and after that—but only after that— independence for the colony. This public declaration is essential. Its absence has already caused major diplomatic difficulties between Britain and Africa, because it leaves open the possibility of a simple return to the pre–UDI status quo in Rhodesia.

It is true that such a declaration would be opposed by South Africa and Portugal, and that the Rhodesian whites would be bitterly hostile. But this is what the present crisis is all about; is Southern Rhodesia to become a nation of equal citizens or is it to become an outpost of white racialism? The fears of Southern Rhodesia's minorities have been dealt with by the many assurances given by Britain about the transitional period after the rebellion comes to an end. It is now time to consider the fears of the African majority, both inside the country and elsewhere in the continent. It is time, in other words, for Britain and the United States of America to make clear whether they really believe in the principles they claim to espouse, or whether their policies are governed by considerations of the privileges of their 'kith and kin'.

By its unilateral declaration of independence, Southern Rhodesia has come out openly in support of racialism in Africa. The rest of Africa cannot, for the sake of its own future, acquiesce in this. But circumstances have meant that Southern Rhodesia's action is also a challenge to Britain and to the West generally. Their future relations with Africa and Africa's future attitude to them, depend upon this challenge being answered effectively. At present the world is willing to support them in meeting this challenge; for once no complications of the 'Cold War' or the 'International Communist Menace' enter into the problem. But if the West fails to bring down Smith, or having defeated him, fails to establish conditions which will lead to majority rule before independence, then Africa will have to take up the challenge. In that case there will be no question of a transition to majority rule. And Africa's economic and military weakness means that she would have to find allies. It is worth considering whether, if that happens, it will then still be true to say that the Cold War does not enter into the situation, and that the 'Communist Bogey' is a nonsensical red herring.

It is vital that Africa's legitimate concern in this matter should be recognized. For each sovereign African nation has had to overcome the power of racialism in order to become independent. It is, to us, the ultimate horror. We can never surrender to it, or allow it to continue unchallenged on the African continent. Our own future is too much involved.

But the United States, Britain, and all other countries of the world are also involved in the issue of racialism. Smith has thrown a challenge at the world, and particularly at the Western powers. He has thrown it on behalf of the whole of Southern Africa. Free Africa is now waiting, with some impatience, to see whether the West really intends to stand on the side of human equality and human freedom.

18

The Tanzanian Economy

On 13 June 1966, President Nyerere addressed the National Assembly at the commencement of its Budget Session. The President explained that he intended to give a general assessment of advances and setbacks in fulfilling the Five-Year Development Plan; this was to be followed by a speech from the Minister responsible for Development Planning, and on the third day the Minister for Finance would introduce the Budget. In his speech President Nyerere outlined the reasons and necessity for self-reliance.

... You will be considering Government's Budget proposals for the coming financial year—in other words, you will be considering how much money should be taken out of the pockets of your constituents and spent by Government, and in what manner any such money should be allocated between one activity or another. No one could doubt the importance of this work and I believe that the voters of Tanzania will be waiting anxiously to see how their representatives are caring for their interests.

I do not myself believe, however, that the people of this country are interested only in not paying taxes! I believe that they are also interested in the development of Tanzania, and that they desire this development to be as rapid as possible. Government's task, with the support of this House, is therefore to account to the people for all plans it makes and to convince them that these plans are reasonable.

Our plans must be seen to be within the capacity of the nation, and such that they will achieve our objects at minimum cost and maximum speed. And because the Budget shows the way in which Government proposes to translate into action a particular phase of the Development Plan, it is important that the Members of this House should know the present economic position of the country and the progress we have made. Only after that can they usefully listen to the Minister for Finance on Budget Day, and assess his proposals.

... 1965 was not an easy year for Tanzania. We experienced two major difficulties—widespread drought conditions which reduced the output of certain important crops, and big decreases in the world market price of certain of our major exports. These two factors have resulted in the slowing down of the speed of our advance towards better economic standards for our people.

But, these difficulties have not stopped this advance. This is very important. Because the people of this country have worked as never before, we have been able to overcome this combination of drought and price-drop without disaster and without having to appeal to other countries for special assistance. This is a matter on which our people are to be congratulated and on which they can take legitimate pride. I shall come back to this point.

These difficulties were beyond our control. Government cannot do anything about the weather, and unfortunately neither can it control world prices—although we continue to work for an international system of price stabilization for primary commodities. Matters such as the organization of our economy and arrangements for economic co-operation with other nations are, however, the responsibility of the Government, and these can also vitally affect the success of our people's efforts. And in these respects we certainly made improvements last year or prepared the ground for improvements in the coming twelve months.

Thus, for example, Members of the House will be aware of the Government's recognition that existing arrangements for East African co-operation were militating against the proper development of Tanzania. This awareness did not, and does not, indicate any lack of desire to co-operate with our brothers in Kenya and Uganda, nor does it indicate a failure to recognize that only through united action can Africa as a whole really make progress. But while African states remain separately sovereign, then each of the Governments has an exclusive responsibility to its own people. It must therefore insist that co-operation brings benefit not just to the area as a whole, but also to its own particular country. For this reason Tanzania has pressed for revisions in the arrangements of the Common Market and the Common Services which were agreed in 1961. It is just not possible for us to continue indefinitely to provide an ever-increasing market for the products of our neighbours without achieving a similar East African market for our own goods. And the fact is that Tanzania's trade deficit with Kenya has continued to grow so that last year it mounted to more than Shs. 200,000,000/-. With East Africa as a whole our deficit was more than 225 million shillings.

As Members know, the Governments of Kenya and Uganda understood our position, and we jointly appointed a commission under the chairmanship of Mr. Kjeld Philip to investigate and make recommendations. Our three Governments have now received the report and it is under urgent consideration. Presidents Kenyatta, Obote, and myself will be discussing the recommendations and outstanding matters at the next Authority meeting later this month.

Let me stress that in these discussions the purpose of Tanzania will be to achieve the maximum inter-African co-operation and trade which is consistent with the development of this country. It is not our purpose to break up existing institutions; it is our purpose to share fairly in their benefits. Neither do we believe that these 'fair shares' have to balance each year; it is inevitable that over certain periods one country will receive more benefit than another from international co-operation. But we believe that it must be possible for the legitimate interests of each country to be safeguarded and for the arrangements to be such that no one partner has a permanent and ever-increasing advantage over the others. It is in this spirit of co-operation and conciliation that your Government will be considering the Philip Report along with the Governments of Kenya and Uganda.

There have been internal arrangements also which time has shown to require further attention from Government. After the first few months of operation of the Five-Year plan it became clear to us that the whole question of the organization and administration of development planning must be re-examined. This was therefore made the subject of detailed investigation by a team of British experts, headed by Professor Ross of the University of East Anglia. Their report has been considered by the Economic Committee of the Cabinet chapter by chapter, and many of its administrative recommendations have now been implemented—or have led to revisions in procedure which should, over time, help us to achieve the development we aim at. It is not Government's intention to publish this detailed and extremely valuable document.

Of more direct relevance and interest to this House, however, will be the reports of the Presidential Commission of Enquiry into the Co-operative Movement and NUTA. The Co-operative Commission has already reported to Government: its document is frank, hard-hitting and extremely well written. It is Government's intention to submit this report to the House in due course and after a Swahili version has been adequately prepared. I believe that the views of Members will be of great assistance to Government in the careful consideration which it intends to give to the commission's recommendations. The same procedure will be adopted when the NUTA Report is submitted.

REVIEW OF THE YEAR

What then did we achieve in 1965? First of all, we have to accept that in monetary terms our national income did not increase to any significant extent. The drought and world prices are responsible for this. That is disappointing after the great efforts which everyone made. Yet it should not be a cause for despondency. In a year when it would have been acceptable if we had experienced a fall in our overall economic standards because of these factors beyond our control, we nonetheless held our position. More, in real terms we improved it. Our total output of most goods increased considerably so that while at current prices our gross domestic product remained about the same as 1964, in terms of constant prices our national income increased by almost 2 per cent in 1965. This increase made it 16 per cent higher in 1965 than it was in 1960, and 20 per cent higher than 1961 when our country was hit by an even bigger climatic disaster.

What do these figures mean? The gross domestic product is the sum total of all goods and services which were produced in the country during the year. It is the total wealth which is available for distribution among our people and for investment in the future, leaving aside any question of grants or loans from outside. Thus, to say that we increased our gross domestic product (or national income) in terms of constant prices, means that we increased the amount of goods available for distribution. To say that the gross domestic product remains static in terms of current prices means that those goods which we produced for sale on the world market averaged a lower price than the previous year, so that the total amount of goods we could purchase from outside went down by the same amount as the value of the increase in the number of goods which we produced.

Our nation was thus in the same position as a canoe which is moving between the same two ports two years running. The first year the crew work hard and cover the distance in 10 hours. The second year they work harder because they want to arrive more quickly but the wind and tide are unexpectedly against them, so that, although they do work harder, they still take 10 hours to reach their destination. The difference which their hard work has made is that the adverse weather and water conditions did not make them take longer than before, and nor did they result in the canoe being waterlogged or overturned.

About the hard work of our people in 1965, there can be no doubt. It covered the whole country, although in relation to maize and rice, as well as sisal and one or two other crops, the result was a smaller output because of the drought. But we succeeded in producing almost 20 per cent more cotton than in 1964, 18 per cent more tea, 52 per cent more pyrethrum, and we more than doubled the output of tobacco. Part of these increases was due to the use of fertilizers and better seed; some of it was due to sheer physical labour and sweat. The farmers of Tanzania have undoubtedly played their part, and they have deserved the congratulations of the Government and of this House. I am confident that in the coming year they will increase the amount of their production still further, in particular by the use of better methods of husbandry and wider use of fertilizers.

The output and sale of minerals also increased in 1965, with a 25 per cent increase in the quantity of diamonds, and a 19 per cent increase in the quantity of salt. Unfortunately, the extra cost of working some of the mines now that the most productive seams are exhausted, meant that the total value added to the economy by mineral production increased only slightly despite better prices for tin and mica.

Particularly encouraging, however, was the considerable increase in the output of industrial goods. The total value of manufactured output last year was £10,000,000 (Shs. 200/- million), which is 16 per cent in value terms, and 10 per cent in quantity terms, above the production of 1964. This is very important, because although the industrial sector still accounts for only about 5.7 per cent of our total national product, this proportion is increasing and must increase if our Plan objectives are to be fulfilled. The number of new factories which started working or which began building operations last year, gives hope that this rate of increase will continue or even get faster. I think we should use this opportunity to congratulate those private investors who made it possible for us to record these achievements. They are helping us at the same time as they are helping themselves.

Let me also mention the work of the National Development Corporation. This national institution came into being only on January 1st, 1965, but even so more than three quarters of a million pounds (Shs. 15/- million) was invested by them during that year and they claim direct responsibility for a further £1.3 million (Shs. 26/- million) of actual private investment during the year. Government has now instructed this Corporation to concentrate more on direct public investment, so that the public sector of our economy grows alongside the private sector; but this does not mean that we are critical of what the NDC has already achieved, nor that we are unwilling to go into joint operations with private companies. We have merely told the NDC to shift its emphasis; but it is important to remember that it will only be able to expand the Government-owned sector as fast as it is given money to do so, that is, as fast as the nation collectively makes available money for new investment by restraining itself from spending on current consumption.

In almost all branches of production, therefore, the people of Tanzania have the right to feel proud and happy about their efforts in 1965. It was no small achievement to overcome the 35 per cent fall in the world price of our biggest single export commodity, sisal. It was an even bigger achievement that, during the same year, we were able to get through a period in which rice production was almost halved by bad weather, and maize production was inadequate for the same reason, without having to ask for outside help from any nation or international agency to meet this emergency. We did it ourselves this time. We imported rice and maize, but we paid for them ourselves. True, the problem was not as big as in 1961, but it would have forced us to look for outside charity in any of the past years. Only the hard work of our people enabled us to surmount it. Clearly we have come some way towards the position where we shall feed ourselves and also build up reserves which can be used against domestic disaster, or made available to other peoples in time of famine.

On all these things we can congratulate ourselves. But we have a long way to go before we can be satisfied even with our rate of progress. For the past year revealed other things too. The cost of living for urban workers went up, and although it is true that on average the lower paid workers improved their wages more than the amount of the increase in costs, this did not apply to everyone. There are still many workers in Tanzania who are not receiving a wage sufficient to keep themselves and their families healthily fed and clothed. There are still too many of our people living in hovels, and who could not afford to pay an economic rent for a decent house even if one were available. We must deal with this situation. The lowest wages must increase still further.

But let us understand that in saying this we are also saying that the amount of goods produced by each of these workers must also be increased. If a man receives Shs. 100/- a month for producing 10 shirts, an increase in his wages will only mean an increase in the price of shirts unless there is, at the same time, an increase in the number of shirts he makes during the month. And if the price of shirts goes up, the farmer will have to do one of two things. He can produce and sell more of his crop in order to be able to buy the same number of shirts as before; that would mean a redistribution of real income in favour of the wage-earner and away from the farmer. Or the farmer can buy fewer shirts; in that case the number of people employed in shirt-making will decrease. For we cannot say often enough that money is not itself wealth. It is only useful for what it represents in terms of goods. Wealth is things, not money. While the quantity of goods remains the same an increase in the money held by one section of the population simply means that those particular people have a larger share of the wealth and others have a smaller share.

In fact, that is what happened in Tanzania during 1965. Adding together the value of the subsistence crops, and the money received for cash crops, the farmers (as a group) had slightly less wealth available to them in 1965 than in 1964. That was the effect of the poor maize and rice harvests. But the prices of the goods the farmer wanted to buy increased. Therefore, while the nation as a whole was as well off in 1965 as in 1964, the farmers, taken altogether, did not have a very good year.

But this is not true of all farmers. Those who were not hit by the drought, and especially the cotton farmers, received more money in 1965 than ever before. This was because the amount of cotton they produced increased by more than the reduction in the money they received for each pound of cotton. Their total earnings were thus greater. Tobacco farmers, too, found that, although the average price per lb. was lower than in 1964, the total money they received was more because they had produced more. These cases illustrate the attitude which must be adopted in Tanzania, for although we cannot control world prices we can, subject to the weather, control our total output by working harder and more intelligently. And it is a combination of output and prices which determines the actual amount of money we have to spend at the end of the year. Our salvation will thus lie in continuing to extend the quantity of the things we produce.

There is, however, one aspect of the farmers' incomes which we now realize needs further attention from this House and from the Government. That is the question of deductions.

When a farmer sells his crop he finds that a whole list of organizations are taking a cut from his money, so that the amount he walks away with is considerably less than the amount he is shown on paper to have earned for the crop he is selling. There are deductions for research, for education, for local government on perhaps two levels, for a co-operative society and co-operative union and so on, until in some cases as much as half his income is being deducted away! In so far as these deductions are justified the farmer must accept them. Services have to be paid for. But there is some evidence to support the view that in the past, and in some areas, the idea of meeting a financial difficulty by adding a cess to the local crop may have been too easily and light-heartedly adopted. If that is so, then correcting it is the responsibility of the people and their representatives in the bodies concerned. This should be easier in the future because, as I have said, the co-operative movement aspects of this question have been included in the commission's report which we have just received, and about which Government will be communicating with the Assembly. The local government aspect of it will be relevant to the proposals for new local government elections which will come before this House shortly, and which should result in a new closeness between the local government institutions and the people whom they are intended to serve.

CAPITAL FORMATION AND EXTERNAL HELP

Always we come back to the need for money if we want to develop our nation and our particular area. Nothing can be done without money—which is a claim on the total resources of the country. And the truth is that the more wealth we hope to have available in the future, the less of our existing wealth can we use for our food, shelter, and enjoyment now. In this matter the nation is like a farmer who begins a season with a certain crop. He then has to decide how much of that crop he will eat during the coming year, how much he will sell to buy clothes and other goods, and how much he will reserve for seed for the next year's planting. And however much he may need clothes today, or even his food, he must not forget his seed for the next season. It is only in dire necessity that he eats his seed. If the farmer wants to plant two acres next year, then he must leave enough seed for two acres.

Tanzania has decided that it wants to get richer as fast as possible, which means (in terms of the farmer) that he wants to go on increasing every year the amount of land planted. The nation has decided, in other words, that it will spend as much as possible of the current wealth on things which will, in the long run, produce wealth. It does this by building factories, schools, roads, telephones, offices, houses, and so on, instead of increasing the amount of clothes which are available to the people now, or the amount of beer they can drink or cigarettes they can smoke, or even food they can eat. And every year, in order to do this, the nation taxes itself, or the people save by putting money in the Post Office Savings, in the banks, or—if they are individually rich enough—by themselves building factories, etc. By these development taxes and savings the people take away from themselves the opportunity of buying things now, and thus leave available that amount of resources for investment in the future.

And in this respect we have done extremely well considering the low level of our national income. By our taxation alone, we have made available £3 million (Shs. 60,000,000/-) in each of the last two years, for spending on development work. It has been hard, but in time to come we shall know that it was worth it. And we must continue along this same road.

There is only one way in which a nation—or a farmer—can invest in the future without refraining from consuming all his current income. That is by receiving gifts, or loans, from other people. If such things are obtained, then investment can be made without present sacrifice.

Over the past year Tanzania did receive capital assistance from abroad; for technical reasons it is not possible to say exactly the amount, but it was something like £5 million if grants in money and in kind, loans and credits, on an official or government-to-government basis are added up. This was a great help to us, and we appreciate it. But it is important that we should understand what it means in real terms and in comparison with our needs. For the truth is that the total amount of external capital aid was less than the amount by which our sisal earnings went down because of the fall in international prices. That is to say, instead of this external aid resulting in an increase over the previous year in the total resources available for investment, it did not even make up for the reduction in our total purchasing power which was caused by the fall in the price of just one of our major exports. It would have been far better if we had received no aid at all, but the prices of our commodities had not fallen.

Further, although we may expect some increase in this figure of external aid when we use more of the credits which have been negotiated recently, experience indicates that we would be stupid to rely on this kind of help. Quite apart from the problems of unacceptable political conditions which possible donors have tried to attach to capital assistance, and which have caused us to receive less than we at one time hoped, there are hard facts to be faced about the amount of international aid likely to be available. For the truth is that since 1961 the amount of capital assistance given by the wealthy countries of the world to the developing countries has not increased at all, despite their own rising standards. It has not even increased to the extent necessary to keep pace with the rising costs of development goods. The amount of aid given in 1965 to underdeveloped countries of the world bought less goods than the amount given in 1961. In terms of goods, aid has decreased—and there is no sign that this trend will suddenly change.

There is no choice for us. We shall be thankful for any outside assistance we receive, but we must not expect it. The only people we can rely upon are ourselves. We simply have to face up to the question: how much of our national income shall we spend on things we want now, and how much of it shall we invest in better living standards for the future?

So far Tanzania has done extremely well. Our people have made the effort, and have faced up to present sacrifice. In 1965 an amount equal to about 19 per cent of our monetary gross income was devoted to gross capital formation. In other words, an amount equal to almost one fifth of the wealth we produced and sold during the year was spent on things which will only bring benefit in the long run, not immediately. This is a much larger proportion than ever before, and I believe that our people are now earning the gratitude which future generations should feel towards those of us who have inherited the opportunity of independence.

There is one other aspect of our development which I wish to raise today because of its relevance to our progress in the coming years. That is the question of foreign exchange. This is as important to us as a nation as cash is to our farmers. At an extremely low level farmers can confine themselves to subsistence agriculture and hardly ever feel the need for cash. But if they want to have good tools to work their farms, if they wish to get a permanent roof for the house, and so on, then they need money. To get it they have to sell some of their crops at whatever price they can obtain. Tanzania too could manage, at an extremely low level, without international exchange. But at the present time we should be unable to make modern roads, build modern schools, obtain metal tools for farm work, or machines for modern industrial production, or do very much of the basic development work we need if we are ever to live at a higher standard. To get these things we sell our goods abroad, and receive in return the foreign currencies we need in order to buy them. And the more we sell abroad, the more we can buy of these overseas goods.

But once again we come to the question of choice. With this foreign currency we can either buy things we want to eat or wear now, or we can buy 'investment goods' like machines. For instance, we must choose between buying another car for the President or a tractor for a maize farm. The more we buy of the goods to enjoy, the less we can buy of the goods which will produce wealth in the future. Yet our position will only improve if we do buy things with which we can, in the future, make and grow our own consumption goods. And if we insist on spending our money on imported products even when a similar thing is produced in Tanzania, then we have—by that act—reduced the amount of overseas money which is available for the things we still do not make here. This is the importance of the 'Buy Tanzanian' campaign which began last week. For we have started some industries of our own; the newspaper supplements last week showed their surprising number and variety considering our recent start. By buying their products we help them to succeed and provide employment for our own people, and at the same time we make it possible to spend more money on the things our nation needs for its development.

Last year, because of this fall in prices of our goods, our balance of payments position was worse than in 1964. That is to say, whereas in 1964 we earned a lot more overseas currencies than we spent, in 1965 we only had a very little more overseas currency than we needed to spend. But, and this is very important now that we are establishing our own currency in 1966, we still had a favourable balance on our current foreign exchange account, and there was still a favourable balance on visible trade between Tanzania and other countries. On capital account our position remained good. Since exchange control was introduced last year, there has been a net inflow on capital account of about £4 million (Shs. 80,000,000/-) from sources outside East Africa.

In the future, however, we shall want to buy more and more machinery and other things for development. It is therefore important that we should do as much as possible to reduce the demands on foreign exchange, especially for consumption goods. We have started along the right path. The oil refinery will mean that we have to spend less money abroad for petrol and diesel. The operation of the cement works will also mean that this essential part of any building programme can be provided from within our country. The textile mills will begin to make their goods available in the next year or so, and so on. But we must do more. It is absurd that this country should still be buying food from abroad, yet last year we

spent outside Tanzania more than £3 million (Shs. 60,000,000/-)
on food products alone.

SELF-RELIANCE

The experience of the past year shows two things. Firstly, that we
cannot rely on outside help. It comes much later than one expects—
the newspaper announcements of loans and credits are usually
months, and sometimes years, in advance of agreement on the
detailed projects, and the actual money comes a long time after
that. It is not always in the form it is wanted; whereas we might
feel that we want a particular kind of machine from country X,
we can only get a different kind of machine from country Y. And
it suddenly becomes 'unavailable' for reasons which have nothing
to do with the economics of our development!

But secondly, the last year shows that we can do more for our
own development than we had thought possible. The investment
which was carried out last year by Tanzanians, either directly or
through their Government and other institutions, was at a higher
level than anyone could reasonably have expected. Our failure to
reach many of the Development Plan targets was due mainly to our
having received a lower level of outside help than we had estimated
for, and to the rather over-ambitious speed at which the Plan
expected us to be physically ready to carry out certain major
investment works.

(Here, let me make it clear that I make that statement not as a
political excuse, but on the basis of an outside intellectual assessment of our achievements and failures. Our local contribution to
development in 1965, and the reasonably anticipated contribution
in 1966, has called forth congratulations from a number of expatriate
economists who have been called to advise on how we can do more!)

But we cannot stop our effort now. We have to increase it.
When you have pushed a load a little way up a hill it is no use relaxing.
You have to go on. Otherwise the load may well fall back to its
original position—and perhaps crush the people in the process.

There is one area in which we, as a people, have to take some
corrective action if these continued efforts for development are to
succeed—and once again, it will be neither easy nor pleasant. We
have to cut back Government expenditure on recurrent services in
some fields, and hold it in others. The Development Plan proposed a

certain annual increase in recurrent expenses—that is, an increase in the cost of running the services of Government—which, together with the proposed rate of investment, would be within the resources of the nation. In practice we have allowed running expenses to increase much faster than we had planned. Now, we must either reduce services, or provide them more economically. We must have more financial discipline within Government and Government institutions. I think it is fair to say that we improved on this last year; but we have proposals in this regard to do more in the time ahead. Further, we have to concentrate our expenditure on those fields which are directly productive; we must streamline our administration, and every Government employee—whether he is cutting grass or working in senior offices—must become more efficient. And however difficult, nothing short of disaster will be allowed to cause any Minister to come to this House with Supplementary Estimates unless he can, at the same time, show an equivalent or greater saving on another Vote in his Ministry.

This question of reducing Government expenditure is very serious, and it is important that everyone understands it. For what is required is not simply an obedience to the letter of the law in this; people must understand the motive of these economy regulations, and they must support their spirit. This applies to everyone; but to politicians and civil servants particularly. It does not always happen; last year I announced two minor economies—in hospitality, and in Government cars. But I have noticed that occasionally expensive wines replace the spirits I banned, and that certain parts of a particular car are sometimes classified as 'spares' so that its price can be within the limit I set!

This year I do not propose to establish new peculiar economies of my own, although I do intend that those of last year should be implemented in the spirit as well as in the letter. But there are two areas which I shall instruct the Minister for Finance and others to watch very closely indeed. Firstly, prestige projects, and secondly, delegations.

Our nation has got a deservedly good reputation for not wasting money on things which someone says are good for prestige; but we must tighten up even further. Our delegations do tend to be rather large, and there do tend to be rather a lot of them! We have to cut them down in size, and we have to think more often about the worth of a particular visit. Neither should we automatically accept invitations if the fares and expenses are paid. When we go under these conditions our freedom is inevitably restricted, and in any case we are not getting on with our regular job—which is therefore being neglected. We cannot afford that.

Of course, this does not mean there will be no more visits abroad by Ministers and officials. The economic Ministers in particular have often to travel if they are to fulfil their function, and foreign affairs matters are often settled more quickly and economically by a visit than by a series of letters and telephone calls. Co-operation with our neighbours, too, demands considerable travel. It is for these reasons that it would not be sensible to limit numbers of personnel or visits to any arbitrary figure. But we have to recognize that in the aggregate they are limited by our resources!

THE COMING YEAR

It is in this spirit of ever-increasing self-reliance that Tanzania must face the coming financial year. This does not mean that we should be isolationist. It means that we must be efficient, and scientific both in our decision-making and in our execution of decisions. When a job has to be done, we must get the right person to do it; it is better to leave a vacancy unfilled or fill it with a competent expatriate than fill a key post with a citizen who is so incompetent that he prevents others from working properly. Neither is there any point in paying the people's taxes out in a salary for someone who is doing nothing useful!

Most important of all, we must work to our economic Plan, as amended and interpreted by the experience of the past two years. And we must work hard, and intelligently.

One of the very important tasks of the Government in the immediate future will be the consideration in conjunction with the Government of Zanzibar, of the Draft Economic Plan for Zanzibar which has just been submitted to us by a team of expatriate experts. It would obviously be wrong of me to comment on this Plan today; there has not yet been time for the Ministers to read it, much less for discussions to start. But I would like to say that the Draft Plan seems to me to be realistic, and to show very real prospects for increasing the prosperity of us all as the economies of the two parts of the Union are linked ever more closely together. The Plan does, in fact, show the very real advantages which can accrue to African peoples by unity, provided this is followed up by detailed and disciplined hard work.

Because this Plan deals with the development of the islands, it will be the prime responsibility of the Zanzibar Government to consider it in detail. On the other hand, it is clear that whatever amendments are made by the Zanzibar administration, the Plan can only be implemented by the joint action of the Union and the Zanzibar Governments. In due course, therefore, the Zanzibar Plan will be published and will be submitted to this National Assembly.

There is another important change taking place in our economic affairs which will affect the whole future of our development. Tomorrow Tanzanian currency notes will be issued for the first time, and in August Tanzanian coins will be issued. These will gradually replace the East African notes and coins which are at present our means of exchange in this country. They will be issued at par—that is to say that anyone taking an East African note or coin to a bank will be given an equivalent amount of Tanzanian money.

This change was not decided upon for prestige reasons; the decision was made because it is impossible to plan economic development properly if currency and credit are not within the control of the planners—that is, of the Government. Had an East African Federation been inaugurated, an East African currency could have continued. Indeed, if Federation does come in the future, the currencies of the countries involved will have to be re-merged. But for the present our Tanzanian currency is essential to us.

Issuing our own money does not, however—as I am sure Members by this time know—mean that we can print notes whenever the Government is short of money. The Tanzanian currency—like that we are now using—will be useful to us only as long as we recognize that it represents goods. We can therefore increase the amount of money issued when the production of goods increases, but not otherwise.

The Tanzanian Government, through the Central Bank of Tanzania which it has established, will safeguard the value of the new currency, both by steps to ensure it has adequate backing, and by the strictest financial discipline throughout the economy. No one need have any more fears about the safety of our new money than they have had about our present money. The present state of our economy, and our continuing favourable balance of payments, means that our currency starts off in a very strong position. Further, as the Governor of the Bank has already announced, the foreign exchange assets of the Bank will amount to between at least £23 and £24 million when all East African notes in Tanzania have been exchanged. Thus, for international purposes, and for internal purposes, there can be full confidence in the Tanzanian shilling.

In order that the Bank may get into full operation as quickly as possible, the Government asks Members of this House to encourage all their constituents to bring for conversion in the next few weeks all the East African notes which they are holding. We know that despite all the arguments against it, some of our people still hoard money rather than put it in the bank or post office. They must be told to bring these hoards to the bank for exchange into the new notes and coins. If they do that quickly they will be helping our country; if they don't do it at all they may find in a year or so that their savings have no value because the East African Currency Board which issued the notes will no longer exist!

Our new currency will, as I have said, start off with strong backing, both because of the assets which our new Bank will inherit from the Currency Board, and because our economy is a very healthy one. In the long run, however, any currency depends for its international and internal reputation on the economic progress of the country. We shall now determine the strength of our currency by our own actions; it is *our* balance of payments, the level of *our* production, and *our* stability, and *our* national integrity, which will determine whether both foreigners and Tanzanians accept our notes in ten years' time in the full confidence that they are meaningful—that they really represent wealth which exists.

I am confident that the Government and people of Tanzania, working together in the future as they have in the past, will continue to strengthen the economy of this country. We have had setbacks since independence, we have encountered difficulties which we did not anticipate. We have made mistakes. But we have also achieved a very great deal indeed. We who live here do not always notice the changes which we have made, just as the man who plants a mango tree does not notice its growth between one week and the next. But those who have been away, and visitors who come here after a long absence, see many changes, and many improvements.

They are often amazed at the speed with which a country which had the reputation of being a 'quiet backwater' is now moving forwards.

In the coming year we must maintain, and even increase, this pace of development. It appears that the prices of our exports will remain low; they may even fall further. We cannot guarantee that the rains will come in the right places at the right times. But we can decide that we will apply in the coming twelve months the lessons we have learnt from the first two years of the Development Plan. We can decide to continue to work hard, and to build for the future. We can accept the fact that although outside events will affect our achievement, only we ourselves will determine our endeavour. We can rely on ourselves, and what we achieve will ultimately depend on that more than on any other factor. For the man who shoots an arrow at a target is the man who really determines whether the target is hit. If the wind blows hard from one direction, then he must take that into account. If the target is moving, then he adjusts his aim accordingly. And always he aims a little higher than the target itself, knowing that only if he does that will he really hit the objective.

Let our motto for the coming year be 'self-reliance', and in that spirit let us pursue our goal of economic betterment for our country and all its people.

Mr. Speaker, I look forward to the wholehearted co-operation of the Members of this House in the work which lies before our nation.

19

Inauguration of the Bank of Tanzania

On Tuesday, 14 June 1966, President Nyerere inaugurated the public activities of the new Central Bank. The Bank of Tanzania, which from its inception was entirely publicly owned, issued the new Tanzanian currency on that day. The President used the opportunity to stress the monetary policy which would be followed by Government.

... To some extent I have mixed feelings in coming here this morning to this short ceremony. I have a feeling of regret and disappointment that this Central Bank is not a federal one. It would have been so much to our heart's desire if it were a Federal President officiating at the inauguration of a Federal Central Bank—and I must say quite candidly that I would have been ready, and in fact happier, to be in the audience to watch him do it. On the other hand, I am glad that at last, as far as Tanzania is concerned, we have now devised an instrument on the monetary and fiscal side, which can effectively contribute to our development without unnecessary handicaps resulting from uncoordinated political and economic policies of three countries. However, I want to take this opportunity to reaffirm what our Government has stated in the past about East African co-operation. If at any time in the future any of our partners in the old East African Currency Board arrangement is ready to merge politically in a Federation with us, the Central Bank and currency we are inaugurating today will be reconstituted to take into account the needs of such a Federation. This should not alarm any members of the staff of the Bank of Tanzania. They would all be absorbed into a Federal Central Bank for, whether as Tanzania or as a Federation, the need for a Central Bank and currency will always be there.

In officially starting the operations of the Bank of Tanzania, I should also say that we are deeply indebted to the East African Currency Board which, despite its handicaps and limitations, served us so well. I am advised that the Board has adapted its policies to the needs and conditions of East Africa, and that because of this adjustment the Bank of Tanzania is not breaking entirely fresh ground. In the next few months the Board's staff will be involved in the complicated exercise of its winding up, and I want to record my own, and Tanzania's, appreciation of the efforts of the Board to see us through to the present extent in our financial and monetary arrangements.

I should also like to take this opportunity to say that the Board and the staff of the Bank of Tanzania are embarking on a very important job. They are to see to it that we get the money we need for our daily use and for development, and that our money is so managed that it will foster rapid growth of the economy in real terms and also maintain its international value. I have no doubt but that this will be done. The Government and people will give full support to the Bank in pursuing these objectives. And we start on a firm foundation.

To back up our new currency we have reserves of foreign assets which are larger in proportion to our trade than the reserves of many countries whose currency is acceptable throughout the world. In addition we have a basically strong economy, which is growing year by year. And our people know that it is their responsibility to increase the wealth of our country, and that this can only be done by producing more goods. We shall not make the mistake of imagining that our problems can be solved by a printing press; we know that real wealth is goods, not money. And the Bank, the Government, and the people, will work together on this basis.

We shall do this because we know that this is the way to serve our country. But in doing so we are, and shall be for some time, using outside expertise to help us on the technical aspects of our task. I am told by the Governor that there are six expatriates on the staff of the management of this Bank, including the Director General, and I would like to say that we value very highly the services of these experts. I know the Minister for Finance has, in the past, publicly expressed our thanks to the organizations which sponsored them and I would like to reaffirm Tanzania's appreciation and gratitude to them here. I am glad to note that, with their assistance, our promise made in June last year that the national currency would come into being in a year's time, has been fulfilled according to plan. It is my hope that it will be easier to attain our other targets in economic development now that the Central Bank has come into being, and the central bankers' expertise will be promptly available on a national basis.

In participating in the issue of the first notes of Tanzania's own currency, I want to ask every Tanzanian with the old notes to come forward and exchange them as soon as possible. This will not only demonstrate our support for the Government's decision to establish this Bank, but it will also enable the Bank to operate normally as a Central Bank. For when the old notes are brought here after the new ones have been given in exchange, the Bank will send them to the East African Currency Board. In return our Bank will receive the sterling assets which are essential to enable it to operate fully. I think also that the need to convert the old currency into the new currency will make those people hoarding money come forward with it. For otherwise their hoards will become useless later on.

I hope, however, that those who bring out their buried money in order to get new notes in exchange, will not then re-bury the new money. It is much better to open a savings account, either in a bank or in the post office. By doing this the owner will earn some interest on his money. Also he will not continue to run the risk of a thief breaking into his house and taking his savings away, nor of himself forgetting where the money is, nor of having his house accidentally burnt down, together with his money.

I should like to stress the question of hoarding. We in Tanzania cannot afford to go round the world begging for money, when under our pillows, in our pots and boxes, we continue to hoard idle money. In fact, at present, some of the money we borrow from abroad finds its way to these hoarders instead of remaining in the banking system for lending to those who need it. This is very bad, and holds back our economic development. I am asking the Bank of Tanzania, from today, to see to it that everybody in the country is made aware of the enormous benefits of placing their money, however small the amount, in a bank or post office, and to publicize the ill-effects and disadvantages of hoarding.

Now I see that we are nearing the time business will start! I am not altogether happy that an important institution like our Central Bank should not start in a building of its own. However, since Tanzania is in a hurry, we could not afford to wait for one to be built. I hope that the plans for the new building will soon be completed so that we can properly house our Central Bank. In the meantime, in spite of this handicap, I trust that the excitement and enthusiasm for this new and important venture will continue to encourage all the staff to work hard to fulfil the task that are required of the Central Bank.

20

The Role of Universities

The World University Service held its General Assembly at Dar es Salaam University College at the end of June 1966. *President Nyerere gave the opening address on* 27 *June, and spoke under the title of 'The University's Role in the Development of the New Countries'.*

It gives me great pleasure to welcome to this conference, and to Dar es Salaam, the delegats and guests of the World University Service. I am told that about 50 countries are represented here, and even more universities and university colleges. We are pleased that the progress of our University College buildings allows us to be hosts on this occasion; we hope that you will be happy and comfortable in these quarters.

Every time I myself come to this campus—which is farly frequently—I think again about our decision to build here, and our decision about the type of buildings. Sometimes I wonder whether we made the right decision, although really I know it is too early for and answer to be given to that question. For the answer depends upon what the graduates of this University College do in the future, and to what extent their actions have been influenced by the expenditure of more than Shs. 50/- million. In other words, the answer depends upon the future—and includes an immeasurable factor anyway!

Yet the question itself is an important one; it involves the whole problem of what a university could, and should, do in a developing society. For I believe that the pursuit of pure learning can be a luxury in society; whether it is or not depends upon the conditions in which that society lives. Perhaps I am being foolhardy in making such a statement at a university gathering, but I am going to repeat it; when people are dying because existing knowledge is not applied, when the very basic social and public services are not available to all members of a society, then that society is misusing its resources if it pursues pure learning for its own sake.

If there are philosophy students among this gathering I suspect that they are already making mental demands that I define my terms: what do I mean by 'pure learning', and 'for its own sake'. And if I hold these reservations about the function of a university in this developing society, why is it that I myself am proud to be Chancellor of the University of East Africa, and Visitor of this University College?

These are valid responses to my rather provocative statement, because one of the very important traditional functions of a university has been this pursuit of pure knowledge—knowledge about things which exist, or happen, just for the sake of finding out more about them. Indeed very many of the advances in the human condition rest upon the foundation of work done at universities which had no apparent relevance to man's life on the earth. I believe that scientists divide their research into two categories—pure and applied—and it is the former which is normally carried out in universities while the latter may also be undertaken in industrial or agricultural complexes. Economists do not—as far as I know—make this same formal distinction, but reading some economists' research papers about theoretical measurements of immeasurable factors it appears that in practice the same division exists! The men and women who seek to solve particular problems of science and society then sometimes use and develop these apparently useless pieces of knowledge, and as a result huge advances are made in dealing with very pressing problems of individuals and communities.

I have no doubt in my mind, therefore, but that the university function of extending the frontiers of knowledge is very important for humanity. I will go further, and say that in the course of time universities in developing countries must also make their contribution to the world of knowledge in this direction. We must not establish in our new young countries institutions of higher learning which simply receive. They must give as well.

But in all things there are priorities, and we have to look at the immediate future, and the immediate present, and decide what it is that universities in our kind of society can at present most usefully give to the world of which we are a part. And it is my conviction that universities in countries like Tanzania have other urgent tasks to fulfil which will test their resources—human and material—to the utmost. I do not believe that they can at this stage pursue 'pure research' and 'knowledge for its own sake' without neglecting other functions which are for the time being more important.

Before I explain what I believe these other functions to be let me make one thing clear. At any good university some of the best brains of the day should be living together. And good brains cannot be turned on and off; a man who thinks about his work will not stop thinking at the end of his day, or when the students are on vacation. If he then finds it relaxing—or exciting, depending upon temperament—to investigate an apparently irrelevant matter, he should certainly be encouraged to do so, and given use of such facilities as are available. And if this means that later he is able to produce a paper explaining, let us say, why certain fish change colour when taken out of water, then he deserves congratulation. My original statement was not that pure learning is useless; it was that it is a luxury under certain conditions. And a man who spends his spare time on this luxury is certainly entitled to our gratitude more than a man who spends his spare time on other equally luxurious, but less constructive, pastimes.

Neither should my assessment of priorities be taken to imply that we expect from our university merely the dissemination of established facts. Whether in a developing country or elsewhere, a university does not deserve the name if it does not promote thinking. But our particular and urgent problems must influence the subjects to which thought is given, and they must influence, too, the approach. Both in university-promoted research, and in the content of degree syllabuses, the needs of our country should be the determining factor.

What are the problems we face in the discipline concerned? What are the obstacles which might prevent the achievement of a particular national goal, and how can they be overcome? Is a particular policy conducive to the attainment of the basic objectives of the society? These are the type of questions to which the university can and should be giving attention. In these fields university staff and students should be co-operating with Government and the people.

There are some people who would undoubtedly challenge this assumption that university should co-operate with Government.

They would say that the task of a university is to seek for truth, and to ignore all other responsibilities, leaving it to those outside the university to accept or reject the result in their practical politics. Yet this is to say that a university could, and should, live divorced from its society. It implies, too, that there is an automatic conflict with Government—that Government is not concerned with truth! It is my conviction that this attitude is based on a half-truth, and has within it great dangers, both for society as a whole and for the university itself.

I fully accept that the task of a university is to seek for truth, and that its members should speak the truth as they see it regardless of consequences to themselves. But you will notice the words 'to themselves'; I do not believe they should do this regardless of the society. A university which tries to put its professors and its students into blinkers will neither serve the cause of knowledge, nor the interests of the society in which it exists. But to try and deal objectively with a particular problem, and in a scientific manner to analyse and describe it—that is one thing. To move from that to an assumption that the consequences are irrelevant is entirely different. What we expect from our university is both a complete objectivity in the search for truth, and also commitment to our society—a desire to serve it. We expect the two things equally. And I do not believe this dual responsibility—to objectivity and to service—is impossible of fulfilment. In this I find support in the speech of the first Principal of the Dar es Salaam University College, Professor R. C. Pratt, who said when the campus was opened:

'We must strive consciously and deliberately to assure that the life and work of the College is in harmony with the central positive objectives that underlie the national policies of our Governments . . . . . . The University of East Africa must be a committed institution, actively relating our work to the communities it seeks to serve. This is in no sense in contrast to, or in contradiction of, the intellectual objectivity and respect for truth which must also be an essential feature of a University. Commitment and objectivity are not opposites, are not in contradiction to each other. Rather the best scholarship is often a product of deep commitment. . .

To question that is, I believe, to pretend that a society can progress if it is based on falsity, or that the truth is so unimportant that it can be buried in intellectual tomes which have no relevance to the work of a people who are trying to revolutionize their conditions of life.

In fact, a university in a developing society must put the emphasis of its work on subjects of immediate moment to the nation in which it exists, and it must be committed to the people of that nation and their humanistic goals. This is central to its existence; and it is this fact which justifies the heavy expenditure of resources on this one aspect of national life and development. Its research, and the energies of its staff in particular, must be freely offered to the community, and they must be relevant.

Applied research, however, is only one aspect of university work. The dissemination of knowledge to undergraduates and other members of society is equally important. But it is not simply facts which must be taught. Students must be helped to think scientifically; they must be taught to analyse problems objectively, and to apply the facts they have learned—or which they know exist—to the problems which they will face in the future. For when a society is in the process of rapid change—which is a definition of a developing society—it is no use giving students the answers to today's problems. These are useful mainly as a training ground; the real worth of the university education will show itself much later when these same men and women have to cope with problems which are as yet unseen.

Yet once again, the real problem in our societies is a different one. For universities all over the world have this task of trying to educate and expand the minds of their students. Universities in developing countries have also another, and in some ways a more difficult problem. It is this same problem of commitment and it brings me back to the question I started with—the question of whether these fine buildings are really the right environment for our new university.

The library, the hostels, the lecture rooms and so on which make up this campus were all designed to enable the students here to work well—to concentrate their energies on learning and thinking. It is because we need young people to do this that we started the University College and devote a considerable proportion of our recurrent revenue to its upkeep. But anyone who walks off this campus into the nearby villages, or who travels up country—perhaps to Dodoma or into the Pare Hills—will observe the contrast in conditions here and the conditions in which the mass of our people live. And the purpose of establishing the university is to make it possible for us to change these poverty-stricken lives. We do not build sky-scrapers here so that a few very fortunate individuals can develop their own minds and then live in comfort, with intellectual stimulus making their work and their leisure interesting to themselves. We tax the people to build these places only so that young men and women may become efficient servants to them. There is no other justification for this heavy call being made on poor peasants.

How can the reality of this responsibility be maintained all the time for students who live here? How can we ensure that they remain—or become—constructively concerned about the task of transforming our national poverty, so that they regard the conditions here as an interim in their lives and not as something to which they are entitled?

What all this really amounts to is not a question about buildings; these are the physical surroundings designed to assist efficiency. The real problem is that of promoting, strengthening, and channelling, social attitudes which are conducive to the progress of our society. For, as I have already said, we in poor societies can only justify expenditure on a university—of any type—if it promotes real development of our people. And the buildings become relevant only because they could introduce one further factor dividing university students from the masses who sent them here. But they do not necessarily have this effect. The factors which really determine whether university students shall remain an integral part of a classless society or become members of an alien elite, are much more subtle—and much more difficult to deal with.

In our traditional societies every member was fully aware of his membership of the society—his responsibility to his fellows as well as their responsibility to him. All individuals lived the same sort of life; it was a hard one in which the need for co-operation was an obvious fact. The social institutions themselves encouraged this psychology of interdependence, and it was part of the environment in which every child grew up. Yet now we take certain of our children and separate them from others by giving them opportunities for secondary schooling which are not available to everyone. Later we choose a still more limited number and send them to universities. And throughout this process we have been taking the individual out of his community, and only too often at the same time encouraging him to work hard by promises of individual advancement if he does so. It is he, as an individual, who is stressed; it is he who alone reads and learns and gets the opportunity for advance. This is inevitable; all of us have different brains, and the complexities of a modern society demand very many different kinds of skills—which require different individual training.

But with all this stress on his individual responsibility how can we at the same time safeguard the individual against the arrogance of looking upon himself as someone special, someone who has the right to make very heavy demands upon society, in return for which he will deign to make available the skills which that society has enabled him to acquire? In particular, what can a university do to ensure that its students regard themselves as 'servants-in-training'?

This is one of the most vital, and most difficult, of the functions of a university in a developing country. For some students this 'lesson' is almost unnecessary. They take for granted the fact that they should work with their fellow citizens in National Service, in lonely up-country posts, and so on. But unfortunately this is not true of all; and certainly as a body there is always a temptation for students to regard themselves as a group which has rights without responsibilities. We have seen how many groups of students demand ever better conditions of study, ever larger allowances. They demand that they should be treated separately from others when questions of National Service arise—not in order to give more, but in order to give less. And most difficult of all they compare themselves as a group, and themselves as graduates individually, with students and graduates of universities in the wealthy countries of the world. Then they feel resentful if their conditions are worse, or their pay lower. And all the time the masses continue to live on an annual income of about £20 per head per year.

A university in a country like Tanzania has to deal with this problem. It has to meet the challenge—'Physician, heal thyself'. For if it is acknowledged that only united effort for development will enable the transformation of the underdeveloped nations of the world, then it must also be acknowledged that the universities of those nations, their staffs and students, must also be united with the rest of those societies in that task. And this can only happen if the university men and women themselves feel their identity with their fellows—including those who never went to school at all. It can only happen if the university graduates merge themselves back into the communities from which they came, and transform them from within.

Many different techniques are used to strengthen and rebuild the relationship between university students and the other members of their society. Work camps, vacation work, National Service, voluntary nation-building and so on are all valuable methods for helping with this problem. Yet it can remain a problem unless the whole atmosphere of the university is one of giving service, and expecting service, from all its members and students; unless, in other words, the prevailing attitude is one of social responsibility. And this must not be the idea of 'giving aid to the poor'. That arrogance has no place in Tanzania at any rate. It must be an attitude of wanting to work, in whatever work there is to do, alongside and within the rest of the community, until finally there is no more distinction between a graduate and an illiterate than there is between a man who works as a carpenter and his fellow who works as a brickmaker. Graduates and illiterates would then accept their tasks as distinctive, and as making different demands on them, but as being in both cases but a part of a single whole.

Mr. Chairman, I have only dealt with a small number of aspects of the many-sided responsibility of a university in a developing society. I have spoken inevitably out of Tanzanian experience of the needs and problems. But I want to close by saying how interested we in the Government are in the subject of your discussions this week. For we believe that our University College can play a very, very important role in our development. Despite the questions I raised we see no reason to revise our confident expectation that it will play this role. Already we have had valuable service from members of faculty; already we have young graduates in law working in our Government offices. And I can assure you that the Tanzanian Government is anxious for the constructive ideas and criticisms which our College, or any other academic institution can give us.

For this is really what I have been saying. The role of a university in a developing country is to contribute; to give ideas, manpower, and service for the futherance of human equality, human dignity, and human development.

21

Principles and Development

In the second quarter of 1966 *certain suggestions were made in the local press and elsewhere to the effect that Tanzania was paying too much attention to principles at the expense of her economic development. Suggestions were also being made that Tanzania had drifted into an 'anti-West' position and was not really non-aligned.*

Although these attitudes were not widespread President Nyerere decided to bring this matter forward for discussion and he prepared the following memorandum for the June 1966 *meeting of the National Executive of TANU.*

It has been suggested, in the press and by a few extremely dedicated patriots, that Tanzania is so concerned with principles—especially in relation to foreign affairs—that our economic development is jeopardized and has already been unnecessarily retarded. This is a very serious matter; if it is true that economic progress has been slowed down by adherence to other principles then people must understand why it has happened and what the alternatives were. If it is not true, then people must be able to answer such allegations.

In fact the answer is not, and cannot be, a simple one. There are three distinct questions which have to be considered. Firstly, there is the question of economic fact. Have the actions of the Government in relation to foreign affairs and other matters really hampered development? If so, by how much? Although a detailed answer in shillings is impossible to give, some assessment of the economic effects of certain policies which were adopted on principle is given at the end of this paper.

The second question is, what are the principles of the Tanzania Government, the pursuit of which has affected economic development, or which may do so in the future? And the third question is whether these principles are so valuable in themselves that any reduction in economic development which they cause is justified for other reasons of national well-being.

A CONFLICT OF PRINCIPLES

First we have to recognize that few issues in the modern world are simple ones, involving only one principle or affecting only one aspect of national life. Nor is it sensible to consider these questions only in the short term; what matters is not only how much economic development we have in the next two or three years, but what kind of life our people will be able to lead in the more distant future— say in the year 1980 and after. We have to recognize too, that in pursuing our goals we must take into account the existence of other forces—for good and evil—in the world, because it is quite impossible for any nation nowadays to live in isolation from the rest.

This means that we have to understand our own objectives, and then assess the best way of reaching them. This will sometimes mean running straight ahead and fighting through obstacles; at other times it will mean manoeuvring to find a better and easier way through. Although it would be a mistake to carry the analogy too far, we can compare our Government with a footballer, whose objective is to see that his team wins. With this objective he sometimes kicks the ball straight at the goal from a long way down the pitch, but more often he does not do this. If the opposing team is strong and active he may dribble the ball forward until he gets into a better position to shoot; but he may also send it backwards away from his goal—so as to ensure that is stays in the control of his own team in the hope that another member may later get in the right position to score. But the one thing that he tries to avoid is letting the ball get in such a position that the other side has a good chance to score; if he can do nothing else he must prevent the issue from being settled by a victory for his opponents. And whereas, therefore, towards the end of a game when the other side is leading he may take considerable risks in order to equalize or to win, at the beginning a good footballer plays carefully. He weighs up the chances of each move, and assesses the relative merits of the different members of both teams, so that he knows which of his own side can be relied upon to outwit the forces which will converge upon him if he gets the ball at his feet.

In the same way, the pursuit—for example—of the principle of anti-colonialism, does not necessarily mean that the nation must go headlong down the pitch regardless of the other forces at work. Sometimes, if it is the only way to prevent disaster this must be done if it is humanly possible. But it would be foolishness if the country with this principle allowed its own economy to be destroyed and all its people's hopes of progress to be sacrificed by a degree of involvement beyond their strength. Yet at the same time, if the principle means anything at all some sacrifice will certainly be demanded. The question becomes whether the sacrifice can be made without disaster, and whether the possible gain from making the sacrifice is—directly or indirectly—great enough to make the risk and the sacrifice worthwhile.

SOME OF THE PRINCIPLES OF TANZANIA

The first responsibility of the Government—its first principle—is the protection of Tanzania's independence and its freedom to determine its own policies, both internal and external. This is really nothing more than a continuation of the freedom struggle under new circumstances. Yet this principle has already cost us aid from West Germany, and is undoubtedly affecting the quantity of aid from other sources.

When our people united behind TANU to win independence they were not interested merely in having a different flag; they were interested in the things which that different flag would symbolize—the ability of the people to decide for themselves what kind of life they would lead. They wanted to have a government responsible to them, so that it would consider their interests and not the interests of people thousands of miles away who had a separate government.

What does this mean in practical terms? The case in which this principle was most openly challenged was the one relating to the recognition of East Germany. When Tanganyika and Zanzibar united, the realities of the world situation meant that Tanzania could only have diplomatic relations with one German state, although up until that time Tanganyika had recognised only the Federal German Republic (West Germany) and Zanzibar only the German Democratic Republic (East Germany). Some practical compromise had to be made, therefore, which would avoid damage to the needs of either part of the new Union. For many months discussions continued about how this problem could be settled to give most advantage to Tanzania without offending the basic principles of either of the two parts of Germany. Finally a formula was worked out by the Tanzania Government, under which only the Federal German Government would be recognized, but the East German authorities would have a Consulate General's office in the Tanzania capital. This formula was operating in Cairo and had already been accepted by both parts of Germany there.

In our case, however, the West Germans demanded more, and put heavy pressure on the Government. When diplomatic pressure failed to move Tanzania from the position taken up in the interests of the Union, the West German Government unilaterally and without notice, broke a five-year training and aid agreement relating to the new air wing, and returned all their technicians overnight. They went further, and threatened to cut all their aid if we continued with our declared policies.

The choice before Tanzania was then clear; we could either accept dictation from West Germany and continue to receive economic aid until the next time we proposed to do something they did not like, or we could maintain our policies and lose the aid immediately. In effect, therefore, we had to choose whether to become a puppet state of Germany in return for any charity she cared to give us.

The Government of Tanzania believed, and still believes, that to have agreed with the West German demands would have been to nullify our real independence. Therefore, although the decision to stand by our very reasonable declared intentions meant a loss of badly needed economic assistance, the Government felt that the real interests of the people of Tanzania left them with no alternative.

It has been suggested, however, that the Government made a mistake by telling the Germans to withdraw all their aid, without waiting for them to do this on their own. Yet even in this regard the Government had little alternative if it was to uphold the dignity of our independent country. For there is no doubt that had we simply maintained our policy and waited for the Germans to react by withdrawing aid as and when they liked, they would have been misled into believing that economic pressure would eventually make us change our minds, and there would have been a great deal of intrigue designed to undermine the unity of the country. It is also clear that only by taking this very strong stand could our determination to defend our independence be recognized—both by the Germans and by others. And in fact this lesson has not been altogether lost on other states which have dealings with us; there is no longer any misapprehension about our sincerity when we say we want aid without strings on our political or economic policies.

Yet it remains true that our total policies do have an effect on other countries' reactions towards us, and therefore on the amount of outside aid we are likely to receive. Thus, for example, discussions in the United States Congress when Overseas Aid Appropriations are submitted may well be affected by powerful Congress groups' dislike of our policy—for example on Vietnam. This is inherent in the American democratic system, and is outside the control of the United States' Government; the President cannot ignore such groups even if he wishes to do so. The question then becomes whether our Government should determine its basic policies in relation to the wishes of legislators in other countries, or whether it should consider the needs, principles, and opinions of the Tanzanian people.

This does not mean that Tanzania must, or should, go out of her way to comment on international matters which do not concern her. If two nations are having a quarrel which does not affect us there is no reason why we should offend either by sitting in judgement upon their quarrel. But the difficulty is that such countries often demand support—not just neutrality, and if we believe them wrong we can surely not give such support? Vietnam is an example of this. It is a very long way away, and is a very complicated issue originating in the anti-colonial struggles of the post-war world even before TANU was formed. Even the question of anti-colonialism itself in that area (and all sorts of other matters are now also involved in the Vietnam question) would not necessarily have demanded action from us—for our priority must be Africa. But we were called upon to endorse various aspects of American policy; it was our refusal to do that which caused us to quarrel with the British Government when they proposed that a particular kind of Vietnam Peace Mission should be sent from the Commonwealth Conference in June 1965. Our refusal to endorse this move also attracted US criticism on us.

The policy of non-alignment between the Cold War blocs, and in relation to any other quarrels which do not concern us, has caused other international difficulties for Tanzania, and has thus indirectly affected the willingness of other countries to co-operate with us in our economic development. It is a natural fact of human nature, and also of international behaviour, that people would prefer to give assistance to those they regard as their reliable friends (who will support them whatever they do) rather than to give to those about whose support they feel more doubtful. This we must understand. The question is, what should we do about it?

The choice before us really amounts to offering to all countries genuine friendship based on equality, or becoming 'reliable allies' to certain large power groups and being therefore more hostile to others. (If we were to adopt the latter policy on economic grounds we should certainly have to choose to be more friendly with the democratic capitalist countries of the West; they are older and more wealthy than the communist countries of the East.) But would taking sides with one power bloc be a sensible choice for us to make? Even economically?

We have declared that we wish to build our economy on the basis of the equality of all citizens, and have specifically rejected the concept of creating a class system where one group of people owns the means of production for the purpose of getting personal profit and another group works for them. We have not excluded private enterprise, and we want people to start their own productive and commercial undertakings. But we have said that the emphasis in our economy should be on ownership by the people, through the people's own institutions. What we are thus trying to do is build a 'mixed economy' which includes both public and private enterprise—with the emphasis on the former—so as to get the most rapid and most beneficial economic development.

Tanzania then finds herself faced with a divided world in which one side combines an economy based almost exclusively on public ownership of the means of production, and a political system which severely curtails individual freedom, and the other side combines a predominantly privately owned economic system with greater individual freedom and a degree of economic inequality which would be unacceptable to us. Tanzania's objectives, therefore, mean that she wants to adapt to her own needs some of the institutions from each side. Clearly she can best do this by having friendly relations with each side of the divided world. Indeed, it is impossible to carry out our economic policy unless we do have relations with both East and West, and unless we attract some economic investment from both. For it is as unrealistic to expect the private enterprise systems of the West to understand the needs of publicly owned industries here, as it is to expect the public ownership systems of the East to establish private firms here.

Thus—given the fact that we are trying to create a society based on human dignity and equality—the economic grounds alone should lead us to support a policy of non-alignment. But in fact it is not only such influences which have determined this policy. For non-alignment comes back to the question of freedom for our nation. If we are to rely upon one of the contending power blocs and be hostile to the other, then we must determine all our policies according to the interests of that bloc, and not according to the special interests of Tanzania. It would be very illogical, for example, to ally ourselves with one bloc for its wealth or protection and then to act contrary to its interests—even when these are inevitably determined almost exclusively by the large powers involved. Thus our freedom to determine our own policies would have to be surrendered.

Yet it is alleged that Tanzania is not 'non-aligned', but 'anti-West', and this belief has certainly influenced some Western countries' attitudes towards us. What is the truth of this?

Historically Tanzania was part of the Western Bloc; this was part of colonialism and there was nothing we could do about it. But to move to non-alignment from being part of one bloc means moving away from that bloc; the question which really matters is whether you move right over to the other side or whether you move into and stay in an independent position. The movement itself is inevitable; and really it is this which has caused a considerable amount of misunderstanding with the West. For until independence the West never had to consider Tanzania at all—it was automatically 'on their side'. Now they find that our support is not assured—and this results in an illogical belief that we have become 'unfriendly'. They have not yet accustomed themselves to the idea that we are independent, and that our friendship will now be genuine but our decisions will be our own.

In support of the allegation that Tanzania is anti-West, it is said that our political leaders, and our Party newspapers, are always attacking the Western countries and never the countries of the Eastern Bloc. And it is true that this is where our emphasis in public speeches has been. There are two reasons for this—one of them shows the obverse side of the Western failure to understand our independence. For it reflects our own failure to grow out of attitudes which we on our side developed during colonial times. Thus, because we ourselves had to fight against Western imperialism we are very conscious of it, and very concerned to safeguard ourselves against its resurgence. We are less conscious of other forms of imperialism, and as a result some of our people are over-sensitive and over-suspicious in one direction only, believing that they are safeguarding their country provided they disagree with whatever the British, or the Americans, do. This attitude we must fight against, for we shall not be a mature state until we have grown out of it.

Yet at the same time it must be recognized that Tanzania's interest in world affairs is primarily an interest in her own needs and those of her continent—Africa. And it is incontrovertible that, both before and after independence, Western countries have interfered more actively—for both good and evil—in Africa than have the Eastern powers. Not only has Africa had more economic and technical assistance from the West; it has also had Stanleyville, Tshombe, and practical support for Verwoerd. If we talk about the first—and we should and do—then we must also talk about the second.

It is also true that the political freedom which exists in the West—and which we wish to emulate here as far as our different circumstances allow—means that disputes between nations are inevitably much more public than in the very different political systems of the East. In the West the newspapers publish very much what they want to publish—regardless of its truth—and sometimes to the embarrassment of their own government. Members of some Western Parliaments are also liable to ask public questions, the answers to which bring out the Western government attitudes. Our own attitudes must necessarily be equally public, and thus both quarrels and disagreements are often conducted where everyone can see them, and where the public in both countries get involved.

The controlled press and the different political systems in communist countries mean that differences of opinion are only brought out into the public eye by the East if the governments concerned wish to do this. Disputes—which are inevitably less in number because of the comparative smallness of communist 'presence' in Africa—are thus conducted on a diplomatic level until and unless they come to a public break of relations. And even if African states make the disagreement public there is no guarantee that the other people will know of it. It is also true that because Eastern countries are not used to deciding what shall happen in Africa, they are less inclined to protest if we decide an issue in a manner which they dislike. And it is clear that former colonial powers are still determined to keep Africa, including independent Africa, as a sphere of influence of the Western world.

Any real discussion of the 'non-alignment' of Tanzania's foreign policy should therefore be based on an examination of what we do, more than on what is said publicly. And the international actions of the Union Government are quite clearly determined by the interests of our country, and the principles of African unity and African freedom.

These two principles of unity and freedom do not need justification to Tanzanians. We know that Africa will only be secure in its freedom, and only allow real economic prosperity for its people, when the present multitude of small states are replaced by one internationally sovereign authority. And we know, too, that until the whole of Africa is free from racialistic minority rule, and alien colonial rule, no part of our continent—united or otherwise—is free from danger from these forces.

Yet it is these principles combined with one other which have caused us to break diplomatic relations with Britain—the country which has, up to now, given us more economic aid than any other. We have asked for a declaration by the British Government that their aim in Southern Rhodesia is independence on the basis of majority rule. We have not asked for assurances about time—simply about the principle. But we have not received these assurances. Then, after UDI, Tanzania—along with other African states—was extremely critical about what we regard as the lack of energy in the fight against the rebel white authorities in that colony. In December the Organization of African Unity passed a resolution calling upon all African states to break diplomatic relations with Britain if by a certain date Smith had not been defeated. We were a party to that resolution.

Thus three separate principles of foreign policy were involved in this matter, leaving us with no real alternative. There was the principle of anti-colonialism—were we prepared to sit back without protest when a racialistic minority tries to seize permanent power over 4 million people? There was the principle of African unity— the fact that our institution for the building of unity in Africa had called for a particular action. And there was the fact that Tanzania had given her support (had pledged her word through her representative) to this resolution, so the question arose of whether our international undertakings were of any value—whether, for example, people could rely on us to observe agreements which we voluntarily entered into. It is difficult to see how Tanzania could ever again expect to be taken seriously in any of these matters if we had not adhered to the spirit of the decision taken at Addis Ababa. We did, in fact, make clear that we were prepared to compromise on the wording; if we had had the assurance about majority rule before independence, or even if new steps had been taken before the deadline date to bring down the Smith regime, we made it clear that we were prepared to accept these as evidence that our principles were accepted. But neither of these things happened.

It has been argued that as other African states did not adhere to their resolution there was therefore no need for Tanzania to do so. But we are responsible only for ourselves. While African states are separately sovereign, each one has to decide for itself whether it will honour its own word and whether it will support the organization we have jointly established. And because a minority of states did act in accordance with the OAU decision, the OAU itself has not been—and cannot be—written off by the rest of the world as a talking-shop from which comes only bluff and bluster. The basis for development towards African unity thus still exists, although its weaknesses have been publicly revealed.

AFRICAN SOCIALISM AND DEVELOPMENT

But it is not only by maintaining our principles in international affairs that the Government is said to have hindered economic development. Our declared aim of African socialism is also alleged to be holding up economic progress.

It is suggested that if Tanzania were to adopt a policy of capitalistic economic development our development would be much faster. In particular our progressive taxation, and our emphasis on the need for public enterprise is said to discourage private capitalists themselves, and also to result in a lack of interest in our needs on the part of international institutions.

First it is necessary to be clear on points of fact. And the truth is that we not only undertake negotiations to attract private investment into certain kinds of industry, but that we have also put on to the statute book several pieces of legislation—for example the Investment Guarantees Act—which are designed to meet the reasonable fears of those who are considering bringing their money into Tanzania from outside. And we have had some large and many small private enterprises started by foreign and local businessmen—the biggest example is the oil refinery. In the course of time these firms will be our best 'public relations officers' with outside capitalists as the safety and profitability of their investment will become obvious to the more timid capital owners.

It is probably true, however, that a taxation policy based on the principle that the wealthy should pay a much higher proportion of their income than the poor does discourage some possible investors. Obviously a balance must be maintained in this matter as in others, but it is important to understand that we want private (foreign or local) investment for a purpose, and only if it fulfils that purpose can we be expected to welcome it.

We want capital investment here so that the amount of wealth which can be produced in Tanzania is increased, and our people will therefore become better off in the future. Yet because we are now a poor nation—in that the efforts of our people do not produce very much wealth—we cannot spend much money on improving our capacity to produce in the future. In other words, we have to use most of the wealth we now produce just on feeding, clothing, and sheltering our people, and we do not have enough left to build all the factories, roads, irrigation projects and so on that we need if our efforts are to produce greater wealth in the future. If, therefore, we can get money for these things from outside the country, or from the few people inside who do have a lot of money, then later—when the investments begin to produce extra goods—we can repay the people who spent their money making these things available to us now, and still be better off ourselves. Or, if they prefer, we can pay them an interest, or a profit, on the money which they invest here, and still be better off than we would have been without the investment. But if we—as a nation—are not going to be better off in the end, then we do not want their money to be spent on that kind of investment in our country. And, equally, if they are not going to get interest on their money, or a profit out of their investment, they will not be willing to bring their money to Tanzania in the first place.

Thus we have to assess the benefits of foreign investment for both sides—because both the private or foreign investor and ourselves are involved. And to us, the benefit will take two forms: the extra wages earned by our people in the factories or on the farms, and the extra revenue earned by our Government through taxation—and thus available for public services like education, hospitals and so on. Therefore, although our taxation system has to allow a fair profit for the foreign investor (and allow him to repatriate that profit if he wishes), it also has to ensure that the people as a whole benefit from the investment and not just the owner of it.

But there is another side altogether to this question of ujamaa. In a country like ours, development depends primarily on the efforts and hard work of our own people, and on their enthusiasm and belief that they and their country will benefit from whatever they do. How could anyone expect this enthusiasm and hard work to be forthcoming if the masses see that a few individuals in the society get very rich and live in great comfort, while the majority continue apparently for ever in abject poverty? If the people do not have reason to believe that the object of their Government is the well-being of the people as a whole why should they be expected to co-operate with that Government in its activities?

In African society in particular this is very important. Traditionally we lived as families, with individuals supporting each other and helping each other on terms of equality. We recognized that each of us had a place in the community, and this place carried with it rights to whatever food and shelter was available in return for the use of whatever abilities and energies we had. The old, and the sick, or those whose crops had been destroyed by natural disasters, were not left alone in their suffering. Other people shared with them, and did so without any feeling on their side that this was 'charity' from the better off, or involved any loss of human dignity for the one who was (through no fault of his own) in need. Certainly, the good hunter, or the good farmer, was honoured in the community, and was usually given specially favoured treatment in return for his great contributions. But the community was a unit in which every individual was important, and among which the goods available were shared without too great inequality.

This attitude is, basically, what we mean by saying that traditionnally African society was a socialist society. And when we say that Tanzania is aiming at building 'African socialism' we mean that we intend to adopt the same attitude in the new circumstances of a nation state which is increasingly using modern techniques of economic production. In the larger national society, where the possibilities of high productivity are exploited, it will be more difficult to organize the fair sharing of both work and reward. It will also require institutions and a degree of understanding which were not necessary when everyone knew everyone else in the family community, and it will take time and experience before we get things working smoothly. But the purpose remains the same as in the traditional society. That is, the welfare of every individual in the context of the needs of the society of which he is a member. It was to build this kind of society that we wanted independence; to build a kind of society in which a few were very rich and the masses desperately poor would be a betrayal of the people. This would be true even if the total wealth of a different kind of society were greater, for our purpose is not the production of wealth for its own sake, or for display, or 'national prestige', but for the benefit of all the people.

If our determination to pursue this objective annoys some people who might otherwise have assisted us in our economic development, what are we supposed to do? Abandon our objective?

ECONOMIC DEVELOPMENT AS PART OF OUR OBJECTIVE

What this means is that despite our great need for economic development, it is not the only thing our people and our nation need. We do need it. We need it because only when we increase the amount of wealth we produce in Tanzania will there be any chance of the mass of our people living decent lives, free from the threat of hunger, or want of clothing, and free from ignorance, or disease. But we also need other things too. We need to live harmoniously among ourselves; we need to safeguard our society, we need to respect ourselves and deserve the respect of others. These things are equally important. 'Man does not live by bread alone'.

Thus, whether or not our Government's actions deserve the support of the people has to be considered both in the light of their effect upon economic development and in the light of their effect upon these other aspects of our social and political development. The valid question is whether or not our people have been asked to sacrifice chances of economic development unreasonably. Or whether so much emphasis has been put on non-economic factors that the efforts of our people to better their standard of living have been wasted?

The Government believes that the answer to both of these questions is 'No'. Government believes that our people recognize that the task of economic development is a long and heavy one, and that it must be shouldered at the same time as they defend their right to determine for themselves what is the right thing to do in any particular circumstance. Government understands that our people do not believe that it is better to be a wealthy slave than a poorer free man. At the same time, the Government believes that the freedom it guards, and the principles it upholds, will in the long run bring economic as well as social benefit to our people.

ECONOMIC EFFECTS OF CERTAIN POLICIES AND DECISIONS

It is impossible to consider all the actions of Government which have been inspired by our national principles and which might have had an effect, one way or another, upon development. Therefore, only major decisions, or decisions which have been a basis for considerable criticism, are discussed.

1. *The boycott of South African goods and the threat to leave the Commonwealth if South Africa remains a member.*

The boycott has cost Tanzania a certain amount of annual income from the remittances of workers who used to go to that country under previous government contracts or who made their way to South Africa.

The boycott has also meant the loss of certain markets for our exports, and has necessitated the importation of certain goods from more expensive sources. The total amount of income loss is difficult to estimate and will be partly offset by the value of the goods which Tanzanian workers have produced at home now that they no longer go to this racially dominated country. The amount of trade with South Africa was, in any case, never very great, and until the boycott received official backing in 1961, showed an annual adverse trade balance for Tanzania (then Tanganyika). The countries to which purchases and exports were transferred are mostly those with which we have a favourable balance of trade. It is thus difficult to say whether there was any real national economic loss once the necessary reorganization had been effected, but if so it would have been very slight indeed.

It must be accepted, however, that as South Africa is the most advanced industrial nation in Africa, and as transport costs from that country to Tanzania are less than those of other industrial nations, co-operation with South Africa could have brought considerable economic benefits to our country. It is in foregoing possible increases in economic development that we have made sacrifices by our policy towards South Africa.

Had the situation arisen where Tanganyika had to refuse to join the Commonwealth, however, the economic loss would have been very great, involving loss of trade preferences and a reduction in the chances of receiving British and possibly Canadian development loans and grants, etc. Fortunately this situation did not arise since South Africa was excluded from the Commonwealth.

2. *Breaking relations with Portugal.*

The refusal to have diplomatic relations with Portugal after independence or to trade with her has not caused any measurable economic effect on Tanzania. Trade with Portugal was always negligible, and even with Mozambique virtually non-existent.

Tanzania could, however, have gained something by a different policy towards Portugal. Had we co-operated it might have been possible for a united stand to have been taken at international conferences and elsewhere on matters concerned with commodity prices for things like sisal and cashew nuts. This might well have strengthened the price of these goods which are very important to our economy, and are also produced by Mozambique. We must face the fact too that with a different policy towards Portugal it might have been possible to have co-operated in the exploitation of the Ruvuma river and its valley—a project which would also certainly have attracted international support.

3. *Our support for the liberation movement of Africa.*

Although this is undoubtedly one of the factors affecting the total Western attitudes towards Tanzania, it is not such an important one as it was now that the only British colony remaining is Rhodesia. But the practical alliances between the Western countries and Portugal and South Africa mean that it remains a factor. The only measurable cost involved is Tanzania's contribution to the OAU Liberation Committee. The annual contribution is approximately £16,000. But there are immeasurable costs. If we were to change this policy we would, over time, find ourselves in more favour with Western governments.

4. *The quarrel with Germany.*

East Germany wanted Tanzania to give diplomatic recognition to her, and West Germany wanted us to ignore the existence of the German Democratic Republic and pretend there is no such administration over the Eastern part of Germany. In fact we refused recognition to the East German authorities but accepted an unofficial Consulate General from them (a formula which had already been accepted in one other African country). As a result of our decision West Germany withdrew some types of aid (unilaterally breaking a five-year air training agreement) and announced that other aid was under threat if Tanzania did not change her policies. Tanzania refused to do this and told the West Germans to withdraw all their federal government aid. This did reduce the amount of capital at the disposal of the Tanzanian Government, but its most important effect was not the withdrawal of monies already promised but the closing down of any possibility of receiving aid for the Five-Year Plan—about which discussions had been proceeding. At that time we had reason to believe that German aid would become very important for they had accepted our request for work on the development of the Kilombero valley, and whatever they had finally decided upon would have involved many millions of pounds. This prospective assistance was lost by our stand.

5. *Disputes with the USA.*

We have twice quarrelled with the US Government, once when we believed it to be involved in a plot against us, and again when two of its officials misbehaved and were asked to leave Tanzania. Both matters have since been cleared up by agreement and in neither case was any existing aid agreement affected. But the disagreements certainly induced an uncooperative coldness between us, thus suspending and then greatly slowing down further aid discussions. A comparison of American aid to Tanzania and to other African countries supports the contention that at any rate our total policies have led to a lower level of assistance than might otherwise have been granted.

6. *Disputes with the British Government.*

We have quarrelled with the British Government on a number of issues, e.g. when we refused to associate ourselves with the Commonwealih communique on Rhodesia in June 1965; when we refused to support the proposed Commonwealth Peace Mission to Vietnam on the grounds that it was neither practical nor genuine; and when we received a Chinese offer to help with the building of the railway to Zambia while still discussing the possibility of British and American help on the same project. The British failed to understand our desire to compare the advantages of different offers before turning any of them down. None of these disputes actually resulted in a loss of agreed aid but they may have adversely affected the amounts of future aid from Britain. It is worth noting, however, that up to now Tanzania has received more aid from Britain than from any other single country.

7. *Breaking diplomatic relations with Britain.*

Tanzania's action in adhering to the OAU decision on Rhodesia has meant that the £7.5 million interest-free loan which had been agreed between the two Governments but not actually signed, has now been 'frozen'. This money is therefore not available to pay for development work within the first two years of the Five-Year Plan. This 'break' will also have adversely affected any question of further aid for the later years of the Plan.

This loss or delay in assistance has implications throughout the Development Plan. For example, although most of the projects for which British aid has been expected have now been stopped certain of them had reached such an advanced stage of building or were so integrated into other parts of a project, that work had to be continued and the money found from local funds. Adopting this policy, however, meant that we may have to refuse other offers of help when these only cover import costs because the local monies which would have been available for the Tanzanian contribution are being utilized to fill the gap which was created by the failure to receive the British money.

8. *Non-alignment.*

Tanzania's obvious refusal to consider the possibility of getting subventions from foreign governments in return for a commitment to support them either in general or on particular issues of world politics, must have resulted in a failure to obtain certain monies. But the amount, and therefore the cost of non-alignment, cannot be even guessed at; a man who does not put himself up for auction cannot tell how much would have been offered if he had done so. But he would clearly have got something! And this we have foregone.

9. *Friendly relations with China.*

The carrying out of our policy to have friendly relations with any country which is willing to be friendly to us has, in relation to China, been an occasion for suggesting that Tanzania has gone communist. The visit of Chou En Lai to Tanzania and President Nyerere's visit to Peking are frequently quoted in this connection, and this widespread though false belief may have adversely affected the attitudes of certain Western countries or organizations towards us. The President's visits to America and Britain do not seem to have counteracted this effect. The effect on Eastern countries of our non-communist friendships and ideology are more difficult to assess; it would be very strange if they had no effect.

10. *The ending of racial segregation in Tanzania.*

The strong action taken to prevent racial discrimination in Tanzania and the ending of segregation in schools and hospitals, etc., has undoubtedly saved money by reducing administrative costs and enabling a more rational allocation of resources. Although a certain number of non-Africans who could not make the adjustment left the country in consequence of this policy, it has enabled us to attract good technical staff on a temporary basis from overseas, and to employ qualified non-African citizens in senior positions when necessary. In fact, the strict adherence to this principle is undoubtedly an economic advantage.

11. *The take-over of the Dar es Salaam Club.*

This was a factor in the resignation of a small number of expatriate officers and may thus have caused some dislocation in certain administrative tasks in Dar es Salaam. As against that however, this action gave the people of Dar es Salaam a meeting plce where all those who could afford Shs. 5/- a month could, regardless of their professional or political rank, meet informally and at the same time inexpensively entertain both Official and private guests. On balance it was undoubtely an economic gain.

12. *Abolishing of freehold land.*

This legislation had no national adverse effect and prevented the growth of a class of land speculators who might, in the future, have held public bodies as well as private citizens up to ransom. The later revocation of leases where development clauses had not been met did lead to misunderstandings and loss of confidence in some areas, particularly after a number of mistakes had been made in one group of revocations. It was the mistakes which had an economic cost in this case, and not the principle itself, and reorganization of this system has since been shown to have taken place to prevent this sort of occasional error occurring in the future.

The administration of this law has, in one other respect, caused loss to local government; that is when leases are revoked in accordance with the law before alternative users are available. This means that rates cease to be paid for a period until the land is re-allocated on a new development clause.

13. *Commitment of African socialism.*

The word itself may have frightened off certain specially sensitive private investors, but most who are really seriously considering investment look at the investment guarantees legislation and the institutions which have been established to help them. There is no evidence of what this commitment to human equality really costs in the way of outside private investment, but it may have discouraged some wealthy businessmen and may have also affected the interest of institutions like the World Bank which put a heavy priority on private as distinct from public investment.

14. *The democratic one-party state.*

There is no evidence that our decision to become a one-party state adversely affected economic assistance from outside Tanzania. On the other hand, the world publicity which was given to the Tanzanian elections and the evidence of national stability which was then apparent have undoubtedly attracted favourable attention from both foreign governments and those foreign investors who are interested in long-term developments rather than the 'get rich quick' type of economic activity. It is also true that the participation by the people in their own Government and a new realization that the Republic's concern is the well-being of the ordinary citizen, has given new impetus to the economic activities of our own citizens.

22

The Dilemma of the Pan-Africanist

President Kaunda of Zambia became the first Chancellor of the University of Zambia when it was inaugurated on 13 July 1966. As Chancellor of the University of East Africa, President Nyerere was invited to attend the ceremony and to give an address to the Congregation. He used this opportunity to discuss the possible conflict between African nationalism and Pan-Africanism.

It is a very great pleasure, and also a privilege, for me to be here today at a ceremony which marks the transformation of one more of Africa's dreams into an African reality. It is an occasion for rejoicing; it is an occasion on which thanks should be tendered to those whose hard work has made the reality possible; and it is an occasion for rededicating ourselves to other dreams—other visions.

Your Excellencies, we have achieved many things in Africa in recent years, and can look back with some pride at the distance we have travelled. But we are a long way from achieving the thing we originally set out to achieve, and I believe there is a danger that we might now voluntarily surrender our greatest dream of all.

For it was as Africans that we dreamed of freedom: and we thought of it for Africa. Our real ambition was Africa freedom an African government. The fact that we fought area by area was merely a tactical necessity. We organized ourselves into the Convention People's Party, the Tanganyika African National Union, the United National Independence Party, and so on, simply because each local colonial government had to be dealt with separately.

The question we now have to answer is whether Africa shall maintain this internal separation as we defeat colonialism, or whether our earlier proud boast—'I am an African'—shall become a reality. It is not a reality now. For the truth is that there are now 36 different

nationalities in free Africa, one for each of the 36 independent states
—to say nothing of the areas still under colonial or alien domination.
Each state is separate from the others; each is a sovereign entity.
And this means that each state has a government which is responsible to the people of its own area—and to them only; it must work
for their particular well-being or invite chaos within its territory.

Can the vision of Pan-Africanism survive these realities? Can
African unity be built on this foundation of existing and growing
nationalism?

I do not believe the answer is easy. Indeed I believe that a real
dilemma faces the Pan-Africanist. On the one hand is the fact that
Pan-Africanism demands an African consciousness and an African
loyalty; on the other hand is the fact that each Pan-Africanist must
also concern himself with the freedom and development of one of
the nations of Africa. These things can conflict. Let us be honest
and admit that they have already conflicted.

In one sense, of course, the development of part of Africa can
only help Africa as a whole. The establishment of a University
College in Dar es Salaam, and of a University in Lusaka, means that
Africa has two extra centres of higher education for its 250 million
people. Every extra hospital means more health facilities for Africa;
every extra road, railway or telephone line, means that Africa is
pulled closer together. And who can doubt but that the railway
from Zambia to Tanzania, which we are determined to build, will
serve African unity, as well as being to the direct interest of our
two countries?

Unfortunately, however, that is not the whole story. Schools
and universities are part of an educational system—a national educational system. They promote, and the *must* promote, a national
outlook among the students. Lessons are given on the Government,
the geography, and the history, of Tanzania, or of Zambia. Loyalty
to the national constitution, to the elected leaders, to the symbols
of nationhood—all these things are encouraged by every device.

This is not only inevitable; it is also right. None of the nation
states of Africa are 'natural' units. Our present boundaries are—as
has been said many times—the result of European decisions at the
time of the scramble for Africa. They are senseless; they cut across
ethnic groups, often disregard natural physical divisions, and result
in many different language groups being encompassed within a

state. If the present states are not to disintegrate it is essential that deliberate steps be taken to foster a feeling of nationhood. Otherwise our present multitude of small countries—almost all of us too small to sustain a self-sufficient modern economy—could break up into even smaller units—perhaps based on tribalism. Then a further period of foreign domination would be inevitable. Our recent struggles would be wasted.

Let me repeat; in order to avoid internal conflict and further disunity each nation state is forced to promote its own nationhood. This does not only involve teaching a loyalty to a particular unit, and a particular flag, although that is serious enough. It also involves deliberately organizing one part of Africa economically, socially, and constitutionally, to serve the overall interests of the people of that part of Africa, and (in case of conflict) not the interests either of another part, or of Africa as a whole.

Thus, each state of Africa devises for itself a constitution and a political structure which is most appropriate to its own history and its own problems. In Tanzania for example, the overwhelming support for our nationalist movement, and the complete absence of a rival to it, meant that from the beginning of independence we had in effect a one-party state. But the continued existence of a political structure which assumed a two-party state meant that we were unable to harness the Party organization, and the enthusiasm of our people, for the new tasks of fighting poverty. There was also some danger that the Party leaders might get out of touch with the people they led because they were able to shelter their own personal shortcomings under the umbrella of the Party. So we worked out a new constitution which acknowledged the sole existence of one Party, and within that framework ensured the people's democratic control of their Government. It is a new arrangement, and so far it seems to be working well. But—and this is my point—it has marked a further differentiation between the political organization of Tanzania and that of other parts of Africa, including that of our neighbours. And the more the people of the United Republic become involved in this system, and the more the peoples of other African nations become involved in the systems they work out for themselves, the greater becomes the division among us.

In economics too, the same thing applies. Each national government of Africa has to work for the development of its own country, the expansion of its own revenues. It must do this. It cannot be content with the development of Central Africa, or of East Africa; it must work for the development of Zambia, or of Tanzania. In certain circumstances the result is not only a failure to grow together; it can be reduction in unity. For example, each East African country is now moving over to its own currency instead of maintaining one common currency. In the absence of a Federal Government this was necessary if each of the governments was to meet its responsibilities to the people who elected it. But it is undoubtedly a move towards nationalism and away from African super-nationalism. Or again, each African government has to work for domestic industrialization; it can only agree to a common super-national industry being sited in another country if there is a clear and obvious compensating advantage in its own favour in another industry, or in some other developmental factor.

Our nationalisms may compete with one another and grow away from one another in international matters too. All of the states of Africa need to attract capital from outside, and all of us wish to sell more of our goods to countries abroad. So we 36 little states each spend money to send our delegations to the wealthy countries, and our representatives to trade talks. Then each one of these national representatives is forced to prove why investment should be made in his country rather than in another, and forced to offer some advantages to the wealthy country if it will buy his goods rather than those emanating from another part of Africa. And the result? Not only worse terms for each of us in relation to aid or trade, but also a kind of fear of each other—a suspicion that the neighbouring country will take advantage of any weakness we have for its own benefit. And my point is that this neighbouring country will do that; it has little choice in the matter. However much it may sympathize with our difficulty, only in rare cases will this sense of 'oneness' be able to transcend the hard necessities of its own economic need.

All that I have been saying so far amounts to this: the present organization of Africa into nation states means inevitably that Africa drifts apart unless definite and deliberate counteracting steps are taken. In order to fulfil its responsibilities to the people it has led to freedom, each nationalist government must develop its own economy, its own organizations and institutions, and its own dominant nationalism. This is true however devoted to the cause of African unity the different national leaders may be. For while it is certainly true that in the long run the whole of Africa, and all its peoples, would be best served by unity, it is equally true, as Lord Keynes is reported to have said, that 'in the long run we are all dead'. The willingness of the people of Africa to make sacrifices for the future is without question; the development plans of our different nations prove this. But the people of this continent have been suffering the effects of poverty too long. They need to see some immediate attack being made on that poverty. They could not, and would not, agree to stagnation or regression while we pursue the goal of unity.

And the truth is that as each of us develops his own state we raise more and more barriers between ourselves. We entrench differences which we have inherited from the colonial period, and develop new ones. Most of all, we develop a national pride which could easily be inimical to the development of a pride in Africa. This is the dilemma of the Pan-Africanist in Africa now. For although national pride does not automatically preclude the development of pride in Africa, it is very easily twisted to have that effect. And certainly it will be deliberately bolstered by those who are anxious to keep Africa weak by her division, or those anxious to keep Africa divided because they would rather be important people in a small state than less important people in a bigger one. Kenyans and Zambians will be told—indeed, are already being told!—that Tanzania is communist and under Chinese control, or that it is so weak that it is the unwilling and unwitting base for Chinese subversion. Tanzanians, on the other hand, are told that Kenya is under American control, and Zambia hostile to it because of its policy on Rhodesia. And so on. Everything will be done and said which can sow suspicion and disunity between us until finally our people, and our leaders, say—'Let us carry on alone, let us forget this mirage of unity and freedom for the whole of Africa'. And then, in 150 years' time, Africa will be where Latin America is now, instead of having the strength and economic well-being which is enjoyed by the United States of America.

But there is another factor which is inimical to an advance to Pan-Africanism through, and after, the development of our separate nationalisms. For good reasons or bad, some African countries are, and will be, wealthier and more powerful than others. It may be the accident of minerals existing in one place and not another, it may be a history of peaceful development in one country and internal divisions and difficulties in another. It may simply be that some of our African states are of a size to become economically viable, while others will never sustain more than a low level of existence. But the net result will be that one state will be more successful than another. And then who makes the move towards unity? If it is the bigger and wealthier, there will be talk of a new imperialism, an attempt to 'take over' the small state. If it is the small nation, there will be talk of betrayal and lack of patriotism. Which of those leaders will then be able to overcome his inhibitions enough even to mention the idea of union? Which of them could risk rebuff? The more genuine their separate desire for real unity on the basis of human equality, the more difficult it is for either of them to make the move.

Yet if to develop our separate nations is to invite the slow dying of our dream of unity, what is the alternative?

Clearly we must first accept the facts which I have outlined. It is no part of transforming dream into reality to pretend that things are not what they are. Instead we must use our present situation to serve us and achieve our purposes. We must face up to the dangers which exist, and overcome them by one means or another.

It is not impossible to achieve African unity through nationalism, just as it was not impossible for various tribal associations or tribally based parties to merge themselves into one nationalist movement. It is difficult, but it can be done if the determination is there. The first thing for Africa, therefore, is to determine that it shall be done. But platitudes are not enough; signatures to the Charter of the Organization of African Unity are not enough. Both these things help, because they maintain the atmosphere and the institutions of unity. But they must be combined with a realization that unity will be difficult to achieve, and difficult to maintain, and that it will demand sacrifices both from nations and from individuals. To talk of unity as though it would be a panacea of all ills, is to walk naked into a den of hungry lions. In its early stages unity brings difficulties—probably more than it disposes of. It is in the longer term, after fifteen or twenty years, that its overwhelming benefits can begin to be felt. Determination that unity shall come must start with a psychological acceptance of its requirements. The African nations, and particularly the African leaders, must be loyal to each other. It is inevitable that some leaders will have a personal liking and admiration for particular other leaders; it is equally inevitable that they will dislike, and perhaps disapprove of others. I do not imagine that all my Regional Commissioners in Tanzania like and admire each other—I hope they do, but I would not guarantee it! But however much they may argue in private, they do not attack each other in public. They may think a particular individual has invited trouble, but if it comes they do not rejoice. They rally round to try and minimize the effect of that trouble on the nation. And African leaders can do likewise for Africa. It is more difficult in that we do not have one common superior body, but it can still be done.

This does not mean that there could be, or indeed that there should be, identical internal or external policies for all African states. While we are separate we can take account of different circumstances in different parts of Africa. Take, for example, differences which exist between some of the policies of Tanzania and Zambia. Both our Governments are concerned to secure control of the national economy and to bend it to serve the masses. But the techniques which are appropriate in Tanzania—where we start almost from scratch, with no inherited industry or mining—would not be right for Zambia, which has to maintain its copper output and use the industry in the transformation of the economy.

Then there is also the question of Rhodesia, and the fact that Tanzania, but not Zambia, has broken diplomatic relations with Britain in the course of this dispute. Naturally, some of our opponents have tried to suggest that this reveals deep-seated differences between the TANU and the UNIP Governments; such a belief by either of us would damage Africa's cause to an incalculable extent. But it is not true, and fortunately both of us know that it is not true. Both of our Governments have one purpose and are equally dedicated to it. That purpose is the ending of the illegal Smith regime and its replacement by majority rule and then independence for Zimbabwe.

But Zambia is a landlocked country with an inherited pattern of trade and communications which made it impossible for her immediately to impose a complete boycott of Rhodesian goods. Tanzania has ports, communications with the north, and never in fact had much trade with Rhodesia. Do such different conditions call for the same reactions to events in Southern Rhodesia? It would be absurd either for Zambia to act as Tanzania does, or for Tanzania to act automatically as Zambia does. what must happen instead is that our two countries must work together, in the closest co-operation and understanding. And in particular Tanzania has a responsibility to do whatever is humanly possible to help Zambia free itself from these inherited chains to the South. Perhaps I could use this opportunity to say this is being done, and will be done, with the whole-hearted support of the whole Tanzania people.

But it is not enough for African states to co-operate in dealing with particular problems. We must deliberately move to unity. To the fullest extent possible we must co-operate in our economic development, our trade, and our economic institutions. We must do this, despite our separate sovereignties, although we have to recognize that there is a limit to the possibilities of economic integration without political union. When that point comes, then we shall either have to stand still—and thus damage our real hopes for Africa—or we shall have to take the plunge into a merger of our international sovereignties.

In some parts of Africa political union will be possible even before there has been great economic integration. It is my firm belief that African states should make such opportunities, or seize them whenever they occur of themselves. The difficulties will remain; Acts of Union do not undo decades or centuries of administrative and political separation. But a government which is responsible to the whole area can deal with difficulties, and elements of separatism, with fairness to all at the same time as it develops new unifying factors. The differences will not disappear if they are left alone; as I have said—they will grow. Thus, for example, it is true that the two component parts of the United Republic of Tanzania are not yet fully integrated. But—and this is the point—there is no question about their being much more integrated than they would have been had two separate Governments merely tried to co-operate. Neither is there any doubt about the benefit which all our people are already feeling as a result of this Union. Certainly no one in Tanzania has any doubts upon this subject. We are now one whole; and as we grow we are growing together.

Political union of neighbours is not, however, always an immediate or possible answer. And economic co-operation is often limited in the short term by lack of communications or other factors. Yet we can still decide whether to go forward to unity or backward to separation. For example, it is entirely Africa's decision whether or not there shall be internal African national disputes. We, the separate states, may be misled about events elsewhere, or we may feel provoked. But it is we who decide what to do in such circumstances. It is Africa which will decide whether to make unclear boundaries an occasion of disunity, or whether they will be settled by conciliation or by law. It is Africa which will decide whether to abandon the only possible base for national boundaries—that is the colonial boundaries—and allow itself to become the plaything of international politics. And in the same way Africa itself can, if it wishes, choose to follow a policy of 'good neighbourliness', and show in actions that the talk of African unity is meaningful.

Talk of co-operation between states, and of good neighbourliness, with resort to courts or arbitration in case of dispute, does not sound very exciting. The heart leaps at the words 'Union Government', and not at these other things which demand patience, self-discipline, and dogged hard work. But if the one thing is impossible —and it is impossible while all African states are unready to surrender their sovereignty to a new body—then this is the only way in which we can move forward instead of backward. It was in recognition of these facts that the Organization of African Unity in 1963 stated its first purpose to be 'to promote the unity and solidarity of the African States'. This was a realistic acceptance of both the facts and the goal. But we must recognize that the statement will not of itself bring the result we need. Only if the OAU is deliberately supported, and strengthened, and only if the spirit of its Charter is honoured in positive action will we begin the long road forward.

And it may be a long road; how long will be settled by our courage and determination. Certainly in the last few years there have been some important advances towards greater co-operation in Africa. But there have also been many setbacks—some of which threaten the very existence of the OAU. And the saddest, and most dangerous of all, is the new tendency to treat the OAU, and all talk of Pan-Africanism, as matters of form—motions which have to be gone through while the serious business of building up states is continued. This would be fatal to Africa. For only through unity will Africa be able to achieve its potential and fulfil its proper destiny.

Mr. Chancellor, those who would like to advocate complete concentration on national interests, and those who would demand the sacrifice of all national interests to the cause of African freedom and unity, both have an easy road to tread. The one can appeal to 'realism' and 'pragmatism', and can appear to be devoted to the practical interests of the people. The other can appeal to the hearts of men, and can appear courageous, self-sacrificing, and revolutionary. But both would lead Africa to disaster—the one to early stagnation and alien economic domination, and the other to chaos and disintegration of the units already existing. No; we must undertake a new and hard way forward and upward. We must avoid the road which goes round the mountain range and leads into the swamp lands; we must avoid also the excitement of the climb up the rockface, for that cannot be negotiated with the load we must carry. Instead, our task is to cut a road up the side of the mountain to the highlands, and cut it gently enough for all our people to travel, even if with difficulty and help over the steep parts. In more realistic language—perhaps more appropriate to the task ahead—we must keep in front of us at all times the goal of unity; we must recognize the danger that without positive action we shall be diverted from it; and we must take that positive action at every possible point. For African unity does not have to be a dream; it can be a vision which inspires us. Whether that is so depends upon us.

Mr. Chancellor, I have not spoken of this dilemma facing the Pan-Africanist without regard to the occasion. I have deliberately chosen this subject because I believe that the members of this university, and of other universities in Africa, have a responsibility in this matter. We present leaders of Africa are grappling with serious and urgent problems within our own states; and we have to deal with dangers from outside. The time available to us for serious thinking about the way forward to Pan-Africanism is limited in the extreme—and when we do take steps in this direction we are always assailed for 'wasting money on conferences', or being 'unrealistic' in our determination to build roads or railways to link our nations. Who is to keep us active in the struggle to convert nationalism to Pan-Africanism if it is not the staffs and students of our universities? Who is it who will have the time and ability to think out the practical problems of achieving this goal of unification if it is not those who have an opportunity to think and learn without direct responsibility for day-to-day affairs?

And cannot the universities themselves move in this direction? Each of them has to serve the needs of its own nation, its own area. But has it not also to serve Africa? Why cannot we exchange students—have Tanzanians getting their degrees in Zambia as Zambians get theirs in Tanzania? Why cannot we share expertise on particular subjects, and perhaps share certain services? Why cannot we do other things which link our intellectual life together indissolubly? These are not things only for Governments to work out. Let the universities put proposals before our Governments and then demand from us politicians a reasoned answer on the basis of African unity if we do not agree!

Mr. Chancellor, I am encouraging trouble for you in another of your capacities! I am urging your new university to be active in this field, just as I want the University College of Dar es Salaam to be active. But I do this with confidence. For I know that you, as much as I myself, want African unity. And I know that you and I, and Zambia and Tanzania, have now bound ourselves together with such bonds that in your country I can speak as I would speak in my own, just as you can say anything in Tanzania which you would say in Zambia.

It is therefore with great feeling, and great sincerity, that I congratulate you, President Kaunda, on your election as Chancellor, and also congratulate the University of Zambia on the Chancellor it has elected. May the University of Zambia go forward under your leadership to great success in the service of this country and of Africa.

23

Africa must not fight Africa

When President Osman of Somalia visited Tanzania in December 1965, a meeting was arranged for him with President Kenyatta in Arusha. Unfortunately it did not prove possible to settle the differences which existed between the two countries, and despite the representation of both Kenya and Somalia at the Neighbourliness Conference in March 1966, tension still existed when President Nyerere paid his return state visit to Somalia in August 1966.

At a banquet in the capital, Mogadishu, on 23 August 1966, President Nyerere made a further appeal for the peaceful settlement of disputes in Africa.

... Tanzania and Somalia are both poor states, both have special problems of their own, and particular political attitudes and organizations. The only reason why you, Mr. President, came to Tanzania last year, and why I have accepted your kind invitation this year, is because we are all Africans, near neighbours, and friends. There is no other reason. And there does not have to be another reason! We exchange these visits because we have woken up to the fact that each part of Africa is involved in the welfare of every other part—that Africa is ONE.

We have not yet succeeded in organizing ourselves on that basis; we still exist as separate sovereign states. But in my experience the peoples of this continent still think of themselves as 'Africans' before they call themselves citizens of this country or that. And this is our greatest hope for the future. Because the truth is that every part of Africa needs Africa as a whole, and Africa as a whole needs every small part of the continent.

We need each other. Each of our separate countries could be a small plaything of the big and powerful nations of the world.

Together we are too big for even the giants to pick up and use. Separately we are shaken by political or economic disasters even when they happen on the other side of the continent; together we could pool our resources to maintain stability and achieve progress at the same time.

Already the African states have begun this work of co-operating together, of acting jointly. It is the disputes between African states which hit the headlines, and it is the quarrels which we ourselves emphasize. But we make a mistake in encouraging this kind of publicity. For the truth is that what really matters to the people of this continent, and to their children, is the progress we make in developing Africa, and maintaining its freedom against outside aggression or infiltration. And to make real progress in this we have to act together. We have no salvation in disunity.

We have all heard the story of the old man who demonstrated to his sons the strength of unity and the weakness of separation by showing that a bundle of sticks *tied together* could not be broken, while separately they could be broken with ease. The states of Africa must never forget the lesson of that story.

Separately each of our nations can lose the reality of its freedom, even if it preserves the trappings of independence—like our flags, our Parliaments, our national anthems and our Ministers. Only if we agree to stand together shall we all be safe and make progress to real greatness. The weakness of Africa is a constant invitation and a constant encouragement to the exploiters of Africa to suck Africa with impunity. Only a strong Africa can stop this. But there can be no strong Africa and no salvation for Africa except in unity.

Mr. President, your Government—like that of Tanzania—has shown by its membership of the Organization of African Unity that it understands the truth of the saying 'unity is strength'. Your Government is associated with that of other states in the attempt to develop a common economic policy for the whole of East and Central Africa. Your Government participated in the inter-Governmental meeting in Nairobi last April. And yet it may be said by some people in Somalia, and by some people in Tanzania, or elsewhere in Africa, that these meetings are no good because the problems we each feel are not solved.

I sometimes wonder whether those who make statements like this are really concerned about the problems, or whether instead they are not really becoming the playthings of non-African forces. For what is the alternative to continued meetings, talks and discussion among African states? How else shall we ever get the unity we all know is necessary but have as yet failed to attain? What is the alternative to patient hard work, and to compromise where two valid principles conflict?

African states are all in Africa. We cannot move ourselves to the moon in order to get away from our neighbours! We have therefore to live together, and somehow we have to find a way of living together. Disputes can only be settled round a table, either bilaterally between the disputing states, or with the help of friends. There is no other way now. In the past our different tribes and clans used to fight over territory or over cattle. I well remember my own father telling me of the battles my tribal people had with our tribal neighbours. Usually these wars were not very serious; a few young men on both sides were killed and cattle stolen or recovered. Indeed, from the way the stories are told now they even sound rather like some excitement in a hard life—although we should remember that they still caused much misery and hardship.

But wars today are not like that. They mean widespread misery, and complete destruction of livelihood for all the peoples involved. And in any case, how would we fight them? None of the free states of Africa can manufacture its own guns, its own ammunition, its own aircraft. If we enter into wars with one another we have no alternative but to buy these things from foreign countries, or allow them to be given to us. And of course we can get such gifts. In my experience the one form of foreign aid which is easy to get from big powers is arms and military training!

But we must all understand why the big powers are interested in supplying weapons, and why they try to persuade each of us that our neighbour has a big army which is threatening us. It is because they welcome the prospect of one part of Africa fighting another part. They know that the net result can only be the weakening of Africa as each nation spends its resources buying arms instead of buying machinery for new factories, or uses the arms it has been given in order to destroy the progress made in another part of the continent.

In fact, the real danger in Africa now is not that our enemies will attack us directly; if that happens to any single state we shall surely all rally round in support. The danger is that the undercover enemies of our continent will intrigue in our separate capitals, and encourage our quarrels until we attack each other. For this purpose they will flatter our national pride, and persuade each of us how evil our particular neighbour is, and how willing they are to help us defend ourselves.

And against whom will these people who call themselves our friends be 'helping us'? Against our brothers!

Really, if Africa once falls into this trap we shall have to call peace conferences, or disarmament conferences, instead of an OAU meeting! Because we are poor and our only strength is in unity we shall then look even more silly than those powers which now spend thousands of millions of their currency on armaments, and a few thousands on talking together on how they can stop doing it!

Of course we in Africa cannot do without arms altogether. Internally each of our states needs a police force with power to uphold law and order. And many of our citizens do need weapons to defend themselves against attacks from wild animals. It is also true, unfortunately, that for Africa as a whole the possibility of attack from the remaining colonial territories in our continent cannot be completely ruled out. But our real security and freedom does not depend on large national armies. It depends on economic progress, on our unity in Africa, and on our united diplomacy. And for these things we need friendship and good neighbourliness as a prelude to united action and ultimate unity.

For let us make no mistake. Africa is not really as weak in relation to the rest of the world as it sometimes appears. It is weak only while our different states allow themselves to be separated from one another. Can anyone really believe that a united African stand on Rhodesia would have had no effect on the British Government and the world? True, even as a united force it may not have been easy for Africa to undertake the military operation which is probably the quickest and still the least painful way of dealing with the Smith regime. But 35 complete diplomatic staffs returning on one day to London could not have failed to wake Britain up to the enormity of her lethargy at this time. She would have been forced to realize Africa's anger at her betrayal of the principles she claims to defend. She would have been forced to act or to admit to the world that she was bankrupt of ideas, power, and will.

But the willingness of Africa to be divided, and the failure of Africa to honour her own resolutions on different subjects, these things are damaging Africa now, and threatening our whole future. We are weakening ourselves because we are unwilling to use our united strength, or to face up to the fact that unity and united action is not, and will not be, always comfortable for individual states. For it means that all of us will be called upon at different times to sacrifice something for the common good in return for the benefit we receive from unity.

Yet I believe the people of Africa are ready for this. In our traditional societies each individual accepted that he could not do exactly what he wanted when he wanted, but that instead he had a loyalty to other members of his community. Who is it then who dares to say that the people of Africa—whether of Somalia, Tanzania, or elsewhere—are not now willing to sacrifice immediate satisfaction for the good of our whole continent? I do not believe our peoples are so stupid that despite everything which has happened they cannot now see beyond their clans, their tribes, or their nations. For we have all of us broken down the old boundaries of family feeling, and extended them to encompass our nations. And yet our new nation states are not the proper boundaries of this extended brotherhood. When you travel in an aeroplane you cannot tell where one African nation ends and another begins; you can only distinguish Africa as a whole, with its rivers, its deserts, its forests, mountains and plains. Africa is one. You and I are really citizens of Africa. We think of ourselves as Africans and the rest of the world thinks of us as Africans before it thinks of us as Somalis or Tanzanians. Our national divisions must therefore be taken for what they are—means of administration. We must not allow them to divide Africa. For in such division comes weakness and then destruction for all of us.

Let us go forward together; let each individual citizen and each leader decide that we will play our part in achieving the unity of Africa. Let us then together enforce our claims to our rightful place in the world as a free and proud people. Mr. President, I believe that Africa can do this, and that our present difficulties are only a challenge which we can, and—God willing—which we will overcome.

24

The Power of Teachers

On 27 *August* 1966, *President Nyerere opened the extensions to the Morogoro Teachers' College,* 120 *miles from Dar es Salaam. While doing so, he paid tribute to the work of voluntary agencies, and then went on to speak of the placing of power in society.*

. . . As it is, we can see around us almost five million shillings—this is what it looks like! And the largest amount of this was contributed, or will be contributed, by the taxpayers of Tanzania. For although some of the three and a half million shillings paid by the Tanzanian Government has come out of past taxation, a large part of it has come from a loan—which will have to be repaid out of future taxation. It is as well to remind ourselves of this, ready for the next time someone asks what is happening to the taxes he is paying!

But in this case Tanzania has received very valuable gifts from abroad to supplement our efforts, and I want to use this opportunity to express our appreciation to the donors. The people of the Federal Republic of Germany have contributed Shs. 1,160,000/- through Misereor to the extension of this college. That is a large gift. But it is not the only one. The people of Austria have sent us Shs. 80,000/-, and a teachers' organization in Holland has given us another Shs. 60,000/-. On behalf of Tanzania I wish to say thank you for these gifts.

Last, but by no means least, there has been the contribution made by the voluntary organization which runs this college on behalf of Government. Every time the Government has paid the money for the salaries of those who teach and work here, a large proportion of the monies due to the Holy Ghost Fathers has been used to expand and improve the college. These individuals, and the society to which they belong, are thus serving us in two ways; first, by teaching and working here, and secondly by giving the money that they have earned back to the taxpayers of Tanzania. It seems to me that this is an appropriate occasion for me to pay tribute to the men and women—here and elsewhere in the country—who express service to God by giving service to our people.

It is of course true that the Holy Ghost Fathers here, and other such workers elsewhere, have come to our country as missionaries for the Christian religion. It is because they are members of particular religious orders that they devote their lives to teaching our children or healing our sick, and their wages to our service. But to us, in independent Tanzania, there is something even more important than that. The voluntary agencies have now accepted that this service is, and must be, the service required by Tanzania.

The days when our people chose between accepting the Christian religion or remaining uneducated have now gone. I am convinced that this is a good thing both for the nation and for the different churches. Serving the needy because they are needy, regardless of race, tribe or religion, can do nothing but good. This attitude may be termed secular, but it is by no means irreligious. All it means is that in our society Muslims, pagans, Hindus, Protestants, and Catholics, all have an equal chance to enter such institutions as this Teachers' College, and that none of them need fear that an attempt will be made to seduce them from their own beliefs. The Morogoro Teachers' College, as much as the Dar es Salaam Teachers' College, is now open to all our educationally qualified citizens regardless of their religion. It is part of our nationally integrated education system.

In saying these things, Mr. Principal, I have said nothing new. I am simply reminding our people of an existing state of affairs—as I know you wished me to do. For the unfortunate truth is that sometimes old ideas do not change as rapidly as the reality changes, and it is important that all of our citizens should realize the effect of our integrated educational system. It was not simply integration of the races—the end of separate racial school systems. It was also the end of rigid religious separation. Now all our citizens can receive their education together under conditions of mutual respect.

Let me now turn to a different subject. For what I really want to talk about today is the *power* which teachers have. We hear a great deal about their responsibility, the important job they are doing, and so on; indeed, I have myself said not a few words on this subject! But I have been wondering why it is that, in the face of that importance, so few of our young men and women really *want* to be teachers. I am not sure, for instance, how many of the students sitting in front of me today did apply for teacher training as their first choice. I would be pleasantly surprised if they are a majority. I have also been wondering why the other side of the coin is true—why, in other words, large numbers of our people regard a man or woman who has entered Government service in the clerical or executive service as having achieved more than one who has entered teaching. For this attitude does exist, and I think it accounts for a large amount of the reluctance of our young people to put teaching as their first choice of career.

It seems to me that an honest answer would express the idea that the civil servant is considered to be more important in terms of power. Up to a certain point it is a civil servant who tells a householder that he may, or may not, build at a particular place. It is the civil servant—again, up to a point—who notifies a parent that his child has, or has not, gained admission to a particular school or college. And so on. The extent to which these civil servants are merely implementing the law, or carrying out the instructions of their Minister, is not obvious to ordinary people. The civil servants appear to be all-powerful—and it is sometimes assumed they are. And the civil servant himself, who knows the extent to which he is governed by the law, by political instructions, or by the sheer bureaucracy of Government, is not always able to explain the limitations of his own position. Indeed—being human—he often does not want to! After all, we all like to have our importance acknowledged by other people, and there are few men or women who are not flattered by being told that they are very powerful.

The same things are not said about teachers, and cannot be said. They do not make rules for society, nor do they act as the spokesmen for those who do. They do not decide who shall have this opportunity, or be denied that. And so it is assumed they are useful but not powerful, important but not worth flattering. And the teachers themselves accept this judgement upon their position, and either become discontented because they feel capable of exercising power, or aggressive and uncooperative as a reaction to being—as they think—denied power.

It is my contention that this whole attitude towards teachers, and by teachers, is based on one of the biggest fallacies of our society.

Our nation—any nation—is as great, as good, as fine a place to live in, and as progressive, as its citizens make it. Its leadership may be good, bad, or indifferent, but if the people are awake and aware of themselves it will not for long be completely unrepresentative of the attitudes in the society. And the truth is that it is teachers more than any other single group of people who determine these attitudes, and who shape the ideas and aspirations of the nation. This is *power* in its reality—much more so than the task of saying 'yes' or 'no' about building a house or getting a licence.

When a child first comes to school at the age of six or seven, it has already developed some character traits, and it has absorbed some ideas through life in the family. But it is usually approaching for the first time all the things which are connected with the community outside the family. Its ideas of what is 'good' and what is 'bad' in non-family situations are mainly unformed. Its mind is still very flexible and can be turned in any one of many different directions. These things are true whether the child is naturally very intelligent or rather dull. In all cases the child is like a young tree which can have its growth stunted and twisted, or which can be fed until it grows beyond its unassisted height, or whose branches can be pruned and trained so that the maximum fruit is obtained at maturity. And the people who have the opportunity to shape these infants—who have that power—are the teachers in our schools.

I do not think I need to explain this point at length. Those of us who left school many years ago have forgotten many of the facts we learned there. But we are what we are in large part because of the attitudes and the ideas we absorbed from our teachers. Our values in life were developed when we were young; the way we regard our fellows, the way we react to events, the things we believe to be right and wrong—all these things have developed from our childhood experiences at home and at school.

Obviously the home environment and the parents' attitudes are very important indeed. They must not be underestimated. But until now we have been inclined to underestimate the importance of school life instead. We have thought of the teachers as imparting knowledge—of arithmetic, reading, writing, and so on. And of course they do, and it is vital. But it is not the only thing or the most important thing which the child learns from the teachers. *What* the teacher presents to the class is important; that is why Government is doing so much work on the curriculum and school syllabuses. But more important still is the question of *how* the teacher teaches.

In this I do not mean simply the techniques of transferring information, although these can encourage or stunt the ability of the child to learn skills. I mean much more than that.

When a teacher comes into a class tired, or looking tired, dispirited and without any enthusiasm for work; when the teacher demands that every bit of physical labour is done by the children while he watches; or when the teacher acts as if every pupil were a nuisance, a dullard; in such cases the children will develop the idea that work is something to be avoided, that learning is simply something which one gets through, and that the way to use authority is to get other people to work for you. The teacher will have encouraged the young minds to develop those ideas simply by the manner in which he has approached his task. Conversely, a bright teacher who works with enthusiasm—and with his pupils, who encourages the children to help each other, who explains why he is doing certain things and why certain rules exist—that teacher will be forming quite different (and very much more constructive) attitudes in the minds of his pupils.

The same thing is true of the teacher's behaviour both inside and outside the classroom. If the teacher fawns on visiting officials, and then treats a poor farmer as though he is dirt, the children will grow up believing that is the proper way to behave in our developing nation. It does not matter what the teacher says in civics classes or elsewhere; they will learn from what he does. But the man who treats everyone with respect, who discusses his position clearly, rationally, and courteously with everyone whatever their position— that teacher is inculcating a spirit of equality, of friendship, and of mutual respect. And he is teaching by being—which is the most effective teaching technique existing!

In 1962, Mr. Principal, I wrote a pamphlet called 'Ujamaa'. And its first sentence began, 'Socialism, like Democracy, is an attitude of mind'. I still believe that to be true. Rules and regulations are necessary in any society, but the real basis of a society of free individuals is the attitude of mind of the individuals who form that free society. And every knowledgeable person now agrees that 'attitudes of mind' are shaped very largely when a person is very young. They *can* alter later, but it is hard, and the early character-forming is usually decisive. The fact is, therefore, that those who have the responsibility to work with the young have a *power* which is second to none in relation to the future of our society. That power is shared by two groups—parents and teachers.

This is what I meant when I said earlier that the assumpton that teachers are not powerful is one of the biggest fallacies of our society For teachers can make or ruin our society. As a group they have a power which is second to none. It is not the power of a man with a gun; it is not a power which can be seen by the fool. But it is the power to decide whether Service or Self shall be the dominant motive in the Tanzania of 1990 and thereafter.

For the fact is that we, the present adults, have a mixed heritage, and it is we more than any other generation who must make this choice. From our traditional African society we inherit concepts of equality, democracy, and socialism as well as economic backwardness. From the colonial period we inherit concepts of arrogant individual-ism and competition as well as knowledge about technical progress. It is our teachers who have the real power to determine whether Tanzania will succeed in modernizing the economy without losing the attitudes which allowed every human being to maintain his self-respect, and earn the respect of his fellows while working in harmony with them. It is they, the teachers now at work and now going through Training College, who are shaping what Tanzania will become, much more than we who pass laws, make rules, and make speeches!

Let me conclude with a two-line quotation which expresses this idea better than I can. It comes from Mark Twain, who said in 1900:

'Soap and Education are not as sudden as massacre, but they are more deadly in the long run.'

Mr. Principal, students of this college, the power of teachers is not the less because it is usually unacknowledged, On behalf of us all, I ask you to use it for good.

25

Foreign Exchange Reserves

On 9 December 1966, President Nyerere laid the foundation stone for the Bank of Tanzania building in Dar es Salaam. After referring to the functions of the Bank and the successful launching of Tanzania's currency he went on to refer to the need to conserve foreign exchange.

... There is one further point I would like to make before I carry out my symbolic contribution to the erection of the Bank building. I want to look a little into the future, for we politicians are often accused of dealing with problems only when and if they arise, and doing nothing to prevent their growth! It is for this reason, and this reason only, that I want to say a word or two about our need to husband the foreign exchange reserves of Tanzania. We are fairly comfortable now; foreign exchange is not one of our present problems. But we have to see that it does not become a problem, and we can do this by increasing and diversifying our exports, and by the deliberate development of import substitution industries. At the same time we have to use our foreign exchange for maximum benefit, and not fritter it away.

What does all this mean? There are many things needed for our development programme which we cannot yet produce in Tanzania. Things like highly complicated machines for our growing industrial sector; steel for building, and so on, will have to be imported for some time to come. We have to buy these with the currencies of other countries—in other words, with foreign exchange. We get these currencies of foreign countries by selling our goods to them; the more we sell, the more foreign currency we have with which to buy these essential elements of our development. And the more of our foreign currencies that we use for things which are not essential—luxuries or other things which we could produce ourselves—the less we have available for the things which we cannot produce, but do need.

Up to the present, and in the near future, we have enough foreign exchange to buy the essential components of our development, and also other things. But as our Five-Year Development Plan progresses, and in the next Plan, we shall need more capital imports. We must be ready for that time. We shall be ready if we save as much foreign currency as we can now, so as to build up a 'Reserve' — in the same way as a thrifty man saves his money in a bank account so that he has a 'reserve' to build a house later. We must also work hard to produce and sell overseas as much as we can. And we must develop import substitution industries, so that gradually we produce more things ourselves and do not have to spend foreign currency on them.

All these policies are being carried out by Government, and will be intensified. Obvious examples of import substitution are the oil refinery and the cement works, but in the industrial areas of Dar es Salaam, Arusha, and Mwanza there are an ever-increasing number of factories which are producing goods we once had to import.

Our exports are increasing too, although in this area we are still very vulnerable to world price fluctuations. The current low sisal prices are very bad for us; but our response must be to sell more sisal, and also to break into new markets with other goods.

Finally, the currency exchange regulations are designed to ensure that our money is not just sent overseas, and that at the least we know what demands are being made on our foreign exchange reserves for spending on imported goods. The Exchange Control is working well; I do not think any good Tanzanian is being seriously inconvenienced by it, and it is helping the Government in its efforts to plan the economic development of our country . . . .

26

The Arusha Declaration:
Socialism and Self-Reliance

When people in Tanzania refer to the Arusha Declaration they are usually speaking of the whole document accepted by the National Executive Committee of TANU in Arusha on 29 January 1967, and not just to The Arusha Resolution which is Part Five only.

The Declaration was discussed and then published in Swahili. This revised English translation clarifies ambiguities which existed in the translation originally issued.

The Declaration is based on a draft submitted to the Committee by President Nyerere, but this was amended in a number of particulars. The Declaration is thus a Party document, not the exclusive work of the President. It is nonetheless reproduced in full because events in Tanzania after 5 February 1967 (when the Declaration was published) cannot be understood except in relation to it.

The Arusha Declaration marked a turning point in Tanzanian politics. The ideology of the country was made explicit by it; also the introduction of 'leadership qualifications', and the measures for public ownership, began a new series of deliberately socialist policy initiatives.

Part One: The TANU Creed

The policy of TANU is to build a socialist state. The principles of socialism are laid down in the TANU Constitution and they are as follows:

WHEREAS TANU believes:

    (a)   That all human beings are equal;

    (b)   That every individual has a right to dignity and respect;

(c)   That every citizen is an integral part of the nation and has the right to take an equal part in Government at local, regional and national level;

(d)   That every citizen has the right to freedom of expression, of movement, of religious belief and of association within the context of the law;

(e)   That every individual has the right to receive from society protection of his life and of property held according to law;

(f)   That every individual has the right to receive a just return for his labour;

(g)   That all citizens together possess all the natural resources of the country in trust for their descendants;

(h)   That in order to ensure economic justice the state must have effective control over the principal means of production; and

(i)   That it is the responsibility of the state to intervene actively in the economic life of the nation so as to ensure the well-being of all citizens, and so as to prevent the exploitation of one person by another or one group by another, and so as to prevent the accumulation of wealth to an extent which is inconsistent with the existence of a classless society.

NOW, THEREFORE, the principal aims and objects of TANU shall be as follows:

(a)   To consolidate and maintain the independence of this country and the freedom of its people;

(b)   To safeguard the inherent dignity of the individual in accordance with the Universal Declaration of Human Rights;

(c)   To ensure that this country shall be governed by a democratic socialist government of the people;

(d)   To co-operate with all political parties in Africa engaged in the liberation of all Africa;

(e)   To see that the Government mobilizes all the resources of this country towards the elimination of poverty, ignorance and disease;

(f)   To see that the Government actively assists in the formation and maintenance of co-operative organizations;

(g)   To see that wherever possible the Government itself directly participates in the economic development of this country;

(h) To see that the Government gives equal opportunity to all men and women irrespective of race, religion or status;

(i) To see that the Government eradicates all types of exploitation, intimidation, discrimination, bribery and corruption;

(j) To see that the Government exercises effective control over the principal means of production and pursues policies which facilitate the way to collective ownership of the resources of this country;

(k) To see that the Government co-operates with other states in Africa in bringing about African unity;

(l) To see that the Government works tirelessly towards world peace and security through the United Nations Organization.

Part Two: The Policy of Socialism

(a) *Absence of Exploitation.*

A truly socialist state is one in which all people are workers and in which neither capitalism nor feudalism exists. It does not have two classes of people, a lower class composed of people who work for their living, and an upper class of people who live on the work of others. In a really socialist country no person exploits another; everyone who is physically able to work does so; every worker obtains a just return for the labour he performs; and the incomes derived from different types of work are not grossly divergent.

In a socialist country, the only people who live on the work of others, and who have the right to be dependent upon their fellows, are small children, people who are too old to support themselves, the crippled, and those whom the state at any one time cannot provide with an opportunity to work for their living.

Tanzania is a nation of peasants and workers, but it is not yet a socialist society. It still contains elements of feudalism and capitalism—with their temptations. These feudalistic and capitalistic features of our society could spread and entrench themselves.

(b) *The major means of production and exchange are under the control of the peasants and workers.*

To build and maintain socialism it is essential that all the major means of production and exchange in the nation are controlled and owned by the peasants through the machinery of their Government and their co-operatives. Further, it is essential that the ruling Party should be a Party of peasants and workers.

The major means of production and exchange are such things as: land; forests; minerals; water; oil and electricity; news media; communications; banks, insurance, import and export trade, wholesale trade; iron and steel, machine-tool, arms, motor-car, cement, fertilizer, and textile industries; and any big factory on which a large section of the people depend for their living, or which provides essential components of other industries; large plantations, and especially those which provide raw materials essential to important industries.

Some of the instruments of production and exchange which have been listed here are already owned or controlled by the people's Government of Tanzania.

(c) *The Existence of Democracy.*

A state is not socialist simply because its means of production and exchange are controlled or owned by the government, either wholly or in large part. For a country to be socialist, it is essential that its government is chosen and led by the peasants and workers themselves. If the minority governments of Rhodesia or South Africa controlled or owned the entire economies of these respective countries, the result would be a strengthening of oppression, not the building of socialism. True socialism cannot exist without democracy also existing in the society.

(d) *Socialism is a Belief.*

Socialism is a way of life, and a socialist society cannot simply come into existence. A socialist society can only be built by those who believe in, and who themselves practise, the principles of socialism. A committed member of TANU will be a socialist, and his fellow socialists—that is, his fellow believers in this political and economic system— are all those in Africa or elsewhere in the world who fight for the rights of peasants and workers. The first duty of a TANU member, and especially of a TANU leader, is to accept these socialist principles, and to live his own life in accordance with them. In particular, a genuine TANU leader will not live off the sweat of another man, nor commit any feudalistic or capitalistic actions.

The successful implementation of socialist objectives depends very much upon the leaders, because socialism is a belief in a particular system of living, and it is difficult for leaders to promote its growth if they do not themselves accept it.

Part Three: The Policy of Self-Reliance

We are at War.

TANU is involved in a war against poverty and oppression in our country; this struggle is aimed at moving the people of Tanzania (and the people of Africa as a whole) from a state of poverty to a state of prosperity.

We have been oppressed a great deal, we have been exploited a great deal and we have been disregarded a great deal. It is our weakness that has led to our being oppressed, exploited and disregarded. Now we want a revolution—a revolution which brings to an end our weakness, so that we are never again exploited, oppressed, or humiliated.

A Poor Man does not use Money as a Weapon.

But it is obvious that in the past we have chosen the wrong weapon for our struggle, because we chose money as our weapon. We are trying to overcome our economic weakness by using the weapons of the economically strong—weapons which in fact we do not possess. By our thoughts, words and actions it appears as if we have come to the conclusion that without money we cannot bring about the revolution we are aiming at. It is as if we have said, 'Money is the basis of development. Without money there can be no development.'

That is what we believe at present. TANU leaders, and Government leaders and officials, all put great emphasis and dependence on money. The people's leaders and the people themselves, in TANU, NUTA, Parliament, UWT, the co-operatives, TAPA, and in other national institutions think, hope and pray for MONEY. It is as if we had all agreed to speak with one voice, saying, 'If we get money we shall develop, without money we cannot develop'.

In brief, our Five-Year Development Plan aims at more food, more education, and better health; but the weapon we have put emphasis upon is money. It is as if we said, 'In the next five years we want to have more food, more education, and better health, and in order to achieve these things we shall spend £250,000,000'. We think and speak as if the most important thing to depend upon is MONEY and anything else we intend to use in our struggle is of minor importance.

When a Member of Parliament says that there is a shortage of water in his constituency and he asks the Government how it intends to deal with the problem, he expects the Government to reply that it is planning to remove the shortage of water in his constituency —WITH MONEY.

When another Member of Parliament asks what the Government is doing about the shortage of roads, schools or hospitals in his constituency, he also expects the Government to tell him that it has specific plans to build roads, schools and hospitals in his constituency—WITH MONEY.

When a NUTA official asks the Government about its plans to deal with the low wages and poor housing of the workers, he expects the Government to inform him that the minimum wage will be increased and that better houses will be provided for the workers— WITH MONEY.

When a TAPA official asks the Government what plans it has to give assistance to the many TAPA schools which do not get Government aid, he expects the Government to state that it is ready the following morning to give the required assistance—WITH MONEY.

When an official of the co-operative movement mentions any problem facing the farmer, he expects to hear that the Government will solve the farmer's problems—WITH MONEY. In short, for every problem facing our nation, the solution that is in everybody's mind is MONEY.

Each year, each Ministry of Government makes its estimates of expenditure, i.e. the amount of money it will require in the coming year to meet recurrent and development expenses. Only one Minister and his Ministry make estimates of revenue. This is the Minister for Finance. Every Ministry puts forward very good development plans. When the Ministry presents its estimates, it believes that the money is there for the asking but that the Minister for Finance and his Ministry are being obstructive. And regularly each year the Minister for Finance has to tell his fellow Ministers that there is no money. And each year the Ministries complain about the Ministry of Finance when it trims down their estimates.

Similarly, when Members of Parliament and other leaders demand that the Government should carry out a certain development, they believe that there is a lot of money to spend on such projects, but that the Government is the stumbling block. Yet such belief on the part of Ministries, Members of Parliament and other leaders does not alter the stark truth, which is that Government has no money.

When it is said that Government has no money, what does this mean? It means that the people of Tanzania have insufficient money. The people pay taxes out of the very little wealth they have; it is from these taxes that the Government meets its recurrent and development expenditure. When we call on the Government to spend more money on development projects, we are asking the Government to use more money. And if the Government does not have any more, the only way it can do this is to increase its revenue through extra taxation.

If one calls on the Government to spend more, one is in effect calling on the Government to increase taxes. Calling on the Government to spend more without raising taxes is like demanding that the Government should perform miracles; it is equivalent to asking for more milk from a cow while insisting that the cow should not be milked again. But our refusal to admit that calling on the Government to spend more is the same as calling on the Government to raise taxes shows that we fully realize the difficulties of increasing taxes. We realize that the cow has no more milk—that is, that the people find it difficult to pay more taxes. We know that the cow would like to have more milk herself, so that her calves could drink it, or that she would like more milk which could be sold to provide more comfort for herself or her calves. But knowing all the things which could be done with more milk does not alter the fact that the cow has no more milk!

What of External Aid?

One method we use to try and avoid a recognition of the need to increase taxes if we want to have more money for development, is to think in terms of getting the extra money from outside Tanzania. Such external finance falls into three main categories.

(a) *Gifts:* This means that another government gives our Government a sum of money as a free gift for a particular development scheme. Sometimes it may be that an institution in another country gives our Government, or an institution in our country, financial help for development programmes.

(b)   *Loans:* The greater portion of financial help we expect to get from outside is not in the form of gifts or charity, but in the form of loans. A foreign government or a foreign institution, such as a bank, lends our Government money for the purposes of development. Such a loan has repayment conditions attached to it, covering such factors as the time period for which it is available and the rate of interest.

(c)   *Private Investment:* The third category of financial help is also greater than the first. This takes the form of investment in our country by individuals or companies from outside. The important condition which such private investors have in mind is that the enterprise into which they put their money should bring them profit and that our Government should permit them to repatriate these profits. They also prefer to invest in a country whose policies they agree with and which will safeguard their economic interests.

These three are the main categories of external finance. And there is in Tanzania a fantastic amount of talk about getting money from outside. Our Government and different groups of our leaders never stop thinking about methods of getting finance from abroad. And if we get some money, or even if we just get a promise of it, our newspapers, our radio, and our leaders, all advertise the fact in order that every person shall know that salvation is coming, or is on the way. If we receive a gift we announce it, if we receive a loan we announce it, if we get a new factory we announce it—and always loudly. In the same way, when we get a promise of a gift, a loan, or a new industry, we make an announcement of the promise. Even when we have merely started discussions with a foreign government or institution for a gift, a loan, or a new industry, we make an announcement—even though we do not know the outcome of the discussions. Why do we do all this? Because we want people to know that we have started discussions which will bring prosperity.

DO NOT LET US DEPEND UPON MONEY FOR DEVELOPMENT

It is stupid to rely on money as the major instrument of development when we know only too well that our country is poor. It is equally stupid, indeed it is even more stupid, for us to imagine that we shall rid ourselves of our poverty through foreign financial assistance rather than our own financial resources. It is stupid for two reasons.

Firstly, we shall not get the money. It is true that there are countries which can, and which would like, to help us. But there is no country in the world which is prepared to give us gifts or loans, or establish industries, to the extent that we would be able to achieve all our development targets. There are many needy countries in the world. And even if all the prosperous nations were willing to help the needy countries, the assistance would still not suffice. But in any case the prosperous nations have not accepted a responsibility to fight world poverty. Even within their own borders poverty still exists, and the rich individuals do not willingly give money to the government to help their poor fellow citizens.

It is only through taxation, which people have to pay whether they want to or not, that money can be extracted from the rich in order to help the masses. Even then there would not be enough money. However heavily we taxed the citizens of Tanzania and the aliens living here, the resulting revenue would not be enough to meet the costs of the development we want. And there is no World Government which can tax the prosperous nations in order to help the poor nations; nor if one did exist could it raise enough revenue to do all that is needed in the world. But in fact, such a World Government does not exist. Such money as the rich nations offer to the poor nations is given voluntarily, either through their own goodness, or for their own benefit. All this means that it is impossible for Tanzania to obtain from overseas enough money to develop our economy.

GIFTS AND LOANS WILL ENDANGER OUR INDEPENDENCE

Secondly, even if it were possible for us to get enough money for our needs from external sources, is this what we really want? Independence means self-reliance. Independence cannot be real if a nation depends upon gifts and loans from another for its development. Even if there was a nation, or nations, prepared to give us all the money we need for our development, it would be improper for us to accept such assistance without asking ourselves how this would affect our independence and our very survival as a nation. Gifts which increase, or act as a catalyst, to our own efforts are valuable. But gifts which could have the effect of weakening or distorting our own efforts should not be accepted until we have asked ourselves a number of questions.

The same applies to loans. It is true that loans are better than 'free' gifts. A loan is intended to increase our efforts or make those efforts more fruitful. One condition of a loan is that you show how you are going to repay it. This means you have to show that you intend to use the loan profitably and will therefore be able to repay it.

But even loans have their limitations. You have to give consideration to the ability to repay. When we borrow money from other countries it is the Tanzanian who pays it back. And as we have already stated, Tanzanians are poor people. To burden the people with big loans, the repayment of which will be beyond their means, is not to help them but to make them suffer. It is even worse when the loans they are asked to repay have not benefited the majority of the people but have only benefited a small minority.

How about the enterprises of foreign investors? It is true we need these enterprises. We have even passed an Act of Parliament protecting foreign investments in this country. Our aim is to make foreign investors feel that Tanzania is a good place in which to invest because investments would be safe and profitable, and the profits can be taken out of the country without difficulty. We expect to get money through this method. But we cannot get enough. And even if we were able to convince foreign investors and foreign firms to undertake all the projects and programmes of economic development that we need, is that what we actually want to happen?

Had we been able to attract investors from America and Europe to come and start all the industries and all the projects of economic development that we need in this country, could we do so without questioning ourselves? Could we agree to leave the economy of our country in the hands of foreigners who would take the profits back to their countries? Or supposing they did not insist upon taking their profits away, but decided to reinvest them in Tanzania; could we really accept this situation without asking ourselves what disadvantages our nation would suffer? Would this allow the socialism we have said it is our objective to build?

How can we depend upon gifts, loans and investments from foreign countries and foreign companies without endangering our independence? The English people have a proverb which says: 'He who pays the piper calls the tune'. How can we depend upon foreign governments and companies for the major part of our development without giving to those governments and countries a great part of our freedom to act as we please? The truth is that we cannot.

Let us repeat. We made a mistake in choosing money—something we do not have—to be the big instrument of our development. We are making a mistake to think that we shall get the money from other countries; first, because in fact we shall not be able to get sufficient money for our economic development; and secondly, because even if we could get all that we need, such dependence upon others would endanger our independence and our ability to choose our own political policies.

WE HAVE PUT TOO MUCH EMPHASIS ON INDUSTRIES

Because of our emphasis on money, we have made another big mistake. We have put too much emphasis on industries. Just as we have said, 'Without money there can be no development', we also seem to say, 'Industries are the basis of development, without industries there is no development'. This is true. The day when we have lots of money we shall be able to say we are a developed country. We shall be able to say, 'When we began our Development Plans we did not have enough money and this situation made it difficult for us to develop as fast as we wanted. Today we are developed and we have enough money'. That is to say, our money has been brought by development. Similarly, the day we become industrialized, we shall be able to say we are developed. Development would have enabled us to have industries. The mistake we are making is to think that development begins with industries. It is a mistake because we do not have the means to establish many modern industries in our country. We do not have either the necessary finances or the technical know-how. It is not enough to say that we shall borrow the finances and the technicians from other countries to come and start the industries. The answer to this is the same one we gave earlier, that we cannot get enough money and borrow enough technicians to start all the industries we need. And even if we could get the necessary assistance, dependence on it could interfere with our policy on socialism. The policy of inviting a chain of capitalists to come and establish industries in our country might succeed in giving us all the industries we need, but it would also succeed in preventing the establishment of socialism unless we believe that without first building capitalism, we cannot build socialism.

LET US PAY HEED TO THE PEASANT

Our emphasis on money and industries has made us concentrate on urban development. We recognize that we do not have enough money to bring the kind of development to each village which would benefit everybody. We also know that we cannot establish an industry in each village and through this means effect a rise in the real incomes of the people. For these reasons we spend most of our money in the urban areas and our industries are established in the towns.

Yet the greater part of this money that we spend in the towns comes from loans. Whether it is used to build schools, hospitals, houses or factories, etc., it still has to be repaid. But it is obvious that it cannot be repaid just out of money obtained from urban and industrial development. To repay the loans we have to use foreign currency which is obtained from the sale of our exports. But we do not now sell our industrial products in foreign markets, and indeed it is likely to be a long time before our industries produce for export. The main aim of our new industries is 'import substitution'—that is, to produce things which up to now we have had to import from foreign countries.

It is therefore obvious that the foreign currency we shall use to pay back the loans used in the development of the urban areas will not come from the towns or the industries. Where, then, shall we get it from? We shall get it from the villages and from agriculture. What does this mean? It means that the people who benefit directly from development which is brought about by borrowed money are not the ones who will repay the loans. The largest proportion of the loans will be spent in, or for, the urban areas, but the largest proportion of the repayment will be made through the efforts of the farmers.

This fact should always be borne in mind, for there are various forms of exploitation. We must not forget that people who live in towns can possibly become the exploiters of those who live in the rural areas. All our big hospitals are in towns and they benefit only a small section of the people of Tanzania. Yet if we have built them

with loans from outside Tanzania, it is the overseas sale of the peasants' produce which provides the foreign exchange for repayment.
Those who do not get the benefit of the hospitals thus carry the
major responsibility for paying for them. Tarmac roads, too, are
mostly found in towns and are of especial value to the motor-car
owners. Yet if we have built those roads with loans, it is again the
farmer who produces the goods which will pay for them. What
is more, the foreign exchange with which the car was bought also
came from the sale of the farmers' produce. Again, electric lights,
water pipes, hotels and other aspects of modern development are
mostly found in towns. Most of them have been built with loans
and most of them do not benefit the farmer directly, although they
will be paid for by the foreign exchange earned by the sale of his
produce. We should always bear this in mind.

Although when we talk of exploitation we usually think of capitalists, we should not forget that there are many fish in the sea. They
eat each other. The large ones eat the small ones, and the small ones
eat those who are even smaller. There are two possible ways of
dividing the people in our country. We can put the capitalists and
feudalists on one side, and the farmers and workers on the other.
But we can also divide the people into urban dwellers on one side
and those who live in the rural areas on the other. If we are not
careful we might get to the position where the real exploitation in
Tanzania is that of the town dwellers exploiting the peasants.

THE PEOPLE AND AGRICULTURE

The development of a country is brought about by people, not by
money. Money, and the wealth it represents, is the result and not
the basis of development. The four prerequisites of development
are different; they are (i) People; (ii) Land; (iii) Good Policies;
(iv) Good Leadership. Our country has more than ten million people*
and its area is more than 362,000 square miles.

AGRICULTURE IS THE BASIS OF DEVELOPMENT

A great part of Tanzania's land is fertile and gets sufficient rain.
Our country can produce various crops for home consumption and
for export.

* 1967 census showed 12.3 million people.

We can produce food crops (which can be exported if we produce in large quantities) such as maize, rice, wheat, beans, groundnuts, etc. And we can produce such cash crops as sisal, cotton, coffee, tobacco, pyrethrum, tea, etc. Our land is also good for grazing cattle, goats, sheep, and for raising chickens, etc.; we can get plenty of fish from our rivers, lakes, and from the sea. All of our farmers are in areas which can produce two or three or even more of the food and cash crops enumerated above, and each farmer could increase his production so as to get more food or more money. And because the main aim of development is to get more food, and more money for our other needs, our purpose must be to increase production of these agricultural crops. This is in fact the only road through which we can develop our country—in other words, only by increasing our production of these things can we get more food and more money for every Tanzanian.

THE CONDITIONS OF DEVELOPMENT

(a) *Hard Work*

Everybody wants development; but not everybody understands and accepts the basic requirements for development. The biggest requirement is hard work. Let us go to the villages and talk to our people and see whether or not it is possible for them to work harder.

In towns, for example, wage-earners normally work for seven and a half or eight hours a day, and for six or six and a half days a week. This is about 45 hours a week for the whole year, except for two or three weeks' leave. In other words, a wage-earner works for 45 hours a week for 48 or 50 weeks of the year.

For a country like ours these are really quite short working hours. In other countries, even those which are more developed than we are, people work for more than 45 hours a week. It is not normal for a young country to start with such a short working week. The normal thing is to begin with long working hours and decrease them as the country becomes more and more prosperous. By starting with such short working hours and asking for even shorter hours, we are in fact imitating the more developed countries. And we shall regret this imitation. Nevertheless, wage-earners do work for 45 hours per week and their annual vacation does not exceed four weeks.

It would be appropriate to ask our farmers, especially the men, how many hours a week and how many weeks a year they work.

Many do not even work for half as many hours as the wage-earner does. The truth is that in the villages the women work very hard. At times they work for 12 or 14 hours a day. They even work on Sundays and public holidays. Women who live in the villages work harder than anybody else in Tanzania. But the men who live in villages (and some of the women in towns) are on leave for half of their life. The energies of the millions of men in the villages and thousands of women in the towns which are at present wasted in gossip, dancing and drinking, are a great treasure which could contribute more towards the development of our country than anything we could get from rich nations.

We would be doing something very beneficial to our country if we went to the villages and told our people that they hold this treasure and that it is up to them to use it for their own benefit and the benefit of our whole nation.

(b) *Intelligence*

The second condition of development is the use of intelligence. Unintelligent hard work would not bring the same good results as the two combined. Using a big hoe instead of a small one; using a plough pulled by oxen instead of an ordinary hoe; the use of fertilizers; the use of insecticides; knowing the right crop for a particular season or soil; choosing good seeds for planting; knowing the right time for planting, weeding, etc.; all these things show the use of knowledge and intelligence. And all of them combine with hard work to produce more and better results.

The money and time we spend on passing on this knowledge to the peasants are better spent and bring more benefits to our country than the money and great amount of time we spend on other things which we call development.

These facts are well known to all of us. The parts of our Five-Year Development Plan which are on target, or where the target has been exceeded, are those parts which depend solely upon the people's own hard work. The production of cotton, coffee, cashew nuts, tobacco and pyrethrum has increased enormously for the past three years. But these are things which are produced by hard work and the good leadership of the people, not by the use of great amounts of money.

Furthermore the people, through their own hard work and with a little help and leadership, have finished many development projects in the villages. They have built schools, dispensaries, community centres, and roads; they have dug wells, water-channels, animal dips, small dams, and completed various other development projects. Had they waited for money, they would not now have the use of these things.

HARD WORK IS THE ROOT OF DEVELOPMENT

Some Plan projects which depend on money are going on well, but there are many which have stopped and others which might never be fulfilled because of lack of money. Yet still we talk about money and our search for money increases and takes nearly all our energies. We should not lessen our efforts to get the money we really need, but it would be more appropriate for us to spend time in the villages showing the people how to bring about development through their own efforts rather than going on so many long and expensive journeys abroad in search of development money. This is the real way to bring development to everybody in the country.

None of this means that from now on we will not need money or that we will not start industries or embark upon development projects which require money. Furthermore, we are not saying that we will not accept, or even that we shall not look for, money from other countries for our development. This is NOT what we are saying. We will continue to use money; and each year we will use more money for the various development projects than we used the previous year because this will be one of the signs of our development.

What we are saying, however, is that from now on we shall know what is the foundation and what is the fruit of development. Between MONEY and PEOPLE it is obvious that the people and their HARD WORK are the foundation of development, and money is one of the fruits of that hard work.

From now on we shall stand upright and walk forward on our feet rather than look at this problem upside down. Industries will come and money will come but their foundation is THE PEOPLE and their HARD WORK, especially in AGRICULTURE. This is the meaning of self-reliance. Our emphasis should therefore be on:

(a)   The Land and Agriculture
(b)   The People
(c)   The Policy of Socialism and Self-Reliance, and
(d)   Good Leadership.

(a) *The Land*

Because the economy of Tanzania depends and will continue to depend on agriculture and animal husbandry, Tanzanians can live well without depending on help from outside if they use their land properly. Land is the basis of human life and all Tanzanians should use it as a valuable investment for future development. Because the land belongs to the nation, the Government has to see to it that it is used for the benefit of the whole nation and not for the benefit of one individual or just a few people.

It is the responsibility of TANU to see that the country produces enough food and enough cash crops for export. It is the responsibility of the Government and the co-operative societies to see to it that our people get the necessary tools, training and leadership in modern methods of agriculture.

(b) *The People*

In order properly to implement the policy of self-reliance, the people have to be taught the meaning of self-reliance and its practice. They must become self-sufficient in food, serviceable clothes and good housing.

In our country work should be something to be proud of, and laziness, drunkenness and idleness should be things to be ashamed of. And for the defence of our nation, it is necessary for us to be on guard against internal stooges who could be used by external enemies who aim to destroy us. The people should always be ready to defend their nation when they are called upon to do so.

(c) *Good Policies*

The principals of our policy of self-reliance go hand in hand with our policy on socialism. In order to prevent exploitation it is necessary for everybody to work and to live on his own labour. And in order to distribute the national wealth fairly, it is necessary for everybody to work to the maximum of his ability. Nobody should go and stay for a long time with his relative, doing no work, because in doing so he will be exploiting his relative. Likewise, nobody should be allowed to loiter in towns or villages without doing work which would enable him to be self-reliant without exploiting his relatives.

TANU believes that everybody who loves his nation has a duty to serve it by co-operating with his fellows in building the country for the benefit of all the people of Tanzania. In order to maintain our independence and our people's freedom we ought to be self-reliant in every possible way and avoid depending upon other countries for assistance. If every individual is self-reliant the ten-house cell will be self-reliant; if all the cells are self-reliant the whole ward will be self-reliant; and if the wards are self-reliant the District will be self-reliant. If the Districts are self-reliant, then the Region is self-reliant, and if the Regions are self-reliant, then the whole nation is self-reliant and this is our aim.

(d) *Good Leadership*

TANU recognizes the urgency and importance of good leadership. But we have not yet produced systematic training for our leaders; it is necessary that TANU Headquarters should now prepare a programme of training for all leaders—from the national level to the ten-house cell level—so that every one of them understands our political and economic policies. Leaders must set a good example to the rest of the people in their lives and in all their activities.

Part Four: TANU Membership

Since the Party was founded we have put great emphasis on getting as many members as possible. This was the right policy during the independence struggle. But now the National Executive feels that the time has come when we should put more emphasis on the beliefs of our Party and its policies of socialism.

That part of the TANU Constitution which relates to the admission of a member should be adhered to, and if it is discovered that a man does not appear to accept the faith, the objects, and the rules and regulations of the Party, then he should not be accepted as a member. In particular, it should not be forgotten that TANU is a Party of peasants and workers.

Part Five: The Arusha Resolution

Therefore, the National Executive Committee, meeting in the Community Centre at Arusha from 26.1.67 to 29.1.67, resolves:

(a) *The Leadership*

1. Every TANU and Government leader must be either a peasant or a worker, and should in no way be associated with the practices of capitalism or feudalism.

2. No TANU or Government leader should hold shares in any company.

3. No TANU or Government leader should hold directorships in any privately owned enterprise.

4. No TANU or Government leader should receive two or more salaries.

5. No TANU or Government leader should own houses which he rents to others.

6. For the purposes of this Resolution the term 'leader' should comprise the following:

   Members of the TANU National Executive Committee; Ministers; Members of Parliament; senior officials of Organizations affiliated to TANU; senior officials of para-statal organizations; all those appointed or elected under any clause of the TANU Constitution; councillors; and civil servants in the high and middle cadres. (In this context 'leader' means a man, or a man and his wife; a woman, or a woman and her husband).

(b) *The Government and Other Institutions*

1. Congratulates the Government for the steps it has taken so far in the implementation of the policy of socialism.

2. Calls upon the Government to take further steps in the implementation of our policy of socialism as described in Part Two of this document without waiting for a Presidential Commission on Socialism.

3. Calls upon the Government to put emphasis, when preparing its Development Plans, on the ability of this country to implement the Plans rather than depending on foreign loans and grants as has been done in the current Five-Year Development Plan. The National Executive Committee also resolves that the Plan should be amended so as to make it fit in with the policy of self-reliance.

4. Calls upon the Government to take action designed to ensure that the incomes of workers in the private sector are not very different from the incomes of workers in the public sector.

5. Calls upon the Government to put great emphasis on actions

which will raise the standard of living of the peasants, and the rural community.

6. Calls upon NUTA, the co-operatives, TAPA, UWT, TYL, and other Government institutions to take steps to implement the policy of socialism and self-reliance.

(c) *Membership*

Members should get thorough teaching on Party ideology so that they may understand it, and they should always be reminded of the importance of living up to its principles.

27

Public Ownership in Tanzania

This article was published in the Sunday News *of 12 February 1967, following a week in which new public ownership provisions were being announced almost daily. It constituted an announcement that the Government had fulfilled its obligations under that part of the Arusha Declaration referring to public ownership and control, and then elaborated on the future position of private enterprise.*

In the past Tanzania has said it is committed to building socialism, but we have not made clear what we mean by this. We have called for private investment in industrial and agricultural activities, but at the same time we have spoken frequently of our determination to control our own economy. We established the National Development Corporation and called it our instrument for socialist development; we gave certain trade monopolies to Cosata and Intrata. But we never laid down our criteria for the division between public and private enterprise. Instead we talked in general terms about the advantages of each—often according to whether the factory we were opening was public or private! We frequently said that we wanted and needed a combination of state and private enterprise but we left it to individuals to judge whether a particular undertaking should be placed in one category or the other. Even when we published the Five-Year Development Plan in 1964, we failed to clarify the position. Indeed, by the heavy reliance on foreign aid and private investment envisaged in that Plan, we implied that it did not matter to us, and that public enterprise would fill the gaps left by private investors.

The purpose of Part Two (b) of the Arusha Declaration was to settle this question, and to make clear the areas where public ownership and control are required, and the areas where private investment is, and will be, welcomed.

Inevitably, however, the first result of such a Declaration was to heighten uncertainty. This was especially true in the minds of those who had already invested in economic undertakings which were referred to in the document, or which might be covered by its general references to 'big factories'. Until they knew their position it was quite obvious that they would not consider any possibility of expansion, and might even consider the desirability of running down their activities. Neither of these things could be in the interests of the Tanzania people, and it was therefore obvious to the Government that immediate action was required to bring uncertainty to an end, so that both private investors and the public at large knew exactly where they stood.

In the space of the past week the Government of the United Republic has therefore taken the decisions necessary to clear up any uncertainties left by the Arusha Declaration. We have put the economy into the position where positive decisions for growth can be made with confidence. The decision-making has now been concluded, and the announcements made.

Since the 5th February we have nationalized all banks operating in the United Republic (except for the Co-operative Bank which continues on its present basis). We have taken into public ownership the following firms which are engaged in the processing of foods normally purchased from or through the National Agricultural Products Board:

Tanzania Millers; Chande Industries; Pure Food Products Ltd.; G. R. Jivraj; Noormohamed Jessa; Kyela Sattar Mills (Mbeya); Associated Traders Ltd. (Mwanza); and Rajwani Mills (Dodoma).

We have also nationalized the National Insurance Corporation Ltd. in which Government previously had a majority shareholding. As from 11th February all new life insurance business in Tanzania will be handled by this Corporation. Existing life insurance policies will, however, continue to be valid and the interests of policy-holders will be protected. Other types of insurance business will also be handled exclusively by the NIC as from a date in the future which will be announced when the Minister presents the enabling Bill to Parliament next week. Then to form the nucleus of the State Trading Corporation which will be the authorized body for external and wholesale trade, we have nationalized the following firms:

Smith Mackenzie & Co. Ltd.; Dalgety (East Africa) Ltd.; International Trading & Credit Co. of Tanganyika; Co-operative Supply Association of Tanganyika Ltd.; A. Baumann & Co. (Tanganyika) Ltd.; Twentsche Overseas Trading Co. Ltd.; African Mercantile Co. (Overseas) Ltd.; Wigglesworth & Co. (Africa) Ltd.

In all these cases we have stated quite clearly and categorically that we shall pay full and fair compensation for the assets acquired, and that we shall honour all existing commitments—with especial reference to commitments to employees. In some cases discussions about these matters have already begun; in the other cases they will be initiated in the very near future.

This list is the complete list of the firms we intend to nationalize in accordance with the Arusha Declaration. Firms which are not included in that list will not be taken into exclusive public ownership.

There is, however, a further list of private firms operating in Tanzania in which the Government intends to hold a controlling share. During the past week this list has also been drawn up, and the firms notified or discussions started. In these cases we shall not be discussing nationalization; we shall be discussing with those concerned the best means by which Government can secure majority shareholding. In some cases this can be effected through Government participation in economically justified expansion plans; in other cases different methods will have to be followed. But in all cases our purpose will be to avoid dislocation of economic production.

The firms affected by this list are as follows:

Beer breweries: Kilimanjaro Brewery and Tanzania Brewery; British American Tobacco; Bata Shoe Company; Tanganyika Metal Box; Tanganyika Extract Company; Tanganyika Portland Cement.

There is only one industry in which the Government intends to take a controlling interest and in relation to which action has not yet been completed. We have informed the Sisal Growers Association of our intention to secure a controlling share in the sisal industry, but the individual firms with whom discussions will take place have not yet been notified. The names of these firms will be announced within the coming week.

All firms not included in the above list, except for sisal estates, may now rest assured that Government does not desire to obtain majority participation in their enterprises. They are free to continue in full private ownership, or with existing minority Government or co-operative ownership.

With these two lists the Government has fulfilled its obligations under the Arusha Declaration, Part Two (b)—that is, the part referring to public ownership and control. All the other industries existing in Tanzania, and to which reference was made, were owned before the Arusha Meeting. For example, Lands, Forests, Mineral Resources, Water, Electricity, Posts, Telecommunications, Radio, Railways, and so on, are in Government hands or Government control. In addition, there are 21 existing firms of various kinds which are already fully Government owned and run under the supervision of the National Development Corporation, and 17 in which NDC hold 50 per cent of the shares or more.

The list of firms whose ownership has been affected by the Arusha Declaration is thus a very small one. It is small because, in the words of Norman Manley, 'You can't nationalize nothing'. The potential of Tanzania is still undeveloped; our real task is to develop it. For this we need hard and intelligent work, and some capital. We have the people who are willing to work hard. We have, or will hire from abroad, the administrators, managers, and technicians that we need. And the capital we shall obtain largely from our own efforts—from re-investing income which we earn from our existing industries—and this means from the products of our agriculture.

Does this imply that Tanzania is no longer interested in receiving capital aid from abroad, or in receiving private investment—either foreign or local? It should be obvious that it does not mean that. We have firmly rejected the proposition that without foreign aid we cannot develop. We shall not depend upon overseas aid to the extent of bending our political, economic, or social policies in the hope of getting it. But we shall try to get it in order that we may hasten our economic progress, and that it may act as a catalyst to our own effort. Similarly with private enterprise: we have rejected the domination of private enterprise; but we shall continue to welcome private investment in all those areas not reserved for Government in the Arusha Declaration.

What does this mean in practice? It means that a potential investor will know that there are certain industries or commercial activities which are reserved for Government. Obviously he will realize that the sectors where we nationalized firms already operating are included in that category. But in addition, of the industries listed in the Arusha Declaration but which do not yet exist, arms are included in this classification. No private investor will be allowed to participate in the industry which manufactures weapons of death.

Secondly, the private investor will know that there is a category of industry and commerce in which Government will insist on having a majority share. This will cover all those economic activities listed in the Arusha Declaration which are not included above. The only one which does not yet exist in any form is the motor-car industry, but of course anyone interested in—for example—establishing another textile mill would realize that they come in this category because those which already existed were converted from majority private ownership to majority Government ownership.

Thirdly, however, the potential investor will know that in all other fields his investment will be welcomed and he will receive full co-operation from the Government and people in establishing a factory. He may do this without any Government or co-operative participation if he wishes. Industries not listed in the Arusha Declaration are open to complete private ownership, and investors are only obliged to abide by the normal law of the land regarding employment conditions, etc.

But it may be that a potential private investor—whether foreign or local—desires Government participation in his undertaking. This we have often found to be the case in the past. In such a case he would approach Government in the normal manner—through NDC—and his request will be given very favourable consideration. If we can co-operate, even on a minority basis, we shall be willing to do so.

There is one further point which it would be useful to clarify. The Arusha Declaration and the subsequent Government action has related to ownership, and this is not always the same thing as management. But policy has to be implemented. This is done by management and staff together, and taking an industry under Government ownership or control does not eliminate the need for skilled work and astute commercial expertise. We shall be asking the existing managers to continue in their present work just as they might do if their firms had changed ownership between two private groups, for we do not as yet have sufficient skilled and experienced people of our own. It is our hope that they will agree to do this, for although we cannot offer a life career to non-Tanzanians we shall be concerned to act fairly towards those who help us through our present needs. This policy is not new, and will not seem strange to our people. Six years after independence we still have expatriates working in the Civil Service and other Government enterprises; firms which are already under Government ownership or control have expatriates in those senior positions for which no Tanzanian is qualified. It is important that all those affected should realize that Government intends to act honestly and fairly towards them, and that it hopes that they will do the same towards the people of the United Republic.

In summary, the actions and announcements of the past seven days amount to this. Tanzania has defined the economic implicotions of her socialist policies, and in doing so has specified the areas of public and the areas of private enterprise. In the division the key positions of the economy have been secured for the nation in the same way as, during a war, an army occupies the sites which dominate the countryside. Our war is a war against poverty, and for the freedom and self-government of our people. In this fight we can now welcome the enterprise of private investors without reservations, because we no longer have any cause to fear the effect of their activities on our social purpose.

It is my hope that the people of this country, including private investors, will take advantage of the situation created by the removal of past uncertainties, and that our nation will now go forward, through hard work, to the brighter future which we can create.

1 In 1966 the President and all members of the Cabinet joined together with members of the National Service for a day's work digging a trench for water pipes.

2 Primary school children taking part in the expansion of their school buildings in accordance with the policies of Education for Self-Reliance.

3 At the National Stadium the President addresses a National Service passing out parade while other members of the National Service and the Army look on.

4 The Tanzania National Service at work on bush clearing for a new farm.

5 The Tanzania National Service on the march.

6 A view of new workers' houses at Magomeni and Kinondoni, near Dar es Salaam, some of the many thousands built since independence.

7 A view of Dar es Salaam's town centre and busy harbour, showing the deep water berths now being extended, and, in the distance, the oil refinery.

8 An aerial view of University College, Dar es Salaam, showing the teaching, library, and administrative buildings on one hill, with student hostels and staff houses on the hills behind.

Part of the crowd at the meeting at Mnazi Mmoja, Dar es Salaam, on 5 February 1967. On that day the President spoke for two hours extempore, introducing and explaining the Arusha Declaration.

This general view of Lumumba street, Dar es Salaam, shows one of the processions in support of the Arusha Declaration arriving at the TANU Headquarters where crowds of people have already gathered. February 1967.

11 A close up of part of the crowd listening to the President after a procession in support of the Arusha Declaration. February 1967.

12 An Arusha Declaration procession is addressed by the President outside TANU Head-quarters.

13 Students of the University College, Dar es Salaam, joined in the Youth Procession in support of the Arusha Declaration.

14 On a tour of Tabora Region the President stops to congratulate the tobacco growers.

15 When the President travels in the rural areas crowds of people gather to greet him at every populous place.

16 A view of Liwete, an ujamaa village in the Ruvuma Region.

17 For more than six months after the Arusha Declaration, groups of youths, women, and even old men, marched from their homes to their Regional Headquarters, or even to Dar es Salaam, to demonstrate support. Some of them walked many hundreds of miles, arriving footsore and weary. To show his support for this spirit of determination the President walked 134 miles to Mwanza in time for the TANU National Conference of October 1967. In this photo the President compares foot troubles with Minister Bhoke Munanka and other members of the party during a halt.

18 Vice President Kawawa, Mrs. Maria Nyerere, President Nyerere, and Father Trevor Huddleston at the opening of the Nurses' Hostel in Masasi District.

19 At the TANU National Conference, October 1967, a delegate, Mzee Diwani, makes a point from the floor.

20 President Nasser listen with attention as President Nyerere addresses the United Arab Republic's National Assembly in April 1967.

21 The landrover frequently provides a platform for President Nyerere during his safari through rural areas. This picture was taken at an unschedulled stop in Tanga Region in January 1967

22 Vice President Karume demonstrating the high quality of rice grown by the people of Zanzibar on a communal shamba after the land redistribution.

28

Socialism is not Racialism

On 14 February 1967, the President published this article in The
Nationalist—*a newspaper which is owned by TANU although it
has an autonomous editorial board. The article was written to forestall
racialism. There had been one or two signs that some individuals
wished to use the self-reliance demands of the Arusha Declaration,
and its public control provisions, as a means of fostering racial hatred,
but this was not the intention or the effect of the measures themselves.*

*By means of this article and the clear intentions of Government
as evidenced by such matters as the composition of management
boards for the new publicly owned industries, the racialists were prevented from nullifying the socialism of the Declaration.*

The Arusha Declaration and the actions relating to public ownership
which we took last week were all concerned with ensuring that we can
build socialism in our country. The nationalization and the taking
of a controlling interest in many firms were a necessary part of our
determination to organize our society in such a way that our efforts
benefit all our people and that there is no exploitation of one man by
another.

Yet these actions do not in themselves create socialism. They are
necessary to it, but as the Arusha Declaration states, they could
also be the basis for fascism—in other words, for the oppressive
extreme of capitalism. For the words with which I began my pamphlet 'Ujamaa' in 1962 remain valid; socialism is an attitude of
mind. The basis of socialism is a belief in the oneness of man and
the common historical destiny of mankind. Its basis, in other words,
is human equality.

Acceptance of this principle is absolutely fundamental to socialism.
The justification of socialism is man; not the state, not the flag.

Socialism is not for the benefit of black men, nor brown men, nor white men, nor yellow men. The purpose of socialism is the service of man, regardless of colour, size, shape, skill, ability, or anything else. And the economic institutions of socialism, such as those we are now creating in accordance with the Arusha Declaration, are intended to serve man in our society. Where the majority of the people in a particular society are black, then most of those who benefit from socialism there will be black. But it has nothing to do with their blackness; only with their humanity.

Some years ago I made the point that fascism and racialism can go together, but socialism and racialism are incompatible. The reason is easy to see. Fascism is the highest and most ruthless form of the exploitation of man by man; it is made possible by deliberate efforts to divide mankind and set one group of men against another group.

In Nazi Germany the majority were incited to join in hostile actions against the Jews—who were a minority religious and ethnic group living among them. 'I hate Jews' became the basis of life for supporters of the Nazi government.

But the man or woman who hates 'Jews', or 'Asians', or 'Europeans', or even 'West Europeans and Americans' is not a socialist. He is trying to divide mankind into groups and is judging men according to the skin colour and shape they were given by God. Or he is dividing men according to national boundaries. In either case he is denying the equality and brotherhood of man.

Without an acceptance of human equality there can be no socialism. This is true however 'socialist' the institutions may be. Thus it was that when Nazi Germany organized the Krupp group of industries no socialist could rejoice; for it simply meant that the fascist state was more highly organized than ever. Nor do socialists welcome the news that South Africa has established an oil trading and refining company in which the state owns a controlling interest. We know that this simply makes that fascist state more efficient in its oppression and more able to defend itself against attack.

We in Tanzania have to hold fast to this lesson, especially now as we advance on the socialist road. For it is true that because of our colonial history the vast majority of the capitalist organizations in this country are owned and run by Asians or by Western Europeans. Twenty years ago we could have said all the capitalists in this country were from those areas; we cannot say this now. For the truth is that capitalism and capitalist attitudes have nothing whatsoever to do with the race or national origin of those who believe in them or practise them. Indeed, nobody who was at Arusha needs any more proof that the temptations of capitalism ignore colour boundaries. Even leaders of TANU were getting deeply involved in the practices of capitalism and landlordism. A few had started talking of 'my Company'. And very many others would have done so if they could; they were capitalists by desire even when they could not be so in practice. Hence the resolution on leadership. Hence the difficulties we must expect in enforcing this resolution.

Socialism has nothing to do with race, nor with country of origin. In fact any intelligent man, whether he is a socialist or not, realizes that there are socialists in capitalist countries—and from capitalist countries. Very often such socialists come to work in newly independent and avowedly socialist countries like Tanzania, because they are frustrated in their capitalist homeland. Neither is any intelligent man blind to the fact that there are frustrated capitalists in the communist countries—just as there will in time be frustrated capitalists in Tanzania. It may even be that some of those frustrated capitalists from Eastern countries come to work with us.

Neither is it sensible for a socialist to talk as if all capitalists are devils. It is one thing to dislike the capitalist system, and to try and frustrate people's capitalist desires. But it would be as stupid for us to assume that capitalists have horns as it is for people in Western Europe to assume that we in Tanzania have become devils.

In fact the leaders in the capitalist countries have now begun to realize that communists are human beings like themselves—that they are not devils. One day they will realize that this includes the Chinese communists! It would be very absurd if we react to the stupidity they are growing out of, and become equally stupid ourselves in the opposite direction! We have to recognize in our words and our actions that capitalists are human beings as much as socialists. They may be wrong; indeed by dedicating ourselves to socialism we are saying that they are. But our task is to make it impossible for capitalism to dominate us. Our task is not to persecute capitalists or make dignified life impossible for those who would be capitalists if they could.

In truth it is necessary for socialists to think about issues—about policies—and about how our institutions can serve the people of our society. To try and divide up the people working for our nation into groups of 'good' and 'bad' according to their skin colour, or their national origin, or their tribal origin, is to sabotage the work we have just embarked upon. We should decide whether a person is efficient in a particular job, whether he is honest, and whether he is carrying out his task loyally. But those of us who call ourselves scientific socialists must be scientific and objective in our thinking and in making such judgements. We must think about men, and an individual man, not about 'Asians', 'Europeans', 'Americans', and so on.

Certainly socialism in Tanzania will be built by Tanzanians. And certainly we are working for the time when all those in our Government employment will be Tanzanians—though they will not all be black Tanzanians. But it is absurd for anyone to suggest that because we now have non-Tanzanians working for Government—or in the newly nationalized industries—that we do not control our own affairs. Only those who are lacking in self-confidence, or who are trying to hide their own shortcomings, could say this now. For all the evidence is against them. We obtained our independence although we were governed by colonialists. We became a Republic although there were many expatriates working here—at that time even in high positions. We effected the Union of Tanganyika and Zanzibar although many Government servants on the mainland came from countries which did not like the Zanzibar Revolution. We have accepted the Arusha Declaration, and in the space of one week have nationalized or taken control of all the large capitalist firms and institutions which could have dominated our economy. In all these activities we have used all the Government servants concerned. And all—Tanzanians and non-Tanzanians alike—are carrying out our decisions loyally, and are working very hard indeed.

The Arusha Declaration talks of men, and their beliefs. It talks of socialism and capitalism, of socialists and capitalists. It does not talk about racial groups or nationalities. On the contrary, it says that all those who stand for the interests of the workers and peasants, anywhere in the world, are our friends. This means that we must judge the character and ability of each individual, not put each person into a prearranged category of race or national origin and judge them accordingly. Certainly no one can be a socialist unless he at least tries to do this. For if the actions taken under the Arusha Declaration are to mean anything to our people, then we must accept this basic oneness of man. What matters now is that we should succeed in the work we have undertaken. The colour or origin of the man who is working to that end does not matter in the very least. And each one of us must fight, in himself, the racialist habits of thought which were part of our inheritance from colonialism.

It is not an easy thing to overcome such habits. But we have always known that it is necessary, and that racialism is evil. We fought our independence campaign on that basis. And the equality of man is the first item in the TANU Creed. For in our constitution we say 'TANU believes (a) That all human beings are equal; (b) That every individual has a right to dignity and respect'.

If we are to succeed in building a socialist state in this country it is essential that every citizen, and especially every TANU leader, should live up to that doctrine. Let us always remember two things. We have dedicated ourselves to build a socialist society in Tanzania. And, socialism and racialism are incompatible.

29

Economic Nationalism

On the 28 February 1967, President Nyerere opened an extension of the Tanzania Breweries plant in Dar es Salaam. This firm was one of those in which Government had announced its intention of securing majority control, and the President therefore began by paying tribute to the work which had been done by the private company, its management and workers. He then proceeded to discuss the nationalism involved in the economic take-over of this and other firms.

... We decided to secure majority ownership in these industries because they are key points in our economy, and because we believe that they should therefore be under the control of Tanzania. Our purpose was thus primarily a nationalist purpose; it was an extension of the political control which the Tanzanian people secured in 1961.

Such an economic expression of nationalism is nothing new in the world; although the manner of the action may have been peculiarly Tanzanian, its motivation is common enough. Every country—whether it be capitalist, communist, socialist or fascist—wants to control its own economy. It does not necessarily exclude foreign participation in economic life, but it does insist as soon as it can that the major means of production, distribution and exchange are in the hands of its own nationals. This is basically what Tanzania was aiming at in the legislation passed earlier this month.

What this means is that Tanzania said: 'Now is the appropriate time for us to secure the control of our economy'. At independence we achieved political control, but all important industries remained in foreign hands. Some—indeed many—have been developing well; but it is not we who have been making the decisions—they have been made for us. We have tried to encourage foreign investors, and we could have prevented any we did not wish to receive. But we were inevitably kept out of positive decisions—a situation which no nation could be expected to enjoy.

This economic dependency was the result of the peaceful methods by which we were fortunate enough to obtain our independence. Countries which are forced to overthrow external or feudalist rulers by force usually secure control of their economy at that time. The Soviet Union and China are obvious examples of this—and I believe that even the American War of Independence resulted in what was called 'some acquisition of enemy property'. But capitalist countries of the West are also now taking steps to ensure that their economies stay in the control of their own nationals. A number of European governments are now empowered to prevent private sales of major industrial or commercial enterprises when this might result in external control of the industry. Sometimes the governments use this power and sometimes they refrain, but the legislation was passed as an expression of the people's national feelings. And in these cases the power has been given to governments despite the total economic strength of the developed capitalist countries—and despite their own parallel investments in foreign countries.

Surely, if it is reasonable or understandable that Britain, Canada, and France, should protect their strong economies against domination by the even stronger American economy, it is also reasonable that Africa should be concerned about these matters? The fact that our national economies are weak does not alter things. On the contrary, the fact that we are undeveloped makes such industry as does exist the more vital to our future. It becomes more essential, not less, that our major means of production should be under the control of the people, and that the people's representatives should determine the policies followed.

As I have said, this economic nationalism has nothing to do with the ideologies of socialism, capitalism, or communism. It is universal among nation states. The time, and the method, of securing such control where it does not already exist will vary. But it would be absurd to expect Africa to accept that the well-being of its people should be indefinitely controlled from outside. Whatever economic system the peoples of different African countries eventually adopt, it is quite certain that sooner or later they will demand that the key positions of their economy are in the hands of their own citizens.

I think this contention is accepted, in theory at least, by all foreign businessmen. When communist countries come to places like Tanzania to participate in the establishment of a new factory or a new industry, they usually operate by making a loan which is to be repaid out of profits once the factory is working. But from the very beginning the factory is owned by the nation in whose territory it is situated. This is unaffected by the nationality of the management or the technicians at any one moment.

Capitalism, too, can make provision for this national control. Major capitalist enterprises are almost always 'public companies' —as Tanzania Breweries has been. This means that members of the public may buy ownership shares in the company. Tanzanians could buy shares in this brewery as much as anyone else—if they had the money to do so. Presumably, therefore, the initiators of this company accepted that at some time in the future the majority of shares may be held by Tanzanians. That is to say, the initiators of this enterprise accepted in theory the possibility of their company coming under the control of Tanzanians.

In other words, ideological differences between countries affect the method, not necessarily the fact, of securing national control. The question is not whether nations control their economy, but how they do so. The real ideological choice is between controlling the economy through domestic private enterprise, or doing so through some state or other collective institution.

But although this is an ideological choice, it is extremely doubtful whether it is a practical choice for an African nationalist. The pragmatist in Africa—the man who is completely uncommitted to one doctrine or another, but claims only to deal with the situation as it is—will find that the real choice is a different one. He will find that the choice is between foreign private ownership on the one hand, and local collective ownership on the other. For I do not think there is any free state in Africa where there is sufficient local capital, or a sufficient number of local entrepreneurs, for locally-based capitalism to dominate the economy. Private investment in Africa means overwhelming foreign private investment. A capitalistic economy means a foreign dominated economy. These are the facts of Africa's situation. The only way in which national control of the economy can be achieved is through the economic institutions of socialism.

To Tanzania this inevitable choice is not unwelcome. We are socialists as well as nationalists. We are committed to the creation of a classless society in which every able-bodied person is contributing to the economy through work, and we believe this can only be obtained when the major means of production are publicly owned and controlled. But the fact remains that our recent socialist measures were not taken out of a blind adherence to dogma. They are intended to serve our society.

Certain things follow from this. It follows that we want the enterprises we control to be efficient. It follows that we shall want them to expand as and when this becomes economically feasible. And it follows that we shall desire to co-operate with all those whose expertise or financial capacity can be of service to our nation.

For these reasons we have acted very fast to make clear what sectors of the existing economy we regard as central, and which must therefore be under the ultimate control of the Tanzanian people. I have stated that there will be no more nationalization or compulsory public participation in enterprises, apart from those covered by our recent legislation—and the only ones which do not yet know their exact position are the individual sisal estates. All others know. If they are not on the list they know they are free to continue in exclusive private ownership if they wish to do so. If at a later date, co-operatives or NUTA wish to participate in existing concerns, they will make a normal commercial approach, through NDC, and the matter will be settled on a willing-buyer, willing-seller basis. And if any private firm wishes public participation, the procedure is the same. I think this is clear. It should also be clear that in certain fields we would welcome new private investment—either foreign or local. And anyone considering this now knows exactly where he is, without possibility of misunderstanding.

It should also be clear that where we have secured majority control, but have not nationalized, we recognize the financial interest of our partners. We recognize that they will wish the firms to make a profit, and our answer is that we too desire these firms to run at a profit. The use of the profits thus gained may be different, but it is not in our interests, any more than it is in the interests of our partners, that these firms should fail.

And finally, it is in the interests of Tanzania that all the firms should be efficiently run. Their management must be good, and their workers must play a full part in securing high production Industrial discipline is an essential part of this process, and so is the fact that the managers should be people of skill and experience. Certainly we are interested in the Africanization of management—a term which incorporates all Tanzanian citizens regardless of colour. But this is nothing to do with our nationalization; we have made it clear for a long time that we expect all enterprises to be preparing Tanzanians to take over management posts. But we are under no illusions. We are not insisting that all the servants of a publicly controlled industry should now be Tanzanians. It is six years since we achieved control of our own Government, yet we still have many Government employees from other countries. And if we are realists as regards the Civil Service, it is surely unlikely that we shall become less realistic when our economy is at stake. The very fact that we as a nation control policy makes it possible for us to employ managers and technicians from other countries for as long as it is necessary for efficiency and economic expansion . . . .

30

Education for Self-Reliance

In March 1967, *President Nyerere issued the first of his 'post-Arusha' policy directives, on education. It analyses the system and attitudes of education as they had evolved in Tanganyika, and then goes on to demand an educational revolution—a re-casting of the system in the light of Tanzania's needs and social objectives.*

After this paper was issued a whole series of working parties—involving teachers and educational administrators—were set up to examine the means of implementing the new ideas. At the same time, many schools in the country—and particularly the secondary schools—began the work of opening farms, establishing workshops, and undertaking 'nation-building tasks'.

Since long before independence the people of this country, under the leadership of TANU, have been demanding more education for their children. But we have never really stopped to consider why we want education—what its purpose is. Therefore, although over time there have been various criticisms about the details of curricula provided in schools, we have not until now questioned the basic system of education which we took over at the time of independence. We have never done that because we have never thought about education except in terms of obtaining teachers, engineers, administrators, etc. Individually and collectively we have in practice thought of education as a training for the skills required to earn high salaries in the modern sector of our economy.

It is now time that we looked again at the justification for a poor society like ours spending almost 20 per cent of its Government revenues on providing education for its children and young people, and began to consider what that education should be doing. For in our circumstances it is impossible to devote Shs. 147,330,000/-

every year to education for some of our children (while others go without) unless its result has a proportionate relevance to the society we are trying to create.

The educational systems in different kinds of societies in the world have been, and are, very different in organization and in content. They are different because the societies providing the education are different, and because education, whether it be formal or informal, has a purpose. That purpose is to transmit from one generation to the next the accumulated wisdom and knowledge of the society, and to prepare the young people for their future membership of the society and their active participation in its maintenance or development.

This is true, explicitly or implicitly, for all societies—the capitalist societies of the West, the communist societies of the East, and the pre-colonial African societies too.

The fact that pre-colonial Africa did not have 'schools'—except for short periods of initiation in some tribes—did not mean that the children were not educated. They learned by living and doing. In the homes and on the farms they were taught the skills of the society, and the behaviour expected of its members. They learned the kind of grasses which were suitable for which purposes, the work which had to be done on the crops, or the care which had to be given to animals, by joining with their elders in this work. They learned the tribal history, and the tribe's relationship with other tribes and with the spirits, by listening to the stories of the elders. Through these means, and by the custom of sharing to which young people were taught to conform, the values of the society were transmitted. Education was thus 'informal'; every adult was a teacher to a greater or lesser degree. But this lack of formality did not mean that there was no education, nor did it affect its importance to the society. Indeed, it may have made the education more directly relevant to the society in which the child was growing up.

In Europe education has been formalized for a very long time. An examination of its development will show, however, that it has always had similar objectives to those implicit in the traditional African system of education. That is to say, formal education in Europe was intended to reinforce the social ethics existing in the particular country, and to prepare the children and young people for the place they will have in that society. The same thing is true of communist countries now. The content of education is somewhat different from that of Western countries, but the purpose is the same —to prepare young people to live in and to serve the society, and to transmit the knowledge, skills, and values and attitudes of the society. Wherever education fails in any of these fields, then the society falters in its progress, or there is social unrest as people find that their education has prepared them for a future which is not open to them.

COLONIAL EDUCATION IN TANZANIA AND THE INHERITANCE OF THE NEW STATE

The education provided by the colonial government in the two countries which now form Tanzania had a different purpose. It was not designed to prepare young people for the service of their own country; instead, it was motivated by a desire to inculcate the values of the colonial society and to train individuals for the service of the colonial state. In these countries the state interest in education therefore stemmed from the need for local clerks and junior officials; on top of that, various religious groups were interested in spreading literacy and other education as part of their evangelical work.

This statement of fact is not given as a criticism of the many individuals who worked hard, often under difficult conditions, in teaching and in organizing educational work. Nor does it imply that all the values these people transmitted in the schools were wrong or inappropriate. What it does mean, however, is that the educational system introduced into Tanzania by the colonialists was modelled on the British system, but with even heavier emphasis on subservient attitudes and on white-collar skills. Inevitably, too, it was based on the assumptions of a colonialist and capitalist society. It emphasized and encouraged the individualistic instincts of mankind, instead of his co-operative instincts. It led to the possession of individual material wealth being the major criterion of social merit and worth.

This meant that colonial education induced attitudes of human inequality, and in practice underpinned the domination of the weak by the strong, especially in the economic field. Colonial education in this country was therefore not transmitting the values and knowledge of Tanzanian society from one generation to the next; it was a deliberate attempt to change those values and to replace traditional knowledge by the knowledge from a different society. It was thus a part of a deliberate attempt to effect a revolution in the society; to make it into a colonial society which accepted its status and which was an efficient adjunct to the governing power. Its failure to achieve these ends does not mean that it was without an influence on the attitudes, ideas, and knowledge of the people who experienced it. Nor does that failure imply that the education provided in colonial days is automatically relevant for the purposes of a free people committed to the principle of equality.

The independent state of Tanzania in fact inherited a system of education which was in many respects both inadequate and inappropriate for the new state. It was, however, its inadequacy which was most immediately obvious. So little education had been provided that in December 1961, we had too few people with the necessary educational qualifications even to man the administration of government as it was then, much less undertake the big economic and social development work which was essential. Neither was the school population in 1961 large enough to allow for any expectation that this situation would be speedily corrected. On top of that, education was based upon race, whereas the whole moral case of the independence movement had been based upon a rejection of racial distinctions.

ACTION SINCE INDEPENDENCE

The three most glaring faults of the educational inheritance have already been tackled. First, the racial distinctions within education were abolished. Complete integration of the separate racial systems was introduced very soon after independence, and discrimination on grounds of religion was also brought to an end. A child in Tanzania can now secure admittance to any Government or Government-aided school in this country without regard to his race or religion and without fear that he will be subject to religious indoctrination as the price of learning.

Secondly, there has been a very big expansion of educational facilities available, especially at the secondary school and post-secondary school levels. In 1961 there were 490,000 children attending primary schools in Tanganyika, the majority of them only going up to Standard IV. In 1967 there were 825,000 children attending such schools, and increasingly these will be full seven-year primary schools. In 1961, too, there were 11,832 children in secondary schools, only 176 of whom were in Form VI. This year there are 25,000 and 830. This is certainly something for our young state to be proud of. It is worth reminding ourselves that our present problems (especially the so-called problem of the primary school leavers) are revealing themselves largely because of these successes.

The third action we have taken is to make the education provided in all schools much more Tanzanian in content. No longer do our children simply learn British and European history. Faster than would have been thought possible, our University College and other institutions are providing materials on the history of Africa and making these available to our teachers. Our national songs and dances are once again being learned by our children; our national language has been given the importance in our curriculum which it needs and deserves. Also, civics classes taken by Tanzanians are beginning to give the secondary school pupils an understanding of the organization and aims of our young state. In these and other ways changes have been introduced to make our educational system more relevant to our needs. At this time, when there is so much general and justified questioning of what is being done, it is appropriate that we should pay tribute to the work of our teachers and those who support their work in the Ministry, in the Institute of Education, the University College and the District Councils.

Yet all these things I have mentioned are modifications of the system we have inherited. Their results have not yet been seen; it takes years for a change in education to have its effect. The events of 1966 do suggest, however, that a more thorough examination of the education we are providing must be made. It is now clearly time for us to think seriously about this question: 'What is the educational system in Tanzania intended to do—what is its purpose?'. Having decided that, we have to look at the relevance of the existing structure and content of Tanzanian education for the task it has to do. In the light of that examination we can consider whether, in our present circumstances, further modifications are required or whether we need a change in the whole approach.

WHAT KIND OF SOCIETY ARE WE TRYING TO BUILD?

Only when we are clear about the kind of society we are trying to build can we design our educational service to serve our goals. But this is not now a problem in Tanzania. Although we do not claim to have drawn up a blueprint of the future, the values and objectives of our society have been stated many times. We have said that we want to create a socialist society which is based on three principles: equality and respect for human dignity; sharing of the resources which are produced by our efforts; work by everyone and exploitation by none. We have set out these ideas clearly in the National Ethic; and in the Arusha Declaration and earlier documents we have outlined the principles and policies we intend to follow. We have also said on many occasions that our objective is greater African unity, and that we shall work for this objective while in the meantime defending the absolute integrity and sovereignty of the United Republic. Most often of all, our Government and people have stressed the equality of all citizens, and our determination that economic, political, and social policies shall be deliberately designed to make a reality of that equality in all spheres of life. We are, in other words, committed to a socialist future and one in which the people will themselves determine the policies pursued by a Government which is responsible to them

It is obvious, however, that if we are to. make progress towards these goals, we in Tanzania must accept the realities of our present position, internally and externally, and then work to change these realities into something more in accord with our desires. And the truth is that our United Republic has at present a poor, undeveloped, and agricultural economy. We have very little capital to invest in big factories or modern machines; we are short of people with skill and experience. What we do have is land in abundance and people who are willing to work hard for their own improvement. It is the use of these latter resources which will decide whether we reach our total goals or not. If we use these resources in a spirit of self-reliance as the basis for development, then we shall make progress slowly but surely. And it will then be real progress, affecting the lives of the masses, not just having spectacular show-pieces in the towns while the rest of the people of Tanzania live in their present poverty.

Pursuing this path means that Tanzania will continue to have a predominantly rural economy for a long time to come. And as it is in the rural areas that people live and work, so it is in the rural areas that life must be improved. This is not to say that we shall have no industries and factories in the near future. We have some now and they will continue to expand. But it would be grossly unrealistic to imagine that in the near future more than a small proportion of our people will live in towns and work in modern industrial enterprises. It is therefore the villages which must be made into places where people live a good life; it is in the rural areas that people must be able to find their material well-being and their satisfactions.

This improvement in village life will not, however, come automatically. It will come only if we pursue a deliberate policy of using the resources we have—our manpower and our land—to the best advantage. This means people working hard, intelligently, and together; in other words, working in co-operation. Our people in the rural areas, as well as their Government, must organize themselves co-operatively and work for themselves through working for the community of which they are members. Our village life, as well as our state organization, must be based on the principles of socialism and that equality in work and return which is part of it.

This is what our educational system has to encourage. It has to foster the social goals of living together, and working together, for the common good. It has to prepare our young people to play a dynamic and constructive part in the development of a society in which all members share fairly in the good or bad fortune of the group, and in which progress is measured in terms of human well-being, not prestige buildings, cars, or other such things, whether privately or publicly owned. Our education must therefore inculcate a sense of commitment to the total community, and help the pupils to accept the values appropriate to our kind of future, not those appropriate to our colonial past.

This means that the educational system of Tanzania must emphasize co-operative endeavour, not individual advancement; it must stress concepts of equality and the responsibility to give service which goes with any special ability, whether it be in carpentry, in animal husbandry, or in academic pursuits. And, in particular, our education must counteract the temptation to intellectual arrogance; for this leads to the well-educated despising those whose abilities are non-academic or who have no special abilities but are just human beings.

Such arrogance has no place in a society of equal citizens.

It is, however, not only in relation to social values that our educational system has a task to do. It must also prepare young people for the work they will be called upon to do in the society which exists in Tanzania—a rural society where improvement will depend largely upon the efforts of the people in agriculture and in village development. This does not mean that education in Tanzania should be designed just to produce passive agricultural workers of different levels of skill who simply carry out plans or directions received from above. It must produce good farmers; it has also to prepare people for their responsibilities as free workers and citizens in a free and democratic society, albeit a largely rural society. They have to be able to think for themselves, to make judgements on all the issues affecting them; they have to be able to interpret the decisions made through the democratic institutions of our society, and to implement them in the light of the peculiar local circumstances where they happen to live.

It would thus be a gross misinterpretation of our needs to suggest that the educational system should be designed to produce robots, who work hard but never question what the leaders in Government or TANU are doing and saying. For the people are, and must be, Government and TANU. Our Government and our Party must always be responsible to the people, and must always consist of representatives—spokesmen and servants of the people. The education provided must therefore encourage the development in each citizen of three things; an enquiring mind; an ability to learn from what others do, and reject or adapt it to his own needs; and a basic confidence in his own position as a free and equal member of the society, who values others and is valued by them for what he does and not for what he obtains.

These things are important for both the vocational and the social aspects of education. However much agriculture a young person learns, he will not find a book which will give him all the answers to all the detailed problems he will come across on his own farm. He will have to learn the basic principles of modern knowledge in agriculture and then adapt them to solve his own problems. Similarly, the free citizens of Tanzania will have to judge social issues for themselves; there neither is, nor will be, a political 'holy book' which purports to give all the answers to all the social, political and economic problems which will face our country in the future. There will be philosophies and policies approved by our society which citizens should consider and apply in the light of their own thinking and experience. But the educational system of Tanzania would not be serving the interests of a democratic socialist society if it tried to stop people from thinking about the teachings, policies or the beliefs of leaders, either past or present. Only free people conscious of their worth and their equality can build a free society.

SOME SALIENT FEATURES OF THE EXISTING EDUCATIONAL SYSTEM

These are very different purposes from those which are promoted by our existing educational arrangements. For there are four basic elements in the present system which prevent, or at least discourage, the integration of the pupils into the society they will enter, and which do encourage attitudes of inequality, intellectual arrogance and intense individualism among the young people who go through our schools.

First, the most central thing about the education we are at present providing is that it is basically an elitist education designed to meet the interests and needs of a very small proportion of those who enter the school system.

Although only about 13 per cent of our primary school children will get a place in a secondary school, the basis of our primary school education is the preparation of pupils for secondary schools. Thus 87 per cent of the children who finished primary school last year—and a similar proportion of those who will finish this year—do so with a sense of failure, of a legitimate aspiration having been denied them. Indeed we all speak in these terms, by referring to them as those who failed to enter secondary schools, instead of simply as those who have finished their primary education. On the other hand, the other 13 per cent have a feeling of having deserved a prize—and the prize they and their parents now expect is high wages, comfortable employment in towns, and personal status in the society. The same process operates again at the next highest level, when entrance to university is the question at issue.

In other words, the education now provided is designed for the few who are intellectually stronger than their fellows; it induces among those who succeed a feeling of superiority, and leaves the majority of the others hankering after something they will never obtain. It induces a feeling of inferiority among the majority, and can thus not produce either the egalitarian society we should build, nor the attitudes of mind which are conducive to an egalitarian society. On the contrary, it induces the growth of a class structure n our country.

Equally important is the second point; the fact that Tanzania's education is such as to divorce its participants from the society it is supposed to be preparing them for. This is particularly true of secondary schools, which are inevitably almost entirely boarding schools; but to some extent, and despite recent modifications in the curriculum, it is true of primary schools too. We take children from their parents at the age of seven years, and for up to $7\frac{1}{2}$ hours a day we teach them certain basic academic skills. In recent years we have tried to relate these skills, at least in theory, to the life which the children see around them. But the school is always separate; it is not part of the society. It is a place children go to and which they and their parents hope will make it unnecessary for them to become farmers and continue living in the villages.

The few who go to secondary schools are taken many miles away from their homes; they live in an enclave, having permission to go into the town for recreation, but not relating the work of either town or country to their real life—which is lived in the school compound. Later a few people go to university. If they are lucky enough to enter Dar es Salaam University College they live in comfortable quarters, feed well, and study hard for their degree. When they have been successful in obtaining it, they know immediately that they will receive a salary of something like £660 per annum. That is what they have been aiming for; it is what they have been encouraged to aim for. They may also have the desire to serve the community, but their idea of service is related to status and the salary which a university education is expected to confer upon its recipient. The salary and the status have become a right automatically conferred by the degree.

It is wrong of us to criticize the young people for these attitudes. The new university graduate has spent the larger part of his life separated and apart from the masses of Tanzania; his parents may be poor, but he has never fully shared that poverty. He does not really know what it is like to live as a poor peasant. He will be more at home in the world of the educated than he is among his own parents. Only during vacations has he spent time at home, and even then he will often find that his parents and relatives support his own conception of his difference, and regard it as wrong that he should live and work as the ordinary person he really is. For the truth is that many of the people in Tanzania have come to regard education as meaning that a man is too precious for the rough and hard life which the masses of our people still live.

The third point is that our present system encourages school pupils in the idea that all knowledge which is worthwhile is acquired from books or from 'educated people'—meaning those who have been through a formal education. The knowledge and wisdom of other old people is despised, and they themselves regarded as being ignorant and of no account. Indeed it is not only the education system which at present has this effect. Government and Party themselves tend to judge people according to whether they have 'passed school certificate', 'have a degree', etc. If a man has these qualifications we assume he can fill a post; we do not wait to find out about his attitudes, his character, or any other ability except the ability to pass examinations. If a man does not have these qualifications we assume he cannot do a job; we ignore his knowledge and experience. For example, I recently visited a very good tobacco-producing peasant. But if I tried to take him into Government as a Tobacco Extension Officer, I would run up against the system because he has no formal education. Everything we do stresses book learning, and underestimates the value to our society of traditional knowledge and the wisdom which is often acquired by intelligent men and women as they experience life, even without their being able to read at all.

This does not mean that any person can do any job simply because they are old and wise, nor that educational qualifications are not necessary. This is a mistake our people sometimes fall into as a reaction against the arrogance of the book-learned. A man is not necessarily wise because he is old; a man cannot necessarily run a factory because he has been working in it as a labourer or storekeeper for 20 years. But equally he may not be able to do so if he has a Doctorate in Commerce. The former may have honesty and ability to weigh up men; the latter may have the ability to initiate a transaction and work out the economics of it. But both qualifications are necessary in one man if the factory is to be a successful and modern enterprise serving our nation. It is as much a mistake to over-value book learning as it is to under-value it.

The same thing applies in relation to agricultural knowledge. Our farmers have been on the land for a long time. The methods they use are the result of long experience in the struggle with nature; even the rules and taboos they honour have a basis in reason. It is not enough to abuse a traditional farmer as old-fashioned; we must try to understand why he is doing certain things, and not just assume he is stupid. But this does not mean that his methods are sufficient for the future. The traditional systems may have been appropriate for the economy which existed when they were worked out and for the technical knowledge then available. But different tools and different land tenure systems are being used now; land should no longer be used for a year or two and then abandoned for up to 20 years to give time for natural regeneration to take place. The introduction of an ox-plough instead of a hoe—and, even more, the introduction of a tractor—means more than just a different way of turning over the land. It requires a change in the organization of work, both to see that the maximum advantage is taken of the new tool, and also to see that the new method does not simply lead to the rapid destruction of our land and the egalitarian basis of our society. Again, therefore, our young people have to learn both a practical respect for the knowledge of the old 'uneducated' farmer and an understanding of new methods and the reason for them.

Yet at present our pupils learn to despise even their own parents because they are old-fashioned and ignorant; there is nothing in our existing educational system which suggests to the pupil that he can learn important things about farming from his elders. The result is that he absorbs beliefs about witchcraft before he goes to school, but does not learn the properties of local grasses; he absorbs the taboos from his family but does not learn the methods of making nutritious traditional foods. And from school he acquires knowledge unrelated to agricultural life. He gets the worst of both systems!

Finally, and in some ways most importantly, our young and poor nation is taking out of productive work some of its healthiest and strongest young men and women. Not only do they fail to contribute to that increase in output which is so urgent for our nation; they themselves consume the output of the older and often weaker people. There are almost 25,000 students in secondary schools now; they do not learn as they work, they simply learn. What is more, they take it for granted that this should be so. Whereas in a wealthy country like the United States of America it is common for young people to work their way through high school and college, in Tanzania the structure of our education makes it impossible for them to do so. Even during the holidays we assume that these young men and women should be protected from rough work; neither they nor the community expect them to spend their time on hard physical labour or on jobs which are uncomfortable and unpleasant. This is not simply a reflection of the fact that there are many people looking for unskilled paid employment—pay is not the question at issue. It is a reflection of the attitude we have all adopted.

How many of our students spend their vacations doing a job which could improve people's lives but for which there is no money— jobs like digging an irrigation channel or a drainage ditch for a village, or demonstrating the construction and explaining the benefits of deep-pit latrines, and so on ? A small number have done such work in the National Youth Camps or through school-organized, nation-building schemes, but they are the exception rather than the rule. The vast majority do not think of their knowledge or their strength as being related to the needs of the village community.

CAN THESE FAULTS BE CORRECTED?

There are three major aspects which require attention if this situation is to change: the content of the curriculum itself, the organization of the schools, and the entry age into primary schools. But although these aspects are in some ways separate, they are also inter-locked. We cannot integrate the pupils and students into the future society simply by theoretical teaching, however well designed it is. Neither can the society fully benefit from an education system which is thoroughly integrated into local life but does not teach people the basic skills—for example, of literacy and arithmetic, or which fails to excite in them a curiosity about ideas. Nor can we expect those finishing primary schools to be useful young citizens if they are still only twelve or thirteen years of age.

In considering changes in the present structure it is also essential that we face the facts of our present economic situation. Every penny spent on education is money taken away from some other needed activity—whether it is an investment in the future, better medical services, or just more food, clothing and comfort for our citizens at present. And the truth is that there is no possibility of Tanzania being able to increase the proportion of the national income which is spent on education; it ought to be decreased. Therefore we cannot solve our present problems by any solution which costs more than is at present spent; in particular we cannot solve the 'problem of primary school leavers' by increasing the number of secondary school places.

This 'problem of primary school leavers' is in fact a product of the present system. Increasingly children are starting school at six or even five years of age, so that they finish primary school when they are still too young to become responsible young workers and citizens. On top of that is the fact that the society and the type of education they have received both led them to expect wage employment—probably in an office. In other words, their education was not sufficiently related to the tasks which have to be done in our society. This problem therefore calls for a major change in the content of our primary education and for the raising of the primary school entry age so that the child is older when he leaves, and also able to learn more quickly while he is at school.

There is no other way in which this problem of primary school leavers can be solved. Unpleasant though it may be, the fact is that it is going to be a long time before we can provide universal primary education in Tanzania; for the vast majority of those who do get this opportunity, it will be only the equivalent of the present seven years' education. It is only a few who will have the chance of going on to secondary schools, and quite soon only a proportion of these who will have an opportunity of going on to university, even if they can benefit from doing so. These are the economic facts of life for our country. They are the practical meaning of our poverty. The only choice before us is how we allocate the educational opportunities, and whether we emphasize the individual interests of the few or whether we design our educational system to serve the community as a whole. And for a socialist state only the latter is really possible.

The implication of this is that the education given in our primary schools must be a complete education in itself. It must not continue to be simply a preparation for secondary school. Instead of the primary school activities being geared to the competitive examination which will select the few who go on to secondary school, they must be a preparation for the life which the majority of the children will lead. Similarly, secondary schools must not be simply a selection process for the university, Teachers' Colleges, and so on. They must prepare people for life and service in the villages and rural areas of this country. For in Tanzania the only true justification for secondary education is that it is needed by the few for service to the many. The teacher in a seven-year primary school system needs an education which goes beyond seven years; the extension officer who will help a population with a seven-years' education needs a lot more himself. Other essential services need higher education—for example, doctors and engineers need long and careful training. But publicly provided 'education for education's sake' must be general education for the masses. Further education for a selected few must be education for service to the many. There can be no other justification for taxing the many to give education to only a few.

Yet it is easy to say that our primary and secondary schools must prepare young people for the realities and needs of Tanzania; to do it requires a radical change, not only in the education system but also in many existing community attitudes. In particular, it requires that examinations should be down-graded in Government and public esteem. We have to recognize that although they have certain advantages—for example, in reducing the dangers of nepotism and tribalism in a selection process—they also have severe disadvantages too. As a general rule they assess a person's ability to learn facts and present them on demand within a time period. They do not always succeed in assessing a power to reason, and they certainly do not assess character or willingness to serve.

Further, at the present time our curriculum and syllabus are geared to the examinations set—only to a very limited extent does the reverse situation apply. A teacher who is trying to help his pupils often studies the examination papers for past years and judges what questions are most likely to be asked next time; he then concentrates his teaching on those matters, knowing that by doing so he is giving his children the best chance of getting through to secondary school or university. And the examinations our children at present sit are themselves geared to an international standard and practice which has developed regardless of our particular problems and needs. What we need to do now is think first about the education we want to provide, and when that thinking is completed think about whether some form of examination is an appropiate way of closing an education phase. Then such an examination should be designed to fit the education which has been provided.

Most important of all is that we should change the things we demand of our schools. We should not determine the type of things children are taught in primary schools by the things a doctor, engineer, teacher, economist, or administrator needs to know. Most of our pupils will never be any of these things. We should determine the types of things taught in the primary schools by the things which the boy or girl ought to know—that is, the skills he ought to acquire and the values he ought to cherish if he, or she, is to live happily and well in a socialist and predominantly rural society, and contribute to the improvement of life there. Our sights must be on the majority; it is they we must be aiming at in determining the curriculum and syllabus. Those most suitable for further education will still become obvious and they will not suffer. For the purpose is not to provide an inferior education to that given at present. The purpose is to provide a different education—one realistically designed to fulfil the common purpose of education in the particular society of Tanzania. The same thing must be true at post-primary schools. The object of the teaching must be the provision of knowledge, skills and attitudes which will serve the student when he or she lives and works in a developing and changing socialist state; it must not be aimed at university entrance.

Alongside this change in the approach to the curriculum there must be a parallel and integrated change in the way our schools are run, so as to make them and their inhabitants a real part of our society and our economy. Schools must, in fact, become communities —and communities which practise the precept of self-reliance. The teachers, workers, and pupils together must be the members of a social unit in the same way as parents, relatives, and children are the family social unit. There must be the same kind of relationship between pupils and teachers within the school community as there is between children and parents in the village. And the former community must realize, just as the latter do, that their life and well-being depend upon the production of wealth—by farming or other activities. This means that all schools, but especially secondary schools and other forms of higher education, must contribute to their own upkeep; they must be economic communities as well as social and educational communities. Each school should have, as an integral part of it, a farm or workshop which provides the food eaten by the community, and makes some contribution to the total national income.

This is not a suggestion that a school farm or workshop should be attached to every school for training purposes. It is a suggestion that every school should also be a farm; that the school community should consist of people who are both teachers and farmers, and pupils and farmers. Obviously if there is a school farm, the pupils working on it should be learning the techniques and tasks of farming. But the farm would be an integral part of the school—and the welfare of the pupils would depend on its output, just as the welfare of a farmer depends on the output of his land. Thus, when this scheme is in operation, the revenue side of school accounts would not just read as at present—'Grant from Government . . .; Grant from voluntary agency or other charity . . .'. They would read— 'Income from sale of cotton (or whatever other cash crop was appropriate for the area) . . .; Value of the food grown and consumed . . .; Value of labour done by pupils on new building, repairs, equipment, etc . . .; Government subvention . . .; Grant from . . .'.

This is a break with our educational tradition, and unless its purpose and its possibilities are fully understood by teachers and parents, it may be resented at the beginning. But the truth is that it is not a regressive measure, nor a punishment either for teachers or pupils. It is a recognition that we in Tanzania have to work our way out of poverty, and that we are all members of the one society, depending upon each other. There will be difficulties of implementation, especially at first. For example, we do not now have a host of experienced farm managers who could be used as planners and teachers on the new school farms. But this is not an insuperable difficulty; and certainly life will not halt in Tanzania until we get experienced farm managers. Life and farming will go on as we train. Indeed, by using good local farmers as supervisors and teachers of particular aspects of the work, and using the services of the Agricultural Officers and assistants, we shall be helping to break down the notion that only book learning is worthy of respect. This is an important element in our socialist development.

Neither does this concept of schools contributing to their own upkeep simply mean using our children as labourers who follow traditional methods. On the contrary, on a school farm pupils can learn by doing. The important place of the hoe and of other simple tools can be demonstrated; the advantages of improved seeds, of simple ox-ploughs, and of proper methods of animal husbandry can become obvious; and the pupils can learn by practice how to use these things to the best advantage. The farm work and products should be integrated into the school life; thus the properties of fertilizers can be explained in the science classes, and their use and limitations experienced by the pupils as they see them in use. The possibilities of proper grazing practices, and of terracing and soil conservation methods can all be taught theoretically, at the same time as they are put into practice; the students will then understand what they are doing and why, and will be able to analyse any failures and consider possibilities for greater improvement.

But the school farms must not be, and indeed could not be, highly mechanized demonstration farms. We do not have the capital which would be necessary for this to happen, and neither would it teach the pupils anything about the life they will be leading. The school farms must be created by the school community clearing their own bush, and so on—but doing it together. They must be used with no more capital assistance than is available to an ordinary, established, co-operative farm where the work can be supervised. By such means the students can learn the advantages of co-operative endeavour, even when outside capital is not available in any significant quantities. Again, the advantages of co-operation could be studied in the classroom, as well as being demonstrated on the farm.

The most important thing is that the school members should learn that it is their farm, and that their living standards depend on it. Pupils should be given an opportunity to make many of the decisions necessary—for example, whether to spend money they have earned on hiring a tractor to get land ready for planting, or whether to use that money for other purposes on the farm or in the school, and doing the hard work themselves by sheer physical labour. By this sort of practice and by this combination of classroom work and farm work, our educated young people will learn to realize that if they farm well they can eat well and have better facilities in the dormitories, recreation rooms, and so on. If they work badly, then they themselves will suffer. In this process Government should avoid laying down detailed and rigid rules; each school must have considerable flexibility. Only then can the potential of that particular area be utilized, and only then can the participants practise—and learn to value— direct democracy.

By such means our students will relate work to comfort. They will learn the meaning of living together and working together for the good of all, and also the value of working together with the local non-school community. For they will learn that many things require more than school effort—that irrigation may be possible if they work with neighbouring farmers, that development requires a choice between present and future satisfaction, both for themselves and their village.

At the beginning it is probable that a good number of mistakes will be made, and it would certainly be wrong to give complete untrammelled choice to young pupils right from the start. But although guidance must be given by the school authorities and a certain amount of discipline exerted, the pupils must be able to participate in decisions and learn by mistakes. For example, they can learn to keep a school farm log in which proper records are kept of the work done, the fertilizers applied, or food given to the animals, etc., and the results from different parts of the farm. Then they can be helped to see where changes are required, and why. For it is also important that the idea of planning be taught in the classroom and related to the farm; the whole school should join in the programming of a year's work, and the break-down of responsibility and timing within that overall programme. Extra benefits to particular groups within the school might then well be related to the proper fulfilment of the tasks set, once all the members of the school have received the necessary minimum for healthy development. Again, this sort of planning can be part of the teaching of socialism.

Where schools are situated in the rural areas, and in relation to new schools built in the future, it should be possible for the school farm to be part of the school site. But in towns, and in some of the old-established schools in heavily populated areas, this will not be possible. In such cases a school might put more emphasis on other productive activities, or it may be that in boarding schools the pupils can spend part of the school year in the classroom and another part in camp on the school farm some distance away. The plan for each school will have to be worked out; it would certainly be wrong to exclude urban schools, even when they are day schools, from this new approach.

Many other activities now undertaken for pupils, especially in secondary schools, should be undertaken by the pupils themselves. After all, a child who starts school at seven years of age is already fourteen before he enters secondary school, and may be twenty or twenty-one when he leaves. Yet in many of our schools now we employ cleaners and gardeners, not just to supervise and teach but to do all that work. The pupils get used to the idea of having their food prepared by servants, their plates washed up for them, their rooms cleaned, and the school garden kept attractive. If they are asked to participate in these tasks, they even feel aggrieved and do as little as possible, depending on the strictness of the teacher's supervision. This is because they have not learned to take a pride in having clean rooms and nice gardens, in the way that they have learned to take a pride in a good essay or a good mathematics paper. But is it impossible for these tasks to be incorporated into the total teaching task of the school? Is it necessary for head teachers and their secretaries to spend hours working out travel warrants for school holidays, and so on? Can none of these things be incorporated into classroom teaching so that pupils learn how to do these things for themselves by doing them? Is it impossible, in other words, for secondary schools at least to become reasonably self-sufficient communities, where the teaching and supervisory skills are imported from outside, but where other tasks are either done by the community or paid for by its productive efforts? It is true that, to the pupils, the school is only a temporary community, but for up to seven years this is the group to which they really belong.

Obviously such a position could not be reached overnight. It requires a basic change in both organization and teaching, and will therefore have to be introduced gradually, with the schools taking an increasing responsibility for their own well-being as the months pass. Neither would primary schools be able to do so much for themselves -although it should be remembered that the older pupils will be thirteen and fourteen years of age, at which time children in many European countries are already at work.

But, although primary schools cannot accept the same responsibility for their own well-being as secondary schools, it is absolutely vital that they, and their pupils, should be thoroughly integrated into the village life. The pupils must remain an integral part of the family (or community) economic unit. The children must be made part of the community by having responsibilities to the community, and having the community involved in school activities. The school work—terms, times, and so on—must be so arranged that the children can participate, as members of the family, in the family farms, or as junior members of the community on community farms. At present children who do not go to school work on the family or community farm, or look after cattle, as a matter of course. It must be equally a matter of course that the children who do attend school should participate in the family work—not as a favour when they feel like it, but as a normal part of their upbringing. The present attitudes whereby the school is regarded as something separate, and the pupils as people who do not have to contribute to the work, must be abandoned. In this, of course, parents have a special duty; but the schools can contribute a great deal to the development of this attitude.

There are many different ways in which this integration can be achieved. But it will have to be done deliberately, and with the conscious intention of making the children realize that they are being educated by the community in order that they shall become intelligent and active members of the community. One possible way of achieving this would give to primary school pupils the same advantages of learning by doing as the secondary school pupils will have. If the primary school children work on a village communal farm—perhaps having special responsibility for a given number of acres—they can learn new techniques and take a pride in a school community achievement. If there is no communal farm, then the school can start a small one of their own by appealing to the older members to help in the bush-clearing in return for a school contribution in labour to some existing community project.

Again, if development work—new buildings or other things—are needed in the school, then the children and the local villagers should work on it together, allocating responsibility according to comparative health and strength. The children should certainly do their own cleaning (boys as well as girls should be involved in this), and shoul learn the value of working together and of planning for the future. Thus for example, if they have their own shamba the children should be involved not only in the work, but also in the allocation of any food or cash crop produced. They should participate in the choise between benefit to the school directly, or to the village as a whole, and between present or future benefit. By these and other appropriate means the children must learn from the beginning to the end of their school life that education does not set them apart, but is designed to help them be effective members of the community—for their own benefit as well as that of their country and their neighbours.

One difficulty in the way of this kind of reorganization is the present examination system; if pupils spend more of their time on learning to do practical work, and on contributing to their own upkeep and the development of the community, they will not be able to take the present kind of examinations—at least within the same time period. It is, however, difficult to see why the present examination system should be regarded as sacrosanct. Other countries are moving away from this method of selection, and either abandoning examinations altogether at the lowest levels, or combining them with other assessments. There is no reason why Tanzania should not combine an examination, which is based on the things we teach, with a teacher and pupil assessment of work done for the school and community. This would be a more appropriate method of selecting entrants for secondary schools and for university, Teacher Training Colleges, and so on, than the present purely academic procedure. Once a more detailed outline of this new approach to education is worked out, the question of selection procedure should be looked at again.

This new form of working in our schools will require some considerable organizational change. It may be also that the present division of the school year into rigid terms with long holidays would have to be re-examined; animals cannot be left alone for part of the year, nor can a school farm support the students if everyone is on holiday when the crops need planting, weeding or harvesting. But it should not be impossible for school holidays to be staggered so that different forms go at different periods or, in double-stream secondary schools, for part of a form to go at one time and the rest at another. It would take a considerable amount of organization and administration, but there is no reason why it could not be done if we once make up our minds to it.

It will probably be suggested that if the children are working as well as learning they will therefore be able to learn less academically, and that this will affect standards of administration, in the professions and so on, throughout our nation in time to come. In fact it is doubtful whether this is necessarily so; the recent tendency to admit children to primary schools at ages of five and six years has almost certainly meant that less can be taught at the early stages. The reversion to seven or eight years' entrance will allow the pace to be increased somewhat; the older children inevitably learn a little faster. A child is unlikely to learn less academically if the studies are related to the life he sees around him.

But even if this suggestion were based on provable fact, it could not be allowed to over-ride the need for change in the direction of educational integration with our national life. For the majority of our people the thing which matters is that they should be able to read and write fluently in Swahili, that they should have an ability to do arithmetic, and that they should know something of the history, values, and workings of their country and their Government, and that they should acquire the skills necessary to earn their living. (It is important to stress that in Tanzania most people will earn their living by working on their own or on a communal shamba, and only a few will do so by working for wages which they have to spend on buying things the farmer produces for himself.) Things like health science, geography, and the beginning of English, are also important, especially so that the people who iwish may be able to learn more by themselves in later life. But most important of all is that our primary school graduates should be able to fit into, and to serve, the communities from which they come.

The same principles of integration into the community, and applicability to its needs, must also be followed at post-secondary level, but young people who have been through such an integrated system of education as that outlined are unlikely to forget their debt to the community by an intense period of study at the end of their formal educational life. Yet even at university, medical school, or other post-secondary levels, there is no reason why students should continue to have all their washing up and cleaning done for them. Nor is there any reason why students at such institutions should not be required as part of their degree or professional training, to spend at least part of their vacations contributing to the society in a manner related to their studies. At present some undergraduates spend their vacations working in Government offices—getting paid at normal employee rates for doing so. It would be more appropriate (once the organization had been set up efficiently) for them to undertake projects needed by the community, even if there is insufficient money for them to constitute paid employment. For example, the collection of local history, work on the census, participation in adult education activities, work in dispensaries, etc., would give the students practical experience in their own fields. For this they could receive the equivalent of the minimum wage, and any balance of money due for work which would otherwise have been done for higher wages could be paid to the college or institution and go towards welfare or sports equipment. Such work should earn credits for the student which count towards his examination result; a student who shirks such work—or fails to do it properly—would then find that two things follow. First, his fellow students might be blaming him for shortfalls in proposed welfare or other improvements; and second, his degree would be down-graded accordingly.

CONCLUSION

The education provided by Tanzania for the students of Tanzania must serve the purposes of Tanzania. It must encourage the growth of the socialist values we aspire to. It must encourage the development of a proud, independent, and free citizenry which relies upon itself for its own development, and which knows the advantages and the problems of co-operation. It must ensure that the educated know themselves to be an integral part of the nation and recognize the responsibility to give greater service the greater the opportunities they have had.

This is not only a matter of school organization and curriculum. Social values are formed by family, school, and society—by the total environment in which a child develops. But it is no use our educational system stressing values and knowledge appropriate to the past or to the citizens in other countries; it is wrong if it even contributes to the continuation of those inequalities and privileges which still exist in our society because of our inheritance. Let our students be educated to be members and servants of the kind of just and egalitarian future to which this country aspires.

31

A New Look at Conditions for Unity

Early in April 1967, *a number of leaders from the African states which had broken diplomatic relations with Britain over Rhodesia met in Cairo. Afterwards President Nyerere stayed on for a state visit, and he used the occasion of his address to the National Assembly of the United Arab Republic (on* 9 *April* 1967) *to discuss the need for a new look at the basis on which African unity could be built. He did this in the context of the difficulties and strains which had been caused by military coups in many African states, and the virtual failure of the* 1966 *meeting of the Organization of African Unity.*

... Today, therefore, I speak as one of 38 family members, and I intend to speak on a subject which affects us all—African unity. I do not speak for anyone but myself and my country. But I speak knowing that the people of Tanzania, and those of every other nation, are involved in the effects of one terrible reality. And that is that hardly a week passes but Africa is humiliated by outside powers. Our interests are ignored, our opinions are brushed aside, and our warnings disregarded. And this happens because the states of Africa are disunited—for no other reason than that.

Africa is ignored and exploited because we ourselves allow it to happen. We refuse to accept the implications of our condition. The power-hungry nations of the world, and the exploiters of the world, must be laughing silently in watching us. For they see 38 different states, which are tied together by the facts of geography and by mutual need, ignore their joint potential in the hopeless chase after the mirage of individual greatness. There is not one which could achieve it. Our separate land area or our population notwithstanding, we are each destined for a constant struggle to maintain our very independence unless we recognize the lesson of our own pasts. This tells us over and over again—unity is strength; division is weakness.

The advantages of continent-wide unity in the modern world do not need listing again. The UAR in particular is well aware of them. Yet the most basic truths can be forgotten if they are not constantly repeated, and in this time of difficulty there is a danger that Africa might forget one thing. That is that the problems which threaten to overwhelm us individually become containable in a wider context. The threat of internecine warfare—of one African state fighting against another—would be greatly reduced if there was one African state of which the contenders were both parts. The cut-throat competition between our poor nations for the economic favours of the rich powers would be eliminated if we dealt with them as a single unit. Our poverty would remain—it would not be transformed by an act of union. New problems of priorities would arise. But the possibility of others exploiting our poverty for their own benefit would disappear in unity, and therefore the road to the future would be opened wider than ever before.

In the early days of this decade the African states acted in recognition of these facts. They recognized that we are all members of one family, which might have internal squabbles, but which should present a united front to outsiders. When the Organization of African Unity was launched in 1963, all those who care for Africa and its people went on their way rejoicing. It appeared that Africa was setting out along the road to its great destiny. But since then—and especially during the last 18 months—we have suffered setback after setback. We have been forced to recognize a fact which our joy concealed from most of us—that Addis Ababa was only the first step on a long and difficult road. And from the euphoric illusions of those days we have now plummetted to the depths of despair.

It is my contention that just as we rejoiced too soon in 1963—just as we overestimated our achievement then—so now we are in danger of despairing too much. African unity is not lost. It will never be lost while there are people conscious of the need for it, and willing to work for it. I believe that there are still many such people in Africa now, and that what is required is more realistic thinking, and a deliberate dedication to this cause.

Such thinking—as always—involves recognizing the facts of Africa as they are, and acting accordingly. It is not necessary that we should like what we see; it is necessary only that we should face up to the facts of the present situation so that we may determine the action which is appropriate for our goal.

There are thus two things about which we have to be clear. The first is the purpose of African unity, and the second is the major obstacles which lie in its way. When we have determined these matters we can search intelligently for the way forward.

All the reasons for African unity can be summed up in one phrase—the welfare of the people of Africa. Their greater freedom is the objective—that is, freedom from outside oppression, from poverty and from the possibility of inter-African wars. There is no other. The people of Africa are the only justification for African unity, and they are also the only means through which it will be attained. No method which disregards their aspirations, their loyalties, and their present conditions,will succeed in reaching the goal.

Yet the truth is that human bein gs realize their social satisfactions most easily in small groups—in societies which they can readily understand, and where they can have an immediate and personal sense of involvement. A common language, a common history, and common symbols of power and life, are great aids to this sense of oneness. And for our peoples in particular, a recognizable and simple structure of authority is imperative. The large size which world conditions and modern technology demand of sovereign states is contrary to these desires. Bigness militates against the desire (which all men have) to know, or know of, those with whom he works in harness. For it is given to comparatively few men to have a really full comprehension of a large social unit. And there is a danger that people may feel that authority is an imposition unless they can know, and can call to account, those who are responsible for decisions whch directly affect their lives.

Thus, for the people of Africa, there may appear to be a conflict between the recognition of the need for all–African unity, and their desire to lead their own lives and control their own destiny. The conflict is, in truth, more apparent than real, but all of us are more conscious of surrendering our own exclusive power over ourselves than we are of obtaining a share in the power over others. Indeed, this desire to have at the same time the advantages of a large unit, and the benefits of a small one, is analogous to man's individual desire to do whatever he wishes, and his simultaneous desire to live in society—where his wishes must sometimes give way to the general good.

Within our separate national states most of us have already faced up to this problem, and made appropriate political and economic arrangements to deal with it. We have local government institutions, local co-operative societies, and so on. These allow our people to deal directly with matters of exclusive local concern, and at the same time ensure that they are integrated into the state apparatus for matters of general interest. By these means we try to find the appropriate balance between the needs of unity and the facts of diversity within our nations.

It is only by some analogous means of accommodating local differences that African unity will be possible. To wait for the time when there are no local differences, suspicions, or hostilities, is to wait for ever. Like-mindedness even on major economic and social questions among all African states is not likely to be achieved even after unity; it will never be achieved before. If we wait for that common approach, then Africa will never be united. We have to accept our differences and accommodate them. There is no other way.

The differences in policy which now exist between different African states are the result of many factors. The objective circumstances—geographic, social, or economic—are different; so too was the method of attaining independence, and so are the backgrounds and philosophical beliefs of those who have been accepted as national leaders. And all these things have had an influence on the present situation which cannot be ignored. For even if circumstances change greatly, and even if leadership changes, the present experience will determine the kind of future, and the kind of attitudes, which the people will adopt.

These facts we have to accept if we are to hope for unity. It is not part of the duty—even if it were within the power—of one African state to interfere with the affairs of another. Even if some of us believe that others are making dreadful mistakes, or being badly misled, we have no right to intervene—any more than they whom we condemn have the right to interfere in our way of conducting affairs. Africa is one; but it is also thirty-eight—and more. Only a recognition of this fact, and its limitations, will allow progress.

Fortunately I think this vital point is now generally acknowledged and accepted in Africa.

For African unity can only come about on the basis of agreement between all the peoples of Africa. And under present circumstances this means agreement by all the nation states of Africa. Not a single state of Africa—not a single people—would accept unity by conquest. It was our fate to be divided by colonialism; no military power can now cause us to unite. Nationalism is a fact—with all its advantages and disadvantages. It has been entrenched through the struggle for freedom, and through the post–independence experiences. Our only way to unified sovereignty is through the sovereign states which exist and which our people have accepted.

This means that unity will be hard to attain. It is never easy for a sovereign unit to surrender its autonomy to a larger grouping. It also means that the inevitable early difficulties of a United Africa will be compounded by the existing nationalisms. To imagine that a merger of sovereignties will automatically solve inter-African conflicts is to invite disaster. Unity will simply change the context in which these problems can be tackled. It will no more bring a solution to all the problems of living together than the formation of the United States of America has solved the problems of 'states' rights' versus the Federal Government. Only the greatest inter-African tolerance, patience, and dedication, will allow unity to advance or, once it is obtained, make it secure.

But to say that tolerance of diversity is essential to both the attainment and the maintenance of unity does not mean that there should be no considerations at all. It would be wrong to say that there are no principles underlying the search for unity. All that I am suggesting is that we have to be very careful in our thinking. We have to be quite clear what are the basic principles which over-ride even our people's need for unity in relation to the outside world. We also have to be clear what are the matters which could be contained, or dealt with, within the diversity of a united Africa.

Thus, for example, it is not possible for African states to compromise on the basic principles of African freedom and African equality. A leader like Tshombe, who was willing to employ South African racialists in order to maintain his own power, and who was willing to dismember an African state if he could not control it—such a man could obviously not bring his nation into a coherent African entity. But the reason is not that his economic policies involved compromise with the exploiters of Africa. The reason is his deliberate betrayal of the basic principles of African freedom and African equality. To negotiate with such a man would be equivalent to negotiating with the present regime in South Africa.

Yet even this question of whether or not an African state has relations with South Africa cannot be a simple criterion of loyalty to the goal of African freedom and unity. The geographical position of countries like Lesotho and Botswana means that they have no alternative but to live with the racialist regime. The real issue in such cases is not whether they are co-operating with South Africa on some things, but whether they are doing so simply to the extent that they must, or whether they are choosing to follow that path. Are these countries, in other words, acting like a man held in the jaws of a beast, who lies still in the hope of avoiding damage until a bid for freedom can be made—or until his friends can rescue him? Cases like this must be judged by Africa in the light of the objective circumstances, and Africa as a whole must try to distinguish between those states which embrace their captors and those which seek merely to survive.

There is all the difference in the world between the inevitable compromises which Zambia makes while preparing herself for the complete break with Rhodesia, and the action of those states which stand aside from United Nations sanctions and extend a hand of friendship to the bitterest enemies of Africa. In the one case Africa must be ready to help; in the other she must recognize a betrayal of the African struggle. But certainly Africa must be cautious about making judgements while it is not in a position to help those of our brothers who are being held to ransom by the South African regime. Countries like Botswana have a right to our sympathy and understanding even when we cannot give them practical help. Treachery we cannot accept; but a beleaguered garrison is expected to do little more than hold on until help arrives.

Africa must never compromise with treachery to our cause. Yet the word 'treachery' is a big, and inevitably a rather vague, term. We must avoid the danger of extending it so that it covers approaches to political and economic questions with which we do not agree. For differences in ideology must not preclude unity. There are, and will be, socialists and non-socialists, democrats and non-democrats in Africa. Some of us may believe—indeed do believe—that others are compromising the future of Africa for the doubtful favour of imperialist powers; some will believe that others are using too short a spoon to sup with communists. Some Africans may believe that other leaders are exploiting their people; some of us may feel bitter hostility towards those who have seized power from the people's democratic leaders. But whatever our feelings or private judgements, we have to accept the existing sovereignty of each African state. If the people of the state concerned acquiesce in the actions of their effective rulers, the rest of Africa does not have to rejoice; it merely cannot intervene. And it does have to accept that the country is still part of Africa. We have either to live with our neighbours or risk the whole future of our continent and its people. Our brothers may be wrong, but they remain our brothers. This appears to me the only attitude open to us on our path to real unity.

It is obvious, of course, that countries which have similarly motivated social and economic policies will build up close relations with each other—just as the UAR and Tanzania are doing. But our friendships must not be exclusive. Our relationships must exist under the umbrella of such institutions of all-African unity as exist at any one time. At present this means under the umbrella of the OAU. And it is particularly important that those of us who are really conscious of the urgent need for all-African unity should not do anything which will weaken it. If some states lose patience, or pursue short-term objectives even when they endanger the solidarity of our Organization, we have to recognize these facts and their effect. But such actions do not justify others treading the same path. On the contrary, it becomes the more important that others stand firm in support of the institution we have established. There can be no 'Organization of Socialist States', or of 'Conservative States' within the OAU. For the OAU is a geographical, not an ideological, grouping. The socialist countries at any rate recognize this. The socialist policies of our own countries must be safeguarded; the African orientated policies of non-socialist states will also have to be safeguarded. It is only after unity that we can each really begin the work of trying to convert Africa as a whole to one ideology or the other. The OAU must remain an all-African organization—and the supreme African organization. Any inter-state co-operation short of the merger of two or more states into one must be under its aegis. But an action by one or more states which reduces the effectiveness of the OAU does not excuse the rest of us from the responsibilities we have taken upon ourselves. The position is the same as that of each individual state when it became clear that there would be a widespread failure to honour the resolution calling for a break in diplomatic relations with Britain; each of us had separately to honour our joint decision or dishonour it. All African states have declared—over and over again—that they want African unity. We now have the duty of accepting the need for tolerance, patience —and hard thinking in its support. None of us is excused by the failures of others—nor even by our own.

This is the more important because of the damage which the OAU has suffered in recent months. We have to understand what has happened to our Organization, and why. Then we must begin to try and rectify the situation. And the truth is that some of us have been impatient. And some of us have not cared enough. Angry words demanding action, and lack of action, can both harm the OAU—and have already done so. Disputes between individual states have been allowed to interfere with African meetings—either preventing them from taking place effectively, or leading to automatic opposition to whatever the so-called 'enemy' proposes. Praiseworthy arrangements of economic co-operation within Africa have been allowed to develop into organizations to which almost exclusive loyalty is given. Goodwill visits to other parts of the world have been allowed to take precedence over our own meetings. And so on.

These are the facts. They are depressing. But they are no reason to abandon the OAU. They are a reason for looking at it afresh, and trying again to make it into a useful body. It has failed in many things; it will probably fail again in the future. But for all its weakness, it exists. It is the only institution for all-African discussion, consultation, and possibly at some time in the future, action. The work of 1963 was no wasted effort just because it has not allowed us to do all the things which need to be done. A man who has been sick for years may well overestimate his strength when he first gets on his feet, so that he falls and hurts himself. But he does not therefore resign himself to the life of a bedridden invalid. He rests a while, and then tries again—more slowly and carefully at the beginning. He learns from his mistakes. Africa must do likewise.

The people of our continent suffered from oppression, from colonialism, and feudalism, for years. In historical terms we achieved freedom peacefully—often (as in the case of Tanzania) by the cumulative effects of strong demonstrations of unity. It is not surprising, therefore, in the exuberance of our first freedom and our first steps towards unity, that we should have underestimated the task before us. Strong words, amounting almost to threats, showed our determination for independence. Africa has been acting on the assumption that this method is appropriate for the new circumstances, and that if we talk big other nations will tremble. We should have learned our lesson. If you talk big you have to be prepared to take big actions. If you know that this is impossible, or too costly, then noisy words from an all-African meeting simply preclude other forms of pressure. It is better to be silent and accept the jeers of the unintelligent while we work for Africa in other ways. For words without actions simply lay us open to ridicule. Unfortunately it is those who do not intend to follow their words with actions who usually shout the loudest. Still waters can run deep, and in time deep waters collect a strength which sweeps all obstacles before it.

Africa must be free. And Africa's freedom will only come through united action. The unity has to come before there will be any great advance against the remaining bastions of privilege and racism. And the unity can be strengthened by many different methods; by economic co-operation, by improved communications, by political unions, and so on. Any step to unity is a help provided that the ultimate goal of a united Africa is not precluded. And every step forward can have intermediate effects of strengthening the freedom fight, and also strengthening our powers of resistance against the pressures of international imperialisms. But we must never lose sight of the ultimate goal, nor mistake interim steps for the achievement.

The true revolutionary in Africa has to do two things at one and the same time. He has to keep his eyes and his attention on the road ahead, and use all the pragmatism of which he is capable so as to negotiate a passage. But at the same time he must keep the goal clearly in his sights, and let it govern his direction at all times. He must, in other words, be a realistic idealist! I should add that I do not myself believe this is a contradiction in terms!

Let us all go forward again; the road to African freedom and unity is long and rocky; but it is not impassable. When a bridge is washed away we can rebuild it. When a mountain blocks our path we can go round it or cut through it. Our tools are our hands, our brains, and our spirit. And these will suffice if we have courage, patience, stamina, and vision.

Let the knowledge of Africa's proper destiny inspire us, and may God help our efforts.

32

The Varied Paths to Socialism

On 10 *April* 1967, *during the same state visit to the United Arab Republic, President Nyerere was awarded an Honorary Degree by the University of Cairo. In his address to the assembled faculty and students on this occasion the President discussed socialism and his rejection of a socialist theology.*

The United Arab Republic and Tanzania are both committed to building socialism, and I would like to use the opportunity of your kind invitation to reflect upon what this means. In particular I wish to direct my remarks to considering its implications for those of us who are—or who may be in the future—in positions of authority or responsibility.

Over time there have been many definitions of socialism, and many books have been written which purport to explain its requirements and implications. Some of these have been valuable analyses of the problems in general, or of problems existing in particular places. We can learn from these writings.

Unfortunately, however, there has grown up what I can only call a 'theology of socialism'. People argue—sometimes quite violently— about what is the true doctrine, or what this or that writer meant when he used a particular phrase. This would not matter if it were simply a recreation of intellectuals, but in fact we have the peculiar position where leaders grappling with existing problems are denounced, or approved, on the grounds that they are—or are not— 'acting in accordance with the book—or one person's interpretation of the book.

Frankly this seems to me to be absurd. I am a Christian and it is part of my belief that the word of God is expressed in the Bible. To me, therefore, in spite of—or even because of—the contradictions of the Bible, it is quite sensible to try to get its full meaning, and, when I am trying to act in accordance with God's wishes, to refer to those who have given the Bible a detailed study. I believe that the same thing is true of those who accept the Koran as the inspired word of God's Prophet Mohammed. But the books on socialism are different. They are written by men; wise and clever men perhaps—but still men. Consequently we should use their books as we use the work of living people—knowing that one individual may contribute greatly to the solution of a problem, but that no man is infallible. Indeed, I think that this idea that there is one 'pure socialism', for which the recipe is already known, is an insult to human intelligence. It seems to me that man has yet to solve the problem of living in society, and that each of us may have something to contribute to the problems it involves. We should recognize that there are books on socialism which can illuminate the problems, and books which chart a way forward from a particular point. But that is all.

It is imperative that socialists continue thinking. And this thinking must be more than an attempt to discover what any so-called socialist Bible or socialist Koran really says and means. It is necessary that those who call themselves scientific socialists should be scientific! In that case they would accept or reject socialist ideas and methods in accordance with the objective circumstances of time and place. They would certainly not be hampered or inhibited by the irrelevancies of a socialist theology.

Let me, hasten to add that, in conformity with this approach to socialism I consider that my remarks here today are simply a contribution to the continuing discussion—no more!

Yet I am not saying that, in my view, socialism is a vague concept which can have as many different meanings and variations as there are people who advocate it. A useful definition of the basic assumption and purposes of socialism is not only possible; it is also essential. And from that basis certain practical principles do inevitably follow. But principles become effective only when they are applied to situations. To say that human life is sacred is to state a principle, but that principle only becomes meaningful when it is applied to saving someone from danger or refraining from such action as might jeopardize someone else's well-being. The principle is essential to social living; but it does not give an answer to every life situation

—for example, what should be done when a psychotic murderer's life threatens the safety of other people.

For socialism the basic purpose is the well-being of the people, and the basic assumption is an acceptance of human equality. For socialism there must be a belief that every individual man and woman, whatever colour, shape, race, creed, religion, or sex, is an equal member of society with equal rights in the society and equal duties to it.

A person who does not accept this may accept many policies pursued by socialists; but he cannot be a socialist. Nor can any socialist organization which is based on inequality justify the support of socialists, whatever its political or economic practices. The so-called 'national socialists' of Nazi Germany were no more socialist than the racialist government of South Africa is socialist—any particular policies of government control of the economy notwithstanding. In socialism there is no room for racialism, and no room either for doctrines of aristocracy. Neither is there any room for that kind of arrogance which leads educated men and women to despise the uneducated. The human equality before God which is the basis of all the great religions of the world is also the basis of the political philosophy of socialism.

Yet socialism is not Utopian. Nor is it unaware that men are unequal in their capacities. On the contrary, it is based on the facts of human nature. It is a doctrine which accepts mankind as it is, and demands such an organization of society that man's inequalities are put to the service of his equality.

Socialism is, in fact, the application of the principle of human equality to the social, economic, and political organization of society. It is a recognition that some human beings are physically strong and others weak, that some are intellectually able while others are rather dull, that some people are skilful in the use of their hands while others are clumsy. It involves, too, a recognition that every person has both a selfish and a social instinct, which are often in conflict. Socialist doctrine then demands the deliberate organization of society in such a manner that it is impossible—or at least very difficult—for individual desires to be pursued at the cost of other people, or for individual strength to be used for the exploitation of others.

For a socialist state these requirements have both a negative and a positive aspect. Men must be prevented from exploiting each other.

And at the same time institutions and organization must be such that man's needs and progress can be co-operatively secured.

There are two paths through which exploitation has been historically secured, and which must therefore be blocked. The first was the use of naked force. Originally through physical strength, and then through a monopoly of weapons of force, men imposed their will upon others. Armies were the instruments by which a minority kept an exploited majority under submission. The kind of revolution which took place in Egypt, where an army converted itself from being an instrument of oppression into being an instrument of the people in opposing oppression, is rare indeed. More usually it is the gradual growth of law, and the principle of equality before the law, which ease the severity of oppression until the people are in a position to take control of their own destiny.

But equality in law—even the theory of equality in the making of law—is not sufficient by itself. For the fact is that equality is indivisible. In practice it is not possible to be equal in some respects but not in others. Thus it is that in aristocratic societies a 'noble' and a 'commoner' are not equal before the law. It will be very unusual for the latter to defeat the former when they go to law for justice, and rare too for each to receive equal treatment for comparable offences against the society. Similarly, a rich man and a poor man are not equally treated for offences, nor equally likely to receive justice from the society in cases of dispute.

The Rule of Law, and Equality before the Law, are one essential means of preventing exploitation. But they are only practical when the society as a whole is based on the principles of equality—when, in other words, a socialist policy is being followed. Human beings being fallible, socialism does not guarantee justice; it has to be worked for and maintained even in a socialist society. But it is certain that it cannot be truly achieved except in that context.

The second major means of exploitation has been through private property. For when one man controls the means by which another earns or obtains the food, clothing and shelter which are essential to life, then there is no equality. One man must call another 'master' —for he is the master of life as truly as if he had the power to kill with a gun. The man whose means of living are controlled by another, must serve the interests of this other regardless of his own desires or his own needs. The nations which experienced feudalism and serfdom know this by experience. But it is as true in capitalist societies where the industries which men depend upon for their wages can be closed, contracted or expanded, and the workers have no voice in the decision and no alternative way of obtaining their food.

If a society is to be made up of equal citizens, then each man must control his own means of production. The farmer must own his own tools—his hoe or his plough. The carpenter must have his own saw and not be dependent upon the whims of another for its use. And so on. The tools of production must be under the control of the individual or group which depends upon them for life.

In African traditional life this was the normal routine. In only a few small areas of Tanzania, for example, was there anything approaching a feudal system. Over the greater part of the country each family worked the land it had cleared, with its own tools, and for its own benefit. But there can be no going back to this system—which has now suffered considerably from the effects of a money economy. It was effective only at a primitive level of life, and left people prey to the vagaries of the weather and subject to other natural calamities.

To secure a good life it is necessary to take advantage of at least some of the modern knowledge and modern techniques. Thus, individual ownership of the tools of production is no longer universally possible; our people want the products of mass production and the easier life which this technology makes possible. Even in agriculture we can no longer rest content with the situation where each farmer owns his own jembe and panga, and uses them as his only tools. By such methods the farmers sweat for very little result. Yet as soon as the more efficient and complicated tools are used, individual ownership becomes either impossible or a great waste of resources. For example, even if it were possible to provide each family in our wheat producing areas with a combine harvester, it would be absurd to do so. If the scale of operations were such that this machine could be economically used, then one family could not by themselves undertake all the other operations which would be involved. The family would have to employ labour to do these other things—and so we would again be in a situation of exploitation, where one man's livelihood depends upon the decisions of another.

In those areas of production where individual ownership of tools is impractical we are therefore forced to the conclusion that group ownership of the means of production is the only way in which the exploitation of man by man can be prevented. This communal ownership can be through the state, which represents every citizen, or through some other institution which is controlled by those involved—such as, for example, a co-operative, or a local authority.

The same thing applies to the question of distribution and exchange. In small peasant societies it is possible for each grower or each producer to bring his goods to a central place and bargain with those who are interested in acquiring them. But the increasing specialization of production which is involved in modern methods requires more sophisticated techniques. And once again, a private individual can then get into a position where he controls the well-being of another. He can do this by his charges for transport, by his commission on sales, or by exploiting a monopoly position which is economically justified.

Communal ownership of the means of distribution—the railways, or the lorries, etc. – and communal enterprise in the act of bargaining, can eliminate this kind of exploitation. At the same time communal ownership in both production and distribution can provide the machinery through which new initiatives for public well-being can be undertaken. For example, a group of farmers together can raise the capital and get access to the technical know-how which is necessary to control a stream and put it to service. Or the residents in an area can together build a road or a bridge, knowing that it will be for mutual benefit. They will not fear that it might just benefit the individual who happens to have a lorry—and who may not reduce his charges although his vehicle no longer suffers damage from fording a stream, and so on.

Yet although the facts of modern technology provide the final justification for the communal ownership of the means of production and exchange, it is not always and everywhere appropriate. The principle of social ownership and control does not provide a detailed answer to every problem. It is possible, as we have found out in Tanzania, for farmers to be exploited even by their own co-operative and their own state if the machinery is not correct, or if the managers and workers are inefficient or dishonest. And it is possible for group ownership to result in a stultification of development, and such stagnation, that in the end the producers would get greater benefit from controlled forms of individual exploitation. For it is not good enough just to deprive people of the incentives of selfishness. Development requires that these should be replaced by effective social incentives. While these do not exist, or to the extent that they do not exist, we have seriously to consider whether, and how far, we can dispense with the incentives of private profit at that time.

So we get problems of what can be and should be socially owned or controlled at each stage in a society's development. Even of things which are quite basic to a nation's economy, public ownership may not necessarily and always be the correct answer for socialists at a particular time. Especially where public ownership means disruption of an existing industry, alternative methods of public control may be appropriate. This can sometimes be exercised through other means—through legislation, veto, consultation, and so on. A decision should depend on the circumstances and the prevailing attitudes—that is, on the success of socialist political education. We have to accept, however, that anything short of ownership often requires a sophisticated and expensive administrative structure if it is not to be simply negative in its effects. In making all such decisions the purpose of socialist organization must be the central factor. That purpose is the service of the people. You do not often serve the people by actions which outrage their feelings, even if those actions are intended to give them collective control over a vital element of their livelihood.

Take, for example, the question of land. In Tanzania we abolished freehold ownership of land shortly after independence. All land now belongs to the nation. But this was not an affront to our people; communal ownership of land is traditional in our country—it was the concept of freehold which had been foreign to them. In tribal tradition an individual or family secured rights in land for as long as they were using it. It became the family land when it was cleared and planted; for the rest of the time it was tribal land, and it reverted to tribal land if the family stopped working it. The only change which our law effected as far as the masses were concerned was that the land became national instead of tribal—and we have been fortunate enough in Tanzania for this transition to be an easy one. Thus only about 1 per cent of our land was really affected by this law, and no Tanzanian who really wants to farm has been unable to find the necessary land—even if not just where he wants it.

These circumstances have meant that the land reforms which were an essential ingredient of the revolution in Egypt would be inapplicable to Tanzania. Equally, our modified traditional ownership system may be quite irrelevant here, or at least quite inappropriate. But the purpose of our different moves has in both cases been socialistic. Both of our states have acted to secure the use of land for the service of the people, and to prevent it providing a basis for inescapable exploitation.

Yet for neither of our countries is the present action the end of all action. Having secured or controlled ownership, we have to decide what is done with the land, and how it is done. And then we have to implement those decisions. This means down-to-earth, village-level decisions which are acceptable to the people there, and at the same time compatible with the larger aims and interests of the society as a whole. And if the correct socialist policy on ownership between two socialist states is different, surely the correct decisions at this lower level will also be different. Indeed, differences may exist at this level even within the one state according to the experiences of the people in a particular place, and the geophysical circumstances existing in that locality.

Of course it is not only in relation to land and agriculture that a socialist policy will vary between different countries. We in Tanzania have recently engaged in a small nationalization exercise, and in other cases have secured majority control in private enterprises. We are now in the stage where people are debating whether we acted correctly or not. Some people criticize us for outright nationalization; some for not nationalizing all industry and commerce; and still other groups criticize us for using former owners as managers of publicly owned industries and businesses. Needless to say, there are other groups which applaud those same actions. We welcome such discussion when it is constructively based on the needs of Tanzania. Out of such discussion what may not have been clear before becomes clear, and rationality continually guides us on our socialist path.

But despite their importance for the future, and despite the attention that our recent public ownership measures have attracted internationally, they are only a small part of the real task Tanzania has now undertaken. In our case agricultural development—and therefore a socialist agricultural policy—is the central issue, and the core of

Tanzania's development of self-reliant socialism. And this we have hardly begun. But we have land in abundance, and traditional agricultural methods which fail to make full use either of the land itself or of the energies of our people. It appears to me that these factors will inevitably cause differences of emphasis and organization between the socialist policies of Tanzania and those of the United Arab Republic. For here, as I understand it, you have the problems of a rapidly rising population pressing heavily upon arable land resources, and agricultural methods already to some extent adapted to the needs of intensive agriculture. These are different problems from ours, and your measures to bring socialism may therefore be different too. And surely, if such different policies are needed between our two parts of the African continent—linked as they are by the Nile waters—even greater differences will be correct socialist policy between either of us and nations elsewhere.

It may be that ultimately—when we have created socialist states instead of being engaged in building them—the institutions and organization in all socialist countries will be very similar. I do not know. The evidence does not yet exist. But I am convinced that the paths to the point where our respective peoples control their own livelihood and their own development will certainly be different. A man coming to Cairo from Dar es Salaam goes in the opposite direction from that taken by a man coming to Cairo from Moscow. What matters is that each should go in the correct direction from his particular departure point! . . . . .

. . . In 1962 I said that socialism is an attitude of mind. I still believe this to be true. It does not mean that institutions and organizations are irrelevant. It means that without the correct attitudes institutions can be subverted from their true purpose. First and foremost, there must be this acceptance of human equality. Then there must be, among the leadership, a desire and a determination to serve alongside of, and in complete identification with, the masses. The people must be, and must know themselves to be, sovereign. Socialism cannot be imposed upon people; they can be guided; they can be led. But ultimately they must be involved.

If the people are not involved in public ownership, and cannot control the policies followed, then public ownership can lead to fascism, not socialism. If the people are not sovereign, then they can suffer under dreadful tyranny imposed in their name. If the people are not honestly served by those to whom they have entrusted responsibility, then corruption can negate all their efforts and make them abandon their socialist ideas.

The political institutions and organizations through which the people's sovereignty is expressed will vary from one state to another, and one time to another, just as the economic institutions of socialism vary. The means most appropriate will depend upon many historical and geographical factors. But ultimately socialism is only possible if the people as a whole are involved in the government of their political and economic affairs. Their efforts must be mobilized. Sometimes this will mean going more slowly, sometimes faster, than academic considerations alone would determine. But the involvement of the people is vital, for socialism is nothing if it is not of the people.

This is a technological age, and many decisions cannot be taken directly by the masses. Tremendous responsibilities therefore rest upon those of us who have had the privilege of higher education. We have been educated out of the resources of the people. Now we have, on their behalf, to deal with complex administrative and technical matters and to make choices which affect their welfare. We have the responsibility to give advice to the people on issues where the implications may not be clear. All these things we must do to the best of our ability. But we must recognize too, that our function is to serve, to guide the masses through the complexities of modern technology—to propose, to explain, and to persuade. For our education does not give us rights over the people. It does not justify arrogance, nor attitudes of superiority.

The only justification for bureaucracies, for industries—or for universities—is the greater well-being of the human beings who constitute the society. And unless we who have power—whether it be political or technical—remain at one with the masses, then we cannot serve them. Our opportunity is unparalleled in man's history. We must meet the challenge with courage, and with humility.

33

Address to the Trade Unions

The biennial Conference of the National Union of Tanganyika Workers was opened by President Nyerere on 27 July 1967. Before a large gathering, which included fraternal delegations from many other countries, the President addressed himself to the responsibilities of wage-earners in Tanzania in achieving the successful implementation of the Arusha Declaration. He then went on:

... Immediately after the Arusha Declaration was announced the Government nationalized the banks, some flour mills and other things, and secured control of a number of factories which had previously been in complete private ownership. That showed that the Government took the Arusha Declaration very seriously. There was, however, one problem resulting from that series of Government actions. Some of our people began to believe that socialism just meant nationalization, and that there was nothing else to do. Some people even believed that by taking over the banks the country had somehow become more wealthy, and that there was some magic involved in taking control of the breweries, shoe factories, and so on, which would enable the prices of all these things to be reduced. That is not so.

The purpose of nationalization of the banks was to ensure that the elected Government of Tanzania has full control over the way money and credit are used, and to ensure also that any profit from running the banks is used within Tanzania and for the benefit of all the people of Tanzania. The purpose of securing majority control in a number of businesses was to ensure that the people of this country are able to decide development policies and to ensure that at least a large proportion of the profits are used for our benefit.

Through public ownership of major enterprises, therefore, we are contributing towards the success of the socialist policies we adopt. But there is much more to socialism than questions of ownership of productive enterprises. For socialism rests upon a basic acceptance of human equality, and involves every man accepting a responsibility for the dignity and the welfare of every other man.

Let me explain briefly what I mean by this idea of accepting responsibility for the welfare of others.

In traditional African society every able-bodied person worked. They did different work sometimes, and some were very clever and quick while others were slower and not so clever. The good hunter was honoured in his society, and so was the good farmer or good housebuilder. Such people were also a little better off than their neighbours because of their work. Yet no one was allowed to go hungry while others had food, even though feeding the unfortunate person might involve sacrifice. There was a sense of mutual responsibility; the man who had food shared what he had, knowing that a time might come when he needed help, and that then he would receive it in his turn. Yet this was done on the assumption and in the knowledge that each person was working to the best of his ability. If there was any man who persistently refused to work, then sooner or later the community dealt with him—sometimes quite roughly because they knew that his idleness endangered them all. Each man received from the society because he contributed to the society as much as he could. No person lived off the work of others unless he was sick, or very old, or very young. There was no exploitation of one man by another.

Traditional African society was not called 'socialist'; it was just life. Yet it was socialist in the principles upon which it was based. It involved human equality, and it involved mutual responsibility, with every member of the community being concerned about the work and the welfare of every other member. Its poverty was the result of ignorance of modern technology, and of the small size of the group which worked together.

The society we live in now is more complicated than that of our forefathers, and therefore gives us an opportunity to defeat the poverty from which they suffered. We now pay people for their work instead of them growing their own crops and exchanging these for other things they need, and so on. But in principle the position is the same. The people of Tanzania can still only eat and use the things which Tanzanians grow or produce. In making this a socialist nation, therefore, we have simply to ensure that modern technology does not destroy the other principles of traditional Africa. That is to say, we have to ensure that now as formerly, every man contributes to society; that each person receives a fair reward in proportion to his contribution and that no man is exploited by another.

It is for this reason that the Arusha Declaration ties the two things together—socialism and self-reliance. Our nation is demanding that every person shall work hard to build our economy and to make us more prosperous. But in the Declaration we are also saying that we must get rid of exploitation; that people must receive an income from their work in proportion to the contribution they make to our society as a whole; and that the old, the sick, and the orphans, must be properly cared for by us all.

We in Tanzania have a long way to go before we achieve these objectives, but we are now moving in the right direction. There are, however, three points I would like to draw your attention to this afternoon because of their special relevance to the work of this congress.

The first point is that the Government of Tanzania is working to prevent exploitation; it depends upon the workers to increase their output. Those people who are still working for private employers need to work hard just as much as those working for Government or public industries. Through minimum wage legislation, through taxation, and through many other methods, the Government will prevent gross exploitation of the workers and people of Tanzania. At the same time it relies upon the workers, and upon NUTA, not to allow industrial disputes of any kind to jeopardize production. If there is a dispute between Government and a private employer, rest assured that the Government will deal with it; if there is a dispute between the workers and the employer, use the machinery which has been set up to get it settled. Strikes and go-slows at this point in time will benefit only those who wish to see the Arusha Declaration fail.

Secondly, the members of NUTA must not think of themselves as the only workers in Tanzania. The vast majority of our people work on their own land; they are not wage-earners but peasants. They do not belong to NUTA, and they have no comparable voice to stand up for their interests, and no similar opportunities to draw attention to their needs and problems. The result has been over the past few years that wage-earners as a group have improved their position at the expense of the farmers. The price of manufactured goods, and the wages of the workers, have increased, while the prices the peasants receive for their output have often decreased; the former have become a little richer relative to the latter. Certainly there are very few NUTA members who are well off. Many are very poor. But in the future their wealth must be increased because our national production has increased, not because the equally hard-working farmers have become even poorer.

Thirdly, when an increase in output in a factory or other institution makes it possible for there to be some slight increase in the return to the workers, that increase must be concentrated at the bottom. It is the lowest paid workers who must have an increase; it should not be a percentage increase for everyone. Independent Tanzania inherited a wage structure where the differential between the skilled and managerial workers on the one hand, and labourers on the other, was much too great. We cannot change this overnight; but any increases which become possible must be given to the lowest paid. . . .

34

The Purpose is Man

On 5 August 1967, President Nyerere spoke at the Teach-In on the Arusha Declaration organized by the Dar es Salaam University College branch of the TANU Youth League. Several hundred young people crowded into the new cafeteria on the hilly College site some eight miles from the city of Dar es Salaam.

The Arusha Declaration is a declaration of intent; no more than that. It states the goal towards which TANU will be leading the people of Tanzania, and it indicates the direction of development. Neither on 5th February, nor on any day since, has Tanzania suddenly become a socialist state, a self-reliant state, or a developed state.

The Arusha Declaration could not achieve these things, and nor would it have been possible for any amount of enthusiasm and energy in implementation to have achieved them in the months since it was adopted by our Party. The Declaration is the beginning, not the end, of a very long and probably extremely hard struggle.

It is necessary that we should be very clear about these things, for otherwise we shall fail to reach the goal stated and shall be liable to do great damage to our nation. We must understand fully what the Arusha Declaration is, what it says, and what it implies for the near as well as the distant future.

WE SHALL REMAIN TANZANIANS

The Declaration is first of all a reaffirmation of the fact that we are Tanzanians and wish to remain Tanzanian as we develop. Certainly we shall wish to change very many things in our present society. But we have stated that these changes will be effected through the processes of growth in certain directions. This growth must come out of our own roots, not through the grafting on to those roots of something which is alien to our society. This is very important, for it means that we cannot adopt any political 'holy book' and try to implement its rulings—with or without revision.

It means that our social change will be determined by our own needs as we see them, and in the direction that we feel to be appropriate for us at any particular time. We shall draw sustenance from universal human ideas and from the practical experiences of other peoples; but we start from a full acceptance of our African-ness and a belief that in our own past there is very much which is useful for our future.

COMMITMENT TO A QUALITY OF LIFE

The Arusha Declaration is also a commitment to a particular quality of life. It is based on the assumption of human equality, on the belief that it is wrong for one man to dominate or to exploit another, and on the knowledge that every individual hopes to live in society as a free man able to lead a decent life in conditions of peace with his neighbours. The document is, in other words, Man-centred.

Inherent in the Arusha Declaration, therefore, is a rejection of the concept of national grandeur as distinct from the well-being of its citizens, and a rejection too of material wealth for its own sake. It is a commitment to the belief that there are more important things in life than the amassing of riches, and that if the pursuit of wealth clashes with things like human dignity and social equality, then the latter will be given priority.

For in a Tanzania which is implementing the Arusha Declaration, the purpose of all social, economic and political activity must be man—the citizens, and all the citizens, of this country. The creation of wealth is a good thing and something which we shall have to increase. But it will cease to be good the moment wealth ceases to serve man and begins to be served by man.

FREEDOM MUST BE MAINTAINED

With our present level of economic activity, and our present poverty, this may seem to be an academic point; but in reality it is very fundamental. For it means that there are certain things which we shall refuse to do or to accept, either as individuals or as a nation, even if the result of them would be a surge forward in our economic development.

For example, even if it were true—which I do not believe—that we could achieve a very great increase in the statistical national wealth and in the income of the majority of our people, we would still reject a proposal that a single foreign country or a group of individuals should establish a complex of agricultural estates, heavy and light industries, etc.

We would reject such a proposal because of its effect upon our national independence, and because large numbers of our people would become the paid servants of another nation or another person. The destiny and the whole life of the people of Tanzania would, in such a case, be controlled by another country or by a few individuals. Either of these things would be inconsistent with our commitment to Tanzanian freedom and to the freedom and human equality of all citizens.

PROGRESS BY EVOLUTION

Yet this does not mean that we have in any way accepted our present poverty. On the contrary, the Arusha Declaration calls for a tremendous human effort for change. We are saying that what has taken the older countries centuries should take us decades. What we are attempting is a telescoped evolution of our economy and of our society. This is not a sociological, or even a biological, impossibility.

It has taken hundreds of millions of years for life on the earth to develop from simple living matter to the complicated and interlinked cell structure which is a human being. Yet a human foetus develops from one to the other in nine months.

The national growth of our country can be telescoped and yet remain organic. It will take more than nine months; but the union of our people and our land, in the light of the human knowledge available in this century, can certainly shorten very considerably the period during which countries like the United Kingdom or the United States achieved their present affluence.

INTEGRATED PROGRAMME BASED ON LINKED PRINCIPLES

The other important fact about the Arusha Declaration is that it is an integrated programme of action based on linked principles. There are some people who would like to support the call for national self-reliance, but have strong reservations about the socialist doctrines and especially the leadership qualifications.

There are others who claim to support the socialist aspects but have reservations about the statement that Tanzania must depend upon its own resources for development and plan accordingly. There are still other people who have tried (usually with ulterior motives) to interpret it as an anti-Asian, or anti-European, document; or who criticize it on the grounds that it supports the interests of these groups against the interests of black people in Tanzania. But the truth is that it is not possible to accept socialism without self-reliance, or vice versa; and it is not possible to talk racialism while still claiming to accept the Arusha Declaration.

Self-reliance in development is merely an application of something we knew in 1954—that only Tanzanians are sufficiently interested to develop Tanzania in the interests of Tanzanians, and only Tanzanians can say what those interests are. And socialism is an application to economic and social life of the doctrine of human equality which we appealed to when we rejected the right of any other nation to govern us.

These two things are but different sides of the single coin—human equality. And most clearly of all, the Arusha Declaration refers to men, and to systems—not to members of particular racial or tribal groups. The person who claims to use it in support of attacks on any particular racial community, is betraying both his ignorance and his rejection of the principles enunciated in it.

THE IMPLICATIONS OF SELF-RELIANCE

What, then, is the meaning of self-reliance, and what are its implications for our future policies? First and foremost, it means that for our development we have to depend upon ourselves and our own resources. These resources are land, and people. Certainly we have a few factories, we have a small diamond mine, and so on. But it is important to realize that (when measured in 1960 prices) out of a gross domestic product estimated at Shs. 4,646/- million in 1966, some Shs. 2,669/- million—that is, more than 57 per cent—was the direct result of agricultural activities. Only Shs. 321/- million was the combined result of mining and manufacturing; that is to say that all the mining and manufacturing of Tanzania produced last year less than 7 per cent of the gross domestic product.

The one thing we certainly do not have is money searching for investment opportunities. The *per capita* income, in terms of 1966 prices, was about Shs. 525/- last year. That does not allow very much to be withdrawn from current consumption and invested in development. Indeed, we did very well last year to find Shs. 135/- million (that is, about Shs. 14/- per person) from internal resources for development.

But to provide one job in a highly mechanized industry can cost Shs. 40,000/- or more. To build the oil refinery cost more than Shs. 110/- million. To build a modern steel mill would cost rather more than that.

DEVELOPMENT THROUGH AGRICULTURE

On the other hand, it is possible to double the output of cotton on a particular acre by spending Shs. 130/- on fertilizer and insecticide; it is possible to double a farmer's acreage under crops by the provision of an ox-plough at a cost of Shs. 250/- or less, and so on. In other words, whereas it is possible to find the sort of investment capital which can bring great increases in agricultural output from our present resources, it is not possible for us to envisage establishing heavy industries, or even very much in the way of light industries, in the near future.

To be realistic, therefore, we must stop dreaming of developing Tanzania through the establishment of large, modern industries. For such things we have neither the money nor the skilled manpower required to make them efficient and economic. We would even be making a mistake if we think in terms of covering Tanzania with mechanized farms, using tractors and combine harvesters.

Once again, we have neither the money nor the skilled manpower, nor in this case the social organization which could make such investment possible and economic. This is not to say that there will be no new modern industries and no mechanized farms. But they will be the exception, not the rule, and they will be entered upon to meet particular problems. They are not the answer to the basic development needs of Tanzania.

AND APPROPRIATE AGRICULTURAL METHODS

This is what the Arusha Declaration makes clear in both economic and social terms. Our future lies in the development of our agriculture, and in the development of our rural areas. But because we are seeking to grow from our own roots and to preserve that which is valuable in our traditional past, we have also to stop thinking in terms of massive agricultural mechanization and the proletarianization of our rural population.

We have, instead, to think in terms of development through the improvement of the tools we now use, and through the growth of co-operative systems of production. Instead of aiming at large farms using tractors and other modern equipment and employing agricultural labourers, we should be aiming at having ox-ploughs all over the country.

The jembe will have to be eliminated by the ox-plough before the latter can be eliminated by the tractor. We cannot hope to eliminate the jembe by the tractor. Instead of thinking about providing each farmer with his own lorry, we should consider the usefulness of oxen-drawn carts, which could be made within the country and which are appropriate both to our roads and to the loads which each farmer is likely to have.

Instead of the aerial spraying of crops with insecticide, we should use hand-operated pumps, and so on. In other words, we have to think in terms of what is available, or can be made available, at comparatively small cost, and which can be operated by the people. By moving into the future along this path, we can avoid massive social disruption and human suffering.

SMALL INDUSTRIES

At the same time we can develop small industries and service stations in the rural areas where the people live, and thus help to diversify the rural economy. By this method we can achieve a widespread increase in the general level of people's income, instead of concentrating any economic improvement in the hands of a few people.

Such capital as we do have will make the widest possible impact by being invested in fertilizers, in credit for better breeding stock, in improved instruments of production, and other similar things. These, although small in themselves, can bring a great proportionate increase in the farmers' incomes.

This does not mean that there will be no new investment in towns, or that there will be no new factories. When you have large numbers of people living together certain public services are essential for public health and security reasons. It would be absurd to pretend that we can forget the towns, which are in any case often a service centre for the surrounding rural areas.

FACTORY SITES

Factories which serve the whole country also have to be sited in places which are convenient for transport and communications. For example, if we had put the Friendship Textile Mill in a rural area, we would have had to invest in special road building, etc. for it to be of any use, and in any case the number of its workers would soon mean that a new town had grown up in that place.

But even when we are building factories which serve the whole nation, we have to consider whether it is necessary for us to use the most modern machinery which exists in the world. We have to consider whether some older equipment which demands more labour, but labour which is less highly skilled, is not better suited to our needs, as well as being more within our capacity to build and use.

TRADE WITH OTHERS

There are, however, two respects in which our call for self-reliance has been widely misunderstood or deliberately misinterpreted. The doctrine of self-reliance does not imply isolationism, either politically or economically. It means that we shall depend on ourselves, not on others.

But this is not the same thing as saying we shall not trade with other people or co-operate with them when it is to mutual benefit. Obviously we shall do so. We shall have to continue to sell enough of our goods abroad to pay for the things we have to acquire. Up to now

Tanzania has always done this; indeed, we have had a surplus of our balance of payments for many years. But the things we sell are the products of our agriculture, and this is likely to continue to be the case despite the problem of commodity prices in the world.

The things we import will increasingly have to be the things which are essential for our development, and which we cannot produce ourselves. Up to now we have been importing many things which a little effort would enable us to provide for ourselves, such as food, as well as luxury items which simply arouse desires among our people which could never be satisfied for more than a tiny minority.

Self-reliance, in other words, is unlikely to reduce our participation in international trade, but it should, over time, change its character to some extent. We should be exporting commodities after at least some preliminary processing, and we should be importing the thing which we cannot produce and which are necessary for the development and the welfare of our whole people.

TANZANIA WANTS CAPITAL ASSISTANCE

The other thing which is necessary to understand about self-reliance is that Tanzania has not said it does not want international assistance in its development. We shall continue to seek capital from abroad for particular projects or as a contribution to general development. It is clear, for example, that if we are to achieve our ambition of getting a railway which links Tanzania and Zambia, we shall have to obtain most of the capital and the technical skill from overseas.

Overseas capital will also be welcome for any project where it can make our own efforts more effective—where it acts as a catalyst for Tanzanian activity. It is for this reason that the Government has made it clear that we shall welcome outside participation—whether private or Government—in establishment of many different kinds of factories, especially those which produce consumption goods or process our crops and raw materials.

Capital assistance for education of all kinds is another of the many fields in which outside assistance can be valuable, provided it is linked to our capacity to meet the recurrent costs. The important thing, however, is that we in Tanzania should not adopt an attitude that nothing can be done until someone else agrees to give us money.

There are many things we can do by ourselves, and we must plan to do them. There are other things which can become easier if we get assistance, but these we should reckon on doing the hard way, by ourselves, only being thankful if assistance is forthcoming.

SKILLED PEOPLE ARE ALSO NEEDED

But it is not only capital which we must welcome from outside; it is also men. Few things make me more angry than a refusal to accept and to work with people from other countries whose participation can make all the difference between our plans succeeding or failing. It is not being self-reliant to refuse to carry out the directions of a foreign engineer, a foreign doctor, or a foreign manager; it is just being stupid. It is absolutely vital that Tanzanians should determine policy; but if the implementation of a particular policy requires someone with good educational qualifications or long experience, it is not very sensible to allow that policy to fail through pride.

We must look at this question of employing expatriates scientifically and without prejudice; we must assess the interests of our development as a whole, not the interests of a particular person who feels that he would like the high post concerned but is neither ready for it nor prepared to go on learning from someone else.

NO FALSE PRIDE IN THIS MATTER

Let us take note of the fact that the developed countries have no false pride in this matter. Western Europe and North America recruit trained people from countries like India and Pakistan, and West European countries complain bitterly about what they call the 'brain drain' caused by the richer United States offering high incomes to educated and skilled people.

It has been alleged that the United States has saved itself billions of dollars by attracting workers on whose education it has not spent one cent. Yet while wealthy and developed countries adopt this kind of attitude, we in Tanzania appear to rejoice when we lose a trained person to Europe or North America.

We rejoice on the grounds that it provides us with an opportunity for Africanization, or for self-reliance! Anyone would think that we have a problem of unemployed experts. It is time that we outgrew this childishness; and we must do so quickly if we intend to tackle this problem of modern development really seriously.

SOCIALISM

What, then, of socialism—the other aspect of the Arusha Declaration? First, it is important to be clear that nationalization of existing industries and commercial undertakings is only a very small part of the socialism which we have adopted. The important thing for us is the extent to which we succeed in preventing the exploitation of one man by another, and in spreading the concept of working together co-operatively for the common good instead of competitively for individual private gain. And the truth is that our economy is now so underdeveloped that it is in growth that we shall succeed or fail in these things.

The nationalization of the banks, of insurance, and of the few industries affected, was important; but much more important is whether we succeed in expanding our economy without expanding the opportunities and the incentives for human exploitation.

Once again this really means that socialism has to spread in the rural areas where our people live. In this we have an advantage over many other countries, just because of our lack of development. Up to now exploitation in agriculture is very limited; the greater part of our farming is still individual peasant farming, or family farming. But although this is not capitalist, neither is it very efficient or productive in comparison with what it could be.

Indeed, it is true that where people work together in groups—and that is mostly in those restricted sectors of capitalist farming—there is often a greater output per worker and per acre. Our objective must be to develop in such a manner as to ensure that the advantages of modern knowledge and modern methods are achieved, but without the spread of capitalism.

HUMAN EQUALITY—THE ESSENCE OF SOCIALISM

Socialism, however, is not simply a matter of methods of production. They are part of it but not all of it. The essence of socialism is the practical acceptance of human equality. That is to say, every man's equal right to a decent life before any individual has a surplus above his needs; his equal right to participate in Government; and his equal responsibility to work and contribute to the society to the limit of his ability.

In Tanzania this means that we must safeguard and strengthen our democratic procedures; we must get to the position where every citizen plays an active and direct role in the government of his local community, at the same time as he plays a full role in the government of his own country. It also means that we have to correct the glaring income differentials which we inherited from colonialism, and ensure that the international imbalance between the wages of factory and service workers on the one hand, and of agricultural workers on the other, is not reproduced within our own nation. We have, in other words, to ensure that every person gets a return commensurate with the contribution he makes to the society.

But at the same time we have to make dignified provision for those whose age or disability prevents them from playing a full role in the economy. We have also to spread—although it can only be done gradually—equality of opportunity for all citizens, until every person is able to make the kind of contribution to our needs which is most within his capacity and his desires. But, most of all, we have to reactivate the philosophy of co-operation in production and sharing in distribution which was an essential part of traditional African society.

CHANGE THROUGH GROWTH

I started this afternoon by saying that the Arusha Declaration is a statement of intent; I hope I have made clear what is intended and have at least indicated some of the implications of this. As I close, however, I want to stress two things.

The first is that the Arusha Declaration lays down a policy of revolution by evolution; we shall become a socialist, self-reliant society through our growth. We cannot afford the destruction of the economic instruments we now have nor a reduction in our present output. The steps by which we move forward must take account of these things. Our change will, therefore, be effected almost entirely by the emphasis of our new development and by the gradual conversion of existing institutions into others more in accordance with our philosophy.

The other thing is that the Arusha Declaration is a general outline. The policy paper on Education for Self-Reliance was an interpretation of its meaning in one field; there will be other papers on other aspects of our development. But the scope for individual initiative within this framework is almost unlimited.

We need people, especially in the rural areas, who accept the underlying doctrines of the Arusha Declaration and who are both willing and able to work with, and to lead, their fellow citizens in the promotion of socialist growth. If we have enough people who are purposeful and dedicated in this manner, we shall succeed.

THE CHALLENGE

The real question, therefore, is whether each of us is prepared to accept the challenge of building a state in which no man is ashamed of his poverty in the light of another's affluence, and no man has to be ashamed of his affluence in the light of another's poverty. Are we prepared to build a society in which all men can treat with others on terms of complete equality and in a spirit of free co-operation? Every one of us has to give the answer to this; but for young people there is a special responsibility. For educated young people there is a special temptation too, because in a capitalist society they would be the ones most likely to attain privilege at the expense of others.

I believe that the young people of Tanzania, educated and uneducated alike, have accepted this challenge. Carrying it through will not always be easy, nor always in every respect popular. In order to do it, it is necessary that there should be a total understanding and acceptance of the objectives and the philosophy of the Arusha Declaration, so that disappointments can be withstood and personal difficulties overcome.

There has to be a recognition that there is a job to be done which will often be difficult, and often demand the renunciation of personal comfort. It will offer in return the challenge and the satisfaction of contributing to the building of a socialist society for the benefit of our children and grandchildren.

35

East African Treaty

When the Central Legislative Assembly of East Africa met in rotation in the different capitals of the partner states, it was customary for the President of the host country to deliver a message or an address on behalf of th East African Authority, that is, himself and his two fellow Presidents.

On 8 August 1967, when the Central Legislative Assembly met in Dar es Salaam, President Nyerere's address was mostly concerned with the Treaty for East African Co-operation which had been signed by the three Presidents in June.

... Honourable Members will remember the many pessimistic prophesies which have been made over recent years about international co-operation in Africa, and about East African co-operation in particular. Every sign of strain and difficulty in the arrangements which had been made in 1961 was pounced upon, and used to justify suggestions that talk of African unity was just words, and meant nothing. But we have always known that there are two ways of dealing with difficulties; you can face up to them and take the necessary correcting action, or you can pretend that they do not exist—until finally arrangements for co-operation break down completely. East Africa has done the former.

It is not necessary for me to go over the details of the arrangements for co-operation and joint activity which are laid down in the Treaty. It is a legal document which is available to Members of this House, and to all others who are interested. What it does is to lay down a realistic basis for the co-operation, on equal terms, of three sovereign states. Its provisions were negotiated by us all, taking into account the problems and the aspirations of each country, and our over-riding recognition of the mutual benefit which can come from united economic action.

I do not wish to suggest to this Assembly that there will in future be no short-term conflicts of interest between Kenya, Uganda and Tanzania. There may well be some. But this Treaty provides for the solution of such difficulties. The machinery devised for the East African Community is realistic; it has been drawn up in the light of experience gained from the present and earlier arrangements for co-operation. The Common Market, and the Common Services, have been greatly strengthened; they should now be able to work with efficiency for our common benefit.

Of particular importance is the introduction of a system of East African Ministers. These three men will be responsible to East Africa, and their concern will be to ensure the smooth running of all the institutions for co-operation. Their task will be a very important one; but I am convinced that they will receive the full co-operation of the Governments and the peoples of East Africa. In particular, it will be important that there should be a close working relationship between the East African Ministers and the various national Ministers who will sit on the different Councils of the Community. These East African Ministers will not be appointed until 1st December 1967. I am happy to report to the Assembly, however, that all three Governments have now designated a Minister to be responsible for the necessary preparatory work. Of course, many of the arrangements laid down in the Treaty will take longer than six months to bring into full operation; the physical movement involved for some offices of the Community is an obvious example. But it will be the task of the East African Ministers, and of the new East African Legislative Assembly, to ensure that the work proceeds as quickly as possible. I am sure this duty will be fulfilled.

There is only one other point in the Treaty which I wish to mention now. That is the fact that provision has been made for other countries to associate themselves with the Community, or to participate in any of the activities of the Community or its Corporations. The importance of this Article is obvious to all those who are concerned with the extension of African unity. It means that neighbouring states can join with East Africa in common projects, or in common economic activities. Such developments could only strengthen us all, and Members may be confident that East Africa will receive with sympathy any such approaches.

The East African Treaty does not inaugurate Federation; neither does it inaugurate an economic Utopia. What it does do is provide a very strong and firm foundation for mutual co-operation and development, on the basis of equality, between the partner states. I believe that this is of fundamental importance, and that the spirit of unity which exists in East Africa will enable us to build rapidly and well upon this foundation. It is therefore with pleasure that I express the Authority's appreciation of the work done by Professor Philip and the members of his Commission. All of them worked extremely hard and well; we are grateful to them.

Mr. Speaker, now that the East African Treaty is signed, there is no barrier in the way of the solid hard work which is necessary to strengthen East African co-operation. The time for talking is past; now it is action which is necessary. I call upon all Members of this Assembly to play their part in the tasks before us.

36

Zambia and Tanzania

In August 1967, President Nyerere led the Tanzanian fraternal dele-gation to the Zambian United National Independence Party Conference at Mulungushi. Then, on 16 August he addressed the 4,000 delegates from the large open air platform, bringing greetings from Tanzania and warning of the dangers of tribalism and inter–African disunity.

I am very proud to have the honour of bringing greetings to this conference. I am proud because I come on behalf of the Tanganyika African National Union, and of the Afro-Shirazi Party of Zanzibar, to express the solidarity of the Tanzanian nationalist movement with the nationalist movement of Zambia. At the same time I speak on behalf of the whole Tanzanian people when I express our admiration and respect for the Government and the people of this country. Not for one day has the life of independent Zambia been easy; always this country has lived in the knowledge that powerful neighbours to the South and West wish harm to the nation and its people. But never has the courage of Zambia faltered; nor has there been any failure in the skill with which Zambia's Government has dealt with threats—both long-term and short-term—to the in-tegrity of this nation. I am proud to bring to you all our congratu-lations and good wishes.

Mr. President, when I come here and see this large gathering of elected representatives my confidence in the future of this country is renewed. That they are all united behind your leadership is only one extra source of satisfaction; indeed, I do not know whether to congratulate the Party on its President, or the President on his Party! I only know that all of us could be happier if these conditions existed everywhere in Africa. If every African state were able to demonstrate this degree of the people's participation in their own

Government, and this degree of unity behind their leaders, then Africa would not be suffering as it is today.

For it is in democratic unity that lies the strength of any African state, and thus the strength of us all. The people of this continent are the weapon with which Africa has to defend itself, and the instrument with which Africa has to develop itself. For what are our guns in contrast to the guns of the big powers—of East or West? Where are our aeroplanes, or missiles, and so on? We do not have them. And where is the capital with which our nations are going to build modern economies? We don't have it. Zambia, Mr. President, is wealthy in comparison with some African states, but we all know that the vast majority of your people too are suffering from the ill-effects of poverty. For Zambia, as for Tanzania, the most important capital is people, not money. If the people are determined to build their nation it will be built and no one can prevent it. If they are not prepared to make the effort and the sacrifices necessary, then no amount of money brought in from outside, or earned from the sale of copper, will lead to national growth.

I believe the existence of this conference, its size, and its representative nature, are an indication that Zambians will respond to the challenge and the opportunity of their independence. For this conference is, and must be, an indication of *unity* in Zambia. I know that there are important questions to be debated here, and also that elections will take place for some of the highest Party offices. Obviously, you will debate these important issues, and obviously not everyone will be equally happy with the results of your Party elections. But this does not mean disunity; it means life and democracy when people who are fundamentally at one talk and argue about how to achieve their common objectives. Maybe the arguing will even become heated—certainly it does in Tanzania on occasions! But the important question is not the words which are said in debate, but the actions which follow decisions. Do the minority accept and work loyally for the decision which has been made, and with the leaders who have been elected? And do the majority accept the right of those who were defeated to have had their own opinion, and to participate in the implementation of the Party decision?

Had UNIP not been doing these things in the past it would not have a conference like the one we see here today. But I believe that there is a special importance, and a special difficulty, for UNIP and for Zambia today. As Zambia goes forward in strength and unity, the apartheid governments in Southern Rhodesia and South Africa know that they are getting weaker, and that their fall is coming nearer. Let us not be confused by their present strength, either economic or military. In the long run they cannot succeed if we succeed—and they know it. It may take years, even decades; but time is on the side of Africa if we use it properly—that is, if we remain united, and exert ourselves for growth on the basis of human principles.

It is for this very fundamental reason that the enemies of Zambia, and of Africa, will make every possible attempt to destroy the unity of Zambia. And to do that they will have to destroy the unity of UNIP. Their methods will be insidious, underhand—and clever. In particular, they will play upon our traditional loyalties to tribes and to men. They will say, 'So-and-so was elected because he was a member of this tribe, and the other tribe—or tribes—are afraid of domination'. And their hope will be that members of these other tribes will look around, and wonder if it is true that their tribe has been defeated by another tribe; and unity will be gone. Or they will say, 'Now that your tribe has been victorious in this election there is an opportunity to get jobs or money which you would not otherwise have had'. Or they will say, 'So-and-so worked hard for UNIP in the past and now he has been defeated; better leave the victorious ones to get on without you'. All these and many other things will be written in their newspapers—the newspapers of our enemies; they will be whispered in the clubs, and at work. And the sole purpose will be the defeat of UNIP and of Zambia—its dissolution through disunity.

Does anyone here think that the South African Government, or the Smith regime, is upset over the fighting in Nigeria? They are rejoicing. They do not care that man is killing man there; they are only happy that African is killing African. For them that is even better than having mercenaries involved, as in the Congo—although that, too, pleases them. And Nigeria is a long way from them; Congo is nearer; but Zambia is on their doorstep. Let Smith make all the pious utterances he wishes; the truth is that chaos in Zambia is his ambition, and he and his supporters will use every opportunity to create it. Only Zambians can prevent it.

But Zambians *can* prevent it. They have already done so, and they can—and I believe will—prevent it in the future. In the past there have been attempts to play upon political party differences, and to tie them to tribal hostilities. The people of Zambia have seen through this attempt and the growing strength of UNIP is the result. Now he will try to use tribalism. I think he will fail. Then again, he will try to loosen the hold of Zambia on the principle of non-racialism. By using white and black racialists he will damage the economy of Zambia, and again set man against man in this country. THIS IS HIS AMBITION. For this conference, this large, united Party representing a united people, is a real danger to him. Much more so than the mouthings of a Prime Minister, bleating about legality from thousands of miles away.

Do not think I am dreaming when I say these things, or that I do not know the strength of Smith. Nor do I imagine that Zambia could invade Southern Rhodesia because you have a large conference here. But Zambia is a danger to Smith because it belongs to Zambians—Zambians of all tribes and all colours. It is a danger to him because Zambians are united in upholding their country, and building their country on the basis of human principles. Certainly Zambia, like Tanzania, still employs non-Zambians with certain skills and experience which its own citizens do not yet possess. But it is Zambia which employs them, and which does so for its own purposes. Zambia may pay these people much higher wages than Zambians get—and this, too, will be used to insinuate doubt about the sincerity of the people's Government in Zambia. But it will be Zambia which decides when these people can be dispensed with, or what they must be offered to secure their services while they are needed.

Let no one doubt this fact for a moment. Zambia belongs to Zambians because they are Zambians, and because they are determined to work together in unity to defend, and to develop, their country. The problems of the nation are very many and very great. They will not be easily or quickly solved—for it is difficult to convert a colonial economy into an economy based on freedom and equality. A large number of the problems will remain for a long time. But the fact that they cannot all be tackled at once is no reason for not tackling any of them—or for pretending that Zambia is not aware of the others. The people of Tanzania have heard me tell the story of the baby millipede; the baby said to its mother, 'With all these legs, which one do I move first in order to walk?' and the mother replied, 'Move, child; move'. So it is with us—with Zambia and Tanzania. We deal with one problem at a time, and do not wait until we are in a position to do everything before we do anything.

But let us realize that while there are problems which we have not yet tackled, so there will be an opportunity for the Smith supporters to mock at us, and try to provoke us into doing other things before we are ready. And they will try. They will provoke our anger in the hope that in the heat of emotion we shall do things we afterwards regret, or do the right things at the wrong time. Their agents will try to act as if our countries belong to them instead of to us; they will do this in the hope that this will make us adopt their racialism and thus give them the justification they seek. And they will do all these things in addition to their spying, and possible attempts to sabotage our efforts for development. Yet every one of these things we can defeat by vigilant unity.

I have spoken at some length on this question. I have not done this because I see any disunity in Zambia. I have done it only because this is the special danger for Africa, and because Zambia's geographical position makes her a prime target for our common enemies.

But I want to add this other thing. Zambia's enemies are Tanzania's enemies too. We are at present two separate countries, but we are united in a common endeavour, and we are involved together. We get strength from one another. It is our hope in Tanzania that we can give Zambia's front line position all the strength which comes from a solid and loyal supporting line. And certainly I know that Tanzania gains strength from Zambia's courage and Zambia's fight.

And, of course, our friendship—our unity—is another temptation to the racialists of Southern Africa. So once again they try to divide us. 'Tanzania is communist', they tell you—and they cite the fact that we have friendly relations with China, and that we have nationalized or taken partnership in the more important of the enterprises in the United Republic. 'Zambia is moderate,' they tell us, citing the fact that you have not done so! But I can give this conference one firm assurance. Neither the Government of Tanzania, nor the Government of Zambia, is made up of fools. We will not be divided.

What stupidity it would be for Tanzania to assume that, because we have taken certain action, therefore that action is appropriate to Zambia, and appropriate now. What stupidity it would be for Zambia to assume that, because something is not right for this country, it is not right for Tanzania now. We know—both our Governments know—that we are leaders elected by the people to pursue their interests to the best of our ability. We both feel that we are responsible to ALL the people of our country—not just to elite groups. And we both know that our different geographical positions, and the different kinds of economy which we inherited from the colonialists, mean that different tactics are required in order that we may reach the same objective. For I believe that our objective is the same. We may word it differently, but what it amounts to is this: the development of a nation, in unity, in which every citizen is an equal member of the society with an equal opportunity to contribute to the best of his ability and an equal right to human dignity and respect. Both UNIP and TANU reject racialism and tribalism, just as we reject discrimination based on religion or anything else except loyalty to our nation and our people.

There is a story however, of two people from distant lands who were going to meet on a fertile mountain-side many miles away from them both. One had to cross a desert before he could start to climb. The other had to thread his way through thick rain forests and cross many rivers and swamps. Only at the last stage of their respective journeys did they both have to climb up the same mountain-side. So each prepared for his own journey. Both carried a rope and a stick for the final climb. But in addition, the first took many water bottles and blankets to protect him from the fierce sun, then walked straight from oasis to oasis. The second travelled light, having first learned how to swim and make boats; he then threaded his way through forest paths, going first west and then east in order to find a passage. It was because of their different preparations, and their different tactics, that they met at their common destination.

The paths of Tanzania and Zambia may at times look different, but we are fellow travellers. One policy may be appropriate for you at one time, and another for us. But it is my conviction that nothing must ever be allowed to divide us. Let us treat with scorn those who try to sow suspicion between our countries, because they do it for their own purposes, not for ours. Our peoples are one. Our two sovereign nations are at the same time one unit. We have a common struggle and a common destiny.

And the truth is that in the current difficulties of Africa, the growing unity between East and Central Africa is of paramount importance. And it will grow. Communications between our four states are improving all the time—and one day we shall get our railway! Trade is increasing and will increase more. These things will continue until finally Zambia is in a position to break the chains that still bind her to the South. But most important of all for Zambia, and for all of us, is the mutual trust and understanding which exist between our peoples, our Parties, and our Governments. In this context we shall grow, and get stronger.

It is the deep desire of TANU, of the Afro-Shirazi Party, and the whole of Tanzania, that the United Republic should be able to contribute to this development. It is for this reason that I have come to this conference on behalf of the Tanzanian people. And in their name I say this: to you, Mr. President, to UNIP, and to the whole people of Zambia, congratulations on your progress so far. Our very best wishes for your continued advance in unity. May we have the privilege of marching with you until our countries reach our common goal—real freedom for all our peoples, and for Africa as a whole.

37

Socialism and Rural Development

The second 'post-Arusha' policy paper was issued by President Nyerere in September 1967, and called for the establishment of 'ujamaa villages'—co-operative communities in which people lived together and worked together for the good of all. This paper analyses the meaning of socialism for the rural areas of Tanzania—that is, for the vast majority of the people of the United Republic.

The traditional African family lived according to the basic principles of ujamaa. Its members did this unconsciously, and without any conception of what they were doing in political terms. They lived together and worked together because that was how they understood life, and how they reinforced each other against the difficulties they had to contend with—the uncertainties of weather and sickness, the depredations of wild animals (and sometimes human enemies), and the cycle of life and death. The results of their joint effort were divided unequally between them, but according to well-understood customs. And the division was always on the basis of the fact that every member of the family had to have enough to eat, some simple covering, and a place to sleep, before any of them (even the head of the family) had anything extra. The family members thought of themselves as one, and all their language and behaviour emphasized their unity. The basic goods of life were 'our food', 'our land', 'our cattle'. And identity was established in terms of relationships; mother and father of so-and-so; daughter of so-and-so; wife of such-and-such a person. They lived together and they worked together; and the result of their joint labour was the property of the family as a whole.

THE ASSUMPTIONS OF TRADITIONAL UJAMAA LIVING

This pattern of living was made possible because of three basic assumptions of traditional life. These assumptions were not questioned, or even thought about; but the whole of society was both based upon them, and designed to uphold them. They permeated the customs, manners, and education of the people. And although they were not always honoured by every individual, they were not challenged; rather the individual continued to be judged by them.

The first of these assumptions, or principles of life, I have sometimes described as 'love', but that word is so often used to imply a deep personal affection that it can give a false impression. A better word is perhaps 'respect', for it was—and is—really a recognition of mutual involvement in one another, and may or may not involve any affection deeper than that of familiarity. Each member of the family recognized the place and the rights of the other members, and although the rights varied according to sex, age, and even ability and character, there was a minimum below which no one could exist without disgrace to the whole family. Even the most junior wife in a polygamous household had respect due to her; she had a right to her own house and in relation to her husband, and she had full access to the joint products of the family group. There was also due to her, and from her, a family loyalty.

While the first principle of the ujamaa unit related to persons, the second related to property. It was that all the basic goods were held in common, and shared among all members of the unit. There was an acceptance that whatever one person had in the way of basic necessities, they all had; no one could go hungry while others hoarded food and no one could be denied shelter if others had space to spare. Within the extended family, and even within the tribe, the economic level of one person could never get too far out of proportion to the economic level of others. There was not complete equality; some individuals within the family, and some families within the clan or tribe, could 'own' more than others. But in general they acquired this through extra efforts of their own, and the social system was such that in time of need it was available to all. Further, the inheritance systems were such that in almost all places death led to the dispersal of, for example, a large herd of cattle, among a large number of people. Inequalities existed, but they were tempered by comparable family or social responsibilities, and they could never become gross and offensive to the social equality which was at the basis of the communal life.

Finally, and as a necessary third principle, was the fact that everyone had an obligation to work. The work done by different people was different, but no one was exempt. Every member of the family, and every guest who shared in the right to eat and have shelter, took it for granted that he had to join in whatever work had to be done. Only by the universal acceptance of this principle was the continuation of the other two made possible.

THE INADEQUACIES OF THE TRADITIONAL SYSTEM

But although these three principles were at the base of the traditional practice of ujamaa, the result was not the kind of life which we really wish to see existing throughout Tanzania. Quite apart from personal failures to live up to the ideals and principles of the social system (and traditional Africa was no more composed of unselfish and hard-working angels than any other part of the world), there were two basic factors which prevented traditional society from full flowering.

The first of these was that, although every individual was joined to his fellows by human respect, there was, in most parts of Tanzania, an acceptance of one human inequality. Although we try to hide the fact, and despite the exaggeration which our critics have frequently indulged in, it is true that the women in traditional society were regarded as having a place in the community which was not only different, but was also to some extent inferior. It is impossible to deny that the women did, and still do, more than their fair share of the work in the fields and in the homes. By virtue of their sex they suffered from inequalities which had nothing to do with their contribution to the family welfare. Although it is wrong to suggest that they have always been an oppressed group, it is true that within traditional society ill-treatment and enforced subservience could be their lot. This is certainly inconsistent with our socialist conception of the equality of all human beings and the right of all to live in such security and freedom as is consistent with equal security and freedom for all others. If we want our country to make full and quick progress now, it is essential that our women live on terms of full equality with their fellow citizens who are men.

The other aspect of traditional life which we have to break away from is its poverty. Certainly there was an attractive degree of economic equality, but it was equality at a low level. The equality is good, but the level can be raised. For there was nothing inherent in the traditional system which caused this poverty; it was the result of two things only. The first was ignorance, and the second was the scale of operations. Both of these can be corrected without affecting the validity and applicability of the three principles of mutual respect, sharing of joint production, and work by all. These principles were, and are, the foundation of human security, of real practical human equality, and of peace between members of a society. They can also be a basis of economic development if modern knowledge and modern techniques of production are used.

THE OBJECTIVE

This is the objective of socialism in Tanzania. To build a society in which all members have equal rights and equal opportunities; in which all can live at peace with their neighbours without suffering or imposing injustice, being exploited, or exploiting; and in which all have a gradually increasing basic level of material welfare before any individual lives in luxury.

To create this kind of nation we must build on the firm foundations of the three principles of the ujamaa family. But we must add to these principles the knowledge and the instruments necessary for the defeat of the poverty which existed in traditional African society. In other words, we must add those elements which allow for increased output per worker, and which make a man's efforts yield more satisfactions to him. We must take our traditional system, correct its shortcomings, and adapt to its service the things we can learn from the technologically developed societies of other continents.

TANZANIA AS IT HAS BEEN DEVELOPING

In recent years this is not what has been happening. Our society, our economy, and the dominant ambitions of our own people are all very different now from what they were before the colonial era. There has been a general acceptance of the social attitudes and ideas of our colonial masters. We have got rid of the foreign government, but we have not yet rid ourselves of the individualistic social attitudes which they represented and taught. For it was from these overseas contacts that we developed the idea that the way to the comfort and prosperity which everyone wants is through selfishness and individual advancement. And, of course, under a capitalist type of system it is quite true that for a few individuals great wealth and comfort is possible. In even the poorest societies— that is, those societies where the total wealth produced and available in the community is very low—a few individuals can be very wealthy, if others are even poorer than they need be. If you abandon the idea and the goal of equality, and allow the clever and fortunate to exploit the others, then the glittering prizes of material success will be attractive to all, and the temptations of individualism will be further increased. No one likes to be exploited, but all of us are tempted by opportunities to exploit others.

One important result of developments over the past 40 years has been the growth of urban centres and of wage employment. In fact only about 4 per cent of our people live in towns, and less than 340,000 people work for wages out of a total adult population of not less than 5 million. Unfortunately, the life of these tiny minorities has become a matter of great envy for the majority. Life in the towns has come to represent opportunities for advancement, a chance of excitement, and the provision of social services, none of which is easily available in the rural areas. Most of all, there is an almost universal belief that life in the towns is more comfortable and more secure—that the rewards of work are better in the urban areas and that people in the rural parts of the country are condemned to poverty and insecurity for their whole lives.

But although the goal of individual wealth has been accepted by our people, and despite their belief that this can be attained by wage employment and by life in the towns, the truth is that it is an unrealistic goal, especially in Tanzania. The vast majority even of our town dwellers live extremely poorly, and in most cases they are on the whole worse off, both materially and in the realm of personal satisfaction, than the people in the rural areas could be. An unskilled worker in the towns or on the agricultural estates earns wages which are hardly sufficient to enable a family to eat a proper diet and live in a decent house. Certainly the concentration of population in a small area makes it essential (for public health reasons) that the community should spend money on making clean water available within easy distance of everyone; certainly, too, the concentration of people makes social life easier, and allows educational opportunities for adults to be more easily available and more varied. Yet, on the other hand, the life of children outside school is often extremely bad, unhealthy and dangerous, and for most people the ever-present threat of unemployment, and consequent real hunger in the midst of apparent wealth, introduces evils which can be excluded from life in the rural areas if this is based on the traditional principles of African society.

CHANGES IN THE RURAL AREAS

Yet it is not only through the growth of towns that our society has changed. Even in the rural areas life has been changing over the past 30 years or so. Self-sufficient family farms producing just their own food with enough over to obtain clothes and pay taxes, are no longer universal. Even where subsistence agriculture is still practised, the young and active men have often left the homestead to go to towns or to seek elsewhere for the modern world.

But the basic difference between Tanzania's rural life now and in the past stems from the widespread introduction of cash crop farming. Over large areas of the country peasants spend at least part of their time—and sometimes the larger part of it—on the cultivation of crops for sale; crops like cotton, coffee, sisal, pyrethrum, and so on. But in the process the old traditions of living together, working together, and sharing the proceeds, have often been abandoned. Farmers tend to work as individuals, in competition and not in co-operation with their neighbours. And in many places our most intelligent and hard-working peasants have invested their money (or money advanced through public credit facilities) in clearing more land, extending their acreage, using better tools, and so on, until they have quite important farms of 10, 20 or even more acres. To do this they have employed other people to work for them. Sometimes—but unfortunately not always—they have paid the Government minimum wages to these labourers for the period over which they were employed. The result has been an increase in production for the nation as a whole—that is, an increase in the amount of wealth produced in Tanzania—and a still further increase in the wealth of the man who owned, managed and initiated the larger farm.

The work of such people as this has shown that in the rural areas of Tanzania it is possible to produce enough crops to give an agricultural worker a decent life, with money for a good house and furniture, proper food, some reserve for old age, and so on. But the moment such a man extends his farm to the point where it is necessary for him to employ labourers in order to plant or harvest the full acreage, then the traditional system of ujamaa has been killed. For he is not sharing with other people according to the work they do, but simply paying them in accordance with a laid-down minimum wage. The final output of the farm on which both employer and employees have worked is not being shared. The money obtained from all the crops goes to the owner; from that money he pays 'his' workers. And the result is that the spirit of equality between all people working on the farm has gone—for the employees are the servants of the man who employs them. Thus we have the beginnings of a class system in the rural areas. Also, the employees may well be paid for working during harvest or during weeding but get no money for the rest of the year.

Let us take an example. A cotton farmer in the Lake Region who works hard and follows all the rules of good husbandry will probably be able to cultivate 3 acres of cotton, in addition to food crops, with just the labour of his own family—assuming that all members will help to pick when the cotton is ready. If he really produces 1,500 lb. to an acre—which some people have already exceeded—and the price he receives after deductions is 46 cents a pound, he will receive Shs. 2,070/- cash. From this he has only to pay his District Taxes; his food is growing, his house is his own and he has no rent to pay, and so on. Apart from a minimum of clothes, repairs to his house, and perhaps very low school fees, the money is at his disposal to spend as he likes. Let us now assume that this man decides that the following year he will plant 6 acres. For this he and his family will have to work harder, but in addition they will employ 3 people during the picking and cleaning for an average period of 3 months during the year. He will thus have to pay out to his labourers something like Shs. 900/-; but in return—because he has used them— he and his family will receive another Shs. 2,070/-. The following year he will thus have Shs. 3,240/- to spend as he likes. He can either expand further—perhaps by acquiring a tractor, or other improved implements—or he can live better, and so on. But the three men whose work at a crucial stage made this extra Shs. 1,170/- possible, will have received between them Shs. 900/- and for the rest of the year they will have to depend upon other kinds of wage employment or find some other way of getting minimum food, clothes and shelter. The one man is progressing very fast—and with increasing speed—and the others are receiving less than they could receive if they worked on their own account.

THE IMPLICATIONS OF THIS KIND OF DEVELOPMENT

If this kind of capitalist development takes place widely over the country, we may get a good statistical increase in the national wealth of Tanzania, but the masses of the people will not necessarily be better off. On the contrary, as land becomes more scarce we shall find ourselves with a farmers' class and a labourers' class, with the latter being unable either to work for themselves or to receive a full return for the contribution they are making to the total output. They will become a 'rural proletariat' depending on the decisions of other men for their existence, and subject in consequence to all the subservience, social and economic inequality, and insecurity, which such a position involves.

Certainly at the moment everyone has a choice between working for others or farming on his own. In Tanzania's circumstances it may therefore seem unnecessary to be worrying about the implications of agricultural capitalist development—implications which will not reveal themselves in their full force until a shortage of land becomes a problem for our nation. But there are already local shortages of land in popular, fertile and well-watered areas. And in any case, if we allow this pattern of agriculture to grow, we shall continue to move further and further away from our goal of human equality. The small-scale capitalist agriculture we now have is not really a danger; but our feet are on the wrong path, and if we continue to encourage or even help the development of agricultural capitalism, we shall never become a socialist state. On the contrary, we shall be continuing the break-up of the traditional concepts of human equality based on sharing all the necessities of life and on a universal obligation to work.

There is, however, another institution in rural life which has brought a very great change to many of our peasants and which does stem from the socialist principles of avoiding the exploitation of man by man. A large part of our farm produce is now marketed by co-operative societies which are owned and governed by the farmers themselves, working together for their own benefit. Many criticisms have been made of the working of our co-operative societies; much practical improvement is necessary if they are really to serve the farmers and not to replace the exploitation of man by man by the exploitation of inefficiency and bureaucratic dishonesty. Yet there is no doubt that marketing by farmers, without the intervention of middle-men who are endeavouring to pay as little as possible to the farmer and receive as much as possible from the consumer, can be to the benefit of both the farmers and the rest of the community. In criticizing the workings of existing co-operative societies, we must not make the mistake of blaming the principles of co-operation. The problems of co-operatives are practical ones, which must be worked out and dealt with by better and more skilled management and commercial machinery.

But although marketing co-operatives are socialist in the sense that they represent the joint activities of producers, they could be socialist institutions serving capitalism if the basic organization of agricultural production is capitalist. It is not inconsistent with the capitalist philosophy of the United States of America that farmers' co-operatives exist there and are quite strong. For a farmers' co-operative marketing society is an institution serving the farmers; if they are capitalist farmers, then the existence of a co-operative marketing society will mean that one group of capitalists—the farmers—are safeguarding their own interests, as against another group of capitalists—the middle-men. It is only if the agricultural production itself is organized on a socialist pattern that co-operative marketing societies are serving socialism.

SUMMARIZING THE PRESENT POSITION

At this point let us try to sum up the present position in Tanzania in a few words. We have the vast majority of our people living in the rural areas, most of them working on their own as farmers who do not employ any labour, but produce their own food and some additional crops which they sell. Many of them try to adopt modern methods, each on his own particular farm and while working in isolation. This is like every worker trying to have his own factory! There are, in addition, a small number of agricultural employers; a few of these are estates employing some hundreds of workers, but increasingly (although still in small numbers) the employers are individuals employing a few people for perhaps only part of the year. Here and there over the country we do have groups of people working on terms of equality and sharing the proceeds in co-operative farms, but these groups are so small in number that they do not yet make a real impact either on our total agricultural output or, except locally, on the social structure which is developing. They are important only as examples of what could be, not as an indication of what is.

Thus we still have in this country a predominantly peasant society in which farmers work for themselves and their families, and are helped and protected from exploitation by co-operative marketing arrangements. Yet the present trend is away from the extended family production and social unity, and towards the development of a class system in the rural areas. It is this kind of development which would be inconsistent with the growth of a socialist Tanzania in which all citizens could be assured of human dignity and equality, and in which all were able to have a decent and constantly improving life for themselves and their children.

TANZANIA AS IT MUST DEVELOP

For the foreseeable future the vast majority of our people will continue to spend their lives in the rural areas and continue to work on the land. The land is the only basis for Tanzania's development; we have no other. Therefore, if our rural life is not based on the principles of socialism our country will not be socialist, regardless of how we organize our industrial sector, and regardless of our commercial and political arrangements. Tanzanian socialism must be firmly based on the land and its workers. This means that we have to build up the countryside in such a way that our people have a better standard of living, while living together on terms of equality and fraternity. It also means that, in the course of time, the advantages of town life in the way of services and personal pleasures and opportunities must become available to those who work in the rural sector as much as those in urban areas.

If we are to succeed in this, certain things are essential. The first of these is hard work by our people. There is no substitute for this, especially as we do not have large accumulations of capital which can be invested in agricultural labour-saving devices or in increased productivity. We have to increase the amount we produce from our land, and we shall have to do it by the use of our own hands and our own brains. No organization of society can do away with this; whether we are capitalist, socialist, communist, fascist, or anything else, only an increase in output can provide the extra goods needed for our people to have the opportunity for a good life. The type of social organization we adopt affects both the distribution of the goods we produce and the quality of the life our people can lead, but it is irrelevant to the central fact that our output of goods has to be increased. Each person has to produce more by harder, longer, and better work.

It is not enough, however, for agricultural production to be increased. Marketing must be properly organized so that, even while our nation is in the grip of international market forces which control world prices, still we get the maximum possible for our goods, and our producers—that is, our farmers—get a fair return for their contribution to the national wealth. The co-operative movement in particular must be made more efficient, both in management and in its democratic machinery.

Not only this, there must also be an efficient and democratic system of local government, so that our people make their own decisions on the things which affect them directly, and so that they are able to recognize their own control over community decisions and their own responsibility for carrying them out. Yet this local control has to be organized in such a manner that the nation is united and working together for common needs and for the maximum development of our whole society.

And finally, the whole rural society must be built on the basis of the equality of all Tanzanian citizens and their common obligations and common rights. There must be no masters and servants, but just people working together for the good of all and thus their own good.

We shall be unable to fulfil these objectives if we continue to produce as individuals for individual profit. Certainly a man who is working for himself and for his own profit will not suffer from exploitation in this employment. But neither will he make much progress. It is not long before an individual, working alone, reaches the limit of his powers. Only by working together can men overcome that limitation. The truth is that when human beings want to make great progress they have no alternative but to combine their efforts. And there are only two methods by which this can be done; people can be made to work together, or they can work together. We can be made to work together by, and for the benefit of, a slave owner, or by, and for the profit of, a capitalist; alternatively we can work together voluntarily for our own benefit. We shall achieve the goals we in this country have set ourselves if the basis of Tanzanian life consists of rural *economic and social communities where people live together and work together for the good of all,* and which are inter-locked so that all of the different communities also work together in co-operation for the common good of the nation as a whole.

The principles upon which the traditional extended family was based must be reactivated. We can start with extended family villages, but they will not remain family communities, and they must certainly be larger communities than was traditionally the case. Also, modern knowledge must be applied by these communities and to them; and the barriers which previously existed between different groups must be broken down, so that they co-operate in the achievement of major tasks. But the basis of rural life in Tanzania must be the practice of co-operation in its widest sense—in living, in working, and in distribution, and all with an acceptance of the absolute equality of all men and women.

This is very different from our present organization of society, and requires a reversal of the present trend. We shall not achieve it quickly. It is different because it involves a determination to maintain human equality. It is different because its dominant characteristic would be co-operation, not competition, and its criteria for individual success would be good service, not the accumulation of private property. The question is how we can organize our acti-vities now so as to eventually reach this goal.

NO SIMPLE OR SINGLE ANSWER FOR ALL CIRCUMSTANCES

It is essential to realize that within the unity of Tanzania there is also such diversity that it would be foolish for someone in Dar es Salaam to try to draw up a blueprint for the crop production and social organization which has to be applied to every corner of our large country. Principles of action can be set out, but the application of these principles must take into account the different geographical and geological conditions in different areas, and also the local variations in the basically similar traditional structures. For exam-ple, in the Kilimanjaro Region not only is the practice of individual land-holding almost universal, but also there is no unused land on the mountain. This affects social attitudes and creates some family problems which do not exist in those parts of Tanzania where a young man can get land of his own quite near to his father's farm as soon as he is ready to start his own family. Again, some parts of our country suffer from great water shortage or uncertainty; their agricultural organization, their density of population—and thus their social organization—must inevitably take account of these facts, just as the organization in well-watered areas must take advantage of its greater potential. All these things affect what can be grown, and the degree of investment in land or implements which is necessary for a given output. It would be absurd to try and settle all these questions from Dar es Salaam, particularly as such variations as those of the type of soil sometimes occur within a very small area. Local initiative and self-reliance are essential.

The social customs of the people also vary to some extent. The Masai are traditionally a nomadic cattle people; their family structure, their religious beliefs, and other things, have been shaped by this fact. They are therefore somewhat different from the social beliefs and organization of, for example, the traditionally agricultural Wanyakyusa. The steps which will be necessary to combine increased output with social equality may therefore also vary; the important thing is that the methods adopted should not be incompatible with each other, and should each be appropriate for the attainment of the single goal in the particular circumstances.

Quite apart from these local considerations, however, there is another factor which would prevent one universally applied method being introduced. For there are some things of which the nation as a whole has great need, but which might not be in the particular interests of any one locality or any particular group of farmers. Thus, for example, it may be necessary for purposes of water control to have forests at the headlands of rivers, and to prevent cultivation or animal herding there. The farmers in these regions might easily feel that this is not in their interests—that they would be economically better off by farming such land rather than leaving it for trees from which no return can be expected for perhaps 50 years. Or, to take another example, tourism brings important foreign exchange into the country, but any individual farmer would prefer to kill off the wild beasts which might eat his produce rather than protect them for other people to look at. Or, again, some crops demand heavy mechanization or other investment if they are to be most economically produced. No single farmer could undertake such work on his own; even a co-operative group would have difficulties at the beginning because of the heavy initial capital requirements and the consequent big burden of debt they would be accepting.

For this kind of over-riding national need it is essential that there should be positive Government action in the field of agriculture, as in other aspects of the economy. There must be state forests and local authority forests of different kinds. There must be national parks controlled and run by the public, acting through Government or the local authority; there must be other areas in which shooting of game is prohibited or controlled. In addition there should be state farms or local authority farms which deal especially with those crops which can be grown most economically for export or for urban sale only on a mechanized or large-scale basis, or where a combination of research and development is required, as for example in the state cattle ranching farm at Kongwa.

In such cases as these traditional agricultural methods can have no place; they are not appropriate. The choice is really only between allowing a few wealthy individuals to undertake the profitable work, if they wish, or reserving all of it for state operation.

In Tanzania it is clear that as a general rule new developments of this kind should be operated by the public, although some private or joint private and public investment may be appropriate in certain cases where expertise or capital is an immediate problem. But certainly it is better that the workers in plantation agriculture should be employed by the community as a whole, or that the community should have a dominant voice in their wages and conditions. By such public or joint public and private employment, the workers on this kind of mass production farm can be sure of fair treatment, and can do their work knowing that any proceeds from the farm go to the community in general or are being used for further investment. The workers will be able to know that their efforts are not just benefiting company shareholders whom they do not know and who do nothing to make the enterprise a success.

Thus, included in the rural and agricultural organization of a socialist Tanzania, there must be some state or other public enterprises, operated under the control of appointed managers and employing labour just as the nationalized food mills do. But this should only be a small part of the agricultural sector in Tanzania. It should not be our purpose to convert our peasants into wage-earners, even on Government farms. To make our socialism and our democracy a reality we should instead adapt to modern needs the traditional structure of African society. We must, in other words, aim at creating a nation in which ujamaa farms and communities dominate the rural economy and set the social pattern for the country as a whole.

UJAMAA AGRICULTURE

In a socialist Tanzania then, our agricultural organization would be predominantly that of co-operative living and working for the good of all. This means that most of our farming would be done by groups of people who live as a community and work as a community. They would live together in a village; they would farm together; market together; and undertake the provision of local services and small local requirements as a community. Their community would be the traditional family group, or any other group of people living according to ujamaa principles, large enough to take account of modern methods and the twentieth century needs of man. The land this community farmed would be called 'our land' by all the members; the crops they produced on that land would be 'our crops'; it would be 'our shop' which provided individual members with the day-to-day necessities from outside; 'our workshop' which made the bricks from which houses and other buildings were constructed, and so on.

Obviously such community activities would need to be organized, would need to have a 'manager' responsible for the allocation of tasks and their supervision. There would need to be a 'treasurer' responsible for the money earned and its administration, and a 'governing committee' which is able to take executive decisions in between general meetings. But all these people could come from among the community, and must do so if it is to be a real socialist unit. They would be members of the community, not outsiders, although at the beginning there may be an advantage in attaching to such schemes some technical and other advisers if the right kind of expert could be found.

Such groups are possible in Tanzania—indeed a few already exist. There is no need to wait for the Government to organize them and give all the instructions. Nor would it be sensible to expect everyone who joins such a group to be willing to think only of the community interest and never of his own. Such unselfishness is rare in man, and no social organization should be based on the expectation that all members will be angels. What is required is a sensible organization which can be shown to be to the benefit of all members. This can be done if every member has certain responsibilities to the community, and is able to see his benefits from it because they are benefits to himself and to his own village.

The essential thing is that the community would be farming as a group and living as a group; investment in the community farm would be investment in the farm of every member; investment in the village—such as a clean water supply—would be of benefit to every member. The return from the produce of the farm, and from all other activities of the community, would be shared according to the work done and to the needs of the members, with a small amount being paid in taxes and another amount (which is determined by the members themselves) invested in their own future. There would be no need to exclude private property in houses or even in cattle; some energetic members may wish to have their own gardens as well as share in the community farm. The extent of the private activities may well vary from one village to another, but always on the basis that no member is allowed to exploit another—nor to exploit a non-member—and that all must play a fair part in the life of the community from which they all benefit.

Such living and working in communities could transform our lives in Tanzania. We would not automatically become wealthy, although we could all become a little richer than we are now. But most important of all, any increase in the amount of wealth we produce under this system would be 'ours'; it would not belong just to one or two individuals, but to all those whose work had produced it. At the same time we should have strengthened our traditional equality and our traditional security. For in a village community a man who is genuinely sick during the harvest would not be left to starve for the rest of the year, nor would the man whose wife is ill find the children uncared for—as he might do if he farms on his own. Traditional African socialism always made such questions as these irrelevant, and our modern socialism, by resting on the same foundations, will also make them irrelevant. For in each ujamaa village the man who is sick will be cared for; a man who is widowed will have no difficulty in getting his children looked after; the old, the unmarried, the orphans and other people in this kind of trouble will be looked after by the village as a whole, just as was done in traditional society.

Group work of this kind, too, would almost certainly allow for greater production and greater services in the community, with a consequent benefit to all members. It would be possible to acquire some modern tools if the members were willing to invest in them; some degree of specialization would be possible, with one member being, for example, a carpenter who makes the tables, chairs, doors and other things needed by the community, and works on the land only during times of greatest pressure, like the harvest. Another member could be responsible for building work, another for running a nursery where the children could be cared for and fed while most of the mothers are in the fields, and so on. By such division of labour arranged by the members according to their own needs, the villagers could make their whole lives more fruitful and pleasant.

UJAMAA SOCIALISM IN PRACTICE

A nation of such village communities would be a socialist nation. For the essential element in them would be the equality of all members of the community, and the members' self-government in all matters which concerned only their own affairs. For a really socialist village would elect its own officials and they would remain equal members with the others, subject always to the wishes of the people. Only in relation to work discipline would there be any hierarchy, and then such officials would be merely acting for the village as a whole.

Let us take an example. It would be a meeting of the villagers which would elect the officers and the committee, and a meeting of the village which would decide whether or not to accept or to amend any detailed proposals for work organization which the committee had drawn up in the light of general directions given by earlier meetings. Let us assume that a forty-member village meeting agrees to a cotton farm of 40 acres and a food farm of 40 acres. It would be the committee's job to propose where in the land available these different crops should be planted, and to propose the times and organization of joint work on the land. At the same time the committee would have to make proposals for the other work which had been decided upon—perhaps the digging of a trench for a future piped water supply, or the making of a new road, or the improvement of village drainage. These detailed proposals they would bring to the next village meeting, and once they had been accepted it would be a job of the officers to ensure that all members carried out the decisions, and to report to a general meeting any problems as they occurred. As the village became more established and the need for a village carpenter, or a village nursery, or a village shop became more pressing, the committee would work out proposals as to how these could be organized and run by a member for the common benefit. The village officials would also be responsible for liaising with other villages and with the general machinery of government. Thus they would be responsible for making any requests for outside assistance about schooling, credit, agricultural advice, and so on, which the village had decided it needed, as well as arranging the selling of crops, the organization of taxes, payments, etc.

By such means as these there would be re-established all the advantages of traditional African democracy, social security and human dignity, and at the same time we would have prepared ourselves to take advantage of modern knowledge and the advantages which this can bring. For there is no reason why, in the course of time, such villages should not become more than simple agricultural communities, selling their crops and buying everything manufactured from outside. Certain things will always be available more cheaply if they are mass produced; but an established village could easily organize the production of other things for itself. And in co-operation with other nearby villages of the same kind, a system of locally-based small industries would be possible for the benefit of all involved. Thus a group of villages together could organize their own servicing station for agricultural implements and farm vehicles; they could perhaps make their own cooking utensils and crockery out of local materials, or they could organize the making of their own clothes on a communal basis. Such villages could also organize together for social, political and educational purposes, so as to bring to all members in their rural area some of the opportunities which can come from living in communities. But all these things would depend upon the democratic decisions of the members themselves. The Government or local authority would become involved only where a decision involved them in responsibilities—as, for example, in the provision of a teacher if a school were planned, or where a proposal might affect the interests of people outside the village or villages directly concerned.

Government personnel and the local government would, of course, have a definite role to play in a society organized on the basis of such communal villages. Just as each village would be able to do certain things on its own, and for others would benefit from co-operating with similar villages nearby, so there are some things in which the nation as a whole has to co-operate. National defence, education, marketing, health, communications, large industries—for all these things and many more, all of Tanzania has to work together. The job of Government would therefore be to help these self-reliant communities and to organize their co-operation with others.

But it would certainly be easier for the members of the villages to take full advantage of Government's services and to co-operate with their fellow citizens if they are living and working together in their small groups. An agricultural field worker, for example, would be teaching new techniques to about 40 people together, instead of one family at a time; he could thus spend more time and give more expert help to the village farm than he could ever give to any individual farmer. Or, again, Government could not hope to give a water pump to every separate house in a scattered community, nor provide the miles of pipes which might be necessary in order to service one isolated house. But it would be able to co-operate much more quickly in the supply of a pump or pipes for a village of 30 to 40 families who were willing to do the physical labour themselves.

The country would also become more democratic through this organization of ujamaa communities. The Member of Parliament, or of the Local Council, would more easily be able to keep informed of the people's wishes and their ideas on national issues if they are living together than if the people do not get a daily opportunity to discuss important issues together. This means that not only would the people be governing their own lives directly in village matters, but they would also be playing a more effective role in the Government of their country.

HOW DO WE GET TO THIS POSITION?—PERSUASION NOT FORCE

It is one thing to argue the advantages of this type of rural organization; the question is how can we move from our present position to make it into a reality? The farmers in Tanzania, like those elsewhere in the world, have learnt to be cautious about new ideas however attractive they may sound; only experience will convince them, and experience can only be gained by beginning.

Yet socialist communities cannot be established by compulsion. It may be possible—and sometimes necessary—to insist on all farmers in a given area growing a certain acreage of a particular crop until they realize that this brings them a more secure living, and then do not have to be forced to cultivate it. But living together and working together for the good of all is not just a question of crop output. It depends on a willingness to co-operate, and an understanding of the different kind of life which can be obtained by the participants if they work hard together. Viable socialist communities can only be established with willing members; the task of leadership and of Government is not to try and force this kind of development, but to explain, encourage, and participate. For a farmer may well be suspicious of the Government official or Party leader who comes to him and says, 'Do this'; he will be more likely to listen to the one who says, 'This is a good thing to do for the following reasons, and I am myself participating with my friends in doing it'. Individuals can have a very great effect in this work, whether or not they have any official position. Government can help to get such communities established by encouragement, and by giving priority in service to those groups who have committed themselves to this type of development. But it is vital that whatever encouragement Government and TANU give to this type of scheme, they must not try to run it; they must help the people to run it themselves.

It would also be unwise to expect that established farmers will be convinced by words—however persuasive. The farmers will have to see for themselves the advantage of working together and living together before they trust their entire future to this organization of life. In particular, before giving up their individual plots of land they will wish to see that the system of working together really benefits everyone. Groups of young men may be willing to experiment and this should be welcomed; we must encourage such young people. But what we are really aiming at is balanced communities where young and old are all involved together. Progress may thus be quite slow at the beginning, yet that is no reason for surrendering the goal. The man who creeps forward inch by inch may well arrive at his destination, when the man who jumps without being able to see the other side may well fall and cripple himself.

STEP-BY-STEP TRANSFORMATION

Where necessary, then, progress can be made in three stages. The first may be to persuade people to move their houses into a single village, if possible near water, and to plant their next years' food crops within easy reach of the area where the houses will be. For some peoples in Tanzania this will be quite a change in living habits, so that in certain areas this may be the second rather than the first stage in the progress. For another step is to persuade a group of people—perhaps the members of a ten-house cell—to start a small communal plot (or some other communal activity) on which they work co-operatively, sharing the proceeds at harvest time according to the work they each have done. Alternatively, it might be that the parents of children at a primary school could start a community farm, working together with the children, and jointly deciding what to grow and how to share out the proceeds. In either of these cases, and whether or not the people are living together in a village at this stage, the people would keep their individual plots; the community farm would be an extra effort instead of each family trying to expand its own acreage. Once these two steps had been effected, the final stage would come when the people have confidence in a community farm, so that they are willing to invest all their effort in it, simply keeping gardens around their own houses for special vegetables, etc. Then the socialist village will be really established and other productive community activities can get under way.

It is obvious, however, that with the variations in potential, in soils and in social customs, it would be absurd to set down one pattern of progress or one plan which must be followed by everyone. What is necessary is the objective of an ujamaa community. The interim steps and the detailed organization should be adapted to the local circumstances—which includes an understanding of the people's traditional attitudes as well as the degree of the people's political understanding and their acceptance of this social objective.

The important thing is that the work should begin. For this it is no use waiting for the Ministry of Lands, Settlement and Water Development to send out its officers to lay out villages, to explain, and so on. If this type of organization is to spread, every rural worker who understands the objective must play his part. The TANU cell leader may in some cases be able to persuade the members in his cell to make a beginning; the Agricultural Officer may be able to persuade a group of farmers how much more he would be able to help them if they were living and working together; the Community Development Officer who has won the confidence of the people in his area may be able to do it; or the TANU official at any level. The teacher in a primary school could help, or any individual Tanzanian who understands (even if he is a Sheikh or a Padre), and whether or not he has an official position. The important thing is that everyone should understand that this is no alternative to hard work; it is simply a more intelligent and more productive form of hard work which, if the weather is good, will lead to better results for all those participating. Promises of miracles, even promises of great Government help, will only lead to disaster.

The first few years of ujamaa village living will be very hard. The facilities available to the people will not immediately increase by their coming together, and there will be new problems of organization and co-operation. The wealth of each village will not be greater than that of the people at present, and the new possibilities—the vision of what can come in the future—may tempt the members to be more dissatisfied than they are at the moment, and to give way to the temptations of impatience. These socialist villages must grow from an application of the principle of self-reliance; they must grow through the efforts of their own members, and that means hard work which brings results only after a few years. Only a full realization of the problems as well as the possibilities of ujamaa communities will enable them to get firmly on their feet. This is why it is so important that each community should start with a mixture of private and co-operative living if the former has been the custom of the people, gradually increasing the level of co-operative working as the members sort out the problems which occur and find a method of organizing their communal activities which best suits them.

This is not to say that the different Ministries of Government have no role to play. But the basis of the growth of such ujamaa communities and of their strength, can only be the work and the understanding of the participants. Government advice and help can only be of marginal importance; it must not be expected everywhere, for if all our two million families started such communities, it would clearly be impossible to help all their schemes at once. Even without everyone starting such schemes, the Government will not be able to give much help to any one that is established.

DISTRIBUTION OF RETURNS IN AN UJAMAA VILLAGE

It is also important that the principles on which any returns from the community farm will be distributed should be just, simple and easily understood from the beginning. The basis must be to share according to the work done, for although in a family everyone shares equally whether they turned out for work every day or not, energetic people would understandably be unwilling to carry lazy people who were not members of their own family. Yet at the same time some proportion of the total return, at least once the village is properly established, should be set aside to help those in genuine difficulties—the sick, the crippled, the old, and orphaned children. It is also important that from the beginning the idea of putting some part aside for expansion or investment should be accepted. When the farm first begins, it might be possible in certain places for most of the return to be devoted to communal purposes, like buying pipes for water supplies, or building a new classroom, a community centre, and so on. This will be especially true while people keep their individual plots, although even here some personal return commensurate to the work done will probably be necessary.

All such decisions, however—how to share out as well as how much to grow, the arrangements for the children, the crippled and old—must be made by the arreement of all the participants. Village democracy must operate from the beginning; there is no alternative if this system is to succeed. A leader will have an opportunity to explain his ideas and to try to persuade the people that they are good; but it must be for the people themselves to accept or reject his suggestions. It does not matter if the discussion takes a long time; we are building a nation, and this is not a short-term thing. For the point about decisions by an ujamaa village is not just whether the members do or do not decide to dig a well or clear a new shamba. The point is that by making this decision, and then acting upon it, they will be building up a whole way of life—a socialist way of life. Nothing is more important than that, and it is not the work of a few days, nor of a few people. An ujamaa village is the village of the members, and the life there is their life. Therefore everything which relates exclusively to their village, and their life in it, must be decided by them and not by anyone else.

SOME SPECIAL PROBLEMS: LOCAL LAND SHORTAGES

There are, however, some areas where local land shortage makes it impossible to move towards co-operative living and working through the opening of entirely new community farms. In such areas as Kilimanjaro, for example, every piece of land is already intensively cultivated, with barely enough open spaces left for public purposes like schools, community centres—and so on. Furthermore, these areas are almost always farmed on the basis of individual plots, usually with each farmer living on his own plot and not in villages with his neighbours.

In areas like these there is already a social problem. Young men and women find that there is no work for them to do on their father's land, and no place nearby where they can start to farm on their own. Up to now they have, as a result, tended to drift to the towns looking for wage employment—which they are often unable to find. There is no easy answer to this; the only answer is through new settlements in other areas. It is impossible to expand the land on the mountain, and the only way forward for the growing population is to go to some other part of Tanzania and start afresh. This is necessary whatever form of agricultural organization is adopted. Government must help the extra population from these areas to settle and to farm.

In the future, however, this assistance for resettlement should be on the basis of settlement in villages which can develop into ujamaa communities. This does not mean that the Government should build modern expensive houses and complete villages for the new settlers to move into. That assumption has been our mistake in the past. Instead we must organize two 'moving days'. The first should be during the beginning of the dry season when active men and women are taken to the new area and loaned tents for a few weeks while they build temporary houses for themselves and their families, who will move in later and begin land clearing ready for the rains. When accommodation is ready the second 'moving day' should be instituted, with the families brought to begin their new life in the village.

For those people whose relatives cannot help them, the Government should provide food until the first harvest; it should also provide credit for poles, permanent roofing, etc., for the houses, and give a grace period of three years before repayment begins. In such settlements, too, it would be essential that agricultural advice be available, because the farmers would be unfamiliar with the crops and the soil requirements of the new area.

It is in circumstances like these that Government should try to provide a Community Development Officer or a TANU official familiar with the potential of living and working together, who would help the new settlers in the initial organization of their village committees, etc. Even so, if the new settlers come from areas of exclusively private farms, it would be a mistake to exclude individual plots at the beginning. Some large areas of land should be reserved for a community farm, but if the settlers wish it they should be allowed to clear first—although as a group—the land which they will each cultivate privately. In order to avoid the need for big capital investment, it is also necessary that the first effort should be made in the direction of the village growing its own food; land clearing and planting of cash crops should be the second priority, not the first.

The need for new settlement from areas of land shortage does not mean that the land shortage areas should be excluded from socialist development. It must be accepted, however, that socialist progress in these areas will be more difficult to achieve, for when vacant land is not available there is only one way to create a community farm; that is by individual farmers coming together and joining their pieces of land and working them in common. Furthermore, many of these areas are under permanent crops, like coffee. A farmer entering an ujamaa village under these circumstances will thus be investing at least part of his existing capital in the new project, not simply investing his effort in making an expanded farm. This will mean that a greater amount of socialist and technical education will be necessary before the first steps are undertaken, for the farmer must be convinced that working together with others, pooling his coffee trees with others, will still bring greater benefits to himself and his family.

It may be that the way to start under these circumstances is to operate first on the basis of working groups, but with the individual plots retained—that is, on the basis of mutual help. This would be simply a revival, and perhaps an extension, of the traditional system of joint activity, making it applicable to existing farms and not just to land clearing or house building. By working together on their private farms the farmers will be able to finish different jobs more quickly, or to do things which would be too difficult for any of them individually. They will then have time to do other useful things—either by themselves or co-operatively.

This first step of mutual help can be followed by others. The farmers could buy certain essential goods co-operatively—things like fertilizers, for example—or they could together build a store for their coffee, or something else which is of use to them all. By doing such things together the farmers will be gradually moving towards an acceptance of ujamaa socialism.

In areas of land shortage like this, the way for people to begin to work together may, however, not be in agriculture at all. Instead, a group of them may come together to start a small 'industrial' or 'service' project in which they all work for the good of all. Thus, for example, in Kilimanjaro a group of farmers may get together and jointly organize and run a modern poultry unit, or a communal tannery, or a communal woodwork shop. Or, again, they may come together to share the use of a truck which they jointly own, or to organize some new irrigation—perhaps with a water-wheel which they jointly own—which will benefit all of them. If people start working together in this way, it will be possible for these densely populated areas to become areas of rural industrialization, thus reducing their dependence on world prices of their cash crops, and also providing a new impetus to community activity and community life.

Rural industrialization projects must not be thought of in terms of large modern factories, but more in terms of 'cottage industries'. Yet it would be a mistake for such work to be done by separate families in their own homes; if the shirt-making or the knitting of sweaters and blankets is to be the project for a particular group, they should work together in one place so that they can help each other and each specialize on certain aspects of the work. Neither should great capital investment be considered. We have many traditional manufacturing activities which we can revive, and which we should revive. Government also intends to take further steps which we hope will, in a year or so, enable advice and ideas to be given to people in circumstances like these. But the important thing is that such 'village industries' must be organized and run on the same basis as community farms, that is, with the members making their own decisions, electing their own officers, and sharing the proceeds in accordance with what they themselves believe to be justice.

ANIMAL HUSBANDRY AREAS

Another special problem may well occur in those areas where animal herding is an important economic activity, if not the only one. Certainly no one can expect that all the farmers in such an area will straight away merge their herds into a common pool. But here, too, we can start gradually and build up socialist herding step by step while the farmers learn the full benefits of it. First we can start by mutual help in herding; the herders will mix up a group of farmers' cattle and take them all out together so that a smaller number of people are out at any one time. This, in fact, is quite customary for many of our people, and it would be comparatively simple to introduce the system where it has died out or never been practised. And it will mean that each farmer will have a little more time to do other work either on his own or—better still—in co-operation with others for the benefit of the community as a whole.

Another method of advance is for a number of cattle owners to each contribute one or two head of cattle so as to make up a community herd, which is then cared for by modern methods and which perhaps has a reserved grazing area. Each farmer would, at this stage, also keep his own herd. But gradually the improvement of the community herd, and the visible experience of the communal benefits from it will probably lead them to build up the community herd and reduce the size of their separate cattle ownership. The participants would, of course, use the income from the community herd as they pleased. They may decide to use the milk for school feeding; they may decide that the income from the herd should be used to build a cattle dip, or a dam which will provide regular water for people and cattle alike; or they may decide to spend the income on improving the village or helping those members of their community who are in some kind of trouble.

In both of these special circumstances the move into a village, so that people live together as well as work together, may have to be accomplished gradually. But until it is done, real democratic and socialist living is impossible.

PROBLEM OF CAPITAL

A very important fact about this method of gradual progress into ujamaa communities is that there is no necessity for great capital investment before they can start. They can be, and—except where a completely new area is being started up to deal with people moving from overpopulated areas—should be, started by the people from their own efforts. New land can be cleared by people using their own tools—the tools they use now on their individual plots. Often they themselves will be able to provide the seed for the community farm from their own stocks, or they can get an advance for the purchase of seed, fertilizers, etc., from their co-operative society or perhaps from the National Development Credit Agency. On that basis alone they can start, and the first year's profits from the community farm can then be used to purchase simple tools—perhaps an ox-plough—and so on, for expanded community effort in the coming years. Again, if there is a Savings and Credit Society existing in the area—and these should be encouraged whether or not there is an ujamaa community—the members of that society may agree to lend their savings for the purpose of starting or expanding an ujamaa community. The important thing is that there should be no reliance on great outside capital injection. We have already seen (in the original Government Settlement Schemes) the great dangers of heavy initial capitalization and the great burden of debt which it leaves for the farmers. And the truth is that in any case our nation does not have large amounts of capital. We have to create our own, and we can do this if we work together using at the beginning simply the resources we already have—that is, our labour, our land, and our willingness to work together.

THE ROLE OF GOVERNMENT

Ujamaa villages will have to be established, and will grow through the self-reliant activities of our people. They will be created by the village people themselves, and maintained by them. It must be done from their own resources.

The Government's role is to help people to make a success of their work and their decisions. Further, where a village community has been established, the Ministry of Agriculture and Co-operatives should ensure that the necessary agricultural advice—about the best crops to plant on the community farm, and how to plant them for greatest success—is available to the villagers. If necessary, in a large village an Agricultural Field Officer could be stationed permanently so that his advice is available whenever required. Alternatively, if there is a member of the scheme who is qualified to receive special training, the Ministry must provide training for him; it must make available a place at an existing institution, or run special courses for such people.

The Ministry of Local Government and Rural Development, too, must be active in these villages; their field workers should be available to help the people to organize themselves, to advise them on how they can become eligible for advances for seed, or for small loans for farm equipment. It would be this Ministry, too, which should draw up a model constitution for the villages at different stages, although it must be stressed that no one model should be imposed on any village. Any model which is drawn up should just be a guide which draws the attention of the people to the decisions which have to be made by them; each village community must be able to make its own decisions. Nonetheless, the experience of existing ujamaa villages, such as those now operating within the Ruvuma Development Association, could be helpful, and the Ministry of Local Government and Rural Development should try to make this experience available to people from different parts.

But the most important thing is not that the Government should do this or that for all villages, but that within its resources it should give priority to requests which are received from villages where the people are living together and working together for the good of all.

CONCLUSION

What is here being proposed is that we in Tanzania should move from being a nation of individual peasant producers who are gradually adopting the incentives and the ethics of the capitalist system. Instead we should gradually become a nation of ujamaa villages where the people co-operate directly in small groups and where these small groups co-operate together for joint enterprises.

This can be done. We already have groups of people who are trying to operate this system in many parts of our country. We must encourage them and encourage others to adopt this way of life too. It is not a question of forcing our people to change their habits. It is a question of providing leadership. It is a question of education. And it is a question of all of us together making a reality of the principles of equality and freedom which are enshrined in our policy of Tanzanian socialism.

38

Policy on Foreign Affairs

In October 1967 the biannual National Conference of TANU met in Mwanza, on the southern edge of Lake Victoria. Almost 2,000 people were involved in this conference, and President Obote of Uganda, and President Kaunda of Zambia brought fraternal greetings to its opening sessions. High-ranking fraternal delegations from Burundi, Congo, Guinea, Kenya and Rwanda also attended.

President Nyerere began his opening speech on 16 October 1967, by welcoming the delegates and the distinguished guests. The rest of his address is now reproduced in full.

... The task of this National Conference is to consider the progress which Tanzania has made towards the second objective of TANU. The first objective—independence—was achieved six years ago. The second is that of building a socialist nation in which all citizens live in decent conditions of human dignity, with as much personal freedom and freedom from hunger, disease, and ignorance as is consistent with equal freedom for all other citizens.

As the supreme body of the Party in a one-party state, this conference has to consider the direction in which we are moving, and decide whether the nation is on the right path. It has to lay down the principles of action, and give guidance and leadership to the people. Its functions are thus of vital importance; but they are not unlimited. For the delegates here come from the people, and are responsible to them. It is impossible for us at this meeting to take over their responsibilities, or to act as if we had some God-given right to force goals of our choosing upon the people. It is impossible, and it would be wrong to try. Our task is a different one; it is to give leadership and guidance along the path which both the people and TANU have already accepted. That is, the path which leads to human equality, to democracy, and to socialism in Tanzania. If the Party succeeds in this, then the people have already shown that they will succeed in their task—which is to guard and to develop our count.

The TANU National Conference, then, has the duty of considering the whole range of policies and affairs, both domestic and foreign. For all these things affect the kind of society ours will become, as well as the speed and direction of our economic development. Domestic and foreign policies are inter-related, both are aspects of one overall task. It is obvious, for example, that international friendships or hostilities affect our internal progress. They do this even if by no other means than leaving us free to concentrate on development problems, or diverting our attention and our resources from them. It is my intention at this conference, therefore, to speak on both aspects of our policy. But I shall do this on two separate occasions; today I shall concentrate on foreign policy questions; and at another session I will direct my attention to domestic affairs.

My task now, therefore, is to survey the international scene as it appears from Tanzania, to indicate some of the problems in which we are involved, and to outline the attitudes and policies we are adopting in the face of them. I shall do this from the basis of the fundamental principles of foreign policy which have been accepted by this country since independence—and which have not changed. For we have still to guard the integrity and security of our country; we persist in our attempt to follow a policy of non-alignment in the ideological and power quarrels of the world, committing ourselves to no great power alliance; we continue to support, and to seek to strengthen, the United Nations in its search for peace and justice; we maintain our belief in African unity as a vital objective for Tanzania and the whole continent; and we continue to support the movement for African liberation and freedom for racialist oppression.

NON-ALIGNMENT

Let me first look at some of the problems of non-alignment. Tanzania has, over recent years, had so many quarrels with big powers which are part of the Western Bloc, that it is useful for us to stress, once again, that we have no desire to be, and no intention of being, 'anti-West' in our foreign policies. We shall deal with each problem as it occurs, and on its own merits. We shall neither move from particular quarrels with individual countries to a generalized hostility to members of a particular group, nor to automatic support for those who also happen to be, for their own reasons, quarrelling with the same nations. We wish to live in friendship with all states and all peoples.

Before independence we had no direct contact with Eastern Bloc countries. After independence we began to establish such contacts and we shall continue to strengthen them. We desire friendship with these non-Western nations as well as with Western states, and on the same basis of mutual non-interference with internal affairs. We shall not allow any of our friendships to be exclusive; we shall not allow anyone to choose any of our friends or enemies for us.

It should also be clear that we shall not allow anyone—whether they be from East or West, or from places not linked to those blocs—to try and use our friendship for their own purposes. Differences of opinion and clashes of interest between Tanzania and other nations are bound to occur—the more so as contact increases. We understand that because we understand that it is the responsibility of every government to look after the interests of their country as they see them. But we shall always try to limit the effect of differences which occur, and to settle them by discussion and negotiation.

Only in the case of South Africa, the racialist colonialism of Portugal, and the Smith regime of Southern Rhodesia, does such settlement of differences seem inherently impossible. With those countries we can never negotiate until they abandon their present rejection of the basic principle of human intercourse—the equality of men. But in all other cases we believe that differences should be able to be settled without compromising the principles of our society, for the interests of every country are best served by mutual friendship and the peaceful settlement of disputes.

Our desire for friendship with every other nation does not, however, mean that we can be unconcerned with world events, or that we should try to buy that friendship with silence on the great issues of world peace and justice. If it is to be meaningful, friendship must be able to withstand honesty in international affairs. Certainly we should refrain from adverse comment on the internal affairs of other states, just as we expect them to do with regard to ourselves. But to stay silent on such issues as Vietnam because one or more powerful nations do not like what we say would be a disgrace.

It is, I think, difficult for us in Tanzania to comprehend the full sufferings of the people of Vietnam in what is probably the most vicious and all-enveloping war which has been known to mankind. There is no security there—for anyone, anywhere in that country. Men, women and children, are all involved, peasants and workers, urban and rural dwellers—all of them live every hour of every day under the threat of death, or injury, or the destruction of their means of livelihood. It is said that more bombs have been dropped on the small country of Vietnam in the last two years than were used in the whole Pacific theatre of war from 1942 to 1945.

World-wide concern has been expressed about the dangers which would follow from bombs falling—accidentally or on purpose—on the territory of the People's Republic of China. We in Tanzania share that concern, for such an event could only lead to a world-wide conflagration. But the fact that Vietnam is a small, and under-developed, nation does not mean that her people are immune from the effects of high explosive, or that other small nations can turn their heads away as if this conflict is at present unimportant.

We are told that great principles are involved, and that the richest nation on earth is defending those principles against attack. What are these principles? There is the principle of self-determination for the people of Vietnam. For twenty years, with unparalleled courage and determination, the people of Vietnam have been fighting for a chance to implement this principle—first against the French, and now against the Americans. Certainly there are Vietnamese on both sides, some are conscripted, or try to find security with those who are strongest in their particular area. But if this is a civil war, what are outside nations doing in that conflict?

Again, we are told that democracy is being defended, and only last month there were some 'elections' in South Vietnam. But these elections only covered the 'pacified areas', and no candidate could stand on a clear platform of opposition to the war! And in any case these were the first elections since 1956, when South Vietnam came into existence, and no one could possibly call the governments of Mr. Diem, or his military successors, democratic.

Or we are told that the outside power responded to a request for assistance from a legitimate government which was threatened by aggression. One can only look at the figures of soldiers operating in South Vietnam and ask whose aggression?

I believe that two things are essential: first, an immediate and unconditional end to the bombing of North Vietnam. And second: a settlement should be reached on the basis of the 1954 Geneva Agreements. Neither North Vietnam nor the Vietcong can be forced to the conference table; that should by now be clear. The USA must recover from the delirium of power, and return to the principles upon which her nation was founded. Those millions of Americans who are now opposing their government's policies in this matter, and calling for peace, are working for the honour of their country. We pray that they triumph soon.

In the Middle East we have seen yet another outbreak of dangerous and destructive war in recent months. The fighting there was brought to a halt very quickly, but the situation remains one of great danger to us all. Large areas of the UAR, Syria and Jordan, remain under Israeli occupation. The Suez Canal is closed, and will obviously remain closed for some time to come; this affects Tanzania's trade by increasing the costs of our imports and reducing the price we obtain from our exports. We are thus very obviously concerned in the matter. But we have other interests too. It is not, and should not be, part of our policy to gloss over an act of aggression because we recognize and have diplomatic relations with the country which commits such aggression.

The establishment of the state of Israel was an act of aggression against the Arab people. It was connived at by the international community because of the history of persecution against the Jews. This persecution reached its climax in the murder by Nazi Germany of six million Jewish men, women, and children—a number equal to half the population of Tanzania, and more than that of many independent African states. The survivors of this persecution sought security in a Jewish national state in Arab Palestine. The international community accepted this. The Arab states did not and could not accept that act of aggression. We believe that there cannot be lasting peace in the Middle East until the Arab states have accepted the fact of Israel. But the Arab states cannot be beaten into such acceptance. On the contrary, attempts to coerce the Arab states into recognizing Israel—whether it be by a refusal to relinquish occupied territory or by an insistence on direct negotiations between the two sides—would only make such acceptance impossible.

In expressing our hope that a peaceful settlement of this terribly difficult situation will soon become possible, it is necessary for us as accept two things. First, that Israel's desire to be acknowledged to a nation is understandable. But second, and equally important, that Israel's occupation of the territories of UAR, Jordan, and Syria, must be brought to an end. Israel must evacuate the areas she overran in June this year—without exception—before she can reasonably expect the Arab countries will begin to acquiesce in her national presence. Israel has had her victory, at terrible cost in human lives. She must now accept that the United Nations which sanctioned her birth is, and must be, unalterably opposed to territorial aggrandizement by force or threat of force.

That is Tanzania's position. We recognize Israel and wish to be friendly with her as well as with the Arab nations. But we cannot condone aggression on any pretext, nor accept victory in war as a justification for the exploitation of other lands, or government over other peoples.

THE UNITED NATIONS

In the face of these two great international conflicts, and with many other dangerous situations, the United Nations has been able to do very little. On Vietnam in particular it has been completely helpless; its Secretary General has tried time and again to intervene in the cause of peace, and every time he has been rebuffed. Yet it is important that we should not in consequence lose faith in the United Nations, nor reduce our support for it. The United Nations is weak when powerful states wish to ignore it. Its servants can only act when the sovereign and independent member nations agree that they shall do so. But these limitations must be treated as a challenge to us, and as reasons for Tanzania to give the United Nations all the support, and all the strength, which it is within our power to do. For there is no other instrument for international peace even as effective as this. Rather than abandon the United Nations we must work steadfastly and persistently towards strengthening it, and increasing its powers. This will not be easy. For big powers can live with the illusion of self-sufficiency; even now it is possible for them to imagine that the rest of the world is unimportant to them. They are therefore anxious to limit the powers of an international body, But we small powers can have no such illusions. Only in an organization such as the United Nations can we hope to make our voice heard on international issues, and only through the implementation of the principles upon which it is based can we hope to survive and grow in peace.

There is, however, one further point I must make with reference to the United Nations. For it has, at present, a basic weakness which is nothing to do with its structure, but everything to do with the independence of the member states. That is the fact that the People's Republic of China is still excluded from the United Nations, and the Chinese seat occupied by representatives of a Government which was overthrown eighteen years ago. This is absurd. While the most populous nation on earth is excluded the United Nations will continue to be hamstrung on all Far Eastern questions, and many other vital international matters. Tanzania will continue to advocate China's admission to her rightful place in the United Nations. We shall continue with our efforts to persuade our friends that whether or not they like or approve of the Government of the People's Republic of China, its existence must be accepted.

AFRICA IS OUR IMMEDIATE CONCERN

But while our concern with world events is real and important, the events in Africa are of even greater and more direct relevance to us. Total African liberation, and total African unity, are basic objectives of our Party and our Government. We recognize that our ong-term interests, as well as those of all other African peoples, are involved in these things. Certainly we shall never be really free and secure while some parts of our continent are still enslaved. If anyone had doubts about this in the past they can have none now. We have only to look at the threats which have been made against the Republic of Zambia in recent weeks—to say nothing of the constant threats to her power supplies since November 1965. Or we can look at the mines which have been laid in Tanzanian territory by the Portuguese colonialists, and which have resulted in the death of some of our citizens. Or again, we can look at the positions in which Botswana and Lesotho find themselves. Nominally independent, they have no real freedom to determine their own policies—either domestic or external—because they are held in thrall by the Union of South Africa.

The total liberation of Africa must be a continuing concern of every independent African state. And legal independence is not enough; legally the Union of South Africa is a sovereign state. The freedom we seek must be freedom for the peoples of Africa without distinction of race, colour, or religion. Racialist minority governments cannot be acknowledged because they are a negation of the very basis of our existence. Co-existence is impossible; for if the African peoples of South Africa and Rhodesia have no human right to govern themselves, then what is the basis of Tanzania's existence, of Zambia's, of Kenya's, and so on? If the principle of white supremacy is accepted anywhere in Africa it will seek to spread, and there will be no peace for any of us.

The struggle for freedom must go on. Our preference, and that of every true African patriot, has always been for peaceful methods of struggle. We abhor the sufferings and the terror, and the sheer waste, which are involved in violent upheavals, and believe that peaceful progress is worth some sacrifice in terms of time. But when the door of peaceful progress to freedom is slammed shut, and bolted, then the struggle must take other forms; we cannot surrender.

This has been the choice before Africa in relation to the Portuguese occupied territories. The metropolitan government claims that Mozambique, Angola and 'Portuguese Guinea' are part of Portugal; there can therefore be no question of independence—and a call for it is regarded as treachery. Further, Portugal is itself a dictatorship; nothing can be achieved even through an involvement in their domestic politics. The only choice available is a violent struggle for freedom, or continued acquiescence in slavery.

The peoples of all the Portuguese colonies have now chosen; they are fighting. And they are doing their own fighting—let there be no mistake about that. Neighbouring territories give moral support to the freedom fighters; we support their cause in the councils of the world. But no outside person, however sympathetic, can make a person free; this they have to do for themselves, with their own hands and brains, and their own sufferings.

I ask this conference to join with me in congratulating the freedom fighters for their successes so far. And I ask the conference to send condolences to all those who have been injured in the fighting, and to the relatives of those who have given their lives for their country's freedom. The task of the freedom fighters is not easy. Portugal may be a poor country in European terms, but the resources at its command are not small, and recent military discussions between the three bastions of racialism in Southern Africa can only make the struggle harder But if the African peoples of this continent, and of those areas in particular, are determined to be free—then in the end nothing will stop them.

SOUTHERN RHODESIA

Recent weeks have also seen the outbreak of fighting in Southern Rhodesia—fighting which was so intense that Smith had to call upon his blood-brothers from South Africa for assistance. Once again the situation is such that Africa has no alternative but to welcome this development. For years we urged patience upon the nationalist movements of Southern Rhodesia; we pointed at the official British policy of colonial freedom, and joined with them in putting pressure upon successive British Governments with the aim of achieving a prospect of peaceful advance. Even after Smith's declaration of independence, we urged that the responsible authority for dealing with this is the British Government. We did everything possible to avoid the dangerous necessity of guerrilla fighting of black against white, for we are aiming at human dignity, not racial wars. But it is now quite clear that only the African people's own efforts can turn the tide in Southern Rhodesia.

It may be that external developments will even now be able to limit the necessity for military action by the people of Southern Rhodesia. The whole of Africa must work for that end. But it is beyond our power to ensure success in obtaining the necessary international action. In the meantime we are therefore forced to welcome the fact that Smith can no longer bemuse the world by claiming that the Africans of Southern Rhodesia support his regime. Now he is forced to devote resources to try to put down the uprising of the people he claims as 'his'.

We hope that the freedom movement will grow stronger; we hope that the nationalist movements of Southern Rhodesia will unite for greater effectiveness. But in any case we must continue to support the struggle against racialism and minority control in that colony. We cannot acquiesce in the establishment of another South Africa in our continent.

Delegates to this conference will remember that it was on this issue that Tanzania broke diplomatic relations with Britain. We took this action because we believed that we had committed ourselves to it when we put our name to the OAU resolution in December 1965. This called upon all African states to break diplomatic relations with the country which claimed sovereignty over Southern Rhodesia, but which was doing virtually nothing about the illegal assertion of power by the racialist white minority. We believed also that the full implementation of that resolution would bring effective pressure to bear on Britain, and make her Government wake up to its world responsibilities. And at the same time we drew attention to the fact that even then Britain had still not stated her own policy objectives in Southern Rhodesia. We therefore demanded, once again, a commitment to the principle of no independence before majority rule.

These things mean that Tanzania's action in breaking diplomatic relations with Britain had two facets. The first was one of principle —that we had to honour our word to the OAU. The second was one of tactics—that we would be taking part in what we hoped would be an effective exertion of African pressure on the United Kingdom Government. That was two years ago. The question we have to consider now is whether our cause is best served by continuing with this policy, or whether some other might be more effective.

So far just one of our objectives has been achieved—and that in words only. In December last year the British Government, with great and obvious reluctance, finally said that all past constitutional offers to the Smith regime were withdrawn, and that a settlement would have to be based upon the principle of majority rule before independence. We gave a cautious welcome to that statement—and our caution has been justified. There has already been a resumption of what is called 'informal contact' with Smith, on the basis of quite different proposals! But still the commitment stands, and it will not be easy for the British Government to get out of it without further international disgrace.

For the rest, Smith continues in command, with ever-increasing support from South Africa and Portugal. International sanctions— in the manner in which they have so far been applied—have proved ineffective. Most other African states took a different view of the OAU resolution than we did, and of those that acted with us some have now reconsidered their position. In these circumstances it will be for the Tanzanian Government in coming months to consider what action will best serve our continuing purposes. For the one thing delegates may be absolutely certain of is that Tanzania will not change its objective in Southern Rhodesia. Our aim is to contribute to, and to assist in, the achievement of democratic independence in Southern Rhodesia.

AFRICAN UNITY

In the light of this continuing problem it is doubly unfortunate that over the last two years so many independent African states have been involved in domestic upheavals and internal conflicts. It is not our business to comment on those changes of government which have not directly affected the total African scene, much as we may regret some of them. But there have been others in which we do have a direct interest. No one, for example—and certainly not a neighbour—could have failed to rejoice when President Mobutu replaced Moise Tshombe as the effective ruler of the Democratic Republic of the Congo. By that change Africa moved from the position where an African traitor was in charge of one of the largest, and potentially most powerful, of its states, to a position where an African nationalist and patriot took control. President Mobutu's accession to power did not mean an end to the difficulties of the Congo; these are not ended yet. But the difficulties now are those of progress and reconstruction. The last mercenary revolt was a rearguard action of men who knew that their reign was being brought to an end. We wish President Mobutu and his colleagues all success in their continuing struggle for the real freedom and independence of their country.

Burundi is another neighbour of ours which has experienced a change of political system since our last ordinary meeting. The present republican regime there has replaced a feudal monarchy, and now has the heavy task of reorganizing the nation on different principles at the same time as it deals with serious economic problems. We are extremely sorry that the effects of his motor-car accident have prevented President Micombero from joining us this week, and on your behalf I would like to wish him a speedy and complete recovery.

Uganda too has changed its type of Government. From being something of a hybrid—neither monarchy nor republic, but with elements of both—it is now beginning with a new system which promises to be more stable. I think all of us understood the motives which caused the Uganda people to try a unique type of constitutional arrangement; I think we can all sympathize with them on the circumstances of its failure. All these matters are the exclusive responsibility of President Obote and the citizens of Uganda, but I do not think I will be misunderstood when I express Tanzania's interest in the unity and progress of our East African partner. Differences of economic and political organization can certainly be accommodated within the arrangements for East African co-operation; yet it would be stupid to pretend that the feudalism, and parochialism, which were enshrined in the old Uganda constitution did not have some effect on the degree of unity which was possible between our three states.

But although these three developments—unpleasant as they were in their immediate effects—were both inevitable and probably necessary for progress in Africa, many other political developments in Africa have to be deplored without reservation. The cumulative effect of them was such that until two months ago it appeared that all hope of African unity, and even the existence of the OAU, was in jeopardy. Every African leader knows that separately our individual states are appallingly weak in the face of any political or economic pressure from outside our continent. All of us must know that in unity we could be incomparably stronger. Yet our petty inter-African difficulties, and our internal squabbles, have time and again overshadowed the most basic requirements of the greater goal. African diplomats have been incarcerated by other African states on their way to and from international gatherings; boundary disputes have been allowed to poison all-African meetings; economic favours of a European power have seduced some of us from our loyalty to the wider African community.

In the face of all these difficulties—to say nothing of the tribal massacre and civil war in Nigeria, and the strong but conflicting views of different states on Middle East questions—optimism about the Kinshasa OAU Meeting was impossible. But that meeting was a success. Africa is now looking forward again—working to settle its own disputes, making arrangements for practical co-operation in small but vital matters, and so on. Delegates will know that, with great reluctance, I decided that it was my duty to stay in Tanzania at the time of that Heads of States Conference. Therefore I need have no hesitation in paying an unreserved tribute to all the participants. In particular I would like to congratulate President Mobutu, the chairman of the conference, and Presidents Kaunda and Obote whose work contributed greatly to the success achieved.

But this does not mean that the path to African co-operation and unity is now clear. Many difficulties remain, and others will undoubtedly occur. What has been demonstrated, however, is that we must never give up. However far back from our goal we seem to have drifted, we must keep working for unity and co-operation. Yet we must not indulge in day-dreams, nor imagine that unity and harmony are round the corner. We have, instead, to look hard at the current situation, and work forward from a full acceptance of it. Conflicts do not disappear because they are a nuisance; nor are they less important to the people involved because others are unconcerned or think them due to a misunderstanding. Indeed, many disputes in Africa are caused by very real short-term conflicts of interest; that they could be overcome in the long term by greater unity, or even greater goodwill, does not mean that they can be dismissed now. The only way forward to African unity is a prior acceptance of Africa as it is—misunderstandings, disputes, and differences of beliefs, loyalties, and international economic links included.

For us in Tanzania this means that the first thing we have to recognize is that Tanzania is responsible to Africa for Tanzania, and for Tanzania's actions towards her neighbours and towards the liberation of Africa. We are not responsible for any other nation. We must accept the full implications of the existing separate sovereignty of all African states. We have to recognize that whether or not we like the government and policy of another African state, it is still the government of that state, and has full freedom to make its own decisions.

We have to accept Africa as it is, and not imagine that we have any more right to interfere with the internal affairs of others than they have to interfere in ours. Of course there will be some governments and policies which we like and approve of more than others, and it would be absurd to ask any one state to be equally friendly and sympathetic to all others. But we must be ready to co-operate with all African states in African affairs regardless of our opinion of their internal—or even their external—policies. Only where a free African state is betraying the liberation of Africa or deliberately and avoidably damaging the degree of co-operation which already exists, has Africa, or any African state, the right to protest. And even then we should make our protests as one brother to another—in private and in a fraternal spirit.

Socialism or capitalism is a matter for each separate nation; the interpretation of our common policy of non-alignment is a matter for each government and people—at least at this stage of our development. Only co-operation in the enslavement of our brothers in Southern Africa must be excluded from our mutual toleration.

It is important too that we in Tanzania, as well as other nations, should learn a little humility in considering the actions of other African states. Certainly we must make judgements about all sorts of things; but we must remember that our decision may sometimes be proved wrong! We must never be unwilling to revise our judgements of other countries, other governments, or other policies. And we must try to understand the practical difficulties which face other countries, not hasten to condemn them from our own different position.

All independent Africa, for example, calls for the complete trade boycott of South Africa and Southern Rhodesia. But if Lesotho or Botswana tried to implement it they would be condemned to complete economic collapse—and might even be militarily occupied by South Africa as well. In neither case could the rest of Africa do anything effective to help. The job of these two countries is to survive with as little co-operation as is consistent with that survival. We can ask that they should not embrace the racialist states which surround them; we can ask that they should do everything possible to assert the principle of human dignity. But we should not ask them commit suicide.

Our neighbour, Zambia, also has real and practical difficulties which prevent her full and immediate implementation of such policies. But the fact is that no state could be doing more to extricate itself from its economic and communications inheritance, or could act with greater courage than Zambia has been doing. It is Tanzania's responsibility to do everything in our power to help in her efforts to establish new trade and communications patterns. And in the meantime I hope that we shall agree to send a message of full support to our sister Party—UNIP—and that this TANU National Conference will rededicate itself, and all TANU members, to work for the speedy fulfilment of the tasks which lie ahead for our two countries.

NEIGHBOURLINESS

But talk of all-African co-operation and understanding can only too easily degenerate into meaningless cliches. If it is to become meaningful it must be put into practice at a neighbourhood level. And this demonstrates the difficulties! For it is one thing to say all African states must accept each other as they are; it is another to accept your neighbour if you disagree with what he is doing or saying, or if he seems to be bringing danger to your doorstep. Yet this is what mutual acceptance, non-interference, and African co-operation must mean in practice. It is no use a man preaching goodwill to all men if he spends his time quarrelling with the man who lives in the next house; his words will then be shown to be without meaning.

We have to accept that close contact between any two men, or any two nations, has certain implications. It means greater opportunities for co-operation for mutual benefit. It also means greater possibilities of conflict. Tanzania, for example, has feelings of warm friendship for the Government of Guinea under the leadership of President Sekou Toure; its feelings are less warm towards certain other West African states. But just as the practical effect of our friendship with Guinea is limited by the distance which lies between us, so too our reservations about those other states do not lead to practical conflict. But lack of sympathy for the government of a neighbouring territory is a different matter, wherever it occurs. It means that every little quarrel between citizens on different sides of the border can easily become an international issue; it means that the natural patterns of trade can be interrupted, or can be the cause of heated and public dispute, and so on.

On the other hand, it is neighbours who can make a reality of African co-operation and friendship. If each accepts the full sovereignty of the other, and within this framework endeavours to maximize co-operation in all fields, then African co-operation will be maximized. For we are all neighbours of one another. If Tanzania works in harmony with Kenya and with Zambia, then Kenya and

Zambia are linked together. If Kenya then co-operates with Ethiopia, then Tanzania and Zambia are both linked to Ethiopia—and so on throughout our continent. This is the way forward for Africa now. We can have our all-African meetings, both political and technical. But experience has shown that the success and the effectiveness of these meetings depends upon good neighbourhood relations in all the different parts of Africa. When these exist, then all-African meetings can facilitate and speed developments. If these do not exist, then the all-African meetings have to devote their time to patching and mending the torn fabric of co-operation, instead of helping the move forward.

We in East Africa have, I believe, learned this lesson. The conference of eleven African states which was held in Nairobi in March 1966 under the able chairmanship of President Kenyatta, had the sole purpose of increasing understanding and co-operation between East Africa and its neighbours. It achieved that purpose; indeed the Tanzania delegation was unanimously of the opinion that we had never attended a more useful and constructive political gathering. Of course that meeting did not solve all the problems of this part of Africa; some of them are too deep-seated and too complicated to be susceptible to such treatment. But the meeting did create an atmosphere in which problems could be tackled; it did contribute greatly to our common progress.

ECONOMIC CO-OPERATION

Certainly we in East Africa can take justifiable pride in the degree of international co-operation which has already been achieved, and in the progress we are making in such matters.

The East African Treaty of Co-operation marks a vitally important step forward for Uganda, Kenya, and ourselves. We have now agreed on a thorough and complete reform of the arrangements for economic co-operation which we inherited from our ex-colonial masters; we have established what can become a real common market, and really effective instruments for joint economic services. The discussions were long and sometimes difficult, for there were real short-term conflicts of interest to be accommodated. But I would like to use this occasion to pay tribute to both President Kenyatta and President Obote, and their respective Governments, for the spirit in which these discussions and negotiations were conducted.

I would also like to pay tribute to the work of Minister Amir Jamal who led the Tanzanian delegation, and to his colleagues, Ministers Nsilo Swai and Paul Bomani, and the staff who so ably supported them. Between us all we managed to confound the pessimists and purveyors of gloom who were expecting—or hoping for!—yet another break-down in inter-African co-operation. We have a right to be proud of this, even while we recognize that other difficulties will occur—indeed, we have already made arrangements for dealing with them! But there will be no danger while all problems are approached in the same spirit of friendship and determination to agree which we enjoyed earlier this year.

This is not all. Tanzania is one of eleven nations involved in discussions which could lead to the creation of an Economic Community of Eastern Africa. We have a long way to go and a great deal of hard work to be done before any of us will derive practical benefit. But, if we succeed, we may in time be able to do away with internal tariffs from the Sudan, south and east, up to Zambia. And even if that objective is many years away, practical co-operation in more limited fields is a real possibility. I can assure this conference that Tanzania will endeavour to play a full and constructive role in the discussions which have started.

These discussions, however, do not yet include the Congo or Rwanda, both of whom—along with Burundi—have a direct and continuing interest in practical co-operation with Tanzania, just as we have with them. For the eastern part of the Congo, as well as for Burundi, Dar es Salaam is the most convenient sea port. Even Rwanda finds this outlet useful. It is our responsibility to work with these countries in making that port effective for their needs as well as our own. I can assure delegates and guests that we shall do this to the best of our ability. Detailed arrangements are still being discussed about how our co-operation can best be organized in the long run. But there should be no doubt about Tanzania's full acceptance of the responsibility which the accidents of geography and history have placed upon her.

Dar es Salaam is also, of course, an increasingly important port for Zambia—along with Mtwara in the south. Delegates will have heard with the same joy as President Kaunda and myself that there is a real prospect that the railway linking our two countries will now be built. The engineering survey will start soon; after that we have, from the People's Republic of China, such assurances of further practical and financial help that completion need not be doubted. This project has been talked about for a long time. There have been feasibility studies, economic surveys, and several different estimates of costing. But now we are making progress. Now we shall proceed at maximum speed, and with a full consciousness of the importance, the urgency, and the implications of this project.

CONCLUSION

Distinguished Guests, and Delegates. I could go on longer by indicating the great amount of work which remains to be done, and the great efforts which will be required from us all if this country is to develop the kind and degree of international co-operation which we desire. But I will conclude by repeating the assurance that Tanzania will remain true to the international principles which she has proclaimed.

We shall work for ever-increasing friendship, co-operation, and unity, with our neighbours, and with all other free African states. We shall never give up the struggle against racialism and colonialism. We shall endeavour to play a proper role in the hard struggle for peace and justice in the world. And at all costs we shall defend the integrity and the security of the United Republic against any attack, or any attempt to diminish our sovereign independence.

39

After the Arusha Declaration

On the second day of the TANU National Conference at Mwanza (17 October 1967), the President spoke for almost two hours on the meaning and implementation of the Arusha Declaration and later policy declarations. This speech is important for its elaboration of the slogan 'self-reliance', and its explanation of the problems and policies of income distribution; and finally, for its emphasis on socialism and rural development.

Many things have happened since our last meeting, and it is the job of this conference to examine the most important of them in the light of the objectives we set ourselves when we adopted the Arusha Declaration. For that Declaration was a commitment to the principles of self-reliance and socialism. It did not by itself bring either of these things; only hard thinking, and hard work in the right direction will do that. It is important that we should be very clear about this fact. The Arusha Declaration did not cause miracles. It did not make the crops more fruitful, nor the rains more regular. It did not make everyone wealthy, nor change the level of our education. It did not change the habits of mind we have grown up with, nor create any other miraculous changes in our condition.

Our acceptance of the Arusha Declaration was like a young Christian's confirmation; it is a declaration of intent to live a certain kind of life and to act in a certain kind of manner for desired ends. We have no more become a socialist country because of the Arusha Declaration than a young boy becomes a good Christian or a good Muslim by the act of dedication. The sincere act of dedication is important; but much more important are the actions which follow during his life. The question before us, therefore, is whether we have started to make the right decisions, and the right plans, and whether we have begun to act in a manner which will in time build socialism and self-reliance in Tanzania.

First, let us look at this question of self-reliance, for I believe that this has been widely misunderstood—by ourselves more than others. Some of our people have spoken and acted as though it meant self-sufficiency in manpower and financial resources. It means nothing of the kind. We would be extremely silly if we imagined that the Arusha Declaration had caused us to have more qualified doctors, engineers, teachers, administrators, and so on, so that the Development Plan target of self-sufficiency in skilled manpower by 1980 had suddenly become irrelevant. Self-reliance does not mean that, for self-reliance is not a silly thing. Let us therefore be very clear what we do expect now, and what the policy of self-reliance means in the immediate future, and what it does not mean.

First, it means that we must make maximum use of the resources which we have. We want citizens to be given priority in every field as soon as they are capable of doing the job efficiently. And certainly we must have Tanzanians making policy; Tanzanians must control our country. But this is not an issue now; we have already achieved that. The question at issue is whether we must at all costs have Tanzanian citizens in every executive position. And the answer we give must be a realistic one if we wish to fulfil our ambitions. For the truth is that we do not yet have enough qualified and experienced Tanzanian citizens to do all the jobs which have to be done if the policies we Tanzanians have decided upon are to be implemented.

The question, therefore, is whether we are prepared to make our plans wait until we have educated and trained a Tanzanian for every job which has to be done. And we long ago decided that this would not only be absurd, it would also be unnecessary. An accountant is an accountant, whether he is a citizen or not; a doctor is a doctor; a manager is either efficient or not efficient. What really matters in relation to such people—whether they be citizens or not citizens—is that they loyally and efficiently carry out the decisions made by our Government and our people.

To employ an inefficient person just because he is a Tanzanian, when the job he has to do is crucial for our development, is not self-reliance; it is stupidity. When we or members of our family fall ill, what we want is a competent doctor, not necessarily a citizen. When we have decided to build a bridge, what we want is a competent engineer who will be able to ensure that the bridge will be safe and effective for its purpose.

The questions we need to ask ourselves are these: firstly, is this job essential to our plans? Secondly, do we have a citizen who is qualified and has the necessary experience for this particular job? And if there is no qualified citizen available, thirdly, can we obtain a qualified non-citizen who will be accountable to us for his loyal and efficient carrying out of the job? And fourthly, what plans do we have for the training of citizens to do this kind of work in due course? Then, if we decide that the job is essential, and if there is no qualified citizen available to do it, and if a non-citizen can be obtained, let us pay a non-citizen to do the job for us. By doing this we might, for example, make it possible for a village in an outlying area to become self-reliant because it can sell its increased production and thus support improved conditions for its members. If we do not allow this bridge to be built simply because we have no citizen available to do it, then the village will remain on a low level and without any real possibility of becoming a self-reliant, prosperous community.

But in this country we also have a second thing which we really desire of the people working for us. Ideally we also need socialists in every job—which is not necessarily the same thing as wanting a citizen for every job, because not all Tanzanians are socialists. But if a competent doctor also has socialist attitudes, then he is surely an especially great asset to us. And the truth is that the international reputation of Tanzania is such that many socialists from other countries very much want to come and work with us. One day in the future Tanzanian socialists may be able to assist other socialists to achieve their objectives. Today we should be ready and happy to welcome socialists from other countries who are ready to help us achieve our objectives. And we should remember that many socialists come from capitalist countries; it is sometimes the very fact that they cannot contribute to socialist objectives in their own country which makes them enthusiastic about working with us.

What all this means is that if we are to make progress towards the implementation of our policies of socialism and self-reliance, we should be ready to use all the people who are able to contribute towards these objectives. There are certain jobs which have to be done by citizens. Those we have now filled. There are other jobs which have to be done, and done now or in the next few years, whether or not we have enough citizens or enough socialists. Let us get these jobs done instead of indulging our prejudices or our generalized assessments of people by skin colour or country of origin.

There is another aspect of our self-reliance policy which has also been misunderstood by some people. For the Arusha Declaration does not say that Tanzania refuses outside aid, or that there is something wrong in receiving it. The Declaration says, and I quote: 'We are not saying that we will not accept, or even that we shall not look for, money from other countries for our development. This is not what we are saying'. What the Arusha Declaration says is that the only group of people we will rely upon is ourselves; we will not organize our country and our life in such a way that there will be no development unless we get foreign money. And most of all, we have said very firmly that we shall not bend our political, economic or social policies in the hope of getting overseas aid as a result. But if we get outside assistance to carry out purposes decided by us, then we shall welcome that assistance. Thus we welcome the Chinese decision to help with the Tanzam Railway. Thus we shall welcome an American decision to help build our road from Dar es Salaam to Tunduma.

In fact, self-reliance is not really against anything or anyone, unless there are people who want to re-colonize us. Self-reliance is a positive affirmation that we shall depend upon ourselves for the development of Tanzania, and that we shall use the resources we have for that purpose, not just sit back and complain because there are other things we do not have.

We are saying to ourselves that we are going to build a self-reliant socialist society. We are saying: 'Here is land, here we are; this is the amount of knowledge, skill and experience we have; and this is the amount of money we have to spend on supplementing our skill and knowledge or on buying more advanced machines. Now let us get on with it'. And we are saying to other people: 'This is what we are doing; if you want to help us, do this and this and this, for that is what we need most at this stage'. The really important thing for us to be clear about is that we are not saying to other people (and now, after the Arusha Declaration, we cannot say): 'Please come and develop our country for us, and if you insist we will stop being socialist, or believing in equalibeingty, or anti-colonial'. These things we will never say. We do not believe that anyone else can develop our country for us and, even if they could, we would not be willing to give up the determination of our own policy. It is we ourselves who will develop our country. We may decide to spend some of the resources we have, or the products of those resources, on buying imports of skills or machines from abroad. But our real emphasis will be on using the skills that we already have, and on developing the natural resources that we now possess.

In our situation this means that the emphasis of our development will be in the rural sector, and particularly in agriculture. Further, it means that we shall modernize within our resources. But we must modernize. In many parts of the country we are beginning to follow the advice of our agricultural experts. But our major tool, the jembe, is too primitive for our present-day needs. We must now abandon it and replace it with the oxen-plough. We cannot make progress by waiting until every peasant is able to possess his own tractor which he can drive and maintain. Indeed, if we wait for that we shall never leave the hoe behind us, for our present methods are too inefficient ever to produce the wealth which would enable us to buy tractors for all parts of the country, or to train the people to drive and maintain them. We are not ready for the tractor, either financially or technically; but we are ready for the oxen-plough. We have the animals, and the ploughs can be bought cheaply or even made here. They are simple tools which our peasants can quickly learn to use, and they are appropriate for the kind of small unit farming which is involved in the ujamaa villages to which we aspire, or even to the amount of land an energetic individual peasant family can cultivate.

We have to modernize our farming if we are to improve our standard of living. But we cannot modernize by buying tractors for everyone, because we do not have either the necessary money or the necessary technical skill, or the social organization which would make such implements economic. We have to modernize by utilizing to the full the tools which are within our capacity to buy and to make; which are sufficiently simple for us to use without trouble and break-downs; and which are appropriate to our present and near future social and economic organization. And this we can do. The oxen-plough, the oxen-cart, the use of the donkeys which now eat our grass without working—all these things can make a tremendous improvement in our output and therefore in the lives of our people.

We must move to these techniques with the maximum possible speed. Then, when we have effected this revolution all over the country, we shall be able to move from the oxen-plough to the tractor. But that time is not yet; now we have to concentrate our attention on the immediate objective.

This does not mean that we shall have no tractors or modern machinery working in Tanzanian agriculture. We shall have these things to deal with special problems, or working on large, highly organized state farms where there is all the work discipline of a modern factory. But they are not appropriate at the present time for the majority of our farming units; and in any case we cannot afford them, nor could we use them in such a way as to justify their expense.

For let us be quite clear. Self-reliance is not some vague political slogan. It has meaning for every citizen, for every group, and for the nation as a whole. A self-reliant individual is one who co-operates with others, who is willing to help others and be helped by them, but who does not depend on anyone else for his food, clothing or shelter. He lives on what he earns, whether this be large or small, so that he is a truly free person beholden to no one. This is the position of the vast majority of our people now; it must be the position of all of us.

For a community, self-reliance means that they will use the resources and the skills they jointly possess for their own welfare and their own development. They will not take the attitude that the Government, or Local Council, or anyone else, must come and do this or that for them before they can make any progress. There will be things for which outside assistance in the form of skilled advice or a capital loan is necessary, but they will realize that this has to be paid for, directly or indirectly, by them and their fellow citizens. And outside capital assistance, in particular, will only be requested after all local development with local resources has been undertaken, and only to the minimum extent necessary to effect their purposes.

For the nation self-reliance will come if the individuals and the different communities are self-reliant, and if the citizens altogether recognize that their way forward must be determined by their joint resources and their common efforts. It means choosing the path to development which does not depend upon outsiders. It means a recognition of international involvement and a willingness to give and to receive help. It means a recognition that outside assistance can help to speed up development along the path which we have chosen. But it also means that the path itself must be one which is within our resources.

THE WAR AGAINST EXPLOITATION

Of course, self-reliance was not the only point of the Arusha Declaration. The Declaration also declared war on exploitation of all kinds. The nationalization measures and the Government action to secure majority control in major economic enterprises was one part of the action which has been taken, and has to be taken, against exploitation in Tanzania. Another concern of the Government for many years has been the exploitation of wage-earners by their employers. The minimum wage legislation, the severance pay legislation, and many other Government and NUTA actions have removed the worst examples of this kind of exploitation, although the problem of enforcement still remains in many cases. But the problem which is now worrying many of our people is the prices of the goods we wish to buy in the shops, and the quality of those goods.

Government has established a National Advisory Board on Price Control as a major first step towards dealing with this problem. But we will be making a very big mistake if we just treat this problem in a negative fashion. The distribution of goods, whether they are made in Tanzania or imported, is a service which has to be paid for. It is no use our establishing textile factories in Dar es Salaam, Mwanza and Arusha if the people of Sumbawanga cannot get the cloth in their district and from their village shops. Someone has to arrange to transport that cloth and to hold it in a shop ready for the day when the peasant has some money and needs to buy new cloth for himself or his wife. This distribution service is just as important to the peasant as the actual production of the cloth. It cannot be handled by the state, and it is no use our laying down rules and regulations which are so restrictive that no one can earn his living by transporting the cloth to the outlying areas and selling it there. Yet at the same time we have to take account of the fact that the cost of selling this cloth is very different in Mwanza from what it is in Sumbawanga. There is no reason why a shopkeeper in this town should be allowed to charge the same price as the man in the south-west of our country—unless he is somehow being made to subsidize the extra cost of transporting locally-made produce to far distant places.

What I am really saying here is that price control is not going to be easy. If we simply lay down hard and fast rules for everything, we may finish up with the farmer being unable to buy the things he wants at a convenient place—which is certainly no service to him, and is therefore not the way to prevent him being exploited The best way to deal with this problem is for people to establish their own co-operative shops, controlled by them, where they can see the real cost of obtaining something at a convenient place. Then they will be able to ensure that they are paying the costs of distribution but are not paying for certain people to live in idleness at their expense.

If we do this we may well find that prices in many areas do not come down very much. In 1962 the Government paid for an enquiry into the distribution business; we wanted to see how far it was possible to give better and cheaper service to our people. The conclusion of this enquiry was that, although there are some pockets of exploitation, especially where one shop has a local monopoly, or where credit is given, Tanganyika had, on the whole, what they called a 'low cost distribution system'.

However, we were not satisfied that nothing could be done, and we tried to establish co-operative wholesale and retail shops by Government initiative. Then we discovered some of the problems for ourselves. Many of these co-operatives failed and the shops have had to be closed. The most important reasons for their failure were, in the first place, inexperienced and poor management, and in the second place, the high costs involved in paying reasonable wages to the shop workers. For the truth is that most of Tanzania's private shops, both African and non-African, are family businesses, where all members of the family share in the work and then, as a group, share in any profits. They have no fixed wage, and often earn less than they would if they had to receive the Government fixed minimum wage.

Yet this is no reason for giving up—because some exploitation does still continue. Price control for certain basic commodities is both necessary and practical, and it will be enforced—usually on a regional basis. But in addition, we should look again at the lessons of our experience in co-operative trading and see if we can make a fresh start. Previously these shops were started on Government initiative; they did not spring from the local community, so that the people felt neither loyalty to them nor confidence in them as weapons against exploitation. But suppose a village community, or the people in a group of streets, decided to start their own shop on an ujamaa basis; then it would really be their 'own' shop to which they had a loyalty. They could jointly decide what type of things they wanted to be available and they could arrange to share in the work, the expenses, and the profits of the shop they were using—just as we are suggesting they should do in relation to ujamaa farming.

If such shops start small, and deal first in the basic requirements of their area, without putting their prices too low while they are building up their capital, we may find that a co-operative retail system can grow and be of great service to us. This will only happen, however, if the shops spring out of the people; they cannot be organized for the people by the Government or anyone else. This is, in fact, another case where self-reliant development is the only practical way forward. And even if it does nothing else, the possibility of competition from an ujamaa co-operative will certainly discourage private shops from exploiting their customers. For it is not enough simply to say that the price of such-and-such a commodity is too high. We should be able to say that our co-operative shop sells this commodity at so much; therefore, if the shop next door charges more, its price is too high.

There is another way in which we can reduce the price we pay for the goods we buy in the shops. This is by moving away from the practice of buying almost everything on credit. Let there be a stated price of goods, and let that be a cash price, with the extra cost of credit clearly stated. Then our people will see how much it is costing them to borrow money from the shopkeeper in order to buy his goods—which is what we are doing when we buy goods on credit. In most cases there is really no need for credit buying. We buy on credit because we do not organize our income properly, or because we do not save enough money at the beginning of the month, or at the end of the harvest, to meet the kind of irregular payments which all of us get involved in at some time—things like school fees, wedding costs, burial costs, etc. This is a question of self-discipline. Organizing one's income properly is, of course, a particular problem for farmers, who receive money only once a year—when the crops are harvested and paid for. But such people, as well as wage-earners who are trying to buy some more expensive article, have a solution which they can develop for themselves. The Savings and Credit Co-operative Societies (*Shirika za Akiba*) can be of very great service, both to the individual and to his local community. Many of these societies already exist in Tanzania, but new ones should be started for they can help us very much in our individual and national drive towards self-reliance. Government has ten full-time workers in the Ministry of Agriculture and Co-operatives who are trying to encourage and help these societies; I hope that all TANU leaders will learn about them and see how and when the people in their area can be helped to establish them.

What all this means is that there are many different ways of working against exploitation in our country; and often the least effective are those which simply try to control or restrict the activities of the people. For I say again, it is not enough just to accuse our shopkeepers of exploitation. Instead we have to organize ourselves for our own benefit, and then our shopkeepers will realize that it is to their own best interests to give honest service. The few who really try to abuse their position can then be—and will be—dealt with firmly by Government and people.

RESPONSIBILITIES OF LEADERSHIP

In this field, as in so many others, what is called for is good, honest leadership from people who are really committed to the welfare of the citizens of Tanzania. And the kind of honest leadership which is required is not necessarily the noisiest. If a leader can encourage the people and help them to understand problems and policies by his constructive oratory, that is a very good thing. But it is not entertainment that our people want and expect from their leaders; nor do they want a lot of false promises about a Utopia which someone will bring to them; nor do they want to listen to their leader abusing some person or some group which he has set up as a scapegoat for the problems the people are experiencing.

The leaders of Tanzania—and that includes everyone present at this conference, as well as many other people—have to show, in both actions and words, that they recognize one central fact. Leaders cannot do anything FOR the people. We can only provide the necessary information, guidance and organization for the people to build their own country for themselves. Leaders of Tanzania should not be making promises; we cannot fulfil them for others. We should not be complaining; complaints help no one. We should know the facts of Tanzania's situation, understand them, and give guidance to the people in the light of them.

This is essential. Leaders have to know the reality of our present position, and then show the people how, by our own efforts, we can change our present poverty into something better. It is no use pretending that certain facts are not facts; it is no use talking about 'alleged' low prices of sisal, etc., when the low world price of sisal is a fact, and has been for many years, and a fact which has very important implications for the plans we should be making. Bad things do not disappear because we pretend they are not there, or because we accuse other people of causing them. We cannot run this country by complaining, and we have been entrusted with the responsibility of running this country. Complaining that we are poor, or that world prices are low, is as useless as complaining that the rains do not fall. We have to assess our present situation—which includes many things beyond our control—and work out plans to change the situation and to counteract the effect of the things we cannot alter. Then we have to execute our plans by hard and intelligent work. There is no other way. There is no short cut.

Our people are poor. That is a fact. It is also a fact that every human being finds it easier to see the greater wealth or the greater privilege of other people than he does to see his own advantages. It is not part of a Tanzanian leader's duty simply to encourage the people in envy, or to turn that envy into hostility or hatred against others. But he does have to make it clear to the people that he is not himself among a group which is unfairly privileged. It is for this reason that the leadership qualifications have been laid down in the Arusha Declaration.

For at the very least it must be clear to our people that no leader will become wealthy by abusing his position or by exploiting others. They must know that any wealth he gains will be from wise use of the payment the people make to him in return for his service. But even this is not enough. Leaders must show the way to the development of our country and our people. If ten hunters have trapped a rabbit they are foolish idiots, wasting their energies, if they stop their hunting in order to fight over the distribution of the meat on that rabbit. They would do better to concentrate their energies on working out a better system of hunting so that they can increase the amount of meat available to them all.

That is similar to the position in Tanzania. This is a poor country now. We do not produce enough wealth for all of us to lead a decent life; we are like the ten hunters with one rabbit between them. There is no getting away from this fact. Neither is there any other way for us to increase our wealth except by producing more. In particular we must realize that it is no good our simply increasing the amount of money in the country. Government could easily order the Bank of Tanzania to print more notes and to give everyone a present of so many shilling notes every year. But this would not increase our wealth in the very slightest. The result would simply be chaos.

To get this truth quite clear in our minds, let us take a simplified example. Imagine a village of ten people in the Rufiji Delta which is cut off by floods. Between them these people have Shs. 1,000/- in notes. They also have one bag of rice. If the Government uses a helicopter to drop another Shs. 1,000/- in notes to these people, will they be any less hungry, less cold, or less in danger from the water? Or if the people decide to make a fire and to burn all the notes in the village, will they be any worse off? But suppose the Government drops more rice from the helicopter. In that case the people will have more to eat, quite regardless of the number of notes which they have between them. On the other hand, if there was an accident and the bag of rice was destroyed, then the people would be in serious trouble, regardless of the fact that they still had all their shilling notes. For they cannot eat notes, nor use them as shelter. Money is not wealth.

Of course, it would be a different situation if, in this isolated village, one person out of the ten managed to get hold of the extra Shs. 1,000/- which the Government dropped by helicopter. The total wealth of the ten men would not be any greater, but this particular individual would be able to get more of the rice for himself. The other nine would therefore get less rice because—let me say again— the amount of rice available would not have been increased by the importation of more money to this isolated community. If the lucky man getting all the extra money happened to be the poorest man in the village, then the effect might be that the distribution of the wealth (that is, the rice) was better as a result of the extra money coming in. In such a case the extra money would have been a substitute for a joint decision by the ten people to distribute the rice fairly. But if the man who got the extra money was already as well off as the majority, or even better off, then nothing at all good or socialist would have come out of the extra money being brought in.

OUR WEALTH

It should not be necessary for TANU leaders to understand statistics before they realize that Tanzania is poor. We see, and we live with poverty. Yet sometimes our people get confused by the sight of a few individuals driving private cars, or by figures which the Minister for Finance talks about during the Budget, and they begin to believe that somehow and somewhere there is a lot of wealth in this country and that the poverty they see around them is due to unequal distribution, or to exploitation, or even that the poverty does not really exist!

Let me therefore state, once again, what the real position is. If all the wealth of all the people in this country were put into one big heap, and then divided equally between all the people who live in Tanzania, each person would receive goods to the total value of Shs. 525/-. That is all he would have for a year. Not a month, but a year. This means that the total wealth of the country is valued at about Shs. 5,455,000,000/-. Out of that amount, nearly $10\frac{1}{2}$ million people have to eat and clothe themselves; we have to run our schools, our hospitals, maintain our roads and our houses, pay for our administration, pay our army and police forces, pay for our Government, and do every other single thing which we want to do in this country. But in addition, it is from this same amount that we have to invest for a better life in the future by building new roads and communications, by building factories, houses, new schools, and so on. In fact, the total wealth available to be spent by the people of Tanzania during one year is much less than the amount which the Government of the United States of America spends on its military forces in one week. (This should be remembered by every well-off Tanzanian who likes to live in luxury.)

However we divide our wealth between us, we are a poor nation. There is no getting away from that fact, and anyone who pretends otherwise by promising the people riches is trying to fool the people, and he should be condemned.

This does not mean that the distribution of our total wealth between different groups of people is unimportant. Of course it is very important, and one of the points made in the Arusha Declaration is that there must be greater equality of incomes between the different people of this country. All that I am concerned to stress here is that the amount which we have to distribute is small. We are like the ten hunters with one rabbit, whom I referred to earlier. Our major preoccupation must be to increase our wealth, and the amount of time and energy we spend on squabbling over what we now have should be very limited indeed.

But what have we in fact done, so far, as regards the distribution of incomes in Tanzania? And what are our plans for the distribution of the wealth we create—how do we propose to divide it fairly?

First, ever since independence we have been gradually making our taxation system more progressive, which means that the higher your income the greater the proportion of it you pay in taxes. Thus, for example, there are only ten people in our whole country who have an income of Shs. 300,000/- or more in a year, and these people each pay more than two thirds of that amount to the Government in direct taxation. After that the luxury goods they want to buy are also very heavily taxed. Of course they remain wealthy in comparison with the rest of us. But they are nothing like as wealthy as they would be if they lived in almost any other country of the world. And people with much lower incomes than that also feel the effect of our heavily progressive tax system—and quite rightly. Any senior civil servant, any Minister, or any other highly qualified worker in Tanzania will be willing to give you evidence of this, even if he is too much of a socialist to complain about it! Taxation policy is, and will be, a very important and very effective way of controlling income differentials in this country.

Second, we have put a stop to any future large-scale exploitation of our workers and peasants through the private ownership of the means of production and exchange. In February we rounded off a number of smaller measures which restricted opportunities for exploitation of this type by nationalizing the banks, the insurance business, a number of large firms involved in the food industry, etc. We cut these straws. At the same time we took control of a number of other businesses; in other words, we put our finger on the straw so as to control the amount which goes through it.

Thirdly, we have put a stop to wage and salary increases at the top levels and have even, in the case of people working directly for the Government, succeeded in cutting their incomes. Our job now is to make sure that the top wages of Tanzanians outside the Government sector also get involved in this high-level freeze. For however much our total national income is increased by our efforts in the coming years, it is highly unlikely that the increase will justify any addition to the top salaries in the foreseeable future.

But the number of people involved at this level is very small indeed; probably not more than 35,000 individuals get enough income to be liable to pay income tax, much less surtax. The real problem in Tanzania is not redistribution between the rich and the poor, but a fair distribution of wealth, and of contribution to national expenses, between the very poor and the poor, between the man who can barely feed himself and the man who can barely clothe himself. Yet even so, considerable improvements have been made for that group of our workers whose incomes can be fairly easily influenced by Government and by their own direct action—which is the wage-earners. The cost of employing a worker in Tanzania has more than doubled during the six years since 1961. Cash wages have increased considerably in most cases, and fringe benefits like leave, severance pay, employers' contribution to the Provident Fund, and so on, have all increased the real security and income of the wage-earner.

The incomes of the peasants, however, are not so susceptible to Government action. By encouraging the co-operative movement we have tried to avoid the exploitation of the peasants by middle-men; we are now engaged in trying to improve the efficiency and effectiveness of the co-operative movement so as to ensure that one type of exploitation does not get replaced by another—the exploitation of inefficiency and bureaucracy. Yet for the most part, the peasant's income in this country is determined by his own hard work, combined with the effect of the weather and the world prices of the crops he sells. Government can, and does, help the peasant by teaching new methods of planting, by making better seeds available, and within our resources by providing credit with which he can buy better tools or fertilizers, etc. But neither Government nor peasant can control the weather; nor can either of us control the prices which our exports receive in the world market.

It is true that some of the crops produced by our peasants are consumed within Tanzania, and that for many of these the Government fixes the price. This does not mean, however, that the Government can increase the wealth of our people by increasing the prices of the food crops. If, for example, we set a higher price for maize, what would be the effect? The result would be that the wage-earners who now buy the maize would have to pay more out of their existing incomes in order to eat the same amount. Their real incomes would thus have gone down. In other words, by increasing the incomes of the farmers, we would be decreasing the incomes of the wage-earners. The wage-earners would then naturally demand an increase in their wages on the grounds that the cost of living had gone up. If that demand were granted, the effect would be to increase the cost of the things the wage-earners produce—things like shirts, shoes, and so on, which the peasant buys. So in the end neither the peasant nor the wage-earner would be better off; both would have more money, but neither would have more goods than he had before.

There is no way of improving our incomes until and unless we improve our output. This can be seen very easily in the case of the peasant, because he works on his own land and owns the crops which he grows. He may complain about the prices he receives, just as he complains about the weather. But he can always see the connection between his output and his income. Whatever the price, if he succeeds in growing 12 bags of maize on an acre, he will be richer than if he only grows 4 bags of maize on that acre. Anything which the Government can do to contribute to the better yield on his land is a contribution to his income, provided that he does the necessary work himself.

For the wage-earners the same basic principles apply; output and income are connected. If the worker's income goes up while the value of his output does not go up, or if his income remains the same while the total value of his output goes down, he will then soon begin to get into difficulties. Let us take a simple case of 100 shirt-makers in a factory who produce between them, let us say, 2,000 shirts a month, that is, 20 for each worker. Let us further assume that each of these workers receives Shs. 200/- a month; on that basis the cost of producing each shirt will be Shs. 10/-. (In order to keep the example simple, I am leaving aside all questions of rent for the factory, cost of the machines, transport, etc., etc.) At that price all the shirts which are produced are bought by the consumers of Tanzania.

Let us now see what happens if the wage of each worker in this shirt factory is increased to Shs. 300/- a month without them increasing the number of shirts they produce. Each shirt would then cost Shs. 15/-. But the consumers only have sufficient money to spend Shs. 20,000/- on buying shirts; therefore, instead of 2,000 shirts being sold each month, only 1,333 shirts will be sold each month. But that means that 67 workers only are needed to produce the number of shirts which can be sold. The other 33 workers will be dismissed because no one can buy the goods they produce. The total effect of the increase in wages has therefore been that 67 people are better off; their incomes have increased from Shs. 200/- a month each to Shs. 300/- a month each. But 33 workers who used to receive Shs. 200/- a month each now receive nothing; in addition, the consumers of Tanzania only have 1,333 new shirts every month instead of having 2,000 new shirts every month.

This is, of course, a very simplified example; but it is not a false one. Indeed something like this has been happening in Tanzania since 1961. Altogether wage incomes have risen by something like 80 per cent, while the productivity of the wage-earners as a group has increased by very much less than this. As a result, 93,000 less people are now employed for wages than were employed for wages in 1961. Many of these people lost their jobs because it became less expensive for the employer to buy a machine than to spend money every month on the increased wages of the number of workers necessary to do the same job by hand. That means that in order to keep prices down, some employers sacked workers and bought a machine to do the same job. In many cases there was no alternative if they were to remain in business. In other cases—for example, in domestic employment—the employers did more work themselves; or they simply contracted their activity, because the higher wages made it uneconomic—the sisal industry gives many examples of this. In 1961 128,928 people were employed in the sisal industry, in 1966 the figure had fallen to 64,593, and now it is even lower.

The connection between wage increases without corresponding increases in productivity on the one hand, and the amount of employment available on the other, is very obvious from the statistics.

Thus, for example, in 1963 when the overall wage levels increased most drastically, the number of people in employment dropped by more than any other year. In 1964, when wages rose slightly—probably by about the same amount as productivity increased—the number of people in employment actually increased. Let me put this in figures. Average wages rose by 28 per cent in 1963; and employment fell by 14 per cent. In 1964, on the other hand, average wages rose by about 3 per cent while the number of people in employment also increased by 3 per cent. Obviously the 1964 experience is more in keeping with our ambitions to expand the economy—and nearer to the target of the Development Plan which is for a 6 per cent per annum increase in employment.

Sometimes it is said that the increased wages should be paid out of profits, and that if this is done prices will not have to go up and nor will the peasants be any worse off—only the rich employers. Unfortunately, as I have already indicated, this is not true in Tanzania; it may be true in some other countries, but that is not our concern. The people of Tanzania, through their Government, their local government, their co-operatives, or through the publicly owned industries, are now the biggest employers of wage-earners in the United Republic. Any profits made by publicly owned or controlled industries come back to the people and are spent for our national development and our national welfare. That was the point of the nationalization exercise in February. And it would certainly be very unfair if the few people who happened to be lucky enough to get jobs in a place like Williamson's Diamond Mines (which is 50 per cent publicly owned) were to have all the profits of that place paid out to them in wages. Those profits must be shared amongst us all—and in fact more than three quarters of the profits of this industry now come to the Government or to other national institutions.

Indeed the truth is that employees in Williamson's, and places like it, are already a privileged group of wage-earners receiving very much above the average rates for the kind of work they are doing. We even had the ludicrous position recently where the Government had to decide what to do about a group of people who had been paid by Williamson's while they were on a special course, and who are now pointing out that, by paying them only the wage we have been paying to expatriate workers in another branch of the diamond industry, they would be receiving less income for doing the job than they had received while being trained for it!

Wage-earners obtain their living by being part of a very complex economic organization. They cannot be expected to understand by instinct the very real connection between their output, their wages and their continued employment. It is our job—that is, the job of TANU and NUTA leaders—to understand these things and to explain them. It is our job to show the workers and peasants that there is only one way in which we can increase the amount of wealth available to us. That is by increasing the amount we produce. Out of that increase we can then have a little more to spend on ourselves and our immediate needs—whether these be new schools and hospitals or more wages for every individual. And the rest of the increased wealth we have created by our efforts we can devote to investments, so that it will be easier for us to increase production still more in future years. But we cannot increase wages or other incomes first and hope that increased production will follow. A farmer cannot eat his maize before he has cleared the ground, planted, weeded, and waited for the time when he can harvest his crop.

None of this means that we have done all there is to do in the way of equalizing the incomes in our country. But we must equalize incomes as we make our total wealth grow. It is growth which we must concentrate on. We must then reduce inequalities in incomes by constantly maintaining and bringing up to date our system of progressive taxation. We must do it by the provision of social services which are available to all, regardless of income; for a man who suddenly has new medical services available to him and his family, or a new house, or a new school or community centre, has had an improvement in his standard of living, just as much as if he had more money in his pocket. And we must also concentrate the wage incomes which increased productivity makes possible on to the lowest paid workers in our society.

But it would be quite wrong for us to aim at complete equality of income between all workers. Incomes must depend upon work and output too; there must be an incentive for everyone to work a little harder. The central point about our wages policy must be that, while it prevents gross inequalities, it creates a direct link between productivity and income. Wherever appropriate piece-rates should be employed, or bonuses paid for increased output. And where this is not possible—for example, in jobs like teaching or nursing—we should take account of the social usefulness of the work, and its relative attractiveness in comparison with other opportunities for earning a living—including farming.

This means that there is an important constructive task for NUTA and for TANU. We must recognize that the way to increase our members' standard of living is by helping them to become more productive at whatever job they are doing. Our trade union movement must shake off its British heritage, where it found its justification for existence by quarrelling with the employers. The largest employer in Tanzania now is the people—their Government and their public institutions. NUTA must learn something from the Soviet trade unions, or the Swedish ones. Both of these, in their different ways, are chiefly concerned with ensuring that the wage-earners get a fair share of an increased value of output. Thus they first work to encourage and to help improve productivity, and then argue about its fair distribution. This is, of course, a more difficult task than just making demands for wage increases. But it is a task which is a real service to the members of the trade union movement and to the people as a whole. Nor should this task be left only to NUTA. TANU leaders also have a responsibility, for wage-earners as well as peasants are members of our political movement.

RURAL DEVELOPMENT

I have spent a long time on this matter because it is important that we should all understand these basic economic facts of Tanzania. We are now a poor nation; there is no short cut to prosperity; hard work and a deliberate decision by us to plan for a better future is the only way forward. Once we accept these things then we can work and plan to make sure that our progress takes us in the right direction. We can then ensure that increasing prosperity is used for the benefit of the people as a whole and not concentrated in the hands of a few. We can ensure that we build a society in which men co-operate together for their mutual benefit. And we can nurture the traditional values of Africa—the belief that man as a member of his community must enjoy respect and well-being alongside his fellows, and in proportion to his contribution to the society of which he is a member.

For the vast majority of our people the community will continue to be a rural one, and the means of livelihood will be agriculture. This means that our agriculture must be organized in such a manner that improved conditions become possible for all who are willing to work, and that our rural life must be based on the principles of socialism—that is, on the principles of equality, co-operation, and democracy.

In traditional African life the people were equal, they co-operated together, and they participated in all the decisions which affected their lives. But the equality was an equality of poverty; the co-operation was on small things; and their government was only the government of their own family unit, and of their clan, or at most of their tribe. Our task, therefore, is to modernize the traditional structure so as to make it meet our new aspirations for a higher standard of living.

This can be done provided we hold fast to the basic principles of traditional living, while we adapt its techniques to those of the twentieth century. And the way to do this is to create all over Tanzania economic and social communities where people live together and work together for the good of all, and which are inter-locked so that all of the different communities also work together in co-operation for the common good of the nation as a whole.

This is the objective outlined in the policy paper 'Socialism and Rural Development' to which I wish to direct the attention of this conference. This paper is the application of the Arusha Declaration to the practical needs of our rural life. It is vital that it be clearly understood, and that we should all work for its implementation. For 'Socialism and Rural Development' is an outline of socialism and self-reliance as it applies to Tanzania's rural life and rural people; and that means as it applies to 95 per cent of our population.

In our countryside there will be national projects; state farms, state forests, national parks, and so on. But these will not be the dominating type of organization for the rural areas. They will be created and run to cater for special problems and special needs. The way the majority of our people will live and work in a socialist Tanzania will be in villages which they themselves create and govern, and which are the basis for the productive activities of the members.

Let us put this objective in its simplest terms. A group of families will live together in a village, and will work together on a common farm for their common benefit. Their houses will be the ones they build for themselves out of their own resources; their farm will be owned jointly, and its produce will be their joint property. The activities of the village, and the type of production they undertake as well as the distribution of crops and other goods they produce, will all be determined by the village members themselves. For the land will be 'our land' to all the members of the village; the crops will be 'our crops'; the common herd of animals will be 'our herd'. In other words, we shall have an up-to-date, and larger, version of the traditional African family, where the land was 'ours', crops were 'ours', and so on.

The size and composition of the group of people who live together will vary from one part of the country to another, depending upon the soil, the appropriate crops or animal husbandry, and the social customs of the people. But by living together and working together, all of them will be able to be better off. Instead of 40 different families each living separately and each farming their own land, collecting their own water, and sending their children miles to school, they will come together and live in a village. Then, by their joint efforts, they will—in time—be able to bring water into the village; they will be able to build their children's school conveniently near all of them; they will be able to build a community centre and a store for their mutual convenience, and so on. Also, by working together on one farm they will soon be able to invest in an oxen-plough to do much of the work each had previously to do with his own hoe and panga; they will be able to take full advantage of skilled advice about modern methods; they will be able to increase their joint production and their joint prosperity. They will be able jointly to arrange the sale of their produce, and the purchase of the goods they want to buy from outside—perhaps by running their own ujamaa shop. And so on. In other words, a living and working community will have been created. All members of the community will be equal in status and any variations of income will reflect only differences in the amount of work done. They will be working in co-operation, and not in opposition to each other; and they will be governing their own village affairs as well as being able to discuss together national issues which affect them as citizens of Tanzania.

This is the objective. It is stated clearly, and at greater length, in the policy paper. We must understand it so that we know what we are working towards. But it is not something we shall achieve overnight. We have a long way to go.

For what has been happening over recent years is quite different. We have not been enlarging and modernizing our traditional family unit as much as abandoning it in favour of small-scale capitalist farming. Many of our most dynamic and energetic farmers, especially those with the most initiative and willingness to learn new techniques, have been branching out on their own as individuals. They have not been enlarging their farms by joining with others in a spirit of equality, but by employing labour. So we are getting the beginnings of the development of an agricultural labouring class on the one hand, and a wealthier employing class on the other. Fortunately, this development has not gone very far; we can arrest the trend without difficulty. But we must not make this change by persecuting the progressive farmers; after all, we have been encouraging them in the direction they have been going! Instead we must seek their co-operation, and integrate them into the new socialist agriculture by showing them that their best interests will be served by this development. For energy and initiative such as these farmers have displayed will be very important to our progress. We need these people.

How then do we move from our present system to the system of ujamaa villages? The policy paper outlines some of the steps which may be used in different places, but it is important to remember two things. First, that the appropriate first steps will be different in different places. And second, that the people themselves must decide whether and when they are prepared to make this movement. For we are not simply trying to organize increased production; we are trying to introduce a whole new way of life for the majority of our people. This can only be done once the people understand its purposes and voluntarily decide to participate.

We must not try to rush this development; what matters is not the speed but the direction in which we move. We must encourage and help people, not try to force them. For this kind of village does exist in Tanzania, and the members of them are learning their advantages. But sometimes people have tried to start this kind of thing and have failed. The reason is often that their expectations were too great; they had too much enthusiasm and too much impatience. What is needed is careful thought and planning—by the people themselves. This is why it is better to start slowly, perhaps by working a common plot in addition to private ones, perhaps by undertaking 'mutual help'. Then as the problems reveal themselves, and are solved by the participants, so they will gain confidence and take the next step.

But 'slowly' does not mean 'without determination'. The initiative for movements in the direction of ujamaa villages can be taken by any-one who understands the objective. It does not have to be a TANU leader, or Government official. Anyone can get together with a group of friends and decide to start. For these villages must govern themselves; the participants must control their own activities. No one else can do it for them. Thus a group of young people may decide to start; or the members of a TANU cell; or the members of a church or a mosque. Or the school teacher in a village school can take the initiative by asking the children's parents to work with the school in a common project—and so on.

The job of TANU leaders is to help, and to encourage. This will not always be easy. Sometimes people will be sceptical or they will reject the advice and make mistakes. But if the TANU leaders are themselves participants in such schemes, and are able to demonstrate by example the benefits of, and the best methods for, this kind of activity, then success will be greater. We have to act ourselves, and then others will follow. If every MP or other delegate here from a rural area decides to be a member of an ujamaa village, we shall make a good start. Indeed, no one who can live in an ujamaa village, but does not, should talk about ujamaa!

One other important point for TANU leaders to remember is that there can be no great promises of Government help, nor of immediate prosperity, if such villages are started. It is safer to assume that the Government will be able to give no help at all than to assume that Government will come in with all the advice or capital which could possibly be required! And the truth is that at the beginning life in an ujamaa village will be just as hard as the life of a farmer working on his own. This system is no substitute for hard work. It just means that the hard work will, in time, bring greater returns.

For an ujamaa village, as outlined in this paper, is both a socialist, and a self-reliant, community. It will be using local resources and traditional knowledge, and working up from these to the simple improvements which are possible when people work together. As the villages succeed, the members will graduate from hoes to ox-ploughs, from carrying everything on their heads to using bicycles, or ox-carts. They will work out their own system of social security and assistance in time of trouble. They will be self-reliant ujamaa communities. When the Government and other national institutions come in, they will do so to supplement the activities of the members and assist them to help themselves.

If we succeed in starting ujamaa villages, we shall be able to build up from them to village associations, whereby a number of villages work together for purposes which are too big for any of them separately. And we shall later be able to develop rural industries to diversify and improve life in the rural areas. But all these things depend upon our moving in the right direction, and starting at the bottom with the people coming together in a spirit of equality to work for their common betterment.

CONCLUSION

This conference has a great deal of serious business before it. But one of the most important things is a consideration of 'Socialism and Rural Development'. This paper should be regarded as an integral part of the Arusha Declaration, and we should therefore give it a great deal of attention here. We have already taken many decisions about the industrial and commercial sector of our economy; we have taken decisions about the responsibilities and qualifications of leadership. Now is the time for us to think deeply and seriously about the way forward for the masses of our people, and therefore for us all.

I believe that by accepting this paper, and by returning home with a determination to work for its implementation, we shall be setting a pattern which will be our pride and our satisfaction in the years to come.

40

Progress in Schools

A Conference of Secondary School Headmasters and Headmistresses was opened in Dar es Salaam by President Nyerere on 11 December 1967. He used the occasion both to congratulate them on progress made, and to clear up certain misunderstandings concerning the new policy.

.... As I have been travelling around the country recently, I have come across a number of secondary schools which are beginning to try and implement the policies of self-reliance. I am met by school farms or demonstrations of produce; I see numbers of young people at work. I have even come across one school which has run into trouble with NUTA because the boys are now doing almost all their own domestic work so that the school no longer needs to employ servants! This is good. It is one indication of the change which is beginning to take place in our schools, and which could only have taken place as a result of good leadership by the senior staff.

For what does our new policy amount to? It demands that our educational effort be directed at the needs of the nation and of the majority of the pupils; it demands an identification of the schools with the community and with our current national struggles. It requires that the correct attitudes towards their future work in our Tanzanian society should be inculcated in the students, that they should become enthusiastic exponents of self-reliant economic development—and excited about the opportunity for service which exists for educated people in our predominantly agricultural economy.

All the signs are that we have begun to move in this direction; ...
... There has, however, been some misunderstanding in some places about what exactly is required of schools and headmasters. It must be clear that we are not trying to introduce a new subject

called 'self-reliance', or 'socialism' into the school curriculum, nor just add periods of physical labour for the pupils and staff. What we are aiming at is converting our schools into economic communities as well as educational communities; in other words, into educational communities which are to a considerable extent self-reliant. We want each school—taking pupils and staff together—to be eventually responsible for doing—or meeting the costs of—its own maintenance, apart from the strictly academic expenses. And we want this new responsibility to be accepted as a conscious and proud contribution to our national development and our national self-reliance.

It is while they are practising this self-reliance—and as an important by-product of it—that the pupils will learn new skills which are relevant to their future life, and adopt a realistic attitude to getting their hands dirty by physical labour. They will learn by doing; they will learn also the relevance of the scientific principles and other things which they are taught in their more strictly academic prusuits.

All this does require a very fundamental change in our old educational system, and in the organization and teaching in every school. The Ministry of Education, and yourselves, as school heads, have together to work out what this means as regards the type of examinations, the school years, the staffing problems, and so on. I imagine that some of these problems will be discussed during your conference this week. But to a very great extent the success of our new policy will depend upon the initiative, and willingness to experiment, of the schools themselves—under your leadership.

For the appropriate manner of practising self-reliance will vary between each school. In some cases emphasis can be placed upon a school farm which provides all the food for the school and gives a surplus of cash crops for sale. In other cases this is not very practicali, emphasis will have to be placed upon doing all the school chores; and making things in a workshop which are useful to that school and to others.. . .

. . . There are just two points I would like to stress in this matter, although many of you have already realized their importance. The first is the fact that the pupils must be really involved in this work, from the planning stage up to and including the allocation of the returns of any productive work which is undertaken. They must not see this new development as a sentence of hard labour, but as an exciting challenge to their ability and their dedication to the Declaration and the progress of our country.

It would be a mistake, for example, for the head and teachers just to work out the plans for a particular kind of farm, using particular tools and methods, or plans for a particular kind of workshop and then give these plans to the pupils saying, 'This is what you have to do'. If the approach is made in this way you may well find that the pupils feel like labourers on a farm or in a workshop belonging to someone else. And in that case they will probably act like labourers, conscious of exploitation, and do as little as they can given the amount of supervision provided!

If, on the other hand the problem and the challenge are put to the students at the very beginning, a different attitude can be built up. Alternative plans can be put before them and explained; they can be asked to elect representatives from each class on to a joint staff and student committee, which will work out the details and lay down the order and discipline of work. This committee could remain as a permanent school body, but with frequent reference back to the whole school as work progresses.

Obviously this is only an example of the kind of approach which is needed. You will be able to work out the system most appropriate to your own circumstances. But any attempt to secure complete involvement and participation will have problems and dangers. In particular, there is the possibility that there will be so much talking that there is no time for action! There is also the danger that mistakes will be made which could have been avoided by a more expert direction, or that school discipline will be undermined by the wrong people being elected to the school work committee.

But if there is good chairmanship of the school assembly and committee most of these problems can be avoided or overcome. It should then be possible to give everyone a fair hearing but still get decisions taken. And although really serious mistakes must be avoided on a large scale, it may sometimes be worthwhile allowing pupils to make mistakes on a small area so that they can learn the advantage of taking expert advice—or else prove it wrong! The problem of discipline under these circumstances must also be faced up to. An essential part of the success of our attempt to build a democratic society is the combination of free discussion followed by the full implementation of joint decisions; if the children get used to this at school they will at the same time be learning about the responsibilities of citizens in a free society.

The other point I wish to make now is that this kind of self-reliance activity must be integrated with the school work; the relevance of one to the other must be made clear. For although it is important that we should reduce the financial costs of education to the public, the more basic purpose of the new policy is to help the students to learn and practise attitudes and skills which will be of use to them, and to the society, in the future. They must therefore not only learn what has to be done in that particular community, or by that community for a wider circle, but why it is necessary. They must learn why it is necessary to have a farm or workshop; they must learn why one process is recommended on the farm, or one method used in the workshop—not just be told that it is so. It is not enough, for example, to learn that fertilizer is a good thing; they must learn why it is, and what it does. Otherwise, when they are operating on their own farms later they may think that by simply doubling the amount of fertilizer they will double the crop produced per acre—and disaster will follow! Our educated young people must be being prepared to give practical leadership in their areas; and this means they must be able to explain and to demonstrate, not simply repeat things by rote.

Obviously this means that there must be close integration between the self-reliance activities and the academic learning of the school. It would be in the science lessons, for example, that the properties of chemical fertilizers, or natural fertilizers, would be demonstrated. It would be in the maths classes that the pupils would learn the principles of proportion, and so on.

This kind of thing may necessitate some adjustment in the content of the different subjects taught. But I want to emphasize that we are not asking you to reduce academic standards in your schools. We are asking you to make the academic subjects relevant. After all, there is no reason why standards should drop if you learn about the properties of one chemical rather than another, or practise mathematical exercises arising from the real problems of making desks in the school workshop, rather than something more abstract. That is the kind of thing we are asking for, not that chemistry or mathematics should be dropped or reduced. It will create problems, of course; it makes new challenges, and demands great co-operation and co-ordination between all the different subject teachers in your schools. I imagine it will also create problems about textbooks: your staff may have to work out their own problems, or write their own notes for distribution . . . .

Index

Published by Oxford University Press P.O. Box 72532, Nairobi
and Printed by Tanzania Litho Ltd., P.O. Box 200 Arusha, Tanzania